Tourism and Sustainable Development Goals

This comprehensive volume comprises some of the best scholarship on sustainable tourism in recent years, demonstrating the rich body of past research that provides a fertile and critical ground for studies on the Sustainable Development Goals (SDGs) by tourism geographers and other social scientists in the future.

Since the turn of the 1990s many international development and policy-making organisations have perceived the tourism industry, with its local and regional connections, as a high-potential tool for putting sustainable development into practice. The capacity of tourism to work for sustainable development was highlighted in relation to the United Nations' SDGs, which were adopted in 2015. The SDGs define the agenda for global development to 2030 by addressing pertinent challenges such as poverty, inequality, climate change, environmental degradation, and peace and justice. Tourism geographers and allied disciplines have held strong and long-term interest in sustainability issues, and their chapters in this collection contribute significantly to this emerging and highly policy-relevant research field.

This book was originally published as an online special issue of the journal *Tourism Geographies*.

Jarkko Saarinen is a Professor of Human Geography at the University of Oulu, Finland, and a Distinguished Visiting Professor of Sustainability Management at the University of Johannesburg, South Africa. His research interests include tourism and development, sustainability in tourism, tourism and climate change adaptation, tourism-community relations, and wilderness and nature conservation studies.

Tourism and Sustainable Development Goals

Research on Sustainable Tourism Geographies

Edited by
Jarkko Saarinen

LONDON AND NEW YORK

First published 2020
by Routledge
2 Park Square, Milton Park, Abingdon, Oxon, OX14 4RN

and by Routledge
52 Vanderbilt Avenue, New York, NY 10017

Routledge is an imprint of the Taylor & Francis Group, an informa business

Chapters 1–6, 8–17 © 2020 Taylor & Francis

Chapter 7 © 2018 María José Zapata Campos, C. Michael Hall and Sandra Backlund. Originally published as Open Access.

With the exception of Chapter 7, no part of this book may be reprinted or reproduced or utilised in any form or by any electronic, mechanical, or other means, now known or hereafter invented, including photocopying and recording, or in any information storage or retrieval system, without permission in writing from the publishers. For details on the rights for Chapter 7, please see the chapter's Open Access footnote.

Trademark notice: Product or corporate names may be trademarks or registered trademarks, and are used only for identification and explanation without intent to infringe.

British Library Cataloguing-in-Publication Data
A catalogue record for this book is available from the British Library

ISBN13: 978-0-367-34166-4

Typeset in Times New Roman
by codeMantra

Publisher's Note
The publisher accepts responsibility for any inconsistencies that may have arisen during the conversion of this book from journal articles to book chapters, namely the inclusion of journal terminology.

Disclaimer
Every effort has been made to contact copyright holders for their permission to reprint material in this book. The publishers would be grateful to hear from any copyright holder who is not here acknowledged and will undertake to rectify any errors or omissions in future editions of this book.

Contents

Citation Information vii
Notes on Contributors ix

1 Tourism and sustainable development goals: research on
   sustainable tourism geographies 1
   Jarkko Saarinen

2 Sustainable tourism: a state-of-the-art review 11
   Richard W. Butler

3 Sustainability and self-regulation: critical perspectives 30
   Allan M. Williams and Armando Montanari

4 Inclusive tourism development 45
   Regina Scheyvens and Robin Biddulph

5 Tourism and the Millennium Development Goals: perspectives beyond 2015 66
   Jarkko Saarinen and Christian M. Rogerson

6 Corporate social responsibility in tourism post-2015: a Development
   First approach 74
   Emma Hughes and Regina Scheyvens

7 Can MNCs promote more inclusive tourism? Apollo tour operator's
   sustainability work 88
   María José Zapata Campos, C. Michael Hall and Sandra Backlund

8 Tourism and Poverty Reduction: Issues for Small Island States 111
   Regina Scheyvens & Janet H. Momsen

9 Using indicators to assess sustainable tourism development: a review 131
   Anna Torres-Delgado and Jarkko Saarinen

10 Sustainability indicators of rural tourism from the perspective of the residents 148
   Mercedes Marzo-Navarro, Marta Pedraja-Iglesias and Lucia Vinzón

11	Requirements for Sustainable Nature-based Tourism in Transfrontier Conservation Areas: a Southern African Delphi Consultation *Anna Spenceley*	165
12	Regional network governance and sustainable tourism *Anna Farmaki*	192
13	Mindful deviation in creating a governance path towards sustainability in resort destinations *Alison M. Gill and Peter W. Williams*	215
14	Collaboration and Partnership Development for Sustainable Tourism *Sonya Graci*	232
15	Beyond the Beach: Balancing Environmental and Socio-cultural Sustainability in Boracay, the Philippines *Lei Tin Jackie Ong, Donovan Storey & John Minnery*	250
16	Community sustainability and resilience: similarities, differences and indicators *Alan A. Lew, Pin T. Ng, Chin-cheng (Nickel) Ni and Tsung-chiung (Emily) Wu*	270
17	Evolutionary economic geography: reflections from a sustainable tourism perspective *Patrick Brouder*	280
	Index	291

Citation Information

The following chapters were originally published in *Tourism Geographies*. When citing this material, please use the original page numbering for each article, as follows:

Chapter 2
Sustainable tourism: A state-of-the-art review
Richard W. Butler
Tourism Geographies, volume 1, issue 1 (1999) pp. 7–25

Chapter 3
Sustainability and self-regulation: Critical perspectives
Allan M. Williams & Armando Montanari
Tourism Geographies, volume 1, issue 1 (1999) pp. 26–40

Chapter 4
Inclusive tourism development
Regina Scheyvens & Robin Biddulph
Tourism Geographies, volume 20, issue 4 (October 2018) pp. 589–609

Chapter 5
Tourism and the Millennium Development Goals: perspectives beyond 2015
Jarkko Saarinen & Christian M. Rogerson
Tourism Geographies, volume 16, issue 1 (February 2014) pp. 23–30

Chapter 6
Corporate social responsibility in tourism post-2015: a Development First approach
Emma Hughes & Regina Scheyvens
Tourism Geographies, volume 18, issue 5 (December 2016) pp. 469–482

Chapter 7
Can MNCs promote more inclusive tourism? Apollo tour operator's sustainability work
María José Zapata Campos, C. Michael Hall & Sandra Backlund
Tourism Geographies, volume 20, issue 4 (October 2018) pp. 630–652

Chapter 8
Tourism and Poverty Reduction: Issues for Small Island States
Regina Scheyvens & Janet H. Momsen
Tourism Geographies, volume 10, issue 1 (February 2008) pp. 22–41

Chapter 9
Using indicators to assess sustainable tourism development: a review
Anna Torres-Delgado & Jarkko Saarinen
Tourism Geographies, volume 16, issue 1 (October 2014) pp. 31–47

Chapter 10
Sustainability indicators of rural tourism from the perspective of the residents
Mercedes Marzo-Navarro, Marta Pedraja-Iglesias & Lucia Vinzón
Tourism Geographies, volume 17, issue 4 (October 2015) pp. 586–602

Chapter 11
Requirements for Sustainable Nature-based Tourism in Transfrontier Conservation Areas: a Southern African Delphi Consultation
Anna Spenceley
Tourism Geographies, volume 10, issue 3 (August 2008) pp. 285–311

Chapter 12
Regional network governance and sustainable tourism
Anna Farmaki
Tourism Geographies, volume 17, issue 3 (July 2015) pp. 385–407

Chapter 13
Mindful deviation in creating a governance path towards sustainability in resort destinations
Alison M. Gill & Peter W. Williams
Tourism Geographies, volume 16, issue 4 (October 2014) pp. 546–562

Chapter 14
Collaboration and Partnership Development for Sustainable Tourism
Sonya Graci
Tourism Geographies, volume 15, issue 1 (February 2013) pp. 25–42

Chapter 15
Beyond the Beach: Balancing Environmental and Socio-cultural Sustainability in Boracay, the Philippines
Lei Tin Jackie Ong, Donovan Storey & John Minnery
Tourism Geographies, volume 13, issue 4 (November 2011) pp. 549–569

Chapter 16
Community sustainability and resilience: similarities, differences and indicators
Alan A. Lew, Pin T. Ng, Chin-cheng (Nickel) Ni & Tsung-chiung (Emily) Wu
Tourism Geographies, volume 18, issue 1 (February 2016) pp. 18–27

Chapter 17
Evolutionary economic geography: reflections from a sustainable tourism perspective
Patrick Brouder
Tourism Geographies, volume 19, issue 3 (July 2017) pp. 438–447

For any permission-related enquiries please visit:
http://www.tandfonline.com/page/help/permissions

Notes on Contributors

Sandra Backlund has a master's degree in International Administration and Global Governance. She has worked with the United Nations World Food Programme and Inclusive Business Sweden. Currently, she is a Case Officer at the Swedish Migration Agency.

Robin Biddulph is an Associate Professor of Human Geography at Gothenburg University, Sweden. His recent research projects include analysis of tourism livelihoods in the area around Siem Reap, Cambodia; land reform in Mozambique and Tanzania; and social enterprises in Scandinavia and Southeast Asia.

Patrick Brouder holds the British Columbia Regional Innovation Chair in Tourism and Sustainable Rural Development at Vancouver Island University, Canada. His research in British Columbia focuses on three interrelated areas of innovation in tourism across the province: Indigenous tourism (as a form of endogenous economic development), creative tourism, and tourism evolution.

Richard W. Butler is an Emeritus Professor of Tourism at the University of Strathclyde, Glasgow, UK, and a Visiting Professor at NHTV University, Breda, the Netherlands. He specialises in the geography of tourism and recreation. He is Past President of the International Academy for the Study of Tourism and a Past President of the Canadian Association for Leisure Studies. His main fields of research have been the evolution cycle of resorts, the social impact of tourism, sustainable tourism, and tourism on islands.

Anna Farmaki is a Lecturer in the Department of Hotel and Tourism Management at Cyprus University of Technology, Limassol, Cyprus. Her research interests lie in the areas of tourism planning and development and tourist behaviour.

Alison M. Gill is a Professor with a joint appointment in the Department of Geography and the School of Resource and Environmental Management at Simon Fraser University, Burnaby, Canada. Her research interests lie in tourism planning and the transformations of place, especially in mountain resort destinations.

Sonya Graci is an Associate Professor at the Ted Rogers School of Hospitality and Tourism at Ryerson University, Toronto, Canada. She is also the co-founder of the Icarus Foundation, a not-for-profit organisation that focuses on the sustainability of tourism, and the Director of Accommodating Green, a sustainability consultancy.

C. Michael Hall is a Professor in the Department of Management, Marketing and Entrepreneurship at the University of Canterbury, Christchurch, New Zealand; a Docent in the Department of Geography Research Unit at the University of Oulu, Finland; and a Visiting Professor in the School of Business and Economics at Linnaeus University, Kalmar, Sweden. He has published widely on tourism, regional development, and environmental change.

Emma Hughes is a Research Development Advisor Pacific and Research Development Advisor for the College of Humanities and Social Sciences at Massey University, Palmerston North, New Zealand. Her research looks at the impact of corporate community development in the tourism sector from community perspectives.

Alan A. Lew is a Professor in the Department of Geography, Planning, and Recreation at Northern Arizona University, Flagstaff, USA, where he teaches courses in geography, urban planning, and tourism development. His research interests focus on tourism and community development in East and Southeast Asia.

Mercedes Marzo-Navarro is an Associate Professor in the Department of Marketing Management and Marketing Research at the University of Zaragoza, Spain. She has written numerous articles on relationship marketing, quality in higher education, and services marketing.

John Minnery is a retired urban planning academic who holds adjunct and honorary positions at the University of Queensland, Brisbane, Australia, and Griffith University, Brisbane, Australia. His research interests are in urban policy, urban history, and urban disasters.

Janet H. Momsen is a Professor Emerita at the University of California, Davis, USA. Her research interests focus on gender and development, tourism, and agriculture. She has done field research in the West Indies, Mexico, Hungary, and Bangladesh, and has published many books and papers.

Armando Montanari is a Professor of Geography of Tourism in the Department of European, American and Intercultural Studies at Sapienza University of Rome, Italy, and the Vice President of the innovative Sapienza Rome University Startup ENViMOB srl on nature and tourism-based solutions. He has published more than 190 articles and volumes in Italian, English, French, Spanish, and Japanese.

Pin T. Ng is a Professor of Economics in the W. A. Franke College of Business at Northern Arizona University, Flagstaff, USA, where he teaches mainly business statistics, econometrics, and managerial economics. His research interests span across econometrics, computational statistics, urban and rural economics, international finance, and tourism and leisure studies.

Chin-cheng (Nickel) Ni is a Professor in the Department of Environmental and Cultural Resources at the National Hsinchu University of Education, Taiwan, where he teaches courses in tourism geography, island studies, and urban and rural analysis. His research interests focus on tourism and community development in marginal regions.

Lei Tin Jackie Ong is a Lecturer in Sustainable Tourism Development at RMIT University, Vietnam. Her research focuses on sustainability tourism practices and development in coastal areas in Asia.

Marta Pedraja-Iglesias is an Associate Professor in the Department of Marketing Management and Marketing Research at the University of Zaragoza, Spain. She has written numerous articles on relationship marketing, and price and channels of distribution.

Christian M. Rogerson is a Professor in the School of Tourism and Hospitality Management at the University of Johannesburg, South Africa. His research interests straddle issues of local and regional development, small enterprise development, and tourism in the global South.

Jarkko Saarinen is a Professor of Human Geography at the University of Oulu, Finland, and a Distinguished Visiting Professor of Sustainability Management at the University of Johannesburg, South Africa. His research interests include tourism and development, sustainability in tourism, tourism and climate change adaptation, tourism-community relations, and wilderness and nature conservation studies.

Regina Scheyvens is a Professor of Development Studies and the Co-Director of the Pacific Research and Policy Centre at Massey University, Palmerston North, New Zealand. Her research focuses on the relationship between tourism, sustainable development, and poverty reduction, and she has conducted fieldwork on these issues in Fiji, Vanuatu, Samoa, the Maldives, and Southern Africa.

Anna Spenceley is a Senior Research Fellow at the School of Tourism and Hospitality at the University of Johannesburg, South Africa. She works in southern Africa on sustainable tourism issues, particularly in relation to biodiversity conservation, sustainable livelihoods, corporate social responsibility, and poverty alleviation.

Donovan Storey is the Deputy Director and Urban Lead for Green Cities in the Global Green Growth Institute's Investment and Policy Solutions Division. He also has an Adjunct role as Associate Professor in the School of Earth and Environmental Sciences at the University of Queensland, Brisbane, Australia. His research focuses on how inclusion in planning can lead to more progressive and sustainable cities and island environments in the developing world.

Anna Torres-Delgado is a Researcher in the CETT-UB Tourism and Hospitality Education/Research Centre and an Assistant Professor in the Department of Physical Geography and Regional Geographic Analysis at the University of Barcelona, Spain. She has done a thesis on sustainable tourism indicators while lecturing in the faculty.

Lucia Vinzón is the Director of the Indoamerican Refugee Migrant Organisation, UK. She has a PhD in Economics and Management, with an emphasis in integrated rural tourism, from the University of Zaragoza, Spain.

Allan M. Williams is a Professor and Chair in Tourism and Mobility Studies at the University of Surrey, UK. His central research interests are the relationships between economic development and mobility, and especially the roles of knowledge and risk. He is especially interested in the relationships between tourism and migration, return migration, innovation, productivity, and entrepreneurship.

Peter W. Williams is a Professor Emeritus in the School of Resource and Environmental Management at Simon Fraser University, Canada. His research interests are tourism policy, planning, and management issues, especially strategies that lead to more sustainable use of natural and cultural resources.

Tsung-chiung (Emily) Wu is a Professor in the Department of Tourism, Recreation, and Leisure Studies at National Dong-Hwa University, Hualien City, Taiwan, where she teaches courses in rural tourism, tourism development, and eco-tourism. Her research interests focus on sustainable development, rural tourism, and indigenous tourism.

María José Zapata Campos is an Associate Professor in Management and Organisation in the Department of Business Administration in the School of Business, Economics and Law at the University of Gothenburg, Sweden. She conducts research on environmental governance, urban development, and socio-environmental change.

Tourism and sustainable development goals: research on sustainable tourism geographies

JARKKO SAARINEN

ABSTRACT *Since the turn of the 1990s many international development and policy-making organisations have perceived the tourism industry with its local and regional connections as a high-potential tool for putting sustainable development into practice. Recently, the capacity of tourism to work for sustainable development has been highlighted in relation to the United Nations Sustainable Development Goals (SDGs), which were adopted in 2015. This connection underlines the importance and responsibility of tourism as one of the world's biggest industries to contribute and make a difference to sustainable development both locally and globally. The SDGs define the agenda for global development to 2030 by addressing pertinent challenges such as poverty, inequality, climate change, environmental degradation, and peace and justice. Tourism geographers and allied disciplines have held strong and long-term interest in sustainability issues and have contributed significantly to this emerging and highly policy-relevant research field. Existing scholarship on sustainable tourism demonstrates the rich body of research that provides a fertile and critical ground for studies on the SDGs by tourism geographers and other social scientists in the future.*

Introduction

Tourism represents a tool for change. For individuals, families, and social groups, tourism is an activity providing a way to take a break from everyday life, enjoy a change of routine, and connect with new places and people. For entrepreneurs and businesses, tourists and tourism phenomena are vehicles for making a living and creating surplus and commercial growth. Through this, various changes occur in the socio-ecological and economic environment – both good and bad. Governments and authorities see the tourism industry as an instrument to maintain and create new economic activity and employment, leading to local and regional development. Since the turn of the 1990s many international organisations and policy-makers have increasingly framed the tourism industry and its local and regional development connections as high-potential tools for putting sustainable development into practice. This prospective connection between the idea of sustainable development and the industry serving the needs of tourists and localities has created the widely used and discussed concept of sustainable tourism, referring to tourism development that aims to meet "the needs of present tourists and host regions while protecting and enhancing opportunities for the future" (World Tourism Organization, 1993, p. 7).

In a way, the core of the connection between tourism and sustainable development lies in the production and consumption of tourism, which is largely driven by the tourism industry's role to serve the needs of non-local people, i.e. tourists and visitors, in the tourism system. This production and consumption creates positive and negative externalities for localities and the environment. Because of the challenges of balancing these, while also integrating the needs of the tourism industry with the common good aim of serving current and future generations, sustainable tourism thinking has become very popular in academic tourism research, with high policy relevancy (Hall, 2011; Saarinen & Gill, 2019). In this respect, the capacity of tourism to work towards sustainable development has recently been highlighted in connection with the United Nations Sustainable Development Goals (SDGs) of the 2030 Agenda for Sustainable Development (Hughes & Scheyvens, 2016). This connection underlines the importance and responsibility of tourism, as one of the world's largest industries, to contribute and make a difference to development and sustainability on a global scale. Basically, the UN SDGs are a strategy to create and realise a better and more sustainable future for all of us. One key question is how can the consumption and production of tourism play a constructive role in this strategy?

This chapter serves as an introduction to the *Tourism Geographies* Virtual Special Issue (VSI) on *Tourism and the Sustainable Development Goals*. As indicated by Scheyvens (2018) only a few tourism scholars thus far have engaged with the issues related to the SDGs. The SDGs were established relatively recently, in 2015, but global concern over tourism and sustainable development targets has been a focus of tourism research since the 1990s (see Bramwell, Higham, Lane & Miller, 2017). The United Nations Millennium Development Goals (UN MDGs) preceded the SDGs by several years and provided a context for tourism research focusing on the relationship between tourism and development in the Global South (see Saarinen & Rogerson, 2014). Indeed, despite limited engagement with the SDGs specifically, there has been a long and evolving research interest in sustainable development in geographical studies on tourism.

From this perspective, this VSI aims to provide a context for research on the SDGs in tourism by introducing a selected collection of previously published articles focusing on tourism and sustainability in *Tourism Geographies*. This rich body of research provides a fertile and critical ground for studies on the SDGs in the future. Before introducing the selected articles published in *Tourism Geographies* during the period 1999–2018, the SDGs are briefly introduced with a reference to the role and capacity of tourism for development. The idea of development refers to qualitative dimensions in social and economic processes, such as quality of life and well-being (Saarinen, Rogerson & Hall, 2017). In this respect, development has two connected threads of meaning: development as a discourse and an ideal, and development as a concrete material process (see Lawson, 2007). The SDGs integrate these two threads by emphasising concrete targets, and the idea that states that no one should be left behind (United Nations, 2015). The agenda also indicates the need to rethink the current economic growth ideology with respect to social well-being and environmental needs in development. This is a highly timely and urgent matter in the context of a global tourism industry that reaches new growth records every year!

Sustainable Development Goals

The United Nations member states ratified the SDGs in 2015 (United Nations, 2015). These goals define the agenda for global development to 2030 by addressing challenges related to poverty, inequality, climate, environmental degradation, prosperity, and peace and justice, for example. Specifically, there are 17 goals (Table 1.1) and 169 specific targets, which are set to transform the world by 2030. They relate to earlier UN MDGs, but in contrast to those, the SDGs are truly global by nature. Instead of having a main focus on the challenges of the Global South, as was the case with MDGs, the SDGs holistically include Global North dimensions in their development agenda. This is crucial as many of the global development challenges depend on the impacts and actions taking place in both the Global South and North, such as climate change mitigation and adaptation, and global partnerships.

Table 1.1 The UN Sustainable Development Goals (SDGs)

Goal 1: No Poverty: Economic growth must be inclusive to provide sustainable jobs and promote equality.
Goal 2: Zero Hunger: The food and agriculture sectors offer key solutions for development, and are central for hunger and poverty eradication.
Goal 3: Good Health and Well-being: Ensuring healthy lives and promoting well-being for all at all ages is essential for sustainable development.
Goal 4: Quality Education: Obtaining a quality education is the foundation to improving people's lives and sustainable development.
Goal 5: Gender Equality: It is not only a fundamental human right but a necessary foundation for a peaceful, prosperous, and sustainable world.
Goal 6: Clean Water and Sanitation: Clean, accessible water for all is an essential part of the world we want to live in.
Goal 7: Affordable and Clean Energy: Energy is central to nearly every major challenge and opportunity.
Goal 8: Decent Work and Economic Growth: Sustainable economic growth will require societies to create the conditions that allow people to have quality jobs.
Goal 9: Industry, Innovation, and Infrastructure: Investments in infrastructure are crucial to achieving sustainable development.
Goal 10: Reduced Inequality: To reduce inequalities, policies should be universal in principle, paying attention to the needs of disadvantaged and marginalised populations.
Goal 11: Sustainable Cities and Communities: There needs to be a future in which cities provide opportunities for all, with access to basic services, energy, housing, transportation, and more.
Goal 12: Responsible Consumption and Production: There needs to be responsible production and consumption.
Goal 13: Climate Action: Climate change is a global challenge that affects everyone, everywhere.
Goal 14: Life Below Water: Careful management of this essential global resource is a key feature of a sustainable future.
Goal 15: Life on Land: Sustainably manage forests, combat desertification, halt and reverse land degradation, and halt biodiversity loss.
Goal 16: Peace and Justice Strong Institutions: Access to justice for all, and building effective, and accountable institutions at all levels.
Goal 17: Partnerships to Achieve the Goal: Revitalise the global partnership for sustainable development.

Source: United Nations, 2015

The 17 SDGs in Table 1.1, along with a numerous specific targets, provide a plethora of topics and issues for tourism scholars to focus on, and opportunities for the tourism industry and tourists to contribute to. Related to this, the United Nations General Assembly established 2017 as the 'International Year of Sustainable Tourism for Development', highlighting the importance of international tourism in fostering development and better understanding among people everywhere (UNWTO, 2017). According to the International Year of Sustainable Tourism for Development, the industry could specifically work towards the following three SDGs: Promote sustained, inclusive and sustainable economic growth, full and productive employment, and decent work for all (SDG 8); ensure sustainable consumption and production patterns (SDG 12); and conserve and sustainably use the oceans, seas, and marine resources for sustainable development (SDG 14). These are high-profile and important goals for tourism to focus on, but they only provide a limited perspective on the relationship between tourism and sustainable development.

Based on the International Year of Sustainable Tourism for Development, the World Bank Group (2017), for example, has expanded the connection between tourism and the SDGs. In their list of 20 reasons why tourism works for development, the five core pillars are as follows: (1) sustainable economic growth; (2) social inclusiveness, employment, and poverty reduction; (3) resource efficiency, environmental protection, and climate; (4) cultural values, diversity, and heritage; and (5) mutual understanding, peace, and security. These pillars greatly expand the potential connections between tourism and the SDGs, and each pillar provides a context of reasons why tourism can work for sustainable development. Under the sustainable economic growth pillar, for example, tourism stimulates GDP growth, increases international trade, boosts international investment, drives infrastructure development, and supports low-income economies. The interpretation of these reasons, however, becomes problematic as there seems to be a confusing relationship between development as an ideal and framework, and growth as an action and emphasised target: all of these connections focus on the growth ideology associated with current neoliberal economic thinking. They are also in potential conflict with some of the other SDGs, such as climate action (Goal 13).

Indeed, while many international development agencies, such as the United Nation World Tourism Organization (UNWTO) and the World Bank, consider (sustainable) tourism as a designated tool for achieving the SDGs and "benefitting communities in destinations around the world" (World Bank Group, 2017, p. 5), academic responses have often been more doubtful and critical in regard to the tourism industry's potential role in contributing to sustainable development. There is a widely shared view that the industry has the capacity to contribute to sustainable development, but to do so requires stronger (external) regulatory measures that go beyond self-regulation by the industry itself (see Mosedale, 2014), which often seems to be primarily focused on sustaining the tourism economy and its rights to utilise natural and cultural resources in destination regions. This potential incompatibility between external and internal modes of regulation has led to criticism among scholars of the very applicability of sustainable development thinking to tourism (see Scheyvens, 2009; Sharpley, 2000). From this critical perspective, tourism is seen as a global-scale growth industry, which hides "its unsustainability behind a mask that is all the more beguiling because it appears so sustainable" (Hollenhorst, Houge-MacKenzie and Ostergren, 2014, p. 306). Thus, the growth of the industry, referring to growth in GDP, international trade, investments, and infrastructure, for example, may not necessarily lead to (sustainable) development for localities where tourism takes place (see Schilcher, 2007).

However, a key task for research in tourism is a need to find *sustainable solutions* for the industry, and despite all the criticism and frustrations (see, Liu, 2003; Sharpley, 2009), moving away from sustainable tourism thinking has turned out to be a very challenging task (McCool & Bosak, 2016; Saarinen & Gill, 2019). Sustainability is widely utilised by tourism policy-makers and institutions when defining the goals and governance models for the tourism and development nexus (Hall, 2011). Those models and processes should interest us as they do not only define global discourses on tourism and development but also local realities and practices. Thus, it is important for tourism scholars to try to influence those policies in a way that they would better – and hopefully truly – meet the needs of sustainable development, i.e. quality of life and the well-being of people and the environment. Based on the current scholarship in tourism, this calls for less focus on growth ideology referring to tourist numbers, international trade and foreign direct investments (FDI). It is great that approximately one-third of service exports and every tenth job in the world is based on tourism (WTTC, 2017; UNWTO, 2018), for example, but we should also ask what kind of employment tourism creates (SDGs 8 and 10) and for whom, and who is included in development based on tourism (SDGs 5 and 10), especially in the Global South. In this respect, the United Nations Conference and Trade Development has indicated that 'tourism employment is not gender neutral in Africa, as women and men do not necessarily have the same opportunities in and benefits from the sector' (UNCTAD 2017, p. 90). Indeed, as noted by the UNWTO (2017, p. 4), to make positive contribution to the SDGs 'a well-designed and managed tourism sector' is needed. All this calls for action and practices beyond policies and well-meant statements towards structural analysis and changes that consider 'the material inequalities generated in the tourism economy' (Bianchi, 2009, p. 486).

In her recent commentary, Scheyvens (2018: 341) has called for tourism geographers in particular, and scholars in general, 'to consider how we might utilise the SDGs to analyse the linkages between tourism and sustainable development in a wide range of contexts and at different scales.' Although research on the specific framework of the SDGs and related targets is still in an emerging phase, tourism geographers have held a strong and long-term interest in sustainability, and many of the core issues in the SDGs, including poverty alleviation and inclusive development (Goals 1 and 10), responsibility in tourism (Goal 12), tourism and climate change mitigation and adaptation (Goal 13), and the sustainable use of natural resources in tourism (Goals 14 and 15), have been relatively intensively studied. Obviously, some research fields on the SDGs in tourism geographies are still developing, and some are probably even neglected. Based on the selected articles, this VSI aims to demonstrate the rich body of geographical research on sustainable tourism published in *Tourism Geographies* since 1999. By doing so the volume provides a basis for developing the research on the SDGs in the future.

Sustainable tourism geographies: introducing selected papers

From day one (i.e. volume one, issue one), *Tourism Geographies* has focused intensively on sustainability issues in tourism. The following articles selected for the VSI cover theoretical and conceptual discourses in sustainable tourism, policy issues in respect of the SDGs and UN MDGs, sustainable tourism indicators and governance models, sustainable tourism planning, and new theoretical and conceptual avenues in relation to sustainable development in tourism. The 16 selected papers outline interesting and versatile insights into sustainable tourism geographies that combine both theoretical and empirical studies, although much more had to be left out due to space considerations. The selection emphasises key topical coverages with time and regional dimensions, with papers from different years and geographical and socio-political contexts.

Richard Butler's (1999) widely read review article on sustainable tourism sets the stage for other articles that came after it. Butler introduces the background and development of the term, including connections with the ideas of carrying capacity. The paper reviews the environmental focus of sustainable tourism and emphasises the need to include the human element in core discussions and analysis in sustainable tourism. Butler argues that there is a need to distinguish between sustainable tourism and the development of tourism in the principles of sustainable development. Allan Williams and Armando Montanari (1999) focus on a specific theoretical aspect of sustainability: regulation theory. Their perspective is on self-regulation and its limits in the pursuit of sustainable tourism, which links interestingly with a recent paper by Regina Scheyvens and Robin Biddulph (2018) on inclusive tourism development and what would make the tourism industry more inclusive. Scheyvens and Biddulph refer to the SDGs and challenges in market-driven responsible tourism and how the production and consumption of tourism could regulate itself towards inclusiveness.

Jarkko Saarinen and Christian Rogerson (2014) provide a background to the tourism and SDGs nexus by reviewing the UN MDGs that preceded the SDGs. They discuss the potential contributions of tourism to the UN MDGs, specifically in terms of poverty alleviation, and how the relationship between tourism development and the UN MDGs has been framed in the tourism literature and what issues should be focused on after the UN MDGs. Here, they identify several promising research avenues for interrogating tourism impacts for development, such as inclusive business models. Emma Hughes and Regina Scheyvens (2016) take a step further by focusing on business responsibility in the post-2015 era of tourism planning. They take a critical stand towards corporate social responsibility (CSR). Instead of hegemonic 'Tourism First' planning, they call for a 'Development First' framework for CSR that would be holistic, sustainable, and people-centred in focus. María José Zapata Campos, Michael Hall, and Sandra Backlund (2018) take an inclusive and responsible tourism analysis approach to a specific multinational company's role in sustainable tourism development and CSR work. They demonstrate how the tour operator's sustainability work also results from organisational responses, which do not only emerge from more inclusive practices within the industry but also anticipate future normative pressures (e.g. legislation). These social and structural pressures are crucial for the adoption of more inclusive practices in the tourism industry.

Regina Scheyvens and Janet Momsen (2008) discuss tourism and poverty reduction in the Small Island Developing States (SIDS) context. They suggest a broader development approach to sustainability governance that would not merely focus on economic growth-orientated policies and indicators but also social and environmental sustainability. For this to happen, they argue that governments need to establish stronger regulatory policies and a stricter planning environment for tourism if sustainable tourism and poverty reduction are to be included as developmental targets. In respect of development targets, monitoring the impact of tourism is key. These sustainable tourism indicators are reviewed by Anna Torres-Delgado and Jarkko Saarinen (2014). They note that indicators of sustainability have been widely adopted in tourism planning and governance in principle, but their effectiveness in achieving the ideals of sustainable tourism development is less evident and there are problems associated with data availability and baseline knowledge. There is a need to develop theoretically sound strategic indicators, as otherwise it is a major challenge to achieve practical applications. Mercedes Marzo-Navarro, Marta Pedraja-Iglesias, and Lucia Vinzón (2015) aim to create such applications for sustainability indicators of rural tourism from the perspective of local residents. Based on a case study, they developed measurement models of the social sustainability that are accessible to tourism managers.

One key aspect in sustainable tourism development is governance, as 'destinations wanting to promote sustainable tourism are more likely to be successful when there is effective governance' (Bramwell, 2011, p. 461). Anna Farmaki (2015) identifies this need by evaluating the effectiveness of regional tourism governance in Cyprus. She analyses a public–private network among regional tourism organisations (RTOs), and her empirical findings reveal several challenges for regional network governance. In this respect Farmaki concludes that network governance cannot be considered separately from the socio-cultural, economic, and environmental factors of the socio-spatial and political context. Alison Gill and Peter Williams (2014) take sustainable tourism governance to a resort scale by analysing the transition in governance from growth to sustainability in the Canadian resort of Whistler. The key focus in their evolutionary economic geography (EEG) analysis is the issue of affordable employee accommodation. Their findings demonstrate how, through 'mindful deviation' from a growth model approach, local entrepreneurs were able to employ the collective agency of the community to address the pressing need for affordable housing.

Sonya Graci (2013) analyses governance from the perspective of collaboration and partnership development in sustainable tourism. For her, a major obstacle for sustainable tourism governance is the lack of collaboration among stakeholders. She applies collaborative theory to tourism development on the island of Gili Trawangan, Indonesia, by examining a multi-stakeholder partnership with a demonstrative example of successful collaboration that has led to the implementation of innovative sustainability governance initiatives on that tourism-intensive island. Similarly, Anna Spenceley (2008) evaluates factors that are perceived as essential for sustainable tourism development and governance in trans-frontier conservation areas

(TFCAs) in southern Africa by utilising a Delphi approach with a wide selection of regional tourism experts. The resulting factors relate to governance issues and sustainable tourism indicators. Further related to governance and sustainability indicators, Lei Tin Ong, Donovan Storey, and John Minnery (2011) examine the growth of coastal tourism development and sustainability practices on Boracay Island in the Philippines. They highlight the need to employ a broader socio-economic and cultural focus in tourism governance, concentrating on the management of change on the 'number one beach' of the Philippines.

The final two papers open new avenues in studying tourism, sustainable development, and the SDGs. Alan Lew, Pin Ng, Chin-cheng Ni, and Tsung-chiung Wu (2016) base their approach on resilience, which has characterised recent discussions on tourism and local development. They review some of the key similarities, differences, and indicators of sustainability and resilience thinking. For them, returning to the core definitions of conservation and adaptation helps to identify similarities and differences and to create indicators for understanding how these two frameworks apply to tourism development. They focus specifically on community responses to change with an empirical research case from rural Taiwan. Finally, Patrick Brouder (2017) utilises EEG to understand change in tourism destinations from a sustainable tourism perspective. Like resilience thinking, the EEG approach has received increasing attention in the past few years among tourism geographers. Brouder critically reflects on past EEG research in tourism geographies from a sustainable development perspective, and calls for theoretically informed empirical analysis on EEGs of sustainability in tourism development. Brouder reflects on pro-growth governance models and regional institutional legacies that hinder the development path towards sustainable tourism, and illustrates these challenges using two Canadian case examples (Niagara and Whistler). While the EEG perspective can help to integrate sustainable tourism analysis to structural thinking in political economy studies, Brouder also argues that a sustainable tourism perspective can resolve some of the burning issues in EEG theory. This calls for developing EEG theory within sustainable tourism geographies, including a structural analysis of change in the tourism industry, tourist behaviour, policy-making, and governance that considers both discursive and material justice, along with needs in linking tourism to the UN SDGs.

References

Bianchi, R. V. (2009). The 'critical turn' in tourism studies: A radical critique. *Tourism Geographies, 11*, 484–504.

Bramwell, B. (2011). Governance, the state and sustainable tourism: A political economy approach. *Journal of Sustainable Tourism, 19*(4–5), 459–477.

Bramwell, B., Higham, J., Lane, B., & Miller, G. (2017). Twenty five years of sustainable tourism and the journal of sustainable tourism: Looking back and moving forward. *Journal of Sustainable Tourism, 25*(1), 1–9.

Brouder, P. (2017). Evolutionary economic geography: Reflections from a sustainable tourism perspective. *Tourism Geographies, 19*(3), 438–447. doi:10.1080/14616688.2016.1274774

Butler, R. W. (1999). Sustainable tourism: A state-of-the-art review. *Tourism Geographies, 1*(1), 7–25. doi:10.1080/14616689908721291

Farmaki, A. (2015). Regional network governance and sustainable tourism. *Tourism Geographies, 17*(3), 385–407. doi:10.1080/14616688.2015.1036915

Gill, A. M. & Williams, P. W. (2014). Mindful deviation in creating a governance path towards sustainability in resort destinations. *Tourism Geographies, 16*(4), 546–562. doi:10.1080/14616688.2014.925964

Graci, S. (2013). Collaboration and partnership development for sustainable tourism. *Tourism Geographies, 15*(1), 25–42. doi:10.1080/14616688.2012.675513

Hall, C. M. (2011). Policy learning and policy failure in sustainable tourism governance: From first- and second-order to third-order change? *Journal of Sustainable Tourism, 19*(4–5), 649–671.

Hollenhorst, S. J., Houge-MacKenzie, S., & Ostergren, D. M. (2014). The trouble with tourism. *Tourism Recreation Research, 39*(3), 305–319.

Hughes, E. & Scheyvens, R. (2016). Corporate social responsibility in tourism post-2015: A Development First approach. *Tourism Geographies, 18*(5), 469–482. doi:10.1080/14616688.2016.1208678

Lawson, V. (2007). Geographies of care and responsibility. *Annals of Association of American Geographers, 97*, 1–11.

Lew, A. A., Ng, P. T., Ni, C., & Wu, T. (2016). Community sustainability and resilience: Similarities, differences and indicators. *Tourism Geographies, 18*(1), 18–27. doi:10.1080/14616688.2015.1122664

Liu, Z. (2003). Sustainable tourism development: A critique. *Journal of Sustainable Tourism, 11*(6), 459–475.

Marzo-Navarro, M., Pedraja-Iglesias, M., & Vinzón, L. (2015). Sustainability indicators of rural tourism from the perspective of the residents. *Tourism Geographies, 17*(4), 586–602.

McCool, S. & Bosak, K. (2016). *Reframing sustainable tourism*. Berlin: Springer.

Mosedale, J. (2014). Political economy of tourism: Regulation theory, institutions, and governance networks. In A. A., Lew, C. M. Hall & A. M. Williams (Eds.), *The Wiley Blackwell companion to tourism* (pp. 55–65). Chichester: John Wiley.

Ong, L. T. J., Storey, D., & Minnery, J. (2011). Beyond the beach: Balancing environmental and socio-cultural sustainability in Boracay, the Philippines. *Tourism Geographies, 13*(4), 549–569. doi:10.1080/14616688.2011.590517

Saarinen, J. & Gill, A. M. (2019). Tourism, resilience and governance strategies in the transition towards sustainability. In J. Saarinen & A. M. Gill (Eds.), *Resilient destinations: Governance strategies in the transition towards sustainability in tourism*, 15–33. London: Routledge (in press).

Saarinen, J. & Rogerson, C. M. (2014). Tourism and the millennium development goals: Perspectives beyond 2015. *Tourism Geographies, 16*(1), 23–30. doi:10.1080/14616688.2013.851269

Saarinen, J., Rogerson, C., & Hall, C. M. (2017). Geographies of tourism development and planning. *Tourism Geographies, 19*(3), 307–317.

Scheyvens, R. (2009). Pro-Poor Tourism: Is There Value Beyond the Rhetoric? *Tourism Recreation Research, 34*, 191–196.

Scheyvens, R. (2018). Linking tourism to the sustainable development goals: A geographical perspective. *Tourism Geographies, 20*(2), 341–342.

Scheyvens, R. & Biddulph, R. (2018). Inclusive tourism development. *Tourism Geographies, 20*(4), 589–609. doi:10.1080/14616688.2017.1381985

Scheyvens, R. & Momsen, J. H. (2008). Tourism and poverty reduction: Issues for small island states. *Tourism Geographies, 10*(1), 22–41. doi:10.1080/14616680701825115

Schilcher, D. (2007). Growth versus equity: The continuum of pro-poor tourism and neoliberal governance. *Current Issues in Tourism, 10*(2–3), 166–193.

Sharpley, R. (2000). Tourism and sustainable development: Exploring the theoretical divide. *Journal of Sustainable Tourism, 8*(1), 1–19.

Sharpley, R. (2009). *Tourism development and the environment: Beyond sustainability?* London: Earthscan.

Spenceley, A. (2008). Requirements for sustainable nature-based tourism in Transfrontier conservation areas: A Southern African Delphi consultation. *Tourism Geographies, 10*(3), 285–311. doi:10.1080/14616680802236295

Torres-Delgado, A. & Saarinen, J. (2014). Using indicators to assess sustainable tourism development: A review. *Tourism Geographies, 16*(1), 31–47. doi:10.1080/14616688.2013.867530

United Nations. (2015). *Transforming our world: The 2030 agenda for sustainable development. Resolution adopted by the general assembly on 25 September 2015.* New York: United Nations.

United Nations Conference and Trade Development. (2017). *The economic development in Africa Report 2017: Tourism for transformative and inclusive growth.* New York: United Nations.

UNWTO (World Tourism Organization). (2017). *Tourism and the sustainable development goals – journey to 2030, highlights.* Madrid: UNWTO.

UNWTO (World Tourism Organization). (2018). *Tourism highlights, 2018 edition.* Madrid: UNWTO.

Williams, A. M. & Montanari, A. (1999). Sustainability and self-regulation: Critical perspectives, *Tourism Geographies, 1*(1), 26–40. doi:10.1080/14616689908721292

World Bank Group. (2017). *Tourism for development: 20 reasons sustainable tourism counts for development.* Washington, DC: The World Bank.

World Tourism Organization. (1993). *Sustainable tourism development: Guide for local planners.* Madrid: Word Tourism Organization.

WTTC (World Travel and Tourism Council). (2017). *Global benchmarking report.* London: WTTC.

Zapata Campos, M. J., Hall, C. M., & Backlund, S. (2018). Can MNCs promote more inclusive tourism? Apollo tour operator's sustainability work. *Tourism Geographies, 20*(4), 630–652. doi:10.1080/14616688.2018.1457074

Sustainable tourism:
a state-of-the-art review

Richard W. Butler

ABSTRACT *The topic of sustainable tourism has emerged in the last decade as a result of discussions from the report Our Common Future. This paper reviews the development of the term, beginning with a discussion of the confusion arising from the imprecise and conflicting definitions of the concept, and the need to distinguish between sustainable tourism and the development of tourism on the principles of sustainable development. The paper then reviews the environmental focus of discussions of sustainable tourism and argues for the need to ensure that the concept includes and is applied to the human environment as well as the physical environment. Attention then shifts to problems of carrying capacity, control of tourism development, and the relevance of the term to mass or conventional tourism. The paper concludes with a discussion of the future direction of sustainable tourism and the likelihood of development moving in this direction.*

Introduction

The profound and rapid changes that have taken place in the world in the past two decades have been mirrored in changes in tourism. Global political and economic reorganizations have resulted in the expansion of tourism both in a spatial sense and in terms of a significant increase in the size of the tourist market. Although these changes have been rapid and, in many cases, unanticipated, they have not had revolutionary effects upon tourism; rather, they have enabled it to grow in an evolutionary fashion. Changes in the environmental sphere, however, appear likely to be more fundamental and even revolutionary in terms of their effects upon tourism, perhaps because they have been slower in coming to the fore and could be viewed as long overdue. If there is a single factor that has the potential to change the nature of tourism more than any other, it is the introduction of the concept of 'sustainable development'. Since the appearance of the term a decade ago, it has achieved worldwide recognition and widespread, if superficial, acceptance. Summit meetings of world leaders, policy statements, legislation, the response of industry and marketing shifts - and perhaps even changes in the behaviour of tourists - all suggest that some basic changes may be taking place in specific elements of tourism at different scales.

Geographers have long been interested in the relationships between tourism and the environments, both physical and human, in which it operates, and it is logical that they would be particularly interested in the discussion and application of sustainable development in the context of tourism. This longstanding interest is manifest in the excellent work that has been undertaken by geographers in the field of tourism (e.g. Mathieson & Wall 1982; Murphy 1985; Pearce 1989, 1995; Hall 1994; Hall & Jenkins 1995). With a few exceptions, however, geographers, like many other researchers in tourism, have been reluctant to take a critical view of sustainable development and the way it has been applied to tourism. Perhaps this is because the concept is a particularly attractive one to anyone who has concerns about the abuse of the environment, which includes most geographers, and because many of the principles of sustainable development are in line with many of the basic principles of sensible resource and environmental management. Irrespective of the reason, many writers about tourism appear to have accepted rather unquestioningly the basic proposition that sustainable development is inherently good and appropriate for tourism, and that its adoption will solve many of the negative problems that have resulted from the development of tourism. A few dissenters have argued that this is not necessarily the case (Butler 1993; Wheeller 1993; Wall 1996) and that sustainable development is neither always possible nor even always appropriate in the context of tourism, but the concept still appears to have broad support, often based apparently on little but optimism.

Here, I discuss the state of the art of knowledge and research on sustainable development in the context of tourism with a focus on geographical research. The paper proceeds by first examining the problem of the definition of sustainable development, with the argument that many of the problems relating to the concept owe their origins to the lack of agreement and clarity over the meaning of the concept. This is followed by a discussion of the difference between sustainable development as a concept and its particular application to tourism and the confusion and ambiguity which have arisen in this area. This confusion has been accentuated by the linking of specific forms of tourism, such as 'alternative' tourism, with sustainable development and a willingness to treat these forms as synonymous with the concept. Although further discussion on the meaning of the concept is important, a great deal more attention must be paid to the problem of how to operationalize the concept and make it applicable in appropriate situations to tourism. Related to this is the issue of whether the concept is the same when applied to the human and social world as it is in the context of the environmental sphere, and whether sustainability is achievable within the same parameters in each situation.

Particular attention is paid to three specific features related to the applicability of sustainable development to tourism, namely carrying capacity, control over tourism and mass or conventional tourism. These represent the real challenges to the acceptance and successful application of sustainable development, and to date the problems which they represent have not been fully resolved. The paper concludes with a brief discussion on the future of 'sustainable tourism' and the role in its development that might be played by the geographic academic community.

The meaning of sustainable development

In the preparation of the presentation on which this paper is based, I requested input from colleagues with respect to the content and issues. Several colleagues responded and suggested that a discussion on definitions of sustainable development was not necessary, since its meaning was clear, and that what was more important was a focus on ways in which it could be applied (A.M. Williams, University of Exeter, personal communication). Initially, I agreed with that sentiment, for a great deal has been written on the topic over the last decade (see, for example, articles in the *Journal of Sustainable Tourism*). However, further examination of the literature suggested that some discussion of the meaning of the term - at least in the context of tourism - was warranted, not because there is no definition, but because there are so many (Stabler & Goodall 1996) (Table 1). As other writers have pointed out (Wheeller 1993), that there are so many interpretations of the term has meant that each individual has been able to claim that his or her use of the phrase is appropriate. One result has been that the wide acceptance of the term noted above in many cases is simply acceptance of the phrase but not its implications.

The original definition of sustainable development was provided by the Brundtland Commission in *Our Common Future* as 'development that meets the needs of the present without compromising the ability of future generations to meet their own needs' (World Commission on Environment and Development 1987: 43). This definition has been subject to a wide range of interpretation. On the subject of tourism, as Wall (1996) has pointed out, the Commission was silent, perhaps reflecting the all too

Table 1 Definitions of sustainable tourism

Tourism which meets the needs of present tourists and host regions while protecting and enhancing opportunity for the future. (World Tourism Organization 1993: 7)

Sustainable tourism is tourism and associated infrastructures that: both now and in the future operate within natural capacities for the regeneration and future productivity of natural resources; recognize the contribution that people and communities, customs and lifestyles, make to the tourism experience; accept that these people must have an equitable share in the economic benefits of local people and communities in the host areas. (Eber 1992: 3)

Tourism which can sustain local economies without damaging the environment on which it depends. (Countryside Commission 1995: 2)

It must be capable of adding to the array of economic opportunities open to people without adversely affecting the structure of economic activity. Sustainable tourism ought not interfere with existing forms of social organization. Finally, sustainable tourism must respect the limits imposed by ecological communities. (Payne 1993: 154–5)

Sustainable tourism in parks (and other areas) must primarily be defined in terms of sustainable ecosystems. (Woodley 1993: 94)

Sustainable tourism is tourism which develops as quickly as possible, taking into account of [s/c] current accommodation capacity, the local population and the environment, and:
Tourism that respects the environment and as a consequence does not aid its own disappearance. This is especially important in saturated areas, and:
Sustainable tourism is responsible tourism, (quoted in Bramwell et al. 1996a: 10–11)

---

frequent ignoring or ignorance of tourism by policy makers. The result has been a tremendously varied usage of this definition in the context of tourism, just as the term has met with similar varying interpretations in other contexts. It has become a form of ideology, a political catch phrase and, depending on the context in which it is being used, a concept, a philosophy, a process or a product (Wall 1996).

Coccossis (1996) has suggested that there are at least four ways to interpret tourism in the context of sustainable development: a sectoral viewpoint such as the economic sustainability of tourism; an ecological viewpoint emphasizing the need for ecologically sustainable tourism; a viewpoint of the long-term viability of tourism, recognizing the competitiveness of destinations; and a viewpoint accepting tourism as part of a strategy for sustainable development throughout the physical and human environments. Recognition that the concept is not value-free is crucial to an understanding of the concept, but, as Bramwell points out, this is not a point which is often made in the literature, with the resulting assumption by many that it is a single unified concept (Bramwell *et al.* 1996b: 23). In their review of the principles and practice of sustainable tourism management, Bramwell *et al.* (1996a: 5) note seven dimensions of sustainability: environmental, cultural, political, economic, social, managerial and governmental. It is clear that researchers and decision makers in each of these dimensions have differing interpretations of the concept, which explains its widespread acceptance and equally widespread misuse and abuse.

It is unlikely, therefore, that there will ever be a totally accepted definition of sustainable tourism that is universally applied, because the very success of the term lies in the fact that it is indefinable and thus has become all things to all interested parties. To the tourist industry, it means that development is appropriate; to the conservationist, it means that principles articulated a century ago are once again in vogue; to the environmentalist, it provides a justification for the preservation of significant environments from development; and to the politician, it provides an opportunity to use words rather than actions. Only to the tourist does it really mean or provide nothing other than, in most cases, as Wheeller (1993) has bitingly observed, an opportunity to feel good while enjoying oneself.

'Sustainable' tourism

One of the major problems with the concept of sustainable development has been the way in which the single word 'sustainable' has been applied to a variety of activities based on the assumption that it carries with it the ideological and philosophical implications of the concept (Harrison 1996). In the case of tourism, the result has been the appearance and widespread adoption of the term 'sustainable tourism', often without any attempt to define it (Hunter and Green 1995). I have argued elsewhere (Butler 1993) that this is not only unfortunate but extremely misleading. 'Sustainable' is a widely used term with a specific meaning; it is the adjectival form of the verb 'to sustain ('to maintain or prolong'; *Collins Concise Dictionary* 1995: 1189). In the context of tourism, an appropriate definition of sustainable tourism is 'tourism which is in a form which can maintain its viability in an area for an indefinite period of time' (Butler 1993: 29). Thus, tourism at places such as Niagara Falls in North America, or in London, Paris or Rome, is eminently sustainable. It has been successful in those locations for centuries and shows no signs of disappearing. With such a definition, the emphasis is on the maintenance of tourism, but in many cases tourism is competing for resources and may not be the 'best' or wisest use of resources in these or other locations in the long term.

The above definition, however, is not what is generally implied by the term 'sustainable tourism'. Rather, based on the current literature, what is normally meant by that term is as follows:

> tourism which is developed and maintained in an area (community, environment) in such a manner and at such a scale that it remains viable over an infinite period and does not degrade or alter the environment (human and physical) in which it exists to such a degree that it prohibits the successful development and well being of other activities and processes. (Butler 1993: 29).

The difference between these definitions is not merely a matter of semantics. The definition of sustainable tourism above says very little about anything except the future of tourism. This is, as Wall (1996) has noted, a single sectoral approach, something that is at odds with the concept of sustainable development, which by its very nature is holistic and multi-sectoral. Thus sustainable tourism is not automatically the same as tourism developed in line with the principles of sustainable development. As long as it is taken to be so, then ambiguity and confusion will continue. The need to define the type of tourism being studied or developed beyond the catch-all of 'sustainable' is therefore crucial, if knowledge about the sustainability of tourism is to be expanded.

Alternative forms of tourism and sustainability

Compounding the ambiguities discussed above has been the tendency to link a variety of forms of tourism with the concept of sustainable development. The majority of these are forms of tourism which can be characterized as being 'green' or 'alternative', in the sense that they are not part of mass or conventional tourism (Smith and Eadington 1992). An unfortunate corollary of this linkage has been the automatic assumption that mass tourism is automatically non-sustainable and, therefore, has nothing to do with sustainable development. Indeed, some of the most ardent critics of mass tourism are the most fervent supporters of sustainable development and alternative forms of tourism, in the apparent belief that support of the latter will make the problems of the former disappear (Croall 1995).

This is a problematic development for two reasons. First, it is almost impossible to have a form of tourism development that does not have impacts upon the location in which it occurs. The naive assumption that tourism which is nature-focused will automatically be sustainable may not only be incorrect but also harmful. Small-scale developments of tourism, all other things being equal, could reasonably be expected to have fewer and less severe impacts than large-scale developments, and thus be more sustainable. They may not be fully sustainable, however; and, in reality, all other things are rarely equal. Many forms of alternative tourism, such as ecotourism, are located in highly sensitive and vulnerable environments, some of which cannot withstand even moderate levels of use, and which often have little or no infrastructure to deal with development. The resulting impacts, small though they may be individually, may become serious because of the location in which they occur or because of their cumulative effects.

Second, it has yet to be proven that all examples of mass tourism are unsustainable. While such evidence as exists tends to suggest such a view, the relatively small amount of empirical research into the effects of mass tourism development leaves a great deal unexplained. More importantly, this assumption appears to have led researchers away from the difficult but much more important task of resolving how mass tourism can be made more sustainable (Wheeller 1993; Bramwell *et al.* 1996a; Wall 1996). The key problem with sustainable development in the context of tourism is not ensuring the continued introduction of small-scale, environmentally and culturally appropriate forms of tourism, but how to make existing mass tourism developments as sustainable as possible. Studies on this aspect of sustainable development, such as that by Prat (1996) on the Costa Brava, are extremely rare.

Sustainable development of tourism in different environments

Much of the discussion on sustainable development and tourism has been in the context of the environment in which tourism occurs (Eagles 1994; McCool 1994), and in many cases the settings examined have been in the Third World (Cater and Lowman 1994). This focus probably results from the fact that, in many ways, it is much easier to examine new or proposed developments in virgin or 'greenfield' sites and to argue how they could be made more sustainable, rather than deal with mature and declining urban tourism destinations. In addition, the tourism industry has not been slow to appreciate the marketability of the concept of sustainable development. It has realized that to ignore the groundswell of support for the concept would leave it vulnerable to criticism and possibly stringent regulation, if not prohibition, in certain localities. In many cases, therefore, it has adopted the concept of sustainable development in name if not in operation. Thus many small-scale tourist operations in a wide variety of locations have suddenly begun to call themselves 'sustainable' (and often 'ecotourist') in the hope of successfully competing for the 'appropriate tourist'. In this context, it is important to remember that the tourist industry is comprised of many small but highly competitive operations as well as the well-known and often criticized multinational conglomerates.

Too many inappropriate or poorly operated small-scale developments in the wrong location can be just as harmful and non-sustainable as a single large development.

The overwhelming focus of attention on the environmental context has been effectively criticized by, among others, Craik (1993: 3), who asked the highly pertinent question, 'Why is sustainable development almost invariably reduced to, and articulated in terms of, environmental matters?' One answer to this very valid query is that sustainable development as a concept emerged in the context of the second global wave of environmental concern. It coincided with increasingly obviously visible environmental impacts of tourism in mature destinations, and growing political support for environmental protection. In the context of tourism, however, it should have been clear to all those involved that tourism, like most forms of resource use, straddles both the physical and the human worlds. It can have just as severe and far-reaching impacts upon the human (cultural, social) resources of tourist destinations as it does on the physical (vegetation, wildlife, water, etc.) resources (Mathieson and Wall 1982). Indeed, this principle has been recognized by the World Tourism Organization, which suggested that sustainable tourist development should meet 'the needs of present tourists and host regions while protecting and enhancing opportunity for the future' (World Tourism Organization 1993: 7). However, relatively little attention has been paid to date by researchers in determining how sustainability in the context of the human environment could be determined. Craik (1995) is one of the few to suggest a specific framework for such an approach, although there are indications that other researchers are increasingly accepting that sustainable development must be accepted as having a human component that is equally as important as the more traditionally accepted environmental focus (for examples, see Briguglio *et al.* 1996a, 1996b).

A second aspect of sustainable development that has received little attention is the application of the principles to tourist sites in the developed world, particularly in urban and highly developed areas. Two recent papers (Bramwell *et al.* 1996a; Zelfde 1996) provide some evidence of a development of interest in these areas. The edited volume by Priestley *et al.* (1996) has an encouragingly wide range of topics within it, including several dealing with the human component of tourism in developed areas, although, despite the title of the volume, the discussion on sustainability is rather limited. The fact remains, however, that the bulk of the literature and policies which do exist on tourism and sustainable development have a clear emphasis on environmental matters and new, often small-scale developments, generally related to natural or heritage features (Ecologically Sustainable Development Working Groups 1991; McCool 1994; Croall 1995; Hunter & Green 1995). Relatively few authors have focused attention on the application of the concept to the human and social elements and the different frame works that are required for successful implementation (Nelson *et al.* 1993; Craik 1995; Bramwell *et al.* 1996b; Briguglio *et al.* 1996a, 1996b; Squire 1996), and their efforts have been concentrated in the last few years only. To many people in tourism and other fields, the concept of sustainable development is still, unfortunately, tied firmly and often exclusively to the physical environment.

Major unresolved issues in sustainable development

In the context of tourism there remain a number of key, as yet unresolved, issues with the concept of sustainable development, including its relationship with carrying capacity, with control of development and operation, and with mass or conventional tourism. These issues are clearly related to each other, and arise because of the nature of tourism development, the nature of the tourism industry and the role of the public sector in tourism in many destinations. In addition, and related to the difficulties stemming from the ill-defined nature of the concept, are the problems of measurement and monitoring. Whether the concept of sustainable development is anything new is a subject that needs considerable discussion, but readers familiar with writings on conservation dating back from the turn of the century may be forgiven for thinking that it is simply a version of that concept with a new face. Certainly, the writings of Meadows *et al.* (1972) a quarter of a century ago in *The Limits to Growth* raised very similar issues and sentiments to those expressed in *Our Common Future* (World Commission on Environment and Development 1987).

The key term in this concept is the one of 'limits'. However much proponents of development may ignore the fact, implicit in the concept of sustainable development is the idea of limits. In the case of tourism, this is normally expressed in terms of numbers of tourists, although implicit in this is the associated infrastructure development and landscape modifications. While thinking on carrying capacity has been modified greatly since the 1960s, when researchers were seeking the 'magic number' of visitors who could be accommodated at a specific site, the issue of volume still remains (Butler 1996). Although it is generally accepted that numbers alone are not an entirely satisfactory measure of the effects of tourism, there is little doubt that, in almost all tourism contexts, there is a maximum number of tourists who can be successfully accommodated (however 'successful' is defined). Once this number is exceeded, a range of negative and sometimes irreversible effects take place. These impacts may take some time to manifest themselves in certain areas (e.g. changes in environmental quality), whereas in others their effects may be felt almost immediately (e.g. resident attitudes). In most cases, there is no clear threshold and the effects are often cumulative, sometimes in a linear but not necessarily simple relationship, depending on a wide range of variables. The fact remains, however, that in almost every conceivable context, there will be an upper limit in terms of the numbers of tourists and the amount of development associated with tourism that the destination can withstand (Shipp 1993). Once these levels are exceeded, a number of things occur, normally in undesirable form. The nature of tourism itself changes, the nature of the destination changes, the attractivity and hence the viability of the destination declines, and tourism becomes no longer sustainable in its original form. If overuse and overdevelopment continue unabated, then any form of tourism may become unsustainable in that destination (Butler 1991; Cooper 1996; Zanetto & Soriani 1996).

Given this scenario, one would expect that proponents of sustainable forms of tourism or sustainable development encompassing tourism would include limits to growth in any proposed development. Such limits would be based on the ability (capacity) of the resources (human and physical) to absorb the effects of tourism so that tourism and other activities and attributes would be able to be maintained over the long term. This is a point made by Bramwell *et al.* in their excellent discussion of a framework for sustainable tourism: 'A key element of setting targets for sustainable tourism is the establishing of the tourism carrying capacity of a destination area' (1996b: 61). In fact few, if any, development proposals identify or propose such limits. If sustainable development principles are included in development plans in anything more than name only, they are normally couched in vague terms which are long on emotion and short on specifics. This is explained, in part, by the fact that researchers and policy makers in tourism have never grasped the nettle of carrying capacity or limits and have never produced measures that could be used in such contexts (Butler 1996). The urgent need to take such steps at the local level as well as at more senior levels of government has been stressed more strongly recently (Coccossis & Parpairis 1996; Johnson and Thomas 1996).

This problem relates directly to that noted above of measurement of sustainability. A few examples of proposed measures appeared in the volume *Tourism and Sustainable Development: Monitoring, Planning, Managing* (Nelson *et al.* 1993), including those by Kreutzwiser (1993), Payne (1993) and Marsh (1993), but all of these are speculative and none are based on empirical research. The idea of measures or indicators of the nature of tourism are not new. The need for performance indicators in plans and management strategies for tourism development has been noted by Getz (1982), Gunn (1994), Inskeep (1991) and the World Tourism Organization (1993) among others, and yet these calls have rarely been translated into action. Without such indicators, the use of the term 'sustainable' is meaningless. It becomes hyperbole and advertising jargon of the kind so brilliantly criticized by Wheeller (1993, 1994). In England, the

Countryside Commission concisely summarized the need for, and the result of an absence of, monitoring: 'A commitment to monitoring is essential. Without any commitment to measuring impact on either a qualitative or quantitative basis, it is impossible to decide whether one is moving towards sustainable tourism or away from it' (Countryside Commission 1995: 9).

The points raised in the above discussion stem in many cases from the fact that, despite the many agencies and private sector elements involved in the promotion and development of tourism, there are few bodies whose function is to control tourism once it has been developed. Indeed, one of the key issues is how tourism could be controlled given the nature, variety and motivations of the industry and the participants. Tourism researchers with few exceptions have tended to ignore the issue of control of tourism and, by implication, the politics of tourism. Richter's (1989) early work raised some of the issues in the context of Asian tourism, but not until more recently has there has been an overall review of the political realm of tourism and its implications (Hall 1994; Hall & Jenkins 1995). The absence of research and discussion on the political aspects of tourism - and the reverse, the ignoring of the political implications of tourism development and the changes it brings by decision makers and their advisors - is yet another example of the isolation of tourism from the world in which it exists. While there are examples of good discussion of the policy implications of sustainable tourism (see, for example, Pigram 1990), the links between policy and politics are often not developed. Wall (1996) has commented eloquently on the problems of dealing with tourism from a single sector viewpoint and the need to consider the context in which tourism occurs and the systems with which it interacts. The political system of control is one of these, and a particularly important one when considering controls on the amount, type and rate of development that are inevitable in the case of sustainable tourism development.

This leads to the third major issue identified above, namely the relationship of sustainable development to mass or conventional tourism. Writers critical of mass tourism (e.g. Poon 1993; Croall 1995) often propose what are termed 'sustainable forms of tourism' as the ideal alternative, and in so doing imply, if not state categorically, that the two forms of tourism are incompatible. It is clear that many examples of mass tourism development are not sustainable by any definition of the term, and the difficult position many established destinations find themselves in at the current time is evidence of this (Dickinson 1996; Prat 1996; Vera & Rippin 1996). However, to take such evidence and conclude that sustainable development principles can only be applied to small-scale, sensitive new developments in greenfield sites is shortsighted. In the first case, as many authors have pointed out (Butler 1991; Wall 1993a, 1993b; Wheeller 1993; Pearce 1995), mass tourism is incredibly popular and is not going to disappear or be replaced by 'alternative' tourism.

Tourism is a phenomenon that has demonstrated continuous growth for at least half a century at the global scale, and most of this growth has been in mass tourism. While the most rapid growth in recent years appears to have been in specialized forms of tourism, such as ecotourism, the actual numbers of tourists involved in these forms are very small compared to those engaged in 'mass' tourism (World Tourism Organization 1995). Also, as these new forms of tourism become increasingly popular, there is every likelihood that they will become varieties of mass tourism; indeed, many of them are taking on such characteristics very rapidly as they expand. The increase in numbers, the intensive marketing, the need for large accommodation and transportation units, the changes in the product itself, and the resultant impacts on destinations are all familiar trends in mass tourism. To assume that they will remain sustainable, if indeed they ever were sustainable in anything but name, is naive and not supported by research.

Where tourism has been in existence for long periods of time, for example in capital cities and at specific 'marked' sites such as the Pyramids, Niagara Falls and the Alps, with few exceptions it has continued to survive by changing its products or enlarging its market. Neither of these techniques is sustainable in the strict sense of the term as used by the World Commission on Environment and Development. However, the basic attractions in such places still exist to a large degree, although certainly not in an unchanged or pristine form. Where tourism has existed for a long time based on natural attractions but involving large numbers of visitors, we see major problems in many areas. The numbers of visitors require and generally result in the establishment of facilities and an infrastructure to meet their needs, with the result that the natural areas lose some of their naturalness and hence their attractivity. As tourist numbers and facilities increase, the market changes and many visitors who were attracted by the natural features and the absence of development and large numbers of tourists no longer come, going instead to other, less developed sites. The natural 'capital' of these sites is being reduced by development and they are becoming less sustainable, although numbers may be stable or even still increasing.

The mass market for tourism shows no signs of decreasing; indeed, as new countries of origin in Asia, such as Japan and Korea, provide ever larger numbers of tourists, it shows every evidence of continuing to increase for the foreseeable future. Existing and future destinations of this mass market should be the focus of efforts at achieving sustainability in tourism for two reasons. First, it is simply inappropriate in this day and age to develop destinations that do not strive to be as environmentally and socially benign as possible, and hence as close to sustainability as feasible. The environments and residents of destination areas deserve such consideration, as do the visitors themselves. Second, if such destinations rapidly decline in quality and attractiveness because of poor planning and development, tourists will desert them and seek new destinations at an increasingly rapid rate.

The benefits of tourism will not be maximized but will only be compressed into a short period. New destinations will have to be established to meet the new demand and the same process will continue to escalate until there are literally no more suitable destinations or no areas willing to accept tourism, a process discussed by Plog (1974) more than 20 years ago.

Conclusions

In trying to identify where the state of the art of current research on tourism in the context of sustainable development stands is rather difficult. There is now a sizeable body of literature on this subject, which is growing rapidly. The topic has even resulted in the appearance of a journal *(Journal of Sustainable Tourism)* devoted to this field. A great deal more research by geographers and others has been conducted and is just reaching the publication stage (Pigram & Wahab 1997; Hall & Lew 1998; C. Becker, University of Trier, personal communication). Thus one cannot conclude simply that there is little written and that much remains to be done, nor can one argue that the key questions have been resolved. Although a great deal has been written, particularly in the last 5 years, I feel that much research does still remain to be undertaken.

The key problem, in my mind, is the current inability to define to the satisfaction of all, or even most, of the stakeholders in tourism, exactly what is meant by 'sustainable tourism'. As noted above, this remains a major problem and, because ambiguity exists, almost any form of tourism can, and often is, termed sustainable. Related to this fundamental issue is the question of how sustainability might be monitored and measured if and when a satisfactory definition of sustainable tourism is established and accepted. It is clear that current research in all disciplines involved with tourism has not really tackled the problem of monitoring the effects of tourism in any context. Despite the real need to benchmark and monitor, first called for many years ago (Mathieson & Wall 1982), such efforts have, by and large, been at best sporadic and non-systematic. Given the hype that exists in industry and political circles to persuade people that much is being done to achieve sustainable tourism, there is implicit, if not overt, opposition to research that might show that very little new or existing tourism development is sustainable, or at best that a decision on its sustainability cannot be made for many years to come. Also, many proponents of the idea of sustainable tourism seem unwilling to accept that, because an operation calls itself sustainable, it may not be so in reality.

To assess the real impacts of tourism and the level of sustainability achieved requires in-depth longitudinal research and environmental, economic and social auditing. This requires stable funding and a willingness on the part of researchers to commit to a research programme for a considerable period of time. There is very little evidence that this sort of commitment currently exists and good long-term research on sustainable development in tourism or any other field is extremely scarce (Wall 1996). One can argue, therefore, that the greatest research need is to develop measures of sustainability and to apply these to existing and new forms of tourism development to help determine what affects sustainability and how it can be achieved; in other words, to operationalize the concept and evaluate it in operation. This is far more complex than it sounds because, as discussed above, a multi-sectoral approach is essential, and this requires much more than simply estimating the direct effects of tourism on the physical and human environments of destination areas.

Even when the elements and processes of sustainability are identified and understood, there is still no guarantee that it will be practised in destination areas. It will be necessary, if sustainability is to be achieved, to ensure that all stakeholders are willing participants in the process. If the industry, at all scales, cannot be persuaded that it is in its own direct interest to commit to some principles of sustainability, then efforts of other stakeholders will have little effect. If the public sector is not willing to educate and, if necessary, enforce sustainable policies and actions, then few are unlikely to follow them. Simply listing appropriate actions and strategies and calling for their adoption (Table 2), as some governments have done (Tourism Canada 1990), is but a first step - specific action and enforcement are necessary as well. If local residents cannot see the short-term as well as long-term benefits to themselves of sustainable policies, they will subvert or ignore them. Finally, if the tourists themselves do not enjoy or anticipate satisfaction from sustainable forms of tourism, they will not participate and not visit destinations geared to offer this type of tourism. One of the other tasks facing researchers, if they wish to ensure the application as well as the understanding of sustainable development of tourism, is to find ways to ensure the necessary policies and actions are acceptable to all stakeholders in tourism.

Simply saying that all is well and that sustainable tourism is the way of the future because there is a growing interest in the concept will not ensure its adoption or success. At present, there is a disturbing tendency, in the desire to promote sustainable tourism, to claim that any small-scale, environmentally or culturally focused form of tourism is sustainable, particularly where it is developed by or for local residents. In the absence of accurate and reliable indicators and monitoring, one cannot comment on the sustainability of any enterprise until many years after its establishment, and only then, after comparing its operation and effects, to the state of the environment at the time of its establishment. Given that the term sustainable development did not enter the lexicon until 1987, it is still too soon to say if anything created since then is truly sustainable or not.

Table 2 An action strategy for sustainable tourism development: the role of government

Governments should:
1. Undertake area- and sector-specific research on overall tourism effects
2. Support the development of tourism economic models
3. Assist and support lower levels of governments to develop their own tourism development strategies in conjunction with conservation strategies
4. Develop standards and regulations for environmental and cultural impact assessments, monitoring and auditing of existing and proposed tourism developments
5. Apply sectoral and regional environmental accounting systems for tourism
6. Design and implement public consultation techniques and processes in order to involve all stakeholders in making tourism-related decisions
7. Develop and implement new economic indicators which define national well-being in the sustainable development sense
8. Design and implement educational and awareness programmes which will sensitize people to the issues of sustainable tourism development
9. Develop adequate tools and techniques to analyse the effect of tourism development projects on heritage sites and ancient monuments as an integral part of cultural and environmental impact assessment
10. Develop design and construction standards which will ensure that tourism development projects are sympathetic with local culture and natural environments
11. Ensure that carrying capacities of tourism destinations reflect sustainable levels of development and are monitored and adjusted appropriately
12. Enforce regulations for illegal trade in historic objects and crafts, unofficial archaeological research, the prevention of erosion of aesthetic values and desecration of sites
13. Regulate and control tourism in environmentally and culturally sensitive areas
14. Include tourism in land use planning
15. Create tourism boards that involve all stakeholders
16. Ensure that all government departments involved in tourism are briefed on the concept of sustainable development
17. Ensure that tourism interests are represented at major caucus planning meetings that affect the environment and the economy
18. Ensure that national and local tourism development agreements stress a policy of sustainable tourism development

Source: Tourism Canada (1990).

References

Bramwell, B., Henry, I., Jackson, G., Prat, A.G., Richards, G. and van der Straaten, J., eds. 1996a. *Sustainable Tourism Management: Principles and Practice.* Tilburg, Netherlands: Tilburg University Press.

Bramwell, B., Henry, I., Jackson, G. and van der Straaten, J. 1996b. A framework for understanding sustainable tourism management. In *Sustainable Tourism Management: Principles and Practice*, ed. W. Bramwell, I. Henry, G. Jackson, A.G. Prat, G. Richards and J. van der Straaten, pp. 23–72. Tilburg, Netherlands: Tilburg University Press.

Briguglio, L., Archer, B., Jafari, J. and Wall, G. eds. 1996a. *Sustainable Tourism in Islands and Small States: Issues and Policies,* Vol. 1. London: Cassell.

Briguglio, L., Butler, R., Harrison, D. and Filho, W. eds. 1996b. *Sustainable Tourism in Islands and Small States: Case Studies,* Vol. 2. London: Cassell.

Butler, R.W. 1991. Tourism, environment, and sustainable development. *Environmental Conservation* 18(3): 201–9.

Butler, R.W. 1993. Tourism - an evolutionary perspective. In *Tourism and Sustainable Development: Monitoring, Planning, Managing,* ed. J.G. Nelson, R.W. Butler and G. Wall, pp. 27–44. Waterloo, Ontario: University of Waterloo (Department of Geography Publication 37).

Butler, R.W. 1996. The concept of carrying capacity for tourism destinations: dead or merely buried? *Progress in Tourism and Hospitality Research* 2(3–4): 283–93.

Cater, E. and Lowman, G. 1994. *Ecotourism: A Sustainable Option?* New York: John Wiley.

Coccossis, H. 1996. Tourism and sustainability: Perspectives and implications. In *Sustainable Tourism? European Experiences,* ed. G.K. Priestley, J.A. Edwards and H. Coccossis, pp. 1–21. Wallingford, Oxford: CAB International.

Coccossis, H. and Parpairis, A. 1996. Tourism and carrying capacity in coastal areas: Mykonos, Greece. In *Sustainable Tourism? European Experiences,* ed. G.K. Priestley, J.A. Edwards and H. Coccossis, pp. 153–75. Wallingford, Oxford: CAB International.

Cooper, C. 1996. The environmental consequences of declining destinations. *Progress in Tourism and Hospitality Research* 2(3–4): 337–46.

Countryside Commission. 1995. *Sustaining Rural Tourism.* Cheltenham, UK: Countryside Commission (CCP 483).

Craik, J. 1993. The cultural limits of tourism in pacific rim countries. Paper presented at the International Conference on Sustainable Tourism in Islands and Small States, Valletta, Malta, November 1993.

Craik, I. 1995. Are there cultural limits to tourism? *Journal of Sustainable Tourism* 3(2): 87–98.

Croall, J. 1995. *Preserve or Destroy: Tourism and the Environment.* London: Calouste Gulbenkian Foundation.

Dickinson, G. 1996. Environmental degradation in the countryside: Loch Lomond, Scotland. In *Sustainable Tourism? European Experiences,* ed. G.K. Priestley, J.A. Edwards and H. Coccossis, pp. 22–34. Wallingford, Oxford: CAB International.

Eagles, P.F.J. 1994. Understanding the market for sustainable tourism. In *Linking Tourism, the Environment and Sustainability,* ed. S.F. McCool and A.E. Watson, pp. 23–33. Ogden, UT: USDA (General Technical Report INT-GTR-323).

Eber, S., ed. 1992. Beyond the Green Horizon: A Discussion Paper on Principles for Sustainable Tourism. Godalming, UK: Worldwide Fund for Nature.

Ecologically Sustainable Working Groups. 1991. *Final Report - Tourism.* Canberra, ACT: Commonwealth of Australia.

Getz, D. 1982. A rationale and methodology for assessing capacity to absorb tourism. *Ontario Geography* 19: 92–101.

Gunn, C. 1994. *Tourism Planning.* Washington, DC: Taylor & Francis.

Hall, C.M. *1994. Tourism and Politics: Power, Policy and Place.* London: John Wiley.

Hall, C.M. and Jenkins, J. 1995. *Tourism and Public Policy.* London: Routledge.

Hall, C.M. and Lew, A.A., eds. 1998. *Sustainable Tourism: A Geographical Perspective.* London: Addison Wesley Longman.

Harrison, D. 1996. Sustainability and tourism: Reflections in a muddy pool. In *Sustainable Tourism in Islands and Small States: Issues and Policies,* Vol. 1, ed. L. Briguglio, B. Archer, J. Jafari and G. Wall, pp. 69–89. London: Cassell.

Hunter, C. and Green, H. 1995. *Tourism and the Environment: A Sustainable Relationship?* London: Routledge.

Inskeep, E. 1991. *Tourism Planning: An Integrated and Sustainable Development Approach.* New York: Van Nostrand Reinhold.

Johnson, P. and Thomas, B. 1996. Tourism capacity: A critique. In *Sustainable Tourism in Islands and Small States: Issues and Policies,* Vol. 1, ed. L. Briguglio, B. Archer, J. Jafari and G. Wall, pp. 118–36. London: Cassell.

Kreutzwiser, R. 1993. Desirable attributes of sustainability indicators for tourism development. In *Tourism and Sustainable Development: Monitoring, Planning, Managing,* ed. J.G. Nelson, R.W. Butler and G. Wall, pp. 243–48. Waterloo, Ontario: University of Waterloo (Department of Geography Publication 37).

Marsh, J. 1993. An index of tourism sustainability. In *Tourism and Sustainable Development: Monitoring, Planning, Managing,* ed. J.G. Nelson, R.W. Butler and G. Wall, pp. 255–8. Waterloo, Ontario: University of Waterloo (Department of Geography Publication 37).

Mathieson, A. and Wall, G. 1982. *Tourism: Economic, Social and Physical Impacts.* London: Longman.

McCool, S.F. 1994. Linking tourism, the environment, and concepts of sustainability: Setting the stage. In *Linking Tourism, the Environment and Sustainability,* ed. S.F. McCool and A.E. Watson, pp. 3–7. Ogden, UT: USDA (General Technical Report INT-GTR-323).

Meadows, D.H., Meadows, D.L., Randers, J. and Behrens, W.W. 1972. *Limits to Growth: A Report for the Club of Rome's Project on the Predicament of Mankind.* New York: Universe Books.

Murphy, P.E. 1985. *Tourism: A Community Approach.* New York: Methuen.

Nelson, J.G., Butler, R.W. and Wall, G. eds. 1993. *Tourism and Sustainable Development: Monitoring, Planning, Managing.* Waterloo, Ontario: University of Waterloo (Department of Geography Publication 37).

Payne, R. 1993. Sustainable tourism: Suggested indicators and monitoring techniques. In *Tourism and Sustainable Development: Monitoring, Planning, Managing,* ed. J.G. Nelson, R.W. Butler and G. Wall, pp. 249–54. Waterloo, Ontario: University of Waterloo (Department of Geography Publication 37).

Pearce, D.G. 1989. *Tourist Development.* London: Longman.

Pearce, D.G. 1995. Tourism Today: A Geographical Analysis. London: Longman.

Pigram, J.J. 1990. Sustainable tourism: Policy considerations. *Journal of Tourism Studies* 1(2): 2–7.

Pigram, J.J. and Wahab, S.A.E., eds. 1997. *Tourism, Sustainability and Growth.* London: Routledge.

Plog, S.C. 1974. Why destination areas rise and fall in popularity. *Cornell Hotel and Restaurant Administration Quarterly* (February): 55–8.

Poon, A. 1993. *Tourism, Technology, and Competitive Strategies.* Harmondsworth, UK: CAB International.

Prat, A.G. 1996. Back to a sustainable future on the Costa Brava. In *Sustainable Tourism Management: Principles and Practice,* ed. W. Bramwell, I. Henry, G. Jackson, A.G. Prat, G. Richards and J. van der Straaten, pp. 121–46. Tilburg, Netherlands: Tilburg University Press.

Priestley, G.K., Edwards, J.A. and Coccossis, H., eds. 1996. *Sustainable Tourism? European Experiences.* Wallingford, Oxford: CAB International.

Richter, L. 1989. *The Politics of Tourism in Asia.* Honolulu, HI: University of Hawaii Press.

Shipp, D., ed. 1993. *Loving Them to Death? Sustainable Tourism in Europe's Nature and National Parks.* Grafenau: Federation of Nature and National Parks of Europe.

Smith, V.L. and Eadington, W.R. 1992. *Tourism Alternatives.* Philadelphia, PA: University of Pennsylvania Press.

Squire, S. 1996. Literary tourism and sustainable tourism? Promoting 'Anne of Green Gables' in Prince Edward Island. *Journal of Sustainable Tourism* 4(3): 119–34.

Stabler, M.J. and Goodall, B. 1996. Environmental auditing in planning for sustainable island tourism. In *Sustainable Tourism in Islands and Small States: Issues and Policies,* Vol. 1, ed. L. Briguglio, B. Archer, J. Jafari and G. Wall, pp. 170–96. London: Cassell.

Tourism Canada. 1990. An action strategy for sustainable tourism development. Workshop paper for Globe '90 Conference, Vancouver, BC, Canada, October 1990. Ottawa, Ontario: Tourism Canada.

Vera, F. and Rippin, R. 1996. Decline of a Mediterranean tourist area and restructuring strategies: The Valencian region. In *Sustainable Tourism? European Experiences,* ed. G.K. Priestley, J.A. Edwards and H. Coccossis, pp. 120–36. Wallingford, Oxford: CAB International.

Wall, G. 1993a. International collaboration in the search for sustainable tourism in Bali. *Journal of Sustainable Tourism* 1(1): 38–47.

Wall, G. 1993b. Towards a tourism typology. In *Tourism and Sustainable Development: Monitoring, Planning, Managing,* ed. J.G. Nelson, R.W. Butler and G. Wall, pp. 45–58. Waterloo, Ontario: University of Waterloo (Department of Geography Publication 37).

Wall, G. 1996. Is ecotourism sustainable? *Environmental Management* 2(3–4): 207–16.

Wheeller, B. 1993. Sustaining the ego. *Journal of Sustainable Tourism* 1(2): 121–9.

Wheeller, B. 1994. Ecotourism: A ruse by any other name. In *Progress in Tourism Recreation and Hospitality Management,* Vol. 6, ed. C.P. Cooper and A. Lockwood, pp. 3–11. London: John Wiley.

Woodley, S. 1993. Tourism and sustainable development in parks and protected areas. In *Tourism and Sustainable Development: Monitoring, Planning, Managing,* ed. J.G. Nelson, R.W. Butler and G. Wall, pp. 83–96. Waterloo, Ontario: University of Waterloo (Department of Geography Publication 37).

World Commission on Environment and Development. 1987. *Our Common Future.* New York: Oxford University Press.

World Tourism Organization. 1993. Sustainable Tourism Development: Guide for Local Planners. Madrid: WTO.

World Tourism Organization. 1995. *Summary of Statistics.* Madrid: WTO.

Zanetto, G. and Soriani, S. 1996. Tourism and environmental degradation: The northern Adriatic Sea. In *Sustainable Tourism? European Experiences,* ed. G.K. Priestley, J.A. Edwards and H. Coccossis, pp. 137–52. Wallingford, Oxford: CAB International.

Zelfde, J. van t'. 1996. Environmentality at Disneyland Paris. In *Sustainable Tourism Management: Principles and Practice,* ed. W. Bramwell, I. Henry, G. Jackson, A.G. Prat, G. Richards and J. van der Straaten, pp. 87–102. Tilburg, Netherlands: Tilburg University Press.

Resume: Le tourisme durable: un etat de la question

Le theme du tourisme durable a emerge dans la demiere decennie, sute aux discussions sur le rapport Notre Futur Commun. Cette contribution s'interesse d'abord au developpement du terme lui-meme, en commen?ant par une discussion sur la confusion engendree par des definitions imprecises et controversies du concept, et sur le besoin de distinguer entre tourisme durable d'une part et developpement touristique fonde sur les principes du developpement durable d'autre part. Elle examine ensuite l'aspect environnemental des discussions sur le tourisme durableet plaide pour la necessite d'affirmer un concept, et ses applications, qui conceme l'environnement autant humain que physique. L'attention est ensuite portee aux problemes de capacite de charge et de controle du developpement touristique ainsi qu'a la pertinence du terme pour le tourisme de masse (ou conventionnel). La conclusion discute de l'orientation future du tourisme durable et de la prob- abilite d'un developpement dans cette direction.

Mots-cles: tourisme durable, definitions, developpement, capacite de charge, controle, tourisme de masse

Sustainability and self-regulation: critical perspectives

Allan M. Williams

Armando Montanari

ABSTRACT *This paper considers the limits of self-regulation in the pursuit of sustainable tourism. There is evidence of considerable good practice brought about by selfregulation in many parts of Europe, and this is illustrated by the example of the Alps. However, even a consideration of the traditional division between individual and social costs indicates the limitations to self-regulation. The main emphasis of the paper is on exploring how regulation theory can deepen our appreciation of the constraints on self-regulation.*

Introduction

The concept of sustainability has been at or near the heart of many, if not most, debates on economic development policy since at least the 1987 Report of the Brundtland Commission and the 1992 Earth Summit. It remains questionable whether there has been a paradigm shift in thinking about development, but there can be little doubt that sustainability has found a place on the agenda of discussions about, and informs the implementation of, economic development strategies. It is surprising, therefore, that much of the literature about sustainability has developed in isolation from wider debates concerning the nature of economic restructuring, and there have been few attempts to articulate the links between these two, largely parallel, discourses. These comments apply as much to the broader sphere of sustainable development as to the more specific theme of sustainable tourism.

The lack of engagement between the two sets of literatures stems partly from their very different theoretical and functional roots. Sustainability is based on advocacy and prescription, and is forward-looking. It is a maze of ethics, organizational ideas and implicit welfare economics (de Kadt 1992), and is strong on morality while weak on theory. There have been attempts to provide a theoretical framework for sustainable tourism (see de Kadt, but most of the literature in this field is focused on the design and implementation of policy initiatives, and case studies of particular projects that provide benchmarks of good practice (Williams & Shaw 1996). The theoretical weakness of the sustainability debate has been noted and Wheeler (1991), for example, complains of the neglect of wider social questions. In part, this is symptomatic of the effective traditional ghettoization of tourism as an academic discipline (Shaw & Williams 1994: 3–17), so that tourism research has become detached from wider theoretical discourses on, for example, the changing nature of production, governance and societal organization.

This paper contends that the debate on sustainable tourism can usefully be informed by research on restructuring, particularly regulation theory, which has informed the research in economic and social geography during the 1980s and 1990s. Williams and Shaw (1998) have investigated five aspects of restructuring theory that have a direct bearing on sustainable tourism: intra-generational equity, shifts in modes of production, new forms of consumption, the supposed decline of mass production of tourism, and the limitations to state intervention.

In this paper, we focus on one particular aspect of sustainable tourism - self-regulation - and consider how regulation theory can be used to inform the debates on this. This is timely given the considerable policy emphasis on self-regulation.

Sustainability and self-regulation

One starting point for a discussion of sustainability is the Brundtland Report's definition that this is 'development that meets the needs of the present without compromising the ability of future generations to meet their own needs' (World Commission on Environment and Development 1987). Essentially, this is a definition based on notions of inter- and intragenerational equity in the distribution and management of resources. Intra-generational equity is more implicit than explicit in comparison to the emphasis on inter-generational concerns.

Over time, increasing emphasis has been placed on the need for partnership between interest groups in the implementation of sustainability programmes. The European Union's Fifth Environmental Action Programme, *Towards Shared Responsibility,* states that partnerships are voluntary collaborations between two or more organizations with a jointly defined agenda focused on a discrete, attainable and potentially measurable goal (CEC 1992). Partnerships have the advantages of facilitating:

1 Identification of the key actors in a sustainability programme.
2 Assisting the partners to recognize their respective strengths and weaknesses.
3 Providing a forum for priority setting.
4 Integrating different points of view, thereby reducing the risks of friction between potential partners.

The last point, about reducing friction between partners, takes us back to the notion of equity. However, for the purposes of this paper, the key point is that partnerships should be 'voluntary collaborations' and 'should integrate different points of view', while the advocacy of 'forums' and 'recognizing respective strengths' implicitly assumes that the key to sustainability lies in self-regulation. Self-regulation involves participation and empowerment for the partners, or stakeholders, in any programme designed to facilitate sustainable tourism. Unfortunately, self-regulation is not a clearly elaborated concept. For our purposes here, it can be suggested that self-regulation involves individuals, individual agencies or partnerships taking direct responsibility for managing their use of the environment. In some political uses of the term 'self-regulation', there is also implicit a rejection of state regulation.

Self-regulation has diverse roots. To some extent it is rooted in neoliberal beliefs that individual decision making, based on self-interest, is the most effective means of achieving predetermined goals, including consumer satisfaction. In the case of sustainable tourism, this involves an assumption that individual decision makers are able to assess and act in the interests of both their long-term and their short-term goals. Such views are partly rooted in von Hayek's (1988) writings emphasizing that maximizing individual freedom to take decisions, without state interference, allows markets to work more effectively in the service of individual interests.

A less extreme justification of self-regulation lies in the belief that, in western economies, there are limits to state regulation, for the latter tends to be more effective in the imposition of negative controls than in eliciting positive behaviour by either consumers or producers. This view is reinforced by the fiscal crisis of the state in the last quarter of the twentieth century, which has led to a reduction in the scale and extent of state interventionism. A third, entirely pragmatic, argument stresses that self-regulation will be effective where the parties perceive the alternative to be greater, and potentially more constraining, state-imposed regulation. Although the extreme neo-liberal view assumes away the need for almost any form of state regulation, most proponents of self-regulation consider that this is only one constitutive, if necessary, element in a holistic approach that combines different forms of regulation.

The case for self-regulation is advanced both on the *a priori* grounds of a competing model of societal organization, and on the practical grounds that there is already considerable evidence that sustainable tourism can be advanced through individual examples of voluntaristic projects. In the following section, we review some European examples of self-regulation, before initiating a broader discussion of the constraints on such an approach.

European experience of self-regulation in sustainable tourism

There is no shortage of good practice, both in voluntary codes and in local or sectoral case studies, of the implementation of sustainable tourism in Europe by means of self-regulation. Good practice is particularly dense on the ground in the Alps, where it is possible to identify a hierarchy of initiatives (Williams & Shaw 1996: 173–9; E Zimmermann, University of Graz, personal communication).

At the macro-regional scale, in the absence of any effective means of state intervention (the Alps do not, of course, coincide with EU territorial jurisdiction), the emphasis inevitably is on self-regulation. Perhaps the most important trans-national code is the Alpine Convention, which includes a protocol for tourism: to ensure that tourism and leisure activities are in harmony with ecological and social requirements, while at the same time restricting those activities which are harmful to the environment through restriction of certain zones (Williams & Shaw 1996: 173). Not surprisingly, given the absence of effective means of implementation, this code is couched at a high level of abstraction.

The Tyrol (Austria) provides a good example of action at the provincial level. In addition to state and provincial formal regulation, there is also a provincial-level attempt to promote self-regulation. The Tyrolean Environmental Seal of Quality was initiated to better integrate tourism and environmental management. This is based on persuading business that 'green' behaviour means being 'financially in the black'. In essence, it is a voluntary eco-labelling award scheme: 'In the knowledge that ecology and economy are not antagonists, but partners, the Tyrol wishes to send out signals to emphasize the necessity of environmental action under the motto "Deeds are born of knowledge"' (Williams & Shaw 1996: 174). The scheme operates by setting criteria which firms have to meet to qualify for a Seal of Quality, which is valued as offering comparative marketing advantages. There are three main groups of criteria which firms are assessed against, and these can be seen as conformity, embeddedness and formalization:

- *Conformity:* adherence to all formal state laws and regulations on the environment.
- *Embeddedness:* use of local products.
- *Formalization:* having in place environmental policies for waste treatment, air quality, energy use, the soil, transport and noise, and information provision for visitors and staff.

The effects of the scheme are considered to extend beyond the direct providers of tourism services. It also provides incentives for supply firms to be more aware of sustainability, helps to improve the standing of the industry in the eyes of the local community and tourism workers, and helps to anticipate and thereby negate the needs for statutory regulation.

At the community level, Weisensee (Austria) provides an example of voluntaristic action, being a partnership between the local community and the local tourist board (Williams & Shaw 1996: 174). Together they have developed a Strategic Concept for Weisensee, the key elements of which are: an annual nature forum to discuss future planning; use of a local tourist tax to help fund plant cultivation that is ecologically and culturally important to the area; a ban on further development of mountain transport facilities; restriction of investment to qualitative improvements to existing facilities; and an integrated traffic management plan. The identification of self-interest with this programme of largely self-regulation is reinforced by the high level of local ownership of resources and general acceptance of the marketing advantages of a higher environmental quality tourism product.

In addition to these types of regionally based initiatives, there are also a number of sectoral projects, with territorial associations, such as Green Villages in Austria. This is an association of 36 villages that produces its own marketing materials and acts as a self-regulatory body. To qualify for inclusion, villages have to meet criteria relating to architectural character (height and style of buildings), ecological standards (such as drinking water quality and waste disposal systems), and minimum social and tourism standards (such as population size, proportion of second homes, and community participation in tourism-related decision making).

There are also examples of effective self-regulation by individual companies and industry associations. Hotelplan, Switzerland, is an example of an individual company adopting a mission statement combining ecological and economic objectives (Ecotrans 1995). A code of business ethics is supplemented by a number of specific actions, such as the appointment of one of the senior staff to be an Environmental Delegate, holding a 'green ideas' competition for the staff, the use of 'green' products, differentiated waste collection for recycling, energy conservation, the assessment of water quality in tourist destinations and ecologically responsible promotion. There are also examples of smaller establishments providing benchmarks for sustainable tourism. For example, the Hotel Ucliva in Waltensburg, Switzerland, is architecturally well integrated in its village, has good public transport links, is constructed of ecologically sensitive building materials, is heated by renewable energy sources, uses local produce, and avoids or composts waste as far as possible. Becker (1995: 212) comments that, 'This example is important because it shows that a successful eco-marketing strategy can be pursued by an ecologically committed hotel - although its prices are relatively high, it secures above-average bookings and makes a substantial economic profit'. In other words, self-regulation can be cost-effective - at least in some circumstances.

In practice, most self-regulation, particularly involving associations rather than individual establishments, centres on the design, agreement and implementation of codes of behaviour. These are probably most effective where they are backed up by sanctions, as in the Green Villages scheme, where exclusion is the penalty for failure to maintain standards. However, not all schemes are so robustly managed, and Goodall and Cater (1996: 43) pose an important question: 'Are codes enforced or even enforceable?'. Beyond this lies the further question of how effective such codes are in influencing agents and activities outside of the participating establishments.

Within the sustainability literature, the question of the effectiveness of self-regulation is usually addressed by reference to the division between individual and social costs and benefits. It is possible to identify three very different circumstances under which the balance of individual and social costs and benefits need to be considered. First, adherence to voluntary codes is likely to be most effective where individual actions can be seen to result in cost reductions for individual establishments, as for example in reducing expenditure on individually packed portions of food, or in the amounts of water and energy consumed.

In the second case, there may be no decisive evidence that ecologically sound improvements reduce individual costs but there may be the prospect that they provide marketing advantages. For example, investment in particular types of sewage treatment or in electric vehicles, or the purchase of local produce, may not result in direct reductions in operating costs. However, such investments may qualify the establishment for inclusion in an eco-labelling scheme, which can be used in marketing to attract more and different customers, who are willing and able to pay higher prices for the tourism product. Although there is some cynicism as to the 'window-dressing' nature of many marketing-led voluntary schemes, particularly where the self-regulation is in the hands of individual companies, strongly managed collective schemes, such as the Green Villages, can achieve marked sustainability benefits. An increasing emphasis on total quality management is also encouraging greater commitment to environmental management.

In the third set of circumstances, the costs of sustainable/non-sustainable practices are perceived to be external to the individual establishment. For example, a ban on car use may have major benefit for the environment or for the local community, but – at least in the short term – the costs of failure to implement such a ban are not borne by the individual establishment. Individual business owners may recognize the existence of a number of environmental problems, such as traffic congestion and air pollution, but may be unwilling to link these to tourism or consider that they cannot be remedied by the actions of individuals.

A number of studies have shown that such external costs and benefits can present formidable barriers to sustainable tourism strategies. For example, Goodall and Cater (1996:43) report an attitudinal impasse in their study of tourism in Guernsey (Channel Islands); even where environmental problems were recognized, the business owners argued that their tourism business was not linked with the causes of these. Moreover, de Kadt (1992: 61) exposes the limitations of self-regulation in the face of such externalities:

> Productive enterprises cannot be expected to take account of such externalities when they calculate their costs. On the contrary, normal business practice motivated by profit maximization will attempt to 'externalize' the relevant costs, thereby, for example, causing pollution. Governments, however, can force them to internalize such externalities and can shift the costs back to the problem-causing economic units through regulation or taxation.

In the face of such externalities, increased emphasis has been placed on a holistic approach, so as to commit all those with an interest in tourism in a particular territory to the principle of sustainability. The Group for Development and Environment (1995: 19) stress that resource use is sustainable only if *'all actors* agree that resource use fulfils productive, physical and cultural functions in ways that will meet the long-term needs of the population affected' (emphasis added). In this situation, sustainability becomes a social task, which needs to be 'worked out in a context of democratic public discourse'. It is argued that only in this way can all agencies become committed to a programme for sustainability.

The challenges presented by such a democratic public discourse are considerable if only because of the diversity of agencies, which have an interest in any sustainable tourism programme. It is not simply a question of the private sector being pitted against the public sector, for the private sector involves a diverse set of capitals differentiated by ownership, scale and, most critically, capacity to benefit from a sustainability programme. Similarly, no local community is likely to be homogeneous. Instead, there may be sharp divisions according to whether local residents have a direct or indirect interest in tourism. In addition, empowerment of disadvantaged groups is required - but rarely achieved - if they are not to be swamped by more articulate and powerful elite groups. Divisions may also be found among tourists, according to their commitment to sustainability, and willingness and ability to accept restrictions on, or higher costs of, some tourist activities. This point brings us back to the issue of intra-generational equity.

Given conflicting interests in the development of the tourism industry, as well as the existence of external social costs and benefits, it is not surprising that there is considerable cynicism as to the capacity for effective self-regulation. Pigram (1992: 80) states that, 'Reconciling ethics with economics is never easy; substantial material interests are always involved and emotive appeals to the good nature of developers are unlikely to achieve the desired outcome'. A similarly pessimistic view is expressed by the Commission of the European Communities (1993: 77):

> Neither the market block nor the local population appear to be capable of giving birth to major initiatives aimed at self-regulating environmental resources. This task can and must be carried out by government organization alone in the first stage and in co-operation with the economic actors at a later stage.

The alternative to self-regulation - greater state intervention on behalf of sustainable tourism - does not necessarily offer a more convincing alternative strategy for sustainable tourism. State policies are a contested sphere where the claims of sustainable tourism have to compete with the claims of other forms of tourism, as well as with a range of other non-tourism investment and consumption demands.

Given the perceived limitations of both self-regulation and of state intervention, there have been increasing calls for a more holistic approach to sustainable tourism, combining different interests, agencies and mechanisms in a single programme. In this context, policy implementation is very much a socio-political process, 'a bargaining exercise meshing political and social acceptability with economic and technical feasibility and with administrative reality' (Pigram 1992: 81). However, to understand the potential for sustainable tourism, there is a need not only to be aware of socio-political processes, but also of the wider framework of political economy relationships.

Restructuring and regulation theory

One of the major recent concerns of economic geography has been to understand the implications for local and regional economies of the processes of economic restructuring which are consequent upon a shift from Fordism to some form of (contested) post-Fordism (Amin 1994). This debate has been significantly influenced by French regulationist theory, which is concerned with the correspondence between regimes of accumulation and the modes of regulation necessary for the stability of the social system (see Dunford 1990). This provides a useful framework within which to re-examine the notion of self-regulation.

The critical question for self-regulation and sustainability in terms of a regime of accumulation is whether there is a shift from Fordism to post-Fordist production, leading to the emergence of a more fragmented and dispersed tourist industry. This is important, as some commentators on sustainability hold that, of necessity, a small dispersed industry is more concerned with quality and environmental issues (Welford & Gouldson 1992). Gibbs (1996: 4) emphasizes that such arguments usually focus on the question of local control:

> technological change and a trend towards dispersed small scale businesses is argued to be somehow naturally more environmentally-friendly than large business because dispersal is thought to involve local control.... Such local control is proposed to mean less resource use and pollution than if control operates through distant decision makers with no local roots.... A more self-reliant set of local economies will emerge that combines local control with reduced environmental impacts.

This assumption provides a basis for the advocacy of self-regulation: small firms and local areas are more likely than large companies and higher-order levels of state organization to be environmentally aware; therefore, they should be entrusted with greater autonomy in respect of environmental management. In addition, it can be argued that small firms and local areas are more likely to respond to environmental management challenges if they are given greater responsibility for their own actions, rather than being stifled within the rigid framework of generalized, externally imposed regulations, which may be insensitive to their particular circumstances. These arguments are flawed because, while there is some evidence of the emergence of new forms of tourism consumption consistent with post-Fordism, this is only a tendency. There is no more evidence that the provision of tourism services in Europe had been overwhelmingly based on the Fordist model of mass production (Williams &c Shaw 1998) than there is now evidence that mass tourism is in absolute decline (see Montanari & Williams 1995). Moreover, the idea that small firms are necessarily more sensitive to environmental issues is also flawed. While there are examples of small companies in pursuit of sustainable tourism management (Becker 1995), large companies have greater power to disseminate innovatory practices and to invest in new, more sustainable environmental equipment and infrastructures, as demonstrated in the case of Swiss Air (Wyss & Keller 1992). There is, in fact, no conclusive empirical or theoretical verification that there is a link between scale and sustainability.

More fundamentally, the faith placed in small firms as a vehicle for sustainability is naive, for it does not recognize the underlying structural causes of environmental problems. The environment has been commodified and its use by tourists tends to be regulated by commercial transactions. The shift from Fordism to post-Fordism does involve modifications to the process by which capital is accumulated and surplus value is extracted. There may be a reliance on smaller units (hotels, etc.) but this does not necessarily reduce the flows of tourists to particular areas. It also does not necessarily increase local control. Fragmentation refers to the scale and geographical distribution of production rather than ownership and control. Many smaller firms may be locked into dependent relationships on external capital.

The role of tour companies illustrates some of the constraints on local control. Tour companies tend to operate with relatively short-term horizons because of the pressing need to sell a fixed quantity of holidays, in any one year, which have been sub-contracted to airline and accommodation suppliers. There is certainly evidence that some tour companies are becoming increasingly environmentally aware. For example, Touristik Union International of Germany, the largest tour company in Europe, has an environmental programme that includes training courses for its personnel, provision of information to its partners and suppliers, and establishing minimum ecological standards for its holiday destinations (Ecotrans 1995).

While such programmes are laudable, they are still based on external control and asymmetrical power relationships. If the environmental quality of a destination does deteriorate, then tour companies have the ultimate option to abandon this resort and to sub-contract to a new group of suppliers in other resorts. This short-termism is reinforced by the 'identikit' nature of many Mediterranean and Alpine resorts based on marketing the consumption of generalized 'natural' attributes such as sunshine and sea, or snow and mountains, in isolation of the particularities of place. Resorts become environmental packages to be consumed and there is intense price competition between them given the high degree of product substitutability (Williams 1995). Therefore, the autonomy of local establishments to pursue self-regulation remains severely constrained.

In addition, many of the specific practices of tour companies militate against sustainable tourism. Noel Josephides of Sunvil Holidays (quoted in Williams & Shaw 1996: 42–3) highlights three such practices: prepayment for rooms in hotels which are still under construction, thereby helping to finance the rapid expansion and oversupply of rooms; refusal to share chartered aircraft with other companies, so that the number of flights and volumes of tourist arrivals are forced to increase by whole rather than part aircraft loads; and the practice of 'allocation on arrival', which reinforces tourists' disregard of specific environmental and cultural features while exaggerating the importance of price competition.

The economic system of late twentieth-century Europe is constructed around individual costs and benefits, in which many environmental costs can be externalized. Tour companies and their relationships to local establishments and communities typify such relationships in the case of tourism. It is our belief that neo-liberal tendencies in western, and even more so eastern, Europe, with their emphasis on deregulation and individual freedoms, are tending to intensify this critical disjuncture between individual and external costs. Combined with the immediate pressures of high levels of unemployment, and increasing competition between places that often have very different environmental regulations (and therefore short-term costs), the constraints on self-regulation, related to the regime of accumulation, are considerable.

In addition to the regime of accumulation, there is also a need to consider the mode of regulation; that is, the regulatory mechanisms that are consistent with, and support, a regime of accumulation. This involves 'complex relations - political practices, social norms and cultural forms - which allow the highly dynamic and unstable capitalist system to function, at least for a period, in a relatively coherent and stable fashion' (Hudson & Williams 1995: 19). In particular, the mode of regulation institutionalizes the contest between different interests, especially with respect to the balance between consumption and production. The stability of the economic system is maintained in practice by a variety of regulatory features. Political practices, which refer to a variety of forms of state interventions at different scales from the global to the local, are critical, but they are paralleled by the influences of social norms and cultural forms.

Given the above definitions, the growth of the sustainability movement may well indicate growing tensions arising from the imbalance between production and consumption, particularly in a longer-term perspective. There is little doubt that mass production has been associated with non-sustainable practices. Lipietz (1992) argues that there is a necessary link between mass production and environmental mismanagement, for the former leads to maximization of production and consumption. Critically, 'the reification of social relations - where people relate to one another with money and commodities on the market - causes the natural constrains on production and consumption to disappear from the consciousness of society' (Gibbs 1996: 5).

The question is whether changes in the mode of regulation, concomitant on a Fordism to post-Fordism shift, provide a basis for effective self-regulation with respect to sustainable tourism. The positive argument lies in the proliferation of voluntary codes across Europe (Williams & Shaw 1996) and the growth of critical 'green' consumer movements. The counter-argument lies in the fact that, ultimately, implementation of sustainable tourism depends on private capitals, which, in both Fordism and post-Fordism, have diverse and possibly conflicting goals. There is no compelling argument that, in the post-Fordist period, a critical mass of tourism capitals would be willing to take on board the externalized social costs of current tourism practices. 'Green' consumer movements are helping to reshape demand, but their impact is uneven in terms of market segments and place. Even if critical consumers, autonomous municipalities and far-sighted entrepreneurs manage to bring about significant sustainability gains in some areas of, say, the Alps, the challenges presented by mass tourism in Venice or the Costa del Sol present challenges of a very different order of magnitude. Given the nature of the mode of regulation, there must be severe doubts as to whether self-regulation would be sufficient to bring about sustainable management practices.

There is also a need to consider more critically changes in tourist behaviour, one of the key components of the social norms and cultural values that partly constitute the mode of regulation. On the one hand, the growth of membership of voluntary societies committed to improved environmental practices, such as Friends of the Earth and (in a different way) the National Trust (UK), all indicate the potential for self-regulation. In contrast, tourism is also a positional good subject to the dictates of fashion, and many market segments remain indifferent to the requirements of sustainability. There is also the fundamental question of whether value changes extend to all the non-sustainable tourism behaviour of individuals, such as use of aircraft or cars. This also raises the question of intra-generational equity; if self-regulation is driven by elite groups, and results in higher short-term costs, there are implications both for intra-generational equity and for the necessary wider acceptance of new sets of social norms and cultural values.

Similar doubts about the role of self-regulation have been advanced by de Kadt (1992: 59), who argues that, 'If scaling down is to be effective, new institutions and organizations will be required. In tourism development the questions relate especially to the setting up of cooperative arrangements between small scale enterprises and the strengthening of local planning and regulatory capacities'. Gibbs (1996: 6) concurs, arguing that 'Neither ethical nor purely market-led rules are adequate. Such rules are insufficient without institutionalized rules of ecological behavior. These imperatives must be institutionalized and equipped with sanctions, so that they become behavioral constraints for everyone'. The problem is that there is little in the emerging mode of regulation of post-Fordism to lead us to believe that there will necessarily be such an institutionalization of sustainability beliefs and practices.

Conclusion: limits to self-regulation

The objectives of campaigns for sustainable tourism can be disaggregated *into* the pursuit of good, common and best (implying 'true' sustainability) practices. There is no shortage of good practice in Europe, which can provide benchmarks for their diffusion into common practice. The real challenge is how to convert good practice into common practice. This relates directly to the notion of self-regulation. Good practice can be, and has been, achieved on the basis of self-regulation, but there is no evidence to suggest that this will also deliver common practice, let alone best practice - not even in the most environmentally sensitive of local areas.

Goodall and Cater (1996: 45) consider that the gap between the current level of environmental performance of the tourism industry and of a genuinely sustainable tourism performance level can be disaggregated into three elements:

- a tactical gap between the best and worst performance;
- a strategic gap between best knowledge and current best practice;
- an absolute gap between the technically best environmental option and true sustainability.

They consider that the first gap can be closed in part by environmental awareness programmes (and therefore by self-regulation). The strategic gap can partly be closed by market forces but also requires state intervention. Finally, the absolute gap is unlikely to be closed by either self-regulation or conceivable state regulation in the near future.

However, any analysis that focuses on 'full' or 'pure' sustainability will necessarily lead to such pessimistic conclusions. Instead, we agree with the Group for Development and Environment (1995: 24) that, 'Sustainability is not an absolute standard of measure. At most we can speak only of degrees of sustainability. Defining natural resources and sustainability is a social task'. Sustainability could, of course, be defined in such an unambitious way that it could be achievable by self-regulation, but most of the debates on the goals of sustainable tourism would reject such minimalist aspirations. The value of regulation theory is that it provides a theoretical framework for considering the scope for both self-regulation and other forms of regulation in a particular economic formation. The brief discussion provided by this paper indicates that self-regulation by itself is not a sufficient approach, but neither is formal regulation via legislation and controls. Instead, a totality approach is required which examines the regime of accumulation and the mode of regulation in their entirety, and in this there is broad sympathy with the emphasis on a holistic approach in the debate on sustainable tourism.

References

Amin, A. 1994. *Post-Fordism: A Reader.* Oxford: Blackwell.

Becker, C. 1995. Tourism and the environment. In *European Tourism: Regions, Spaces and Restructuring,* ed. A. Montanari and A.M. Williams, pp. 207–20. Chichester, UK: John Wiley.

Commission of the European Communities. 1992. *A European Community Program of Policy and Action in Relation to the Environment and Sustainable Development.* Brussels: CEC (Com (92) 23 Final).

Commission of the European Communities. 1993. *Taking Account of Environment in Tourism Development.* Brussels: CEC (DG XXIII).

de Kadt, E. 1992. Making the alternative sustainable: lessons from development for tourism. In *Tourism Alternatives: Potential and Problems in the Development of Tourism,* ed. V.L. Smith and W.R. Eadington, pp. 47–75. Chichester, UK: John Wiley.

Dunford, M. 1990. Theories of regulation. *Society and Space* 8: 297–321.

Ecotrans. 1995. *Turismo Compatible.* Milan: Ecotrans.

Gibbs, D. 1996. Integrating sustainable development and economic restructuring: A role for regulation theory. *Geoforum* 27: 1–10.

Goodall, B. and Cater, E. 1996. Self-regulation for sustainable tourism. *Ecodecision* 20: 43–5.

Group for Development and Environment. 1995. *Sustainable Use of Natural Resources.* Berne: GDE, Institute for Geography, University of Berne (Development and Environment Reports No. 14).

Hudson, R. and Williams, A.M. 1995. *Divided Britain.* Chichester, UK: John Wiley.

Lipietz, A. 1992. *Towards a New Economic Order: Postfordism, Ecology and Democracy.* Cambridge: Polity Press.

Montanari, A. and Williams, A.M., eds. 1995. *European Tourism: Regions, Spaces and Restructuring.* Chichester, UK: John Wiley.

Pigram, J.J. 1992. Alternative tourism: Tourism and sustainable resource management. In *Tourism Alternatives: Potential and Problems in the Development of Tourism,* ed. V.L. Smith and W.R. Eadington, pp. 76–87. Chichester, UK: John Wiley.

Shaw, G. and Williams, A.M. 1994. *Critical Issues in Tourism: Geographical Perspectives.* Oxford: Blackwell.

von Hayek, EA. 1988. *The Fatal Conceit.* London: Routledge.

Welford, R. and Gouldson, A. 1993. *Environmental Management and Business Strategy.* London: Pitman.

Wheeler, B. 1991. Tourism's troubled times: Responsible tourism is not the answer. *Tourism Management* 12: 91–6.

Williams, A.M. 1995. Capital and the transnationalisation of tourism. In *European Tourism: Regions, Spaces and Restructuring,* ed. A. Montanari and A.M. Williams, pp. 163–76. Chichester, UK: John Wiley.

Williams, A.M. and Shaw, G. 1996. *Tourism, Leisure, Nature Protection and Agri-Tourism: Principles, Partnerships and Practice.* Brussels: European Partners for the Environment.

Williams, A.M. and Shaw, G. 1998. Tourism and the environment: Sustainability and economic restructuring. In *Sustainable Tourism: A Geographical Perspective,* ed. C.M. Hall and A.A. Lew, pp. 49–59. Harlow, UK: Addison Wesley Longman.

World Commission on Environment and Development. 1987. *Our Common Future* (The Brundtland Report). London: Oxford University Press.

Wyss, E and Keller, L. 1992. Environmentally acceptable air transport: Possibilities and parameters of Swissair's 'Oekkobilanz' environmental audit. In *Strategies for Reducing the Environmental Impact of Tourism* (ENVIROTOUR Vienna 92 Proceedings), ed. W. Pillman and S. Predi, pp. 117–31. Vienna: International Society for Environmental Protection.

Résumé: Durabilité et auto-régulation: perspectives critiques

Cet article traite des limites de l'auto-régulation en vue du tourisme durable. De nombreux cas témoignent d'une bonne pratique en matière d'autorégulation à travers l'Europe, comme le démontre l'exemple des Alpes. Cependant, même une analyse de l'opposition traditionnelle qui existe entre coûts individuels et coûts sociaux montre les limites du processus d'auto-régulation. Le présent article souligne notamment comment la théorie de régulation peut nous aider à mieux appréhender les contraintes qui pèsent sur l'auto-régulation.

Mots-clés: durabilité, auto-régulation, régulation, Europe

Inclusive tourism development

Regina Scheyvens and Robin Biddulph

ABSTRACT
In the light of growing inequality globally, it is important to consider how to make tourism, one of the world's largest industries, more inclusive. This concern is set in the context of, first, the growing use of tourism as a tool for social integration in Europe, not least in relation to making refugees welcome, and second, new expectations in the sustainable development goals (SDGs) that development should be inclusive and that the Global North and the private sector will take more responsibility for this. We provide a definition and suggest elements of an analytical framework for inclusive tourism, and note where inclusive tourism sits in relation to other terms that engage with the social and economic development potentials of tourism. Elements of inclusive tourism are illustrated with reference to a range of examples from around the world. This illustrates how marginalized people might be ethically and beneficially included in the production and consumption of tourism. However, it also demonstrates how formidable the challenges are to achieve substantial social change through inclusive tourism given constraints both within the sector and in the wider political economy.

摘要
鉴于全球范围日趋严重的不平等，考虑如何使全球最大产业之一的旅游业变得更为包容很重要。这个关切鉴于如下背景:首先，发达国家逐渐把旅游业作为社会融合的手段，特别是与使难民受欢迎有关;其次，可持续发展目标有新的期望，即发展应该是包容的，北半球及其私营部门对此要担负更多的责任。我们界定了包容性旅游的定义，提出了包容性旅游分析框架的要素，解释了包容性旅游与涉及旅游业社会经济发展潜力的其它术语之间的关系，参考全球范围的一系列实例解释了包容性旅游的要素。本文也说明了边缘群体如何从伦理和利益方面融入到旅游的生产与消费中。但是,本文也表明,鉴于旅游部门和全球政治经济存在的制约因素,通过包容性旅游实现社会实质性变化的艰巨性。

1. Introduction

One of the most enduring critiques of tourism in social science discourse relates to its exclusive nature. Tourism is accused of providing opportunities for the privileged middle and upper classes to travel and enjoy leisure activities in 'other' places, creating profits particularly for large companies and creating exclusive enclaves for rich, while development opportunities associated with tourism are not open to those who are poor and marginalized (Gibson, 2009, p. 1280; Harrison, 1992; Jamal & Camargo, 2014). In this article, we recognize the validity of these criticisms but start with a different proposition: that the concept of inclusive tourism development can help us to think constructively and critically about ways of approaching tourism that so that it can provide a holistic range of benefits and lead to more equitable and sustainable outcomes.

A concern with inclusiveness enables analytical links to be made between the stated ambitions of global policy-making and a range of grass-roots initiatives. These involve a plethora of different actors in diverse settings seeking to widen the range of people involved in producing tourism, consuming tourism, and benefiting from tourism. In many cases, these initiatives involve challenging existing geographies of tourism. In other words, inclusive tourism development attempts not only to widen access to consumption, production and benefit-sharing in existing tourism sites, but also to re-draw the tourism map in order to create new sites of experience and interaction.

At the global level, inclusion is one of the central principles behind the United Nations' sustainable development goals (SDGs) which were ratified in September 2015. As noted by UNDP, 'Many people are excluded from development because of their gender, ethnicity, age, sexual orientation, disability or poverty… Development can be inclusive – and reduce poverty – only if all groups of people contribute to creating opportunities, share the benefits of development and participate in decision-making' (United Nations Development Program, 2016). Seen in this light, a focus on tourism development as inclusive would include attention to including previously silenced voices in decision-making about tourism, as well as ensuring that a broader spread of the benefits of tourism.

In this article, we will define 'inclusive tourism', and show how it sits in relation to other conceptualizations of socially and economically beneficial tourism development like pro-poor and responsible tourism. We argue that this term can add value to tourism knowledge and understandings by seeking to explicitly overcome the exclusionary tendencies of tourism and to ensure that a wider range of people participate in and benefit from tourism endeavours.

2. Conceptualizing inclusive tourism

Before defining what we mean by inclusive tourism, it is important to distinguish it from some of the ways that the concept of inclusion has previously been linked to tourism and to development more broadly, in both the scholarly literature and in development industry material.

First, when talking about inclusive tourism we are not referring to 'all-inclusives' whereby tourists pay a travel agent in advance for a package including the costs of flights, transfers, accommodation, meals and tours at a foreign destination. In fact, all-inclusive tourism often offers the opposite of what we see as inclusive tourism. For the last two to three decades social scientists have critiqued all-inclusive resorts because they tend to result in enclaves which are out of bounds to the local population, they limit opportunities for local entrepreneurs to benefit by selling goods or services to tourists, and they result in high levels of leakage of tourist spending, with much going to foreign hotel chains and travel agents (Britton, 1982; Gibson, 2009; Scheyvens, 2011). As Saarinen (2017, p. 425) concludes, 'enclave tourism spaces with all-inclusive products can turn out to be all-exclusive for local communities in development'.

Second, tourism is sometimes viewed through an 'inclusive business' lens. Within international development discourse and among businesses wishing to exhibit their social responsibility, a specific body of work has formed around the notion of inclusive business. Here the focus is on how for-profit businesses can contribute to poverty reduction by including people from low-income communities in the value chain (www.businessfordevelopment.org). In tourism, proponents emphasise how low-income populations can benefit from tourism growth (www.inclusivebusinesshub.org; see also www.inclusive-business.org). For example, the ITC training guide examines ways in which handicraft producers can be linked to tourism markets (International Trade Centre, 2012). Growth in tourism, it is proclaimed,

> offers a unique opportunity for unlocking opportunities through inclusive business (IB) models. Tourism can create employment and income-generating opportunities along an expansive value chain... For this growth to create meaningful and sustainable impact for local populations however, innovative inclusive business models need to be put into place that allow low-income people to have better employment and entrepreneurship opportunities and catalyse more systemic poverty reduction effects. (Deutsche Gesellschaft für Internationale Zusammenarbeit, 2016)

The inclusive business approach has much in common with the inclusive growth agenda which is currently a dominant thread in discussions by aid donors and development banks. According to Bakker and Messerli (2017), inclusive growth is based on a long-term agenda to expand employment opportunities and the size of the economy: it is not specifically about redistribution of resources to the poor. These authors believe that the concept of inclusive growth offers more promise to the tourism sector than a pro-poor tourism (PPT) approach. While few tourism scholars have tested the notion of tourism-led inclusive growth, it is significant that Hampton, Jeyacheya, and Long (2017) work in Ha Long Bay, Vietnam, concluded that despite the rapid growth of tourism in this area, the research raised significant doubts about whether tourism could contribute to inclusive growth. In fact, the local supply chain was weakening, and business and employment opportunities were less equitable than in the past.

Notably, the inclusive business approach supports a neoliberal model of economic growth, which assumes that including the poor in the market economy is a direct route out of poverty. It limits itself to economic dimensions and is not linked to a political agenda such as efforts to overcome structural inequalities which are barriers to development for the poor. We support the views of a number of scholars who see flaws in this approach (Blowfield & Dolan, 2014; Kumi, Arhin, & Yeboah, 2014; José Carlos Marques & Peter Utting, 2010). For example, a number of big business actors are primarily interested in the business case for responsible practice: in one study of 40 large corporations the motivation to pursue sustainable and inclusive business practices ranged from 'maintaining competitive position' as the leading motivator, followed by 'avoiding reputational damage,' 'avoiding future supply disruptions,' and 'capturing revenues and building loyalty" (Chakravorti, Macmillan, & Siesfeld, 2014, pp. 2–3). Our understanding of 'inclusive tourism' should thus not be conflated with an inclusive business or inclusive growth approach.

Third, a broader, more holistic perspective on 'inclusive development' has emerged as seen in the following UNDP definition:

> People are excluded from development because of their gender, ethnicity, age, sexual orientation, disability or poverty... Development can be inclusive – and reduce poverty – only if all groups of people contribute to creating opportunities, share the benefits of development and participate in decision-making. (www.undp.org)

Lawson (2010) takes this argument forward, arguing that inclusive development requires an understanding of economic development as being intrinsically embedded in place, politics and society. She completes her critique of the 2009 Human Development Report with the statement that 'Inclusive development begins from an embedded conceptualization of economic development which is informed by an ethical concern for people and care, not just economic growth' (Lawson, 2010, p. 359). International actors, including donors, have become well versed in the language of inclusive development partly through the post-2015 focus on the SDGs. While the notion that economic growth is essential to inclusive development comes through in the SDGs, overall there is a broader perspective of inclusive development than that found in business-centric approaches. There are associated social development objectives embedded in the SDGs including enhancing human dignity and overcoming inequalities.

Inclusive development is, therefore, a more holistic concept than inclusive growth, implying an interest in a broader sense of welfare than one simply measured by per capita GDP. It also goes beyond societal averages (as found in headline Human Development Index figures) or impacts on particular groups (as in pro-poor figures), but takes an interest in whether marginalized groups improve their overall share of welfare, such as narrowing the gap between the poor and the rest of society (Rauniyar & Kanbur, 2010). Drawing on these understandings of the meaning of inclusive development allows us to broaden the scope of inclusive tourism development beyond economic criteria, and to deliberately steer it away from notions of 'inclusive business' and 'all-inclusive' tourism.

3. A definition

The authors have noted that a small group of researchers is starting to link 'tourism' and 'inclusive development', so the following discussion represents our efforts to provide clearer parameters around this term. Inclusive tourism can be understood as

> Transformative tourism in which marginalized groups are engaged in ethical production or consumption of tourism and the sharing of its benefits.

This means something can only be considered inclusive tourism if marginalized groups are involved in ethical production of it, or they are involved in ethical consumption of it, and in either case, marginalized groups share the benefits. Who is marginalized will vary from place to place but this could include the very poor, ethnic minorities, women and girls, differently abled people and other groups who lack power and/or voice. Ethical production and consumption is a key component of the definition of inclusive tourism. This includes responsibility for other people, and for the environment. In terms of 'transformative', this could mean addressing inequality, overcoming the separation of different groups living in different places, challenging stereotypes or generalized histories, and opening people up to understanding the situation of minorities.

A strength of this definition is its applicability to the Global North and South, blurring conventional boundaries. It encourages us to ask the same questions of tourism as an inclusive development activity no matter whether it is occurring in a village in England or a megacity in China, the mountains of Kenya or the coast of Australia.

In social terms, inclusion invites two sets of crucial questions: (1) who is included (and excluded) and (2) on what terms are they included? As such, a discussion of inclusion can never be adequate if it only attends to one case or group. Similarly, if a narrow group of stakeholders are included in a tokenistic way in order to create the impression of progress, or if some marginalized people are included but in a superficial manner – as represented in the literature by terms such as green-wash, pink-wash – then tourism is not being inclusive in any meaningful way. It is, to borrow the terms used by Marques and Utting (2010), ameliorative rather than transformative.

Using 'inclusion' alerts us to who is not there as well. Since the 1970s, tourism has been widely critiqued by academics for being *exclusive*, that is, dominated by multinational interests, mainly accessible to those who are members of national and global elites, exploitative of local people and resources, and leading to dependency. The saga of Ochheuteal Beach in Cambodia, where local stallholders are negotiating under threat of eviction with provincial and national authorities who are seeking to beautify and develop the seafront (Sotheary, 2016), is but one of many examples of struggles around the terms on which local people are included in or excluded from the spaces, activities and benefits of tourism. An interesting prospect is Cukier's notion of the value of 'explosions of niches' in tourism in Cuba, as a contrast to exclusive enclaves (Cukier, 2011). The discussion of inclusive tourism is a direct attempt to acknowledge that many people have been excluded by tourism in the past, and to find ways to overcome this so that more people can benefit from tourism. However, it also acknowledges that some people may choose not to be included because of concerns they have about tourism (Craven, 2016).

Implicit in the concept of inclusive tourism are the following components, which are further depicted in the seven elements of Figure 1:

(1) Overcoming barriers to disadvantaged groups to access tourism as producers or consumers.
(2) Facilitating self-representations by those who are marginalized or oppressed, so their stories can be told and their culture represented in ways that are meaningful to them.
(3) Challenging dominant power relations.
(4) Widening the range of people who contribute to decision-making about development of tourism.
(5) Providing opportunities for new places to be on the tourism map.
(6) Encouraging learning, exchange and mutually beneficial relationships which promote understanding and respect between 'hosts' and 'guests'.

Analytically, then, these elements provide a conceptual framework: the degree to which tourism development is inclusive may be assessed in terms of its ambitions and achievements in relation to these seven elements. There are examples of inclusive approaches to tourism which incorporate these elements in Section 5. Before this,

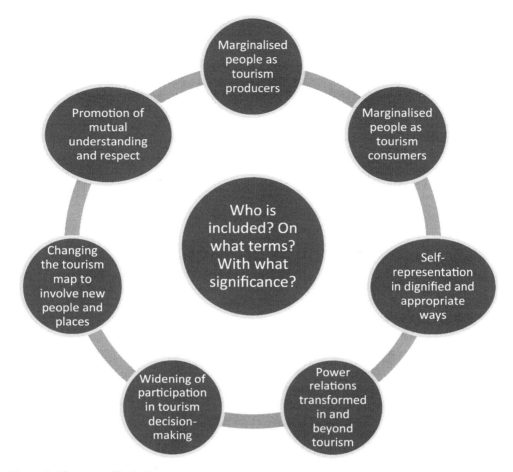

Figure 1. Elements of inclusive tourism.

however, we elaborate on how the concept of inclusive tourism development builds upon and is distinctive from related terms in tourism scholarship and practice.

4. How does 'inclusive tourism' compare with other related terms regarding tourism and development?

The dual notions that tourism itself can be improved, and also that tourism can act as an agent of improvement for wider society, have spawned a broad family of overlapping concepts deployed to varying extents by scholars and practitioners. Some of these, such as responsible tourism and eco-tourism, are part of mainstream practice and will be familiar to many consumers and producers of tourism. Others are probably more recognizable to scholars and policy-makers, such as PPT and social tourism. Others cater for smaller niches, such as tourism for peace and community-based tourism. Such terms are outlined in Table 1, noting their key elements and what makes inclusive tourism distinct from them.

The concept of inclusive tourism adds one more distinctive term to this family of overlapping concepts. As such it does not seek to usurp or supersede any of them. We

Table 1. Distinctions between inclusive tourism and other related forms of tourism.

	Commonalities with inclusive tourism	Inclusive tourism focus is different because:
Accessible tourism	Focuses on access to tourism by differently abled people as consumers of tourism	Inclusive tourism is interested more broadly in access to consumption *and* productive of tourism, by *all* forms of marginalized people
Pro-poor tourism	Focuses on increasing poor people's economic share of benefits from tourism in the Global South	Inclusive tourism focuses on economic and *social* inclusion of poor and other marginalized groups, and applies to both the Global North and South
Social tourism	Focuses on widening access of marginalized groups as consumers of tourism	Inclusive tourism also focuses on widening of access of marginalized people, but as both as *producers* and consumers of tourism, and as *decision-makers*
Peace through tourism	Focuses on tourists as ambassadors for peace	Inclusive tourism is *broader* in focus, but shares this interest in building mutual understanding between hosts and guests
Community-based tourism	Focuses on empowerment and development of community members as producers of tourism	Inclusive Tourism is interested in these things, but not only at the community level; it focuses on *all forms and scales of tourism*
Responsible tourism	Focuses on ethical tourism, with a general interest in improving the terms under which tourism takes place	Inclusive Tourism does not share the focus on environment found in responsible tourism, and is more focused on *quality of relationships and empowerment of hosts*

envisage inclusive tourism to be an analytical term rather than one that will be taken up and used in marketing or certification or campaigning. The distinctive contributions of the term to the analytical mix relate to

(1) focusing attention on an innovation frontier where new people and new places are incorporated into tourism consumption and production, and
(2) using tourism to counter socio-economic exclusions and divisions.

As such the interest is both quantitative (to what extent are new people and places being included) and qualitative (what are the terms and meanings of that inclusion).

4.1. Accessible tourism

When the inclusiveness of tourism is discussed it is often in terms of its accessibility for tourists who are differently abled. The concept has been variously defined in order to pay more or less attention to issues of physical ability, cognitive ability and issues relating to age (Darcy, 2006; Darcy & Dickson, 2009). While accessibility is generally the key term in this literature, inclusive approaches and inclusive attitudes are identified as key to providing accessibility (Darcy & Pegg, 2011; Yau, McKercher, & Packer, 2004).

Accessible tourism is based on advocating for the rights of differently abled people to enjoys holidays and tourism, which necessitates removing barriers which might prevent this from occurring (Pagán, 2012). Others have described inclusive tourism along these lines as well, for example: 'Inclusive Tourism is an environment where people of all abilities are felt welcome and wanted as customers and guests' (TravAbility.com). For us inclusive tourism relates to both production and consumption of tourism, so in terms of differently abled people an inclusive tourism perspective would also focus on their roles as owners, entrepreneurs, employees and regulators. Accessible tourism has value in that it seeks to ensure that tourism is produced with people of all abilities in mind, and can be consumed by people of all abilities. As such, accessible tourism is just one aspect of inclusive tourism as the latter is interested in all forms of social and economic exclusion and division.

4.2. PPT

PPT emerged as an analytical concept around the turn of the century and is associated with some of the same academic-practitioners as responsible tourism (Ashley, Boyd, & Goodwin, 2000; Ashley & Roe, 2002; Goodwin & Font, 2007). It follows a long-term interest arising from the expansion of mass tourism in relatively poor settings in the Global South (Britton, 1982; de Kadt, 1979; Harrison, 1992) and seeks ways of ensuring that a greater proportion of the tourist spend finds its way directly or indirectly into the hands of poor people (Mitchell & Ashley, 2010). An inclusive tourism approach shares this concern with economic inclusion, but also extends it to the Global North, and is interested not only in tourism's economics but also in its potential to promote social inclusion and integration.

4.3. Social tourism

Social tourism is concerned with guests rather than hosts, and has focused more on the Global North rather than the Global South: social tourism is thus almost a mirror image of the concerns of PPT. Historically, social tourism has been concerned with enabling economically disadvantaged people to participate in tourism (Haulot, 1981). Academic interest has focused on eligibility for social tourism, on the particular interests and needs of different age groups, and on the social and economic costs and benefits of social tourism (Caffyn & Lutz, 1999; McCabe & Diekmann, 2015; Minnaert, Maitland, & Miller, 2011; Morgan, Pritchard, & Sedgley, 2015). The interest in overcoming exclusion is a shared perspective with inclusive tourism. Again, though, inclusive tourism's scope is broader, encompassing guests and hosts, the Global North and the Global South, and also being interested in opening new geographical frontiers for tourism.

4.4. Peace through tourism

Peace through tourism has investigated the proposition that tourism can be mobilized as a means of avoiding war or securing peace (Cho, 2007), and is associated with a practitioner-academic movement which seeks to rebrand tourism as the first global peace industry (D'Amore, 2009). Tourism's potentials as a promoter of peace are examined in two ways: firstly, on a structural level where the financial incentives provided and organizational cooperation required by tourism are seen as having potential to steer countries towards peace (Kim, Prideaux, & Prideaux, 2007), and secondly, at a personal level where bringing people together in situations where they better understand and empathize with each other might undermine popular support for conflict (Gelbman, 2008; Sonmez & Apostolopoulos, 2000). To the extent that pro-peace tourism in involves people and places that would not normally be included in tourism (for example in the growth of food tourism and homestays in Palestine), then peace through tourism shares some concerns with inclusive tourism. However, while the peace through tourism literature chiefly engages with theories from international relations (Kim et al., 2007), inclusive tourism's interests are more broadly aligned with sociological and geographical literatures on exclusion and integration (Higgins-Desbiolles, 2003; Lawson, 2010).

4.5. Community-based tourism

Community-based tourism may be motivated by a variety of economic, social, cultural or environmental concerns, and usually involves an element of control over the tourism enterprise by local communities (Okazaki, 2008; Salazar, 2012; Zapata, Hall, Lindo, & Vanderschaeghe, 2011). Community-based tourism is usually small-scale and as such it may be a site for piloting ways of doing things which can be scaled up, but it may also function as a cul-de-sac, as approaches which work in small, resource-intensive, often personalized niches prove difficult to scale up to larger scales and mass markets (Goodwin, 2009). From an inclusive tourism perspective, just as with responsible tourism and PPT, community-based tourism can be a promising site of innovation. However, key questions revolve around the extent to which inclusiveness extends either within the local community (Blackstock, 2005; Manyara & Jones, 2007), or beyond it into areas that are of interest to inclusive tourism such as wider societal structures and industry practices.

4.6. Responsible tourism

One of the broadest and most long-standing concepts associated with tourism and socio-economic improvement is responsible tourism. This was initially adopted in preference to the label 'alternative tourism' (Wheeller, 1990), which it critiqued as being impotent to deal with the fact that mass tourism was already a fact of life and that seeding alternatives would do nothing to curb the negative effects of mass tourism (Wheeller, 1991). Since this time it has become much more broad in its scope, and especially since the establishment of the International Centre for Responsible Tourism centred around Leeds Metropolitan University in the mid-1990s it has become a movement which seeks to influence the behaviour of producers and consumers in the mass market as well as in specialized niche markets (Goodwin & Font, 2007).

Responsible tourism as a concept stresses doing no harm. However, its definition, as laid out by those who propagate it, is not just concerned with the ethics of tourism actors, but with the wider operation of socio-economic processes relating to tourism. Within the Cape Town Declaration (Spenceley, 2012, p. 5), it is clear that responsible tourism includes engendering respect and building local pride, generating greater economic benefits – especially for local people – and involving them in decision-making, encouraging meaningful connections between guests and local people, and respecting cultural and natural diversity. Responsible Tourism requires that operators, hoteliers, governments, local people and tourists take responsibility, and take action to make tourism more sustainable. It has thus become a framework for evaluating any tourism sector from a broad range of research perspectives (Bramwell, Lane, McCabe, Mosedale, & Scarles, 2008). For example, a responsible tourism lens has been applied to cruise tourism (Klein, 2011), slum tourism (Booyens, 2010), and tourism for the promotion of peace (Isaac, 2010). Interpreted broadly, then, responsible tourism is the term which has the largest overlap with the notion of inclusive tourism.

5. Inclusive tourism in practice

We have framed inclusive tourism as comprising a concern with widening the participation of marginalized groups in tourism, on terms that are favourable to them and that might have broader transformative influence within and beyond the tourism industry. Using the elements from our framework above (Figure 1) as sub-headings, we now focus on how inclusive tourism is being sought in practice by drawing on examples from the wider literature, and also noting where barriers exist.

5.1. Marginalized people as tourism producers

In the Global South, the inclusion of local people as producers in and for the tourism market is a long-term and continuing struggle. For example, small farmers are one group which has typically not benefited greatly from growth of tourism, even where there is significant interest in utilizing local fresh produce in tourist restaurants (Telfer & Wall, 2000; Torres, 2002). Thus, many newly emerging inclusive tourism initiatives are concerned with engaging different groups of people as tourism producers. For example, the Fair Trade in Tourism (FTT) movement is actively trying to change the poor deal that some producers get from the tourism industry: specifically, it aims to ensure that tourism producers (of handicrafts, accommodation, produce, etc.) get a fair deal, and to raise the awareness of consumers about FTT. In South Africa, a national FTT organization certifies tourism businesses and thus provides a guarantee for consumers regarding a business's ethics (Scheyvens, 2011, p. 34).

Arguably, one of the biggest challenges for inclusive tourism is to encourage responsible production of tourism by existing tourism businesses. Mainstream operators can take an inclusive approach to tourism production by transforming their core activities, such as providing decision-making roles and ownership opportunities for staff; mentoring local people in relation to starting their own small businesses associated with tourism; introducing inclusive procurement strategies; and offering dignified work, good training, and fair remuneration (Ashley, Haysom, & Spenceley, 2008; Walmsley, 2012; Hughes & Scheyvens, 2016). Interestingly, when inclusive tourism was promoted by local authorities in the rural town of Dullstroom in South Africa, the emphasis was on upskilling of employees for quality jobs, not just on job creation (Butler & Rogerson, 2016).

Tren Ecuador provides an example of a business offering a luxury tourist experience – a train journey across Ecuador, from the Andes to the Pacific – but doing so in a sustainable and responsible way. One of the state-owned business's key goals is to contribute to improving the quality of life of local communities along the length of its journeys (Monge, Yagüe, & Perales, 2016). As such, rather than creating an exclusive comfort zone on board that separates travellers from local populations, Tren Ecuador encourages tourists to eat at restaurants along the way, buy crafts at one of 14 artisan squares, and purchase snacks from over 20 locally run station cafes. It is estimated that Tren Ecuador now supports the livelihoods of over 5,000 people living along its routes, which is why it was awarded 'Best in poverty reduction and inclusion' in the 2016 Responsible Tourism Awards (http://www.responsibletravel.com/awards/categories/economic.htm).

5.2. Marginalized people as tourism consumers

Another way to ensure that tourism is inclusive is through widening access to non-mainstream consumers – building on traditions such as social tourism (for lower socio-economic groups) and accessible tourism (for those with disabilities), as discussed in Section 4. For example, in the United Kingdom it has been found that economically disadvantaged older people gain numerous well-being benefits from the ability to participate in specially designed trips which allow them to escape their everyday lives, reminisce and connect with others (Morgan et al., 2015).

Tourism can also become less exclusive through ensuring that destinations are frequented by both tourists and locals, which can be encouraged through domestic marketing campaigns, encouraging schools to take students on extended field trips, and support for social tourism initiatives. There are both economic and sociocultural benefits of such domestic tourism, including breaking down barriers between different ethnic groups and increasing appreciation of cultural, linguistic and religious differences; helping to build a sense of national pride and identity; revitalizing social ties between extended family and community groups; encourage local servicing of tourist demands; and spreading economic benefits to areas not frequented by international tourists (Mawdsley, 2009; Scheyvens, 2007). Socially and politically, nationals of any country should feel able to enjoy the attractions of their own country but due to neo-colonial attitudes there can be barriers which prevent access. In Fiji, Uprising Resort provides a contrast to the enclave-type development of many other tourist resorts which leave indigenous people feeling unwelcome and excluded, by encouraging Fijians to enjoy the resort's facilities and participate in activities such as sports events (Scheyvens, 2011).

5.3. Changing the tourism map to involve new people and places

We also argue that there is a territorial dimension to inclusive tourism in that it opens up more places and spaces as sites of tourism. As Kitchin and Dodge have argued, '…mapping is a process of constant reterritorialization' (Kitchin & Dodge, 2007, 331). Thus, places not conventionally frequented by tourists – such as under-resourced or lower socio-economic neighbourhoods – can be reimagined as tourist spaces, and included on the tourist map. In doing so, individuals have the opportunity to encounter new locations and landscapes in multiple, nuanced ways (Edensor, 2015).

This process of remapping tourism and involving new people and places is evident in Sweden's second largest city, Gothenburg. Anna Cederberg Gerdrup wrote a book based on riding the No.11 tram line in Gothenburg from one end to the other, passing through a range of socio-economic areas and getting off at each stop to meet people, to eat and to collect recipes which are reproduced in a cookbook. Her book is encouraging residents to explore their own city more actively and make contact with people of different ethnicities and walks of life (personal communication, April 2016).

We do not wish to suggest, however, that the provision of a few 'novel' or 'out of the way' places and spaces for tourism necessarily constitutes 'inclusive tourism'. Favela, slum or shantytown tours are a good case to consider here. Twenty years ago, such tours were virtually unheard of and only the most intrepid tourists would venture into these somewhat marginalized zones of the city, whereas now they are another box to tick on the itinerary of many conventional tourists visiting the likes of Rio de Janeiro, Mumbai or Johannesburg. Whether or not these tours are inclusive, however, depends on how they are established, with whose input, and how they are carried out. Criticisms abound relating to concerns about voyeurism, representation of the poor, exploitation and commercialization of poverty, and lack of direct benefits to the people of these marginalized areas (Frenzel, 2014; Selinger, 2009). In practice, however, some of these tours have enabled poorer residents to be directly involved in the production of tourism by constructing and running tours, or developing small enterprises that engage tourists; meanwhile tourists consuming these tours have the opportunity to deepen their understanding of the history and politics of the people and places visited, in the case of those tours providing good information (Basu, 2012; Mekawy, 2012).

In the Global North, 'changing the tourism map' is sometimes an implicit component of agendas to promote social integration, such as with the Tikitut initiative in Gothenburg, Sweden. Tikitut attracts domestic and international tourists to an outlying district which has previously suffered from a reputation as a deprived and dangerous area. A network of local hosts who are migrants to Sweden and have no background in tourism or hospitality industries offer home stays and cooking experiences (http://tikitut.se/home). This fundamental shift in who produces the tourism product (see Section 5.1) has led to a number of related inclusive tourism benefits such as integration of marginalized groups, and promoting mutual understanding and respect between hosts and guests (see Section 5.5).

5.4. Widening of participation in tourism decision-making

Who controls and makes decisions about tourism development has a big influence on whether tourism will contribute to inclusive development. Tourism industry players are centrally concerned with profit maximization thus if they are left to self-regulate and adopt unmonitored policies on corporate social responsibility (see Section 5.1), it is unlikely that the industry will always act responsibly and reflect the interests of wider society. This is why Pingeot (2014), referring to the influence of big business over the development of the SDGs, cautions against giving corporations 'undue influence on policymaking and ignoring their responsibility in creating and exacerbating many of the problems that the Post-2015 agenda is supposed to tackle' (Pingeot, 2014, p. 6). When we look closely at what is proposed by business actors in relation to the SDGs, self-interest is a clear driver: this is why there is a focus on voluntary change rather than regulation, and soft measures to reduce environmental impacts rather than fundamental changes in production and consumption (Pingeot, 2014, p. 29). This is of even greater concern when we consider that recent years have seen consolidation of the power of the largest tourism-related organizations through mergers and growth, rather than a dismantling of their power (Scheyvens, 2011).

A counter to this, and a strategy for more inclusive tourism, is to enhance citizens' active participation in tourism decision-making. Timothy (2007, p. 203), for example, shows how decentralizing decision-making power by empowering 'people locally on the ground' can lead to more effective development outcomes. After conducting research with Tibetan youths living in a suburban area of Lhasa, Tibet, and asking them to compare the value of two tourism parks in their area, Wu and Pearce (2016) discovered that the young people preferred strong community control over tourism rather than tourism that is managed by an outside company. This might run counter to some people's views that outside companies are preferred because of advantages they bring in terms of investment potential and business know-how; however this does not reflect the views of at least one large segment of the community. It is vital that more research which actively listens to community voices is conducted to counter industry-centric perspectives and inform inclusive approaches to tourism development.

Following on from this point, Smith and Pappalepore (2015) discuss the case of Deptford, an economically marginal area of London's docklands which was controversially promoted as a tourist destination by the New York Times. Their discussions with local residents lead them to recommend that tourism development should be based on the preferences of these people. They note that this is somewhat 'idealistic' thus they pair it with a more practical recommendation of stimulating events as a means of catalysing movement in and out of such areas and thereby allowing a more organic growth of tourism rather than one that is derived from marketing or journalism which may oversell or mis-sell a place (see Section 5.6).

5.5. Promotion of mutual understanding and respect

While government officials are often preoccupied with economic benefits of tourism, the social benefits can be very important too. An inclusive approach to tourism can, for example, result in enhanced unity in rural, urban or beach locations, less crime, a better sense of security, and a more pleasant place to live. With growing inequality and associated social dysfunction in many societies in the Global North and South, there is now greater interest in the value of breaking down barriers between people (including those living in different suburbs within the same city), providing opportunities to develop mutual understanding, and overcoming negative stereotypes. For example, Higgins-Desbiolles (2016, p. 1280) points out that in Australia indigenous festivals can result in 'positive visibility' for indigenous people and even have a 'role of reconciliation' in situations of past harm from a settler society. Much depends, however, on whose interests are reflected in the resulting tourism, and in this case there were concerns that the festival was transformed in ways that grew tourist numbers while undermining the social and cultural value of the festival, especially from an indigenous perspective (Higgins-Desbiolles, 2016).

In South Africa, the government has tuned into the language of inclusive tourism, and sees this as a means of providing opportunities for people on the margins. As South Africa's Minister of Tourism, Derek Hanekom, said in 2015,

> We want to make the entire sector more inclusive and representative by bringing people who have been marginalised in to the mainstream tourism economy (cited in Butler & Rogerson, 2016, p. 265)

When this concept was applied to the town of Dullstroom, mentioned above, which has seen growth in second home tourism, fly fishing and agritourism, Butler and Rogerson (2016) found clear evidence of an inclusive tourism development approach. Surveyed residents noted social benefits as being highly significant to them. Interestingly, apart from oft-cited benefits such as capability and empowerment, these residents valued the enhanced safety of their town associated with growth of tourism, along with important strides to overcome mistrust between ethnic groups (who were now more likely to be working together in tourism enterprises): 'An additional example of social empowerment concerned the development of positive relationships between black and white community members' (Butler & Rogerson, 2016, p. 276).

In recent years, a rise in the share of the votes in elections by anti-foreigner political parties in Europe has coincided with a refugee crisis prompted by the Syrian conflict which has also flowed over into Europe. Rights to asylum have been challenged even in places where they have for decades been taken for granted. Amongst the many efforts seeking to ensure that refugees are given asylum have been those emanating from the tourism sector. Social enterprises such as the Good Hotel in Amsterdam and London and the Magdas Hotel in Vienna have been set up to provide employment for refugees and to create opportunities for social interaction as part of a movement to use tourism to ensure that refugees are welcomed and integrated in European societies (Coldwell, 2016). Similarly, the Kitchen on the Run project saw a small group of Germans build a kitchen in a container which they toured around European cities for five months during summer 2016; they used the container to host several dinner parties per week for 25–35 refugees and locals who cooked together and ate together in 'a space that encourages and supports intimate get-togethers between refugees from all over the world and locals in Europe around the kitchen table' (Kitchen on the run, 2016). They cooked with a total of over 2000 people from 65 different countries, and planned to repeat the initiative with multiple containers taking different routes in 2017 (Persson, 2016).

5.6. Self-representation in dignified and appropriate ways

One persistent critique of tourism is that it has a tendency to objectify and exoticize the 'other'. This is a process that is entrenched. As quickly as tourists move beyond the tourist track in search of 'authentic' interactions, those interactions themselves become susceptible to commercialization and commodification (MacCannell, 1992, 2008). This process of objectification is part of what critics find abhorrent about orphanage tourism and some forms of voluntourism (Guiney & Mostafanezhad, 2015).

One of the foci of inclusive tourism, then, is to find ways that host communities, including indigenous people, and vulnerable and poor people in host communities, can represent themselves in ways that they find appropriate and dignified. Thus, for example, rather than being represented by others as having a 'static', 'traditional' culture, Māori people of New Zealand are, through their tourism businesses, re-negotiating the way in which they are represented to tourists and showing how they interact with and draw from other cultures as well: '…"difference" is not so much a pre-given and static trait of 'fixed' tradition but a complex ongoing negotiation' (Amoamo & Thompson, 2010, p. 47). In another example, Seiver and Matthews (2016) provide a fascinating comparison of representations of Aboriginal people in destination images for four regions in Australia. While one region virtually overlooks Aboriginal peoples, in other destinations Aboriginal tourism incorporates Aboriginal perspectives and presents the culture as living and dynamic, which helps to disrupt stereotypes.

5.7. Power relations transformed in and beyond tourism

All of the elements of inclusive tourism which we have discussed above provide potentially incremental contributions to the larger, long-term goal of transforming power relations and ending social exclusion. Direct attempts at overturning power relations, however, whether within the tourism industry or in wider society, are inevitably battling the odds. Social structures and systems which marginalize and impoverish may have a high degree of resilience and path dependency (Baird, Chaffin, & Wrathall, 2017). Thus some new initiatives such as Private-Community Partnerships in Uganda, which are set up specifically to share ownership of a tourism venture such as a high-end ecolodge, have fallen short in achieving true 'partnership' (Ahebwa, Van der Duim, & Sandbrook, 2012). Nevertheless there are examples of transformations of social and economic life such that marginalized and poor individuals and groups are included on terms that are decent and fair, and of shared ownership which genuinely transfers power to previously exploited groups.

Positive initiatives include those that hand over ownership and control of a tourism business to (former) employees. An interesting example from North Cyprus is the Dome Hotel, which used to be state-owned, and became employee-owned after trade unions and employees sought an alternative to planned privatization of the hotel. It is now owned by 49 hotel employees and the Tourism Workers Union, and operated by Solidarity Tourism Company (Timur & Timur, 2015). Through this system, every full time employee has one vote over decisions which span marketing, wages, profit distribution, and investments. The employee ownership system is widely appreciated by the new owners and by the wider community, which benefits from the hotel's 'support your local economy' policy, and also experiences social benefits such as discounted access to the hotel facilities. Interestingly, the hotel has also gained direct benefits from this, including more stable local employment, more return customers (partly related to the relationships developed with long-term staff), and preservation of an iconic hotel (Timur & Timur, 2015). This may provide a source of inspiration for other similar employee ownership or worker cooperative schemes, to allow them to find a more substantial foothold in the tourism market thus disrupting the consolidation of power in the hands of a small number of major hotel and tour operators.

6. Constraints to achieving inclusive tourism

However, a few success stories are not enough to 'prove' that an inclusive approach to tourism is valuable. The power of larger companies in the tourism sector is becoming entrenched, making it difficult for those wanting to start their own initiatives: 15 per cent of businesses which are internationally branded chains have 52 of the business, thus claiming a 'dominant' position in the industry (Niewiadomski, 2014, p. 50). It is important for us to confront the constraints on inclusiveness in practice, with the key constraint being the prevailing ideology of neoliberalism. Essentially, whether there is a tag-on agenda of poverty-alleviation or sustainability, under neoliberal logic the premise is that economic growth is the basis of development (Mowforth & Munt, 2009, p. 34). Such an approach fails to consider how economic growth can undermine sociocultural well-being and the environment. Thus, encouraging the inclusion of new sites for people to find leisure or escape may compromise quality of life for some people in those locales by impinging on livelihood options (not always positively), overcrowding, limiting public access to social spaces, and so forth. Under neoliberal policy much faith has been placed in private sector entities working as development actors, despite the fact that, for example, global tour operators, multinational hotel chains and the like are not skilled in overcoming inequality, empowering the poor or delivering on socio-economic goals (McEwan, Mawdsley, Banks, & Scheyvens, 2017). Neoliberalism has led to a rise in the number and types of enclavic spaces in tourism, making more places inaccessible to local people (unless they enter as cleaners, gardeners and so forth) (Saarinen, 2017). Allowing markets to drive growth is thus unlikely to work as a strategy to support inclusive tourism; rather, it is more likely to reinforce the wealth of some and entrench the poverty of others.

There are significant barriers to overcome to achieve inclusive tourism in terms of opportunities for those who are poor or marginalized. In many cases, poorer local people, even when in sight of wealthier tourists and without physical or policy barriers erected against them, will lack the language, skills, networks or capital to engage with those tourists on their own initiative (e.g. Biddulph, 2015, pp. 107–9). They also tend to face various forms of discrimination. Even when they have an opportunity to, for example, operate a community-based tourism enterprise, they might simultaneously experience empowerment and forms of disempowerment, the latter because they are still subject to domination by others (Knight & Cottrell, 2016).

Furthermore, a lot of tourism products are still built on difference (between rich and poor, between different cultures) rather than breaking down differences and building mutual understanding. The industry explicitly exploits this 'difference', for example, when rich tourists visit the poor via cultural tourism, and when tourists from urban jungles are enticed to meet the 'primitive' minorities in tropical jungles (Scheyvens, 2011, p. 83). This is what Mowforth and Munt (2009, p. 81) refer to as the 'ultimate aestheticism of reality... [through] which racism and class struggle actually seem to be enjoyed'. Thus initiatives espoused under the banner of inclusive tourism might simply provide a distraction from the fundamental structural inequalities upon which tourism is base. For example, a nice tourism-related social enterprise to help former-refugees in an outer suburb to economically integrate into a new country might deflect attention from more pressing needs and challenges they face in their new communities. Tourism, inclusive or not, will not always be a suitable strategy to achieve holistic development.

7. Conclusion

This article has defined and conceptualized inclusive tourism, demonstrating why the authors feel that it provides a valuable analytical perspective to tourism in the Global North and South. Travel can broaden the mind by exposing the traveller to places and people and perspectives that s/he would not encounter at home. Tourism, by commodifying travel, always risks robbing it of what is most enriching and promising about it. Initiatives to make tourism more inclusive can be seen as attempts to improve the quality of human interaction, and to ensure that tourism delivers benefits to those who have in the past been excluded from, or marginalized by, its production and consumption. Given the fierce competition within the industry with drives to keep the mass market low cost and standardized and the luxury market exclusive and enclaved, such initiatives are likely to be battling against the odds. This is especially the case in a neoliberal climate which expects change to be led not through the consolidated, organized power of the state, but via the fragmentary, uncoordinated decisions of individual consumers.

Nevertheless, the discussion above has demonstrated ways in which an inclusive approach to tourism is playing out in practice in specific locations. Some of the examples could provide inspiration to actors wishing to support more inclusive outcomes from tourism development. We have shown how marginalized people are becoming more involved in the production and consumption of tourism, with Tren Ecuador's support for the livelihoods of thousands of people along its routes and Uprising Hotel in Fiji welcoming indigenous customers while challenging notions of the resort as an exclusive enclave. We have demonstrated why it is important for more people to have a say over decision-making around tourism, whether the economically marginalized of Deptford or the youth of Lhasa. Our examples show that indigenous people are now choosing how they represent themselves to tourists, after years of being misrepresented. We have explained how tourism can be a mechanism for the economic empowerment and social inclusion of refugees, such as through the Good Hotel in Amsterdam, and how a business can come to be owned and controlled by former employees, as with the Dome Hotel in Cyprus.

We believe that inclusive tourism provides a way forward in terms of thinking that will help to overcome some of the barriers noted in the discussion above. Our ambition is not that inclusive tourism will become a source of branding or certification initiatives, but rather that it will provide a source of critical and innovative thinking. We hope that it will prompt a certain analytical restlessness as the questions 'how inclusive is this development?' and 'how could this tourism enterprise be more inclusive?' are repeatedly posed and improvements sought. Furthermore, it is apparent that for inclusive tourism to be fully realized we cannot rely on private sector initiative or good intentions alone, rather, national and international regulatory frameworks have a critical role to play.

Disclosure statement

No potential conflict of interest was reported by the authors.

ORCID

Regina Scheyvens http://orcid.org/0000-0002-4227-4910

References

Ahebwa, W. M., Van der Duim, V. R., & Sandbrook, C. G. (2012). Private-community partnerships: Investigating a new approach to conservation and development in Uganda. *Conservation and Society*, *10*(4), 305.

Amoamo, M., & Thompson, A. (2010). (re) Imaging Māori tourism: Representation and cultural hybridity in postcolonial New Zealand. *Tourist Studies*, *10*(1), 35–55.

Ashley, C., & Roe, D. (2002). Making tourism work for the poor: Strategies and challenges in Southern Africa. *Development Southern Africa*, *19*(1), 61–82. doi:10.1080/03768350220123855

Ashley, C., Boyd, C., & Goodwin, H. (2000). *Pro-poor tourism: Putting poverty at the heart of the tourism agenda*. London:ODI (Overseas Development Institute).

Ashley, C., Haysom, G., & Spenceley, A. (2008). The development impacts of tourism supply chains: Increasing impact on poverty and decreasing our ignorance. In A. Spenceley (Ed.) *Responsible Tourism: Critical issues for Conservation and Development*. London: Earthscan. 129–156.

Baird, T. D., Chaffin, B. C., & Wrathall, D. J. (2017). A disturbance innovation hypothesi s: Perspectives from human and physical geography. *The Geographical Journal*, 183(2), 201–208. doi:10.1111/geoj.12206

Bakker, M., & Messerli, H. R. (2017). Inclusive growth versus pro-poor growth: Implications for tourism development. *Tourism and Hospitality Research*, 17(4), 384–391 doi:10.1177/1467358416638919

Basu, K. (2012). 4 Slum tourism: For the poor, by the poor. *Slum Tourism: Poverty, Power and Ethics*, 32, 66.

Biddulph, R. (2015). Limits to mass tourism's effects in rural peripheries. *Annals of Tourism Research*, 50, 98–112.

Blackstock, K. (2005). A critical look at community based tourism. *Community Development Journal*, 40(1), 39–49. doi:10.1093/cdj/bsi005

Blowfield, M., & Dolan, C. S. (2014). Business as a development agent: Evidence of possibility and improbability. *Third World Quarterly*, 35(1), 22–42. doi:10.1080/01436597.2013.868982

Booyens, I. (2010). Rethinking township tourism: Towards responsible tourism development in South African townships. *Development Southern Africa*, 27(2), 273–287. doi:10.1080/03768351003740795

Bramwell, B., Lane, B., McCabe, S., Mosedale, J., & Scarles, C. (2008). Research perspectives on responsible tourism. *Journal of Sustainable Tourism*, 16(3), 253–257. doi:10.1080/09669580802208201

Britton, S. G. (1982). The political economy of tourism in the third world. *Annals of Tourism Research*, 9(3), 331–358. doi:10.1016/0160-7383(82)90018-4

Butler, G., & Rogerson, C. M. (2016). Inclusive local tourism development in South Africa: Evidence from dullstroom. *Local Economy*, 31(1–2), 264–281.

Caffyn, A., & Lutz, J. (1999). Developing the heritage tourism product in multi-ethnic cities. *Tourism Management*, 20(2), 213–221. doi:10.1016/S0261-5177(98)00075-2

Chakravorti, B., Macmillan, G., & Siesfeld, T. (2014). *Growth for good or good for growth? How sustainable and inclusive activities are changing business and why companies aren't changing enough*. Retrieved from http://www.citifoundation.com/citi/foundation/pdf/1221365_Citi_Foundation_Sustainable_Inclusive_Business_Study_Web.pdf

Cho, M. (2007). A re-examination of tourism and peace: The case of the Mt. Gumgang tourism development on the Korean Peninsula. *Tourism Management*, 28(2), 556–569. doi:10.1016/j.tourman.2006.04.019

Coldwell, W. (2016, 27th June). Floating hotel to open in London as part of social enterprise project. *The Guardian*. 20 June 2016. Retrieved from https://www.theguardian.com/travel/2016/jun/27/floating-hotel-to-open-london-social-enterprise-project

Craven, C. E. (2016). Refusing to be toured: Work, tourism, and the productivity of 'Life' in the Colombian Amazon. *Antipode*, 48(3), 544–562. doi:10.1111/anti.12208

Cukier, J. (2011). Development tourism: Lessons from Cuba. *Annals of Tourism Research*, 38(1), 333–335. doi:10.1016/j.annals.2010.11.004

D'Amore L. (2009). Peace through tourism: The birthing of a new socio-economic order. *Journal of Business Ethics*, 89(4), 559–568. doi:10.1007/s10551-010-0407-3

Darcy, S. (2006). Setting a research agenda for accessible tourism. In C. Coober, T. D. Lacy, & L. Jago (Eds.), *Sustainable Tourism Cooperative Research Centre technical report series*. Gold Coast, Australia.

Darcy, S., & Dickson, T. J. (2009). A whole-of-life approach to tourism: The case for accessible tourism experiences. *Journal of Hospitality and Tourism Management*, 16(1), 32–44. doi:10.1375/jhtm.16.1.32

Darcy, S., & Pegg, S. (2011). Towards strategic intent: Perceptions of disability service provision amongst hotel accommodation managers. *International Journal of Hospitality Management*, 30(2), 468–476. doi:10.1016/j.ijhm.2010.09.009

Deutsche Gesellschaft für Internationale Zusammenarbeit. (2016). *How can we unlock the power of inclusive tourism?* Paper presented at the 2nd Inclusive Business Asia Forum, Manila. http://www.

inclusivebusinesshub.org/wp-content/uploads/2016/05/IBAsiaForumTourismSessionGIZRIBHOutline.pdf

Edensor, T. (2015). The gloomy city: Rethinking the relationship between light and dark. *Urban Studies*, *24*, 422–438.

Frenzel, F. (2014). Slum tourism and its controversies from a management perspective. In M. Gudic, A. Rosenbloom and C. Parkes (Eds.). *Socially Responsive Organizations and the Challenge of Poverty* (pp. 123–135). Leeds: Greenleaf.

Gelbman, A. (2008). Border tourism in Israel: Conflict, peace, fear and hope. *Tourism Geographies*, *10* (2), 193–213. doi:10.1080/14616680802000022

Gibson, C. (2009). Geographies of tourism: Critical research on capitalism and local livelihoods. *Progress in Human Geography*, *33*(4), 527–534.

Goodwin, H. (2009). Reflections on 10 years of pro-poor tourism. *Journal of Policy Research in Tourism, Leisure and Events*, *1*(1), 90–94. doi:10.1080/19407960802703565

Goodwin, H., & Font, X. (2007). *Advances in responsible tourism*. Retrieved from Leeds:

Guiney, T., & Mostafanezhad, M. (2015). The political economy of orphanage tourism in Cambodia. *Tourist Studies*, *15*(2), 132–155. doi:10.1177/1468797614563387

Hampton, M., Jeyacheya, J., & Long, P. H. (2017). Can tourism promote inclusive growth? Supply chains, ownership and employment in Ha Long Bay, Vietnam. *The Journal of Development Studies*. Online advance publication. doi:10.1080/00220388.2017.1296572

Harrison, D. (Ed.) (1992). *Tourism and the Less Developed Countries*. London: Belhaven Press.

Haulot, A. (1981). Social tourism. *International Journal of Tourism Management*, *2*(3), 207–212. doi:10.1016/0143-2516(81)90007-4

Higgins-Desbiolles, F. (2003). Reconciliation tourism: Tourism healing divided societies! *Tourism Recreation Research*, *28*(3), 35–44. doi:10.1080/02508281.2003.11081415

Higgins-Desbiolles, F. (2016). Sustaining spirit: A review and analysis of an urban indigenous Australian cultural festival. *Journal of Sustainable Tourism*, *24*(8-9), 1280–1297. doi:10.1080/09669582.2016.1149184

Hughes, E., & Scheyvens, R. (2016). Corporate social responsibility in tourism post-2015: A development first approach. *Tourism Geographies*, *18*(5), 469–482.

International Trade Centre. (2012). *Linking the handicraft sector to tourism markets*. Geneva. Retrieved from: http://www.intracen.org/uploadedFiles/intracenorg/Content/Exporters/Sectoral_Information/Service_Exports/Tourism/Linking the Handicraft Sector reprint 9 10 2012 for web.pdf

Isaac, R. K. (2010). Moving from pilgrimage to responsible tourism: The case of Palestine. *Current Issues in Tourism*, *13*(6), 579–590. doi:10.1080/13683500903464218

Jamal, T., & Camargo, B. A. (2014). Sustainable tourism, justice and an ethic of care: Toward the just destination. *Journal of Sustainable Tourism*, *22*(1), 11–30.

Kim, S. S., Prideaux, B., & Prideaux, J. (2007). Using tourism to promote peace on the Korean Peninsula. *Annals of Tourism Research*, *34*(2), 291–309. doi:10.1016/j.annals.2006.09.002

Kitchen on the run. (2016). Kitchen on the run. Retrieved from http://www.kitchenontherun.org/about/

Kitchin, R., & Dodge, M. (2007). Rethinking maps. *Progress in Human Geography*, *31*(3), 331–344.

Klein, R. A. (2011). Responsible cruise tourism: Issues of cruise tourism and sustainability. *Journal of Hospitality and Tourism Management*, *18*(1), 107–116. doi:10.1375/jhtm.18.1.107

Knight, D. W., & Cottrell, S. P. (2016). Evaluating tourism-linked empowerment in Cuzco, Peru. *Annals of Tourism Research*, *56*, 32–47.

Kumi, E., Arhin, A. A., & Yeboah, T. (2014). Can post-2015 sustainable development goals survive neoliberalism? A critical examination of the sustainable development–neoliberalism nexus in developing countries. *Environment, Development and Sustainability*, *16*(3), 539–554.

Lawson, V. (2010). Reshaping economic geography? producing spaces of inclusive development. *Economic Geography*, *86*(4), 351–360.

MacCannell, D. (1992). *Empty meeting grounds*. London: Routledge.

MacCannell, D. (2008). Why it never really was about authenticity. *Society*, *45*(4), 334–337. doi:10.1007/s12115-008-9110-8

Manyara, G., & Jones, E. (2007). Community-based tourism enterprises development in Kenya: An exploration of their potential as avenues of poverty reduction. *Journal of Sustainable Tourism, 15*(6), 628–644. doi:10.2167/jost723.0

Marques, J. C., & Utting, P. (2010). *Corporate social responsibility and regulatory governance: Towards inclusive development?* Basingstoke: Palgrave Macmillan.

Marques, J. C., & Utting, P. (2010). Introduction: Understanding business power and public policy in a development context. *Business, politics and public policy* (pp. 1–29). New York: Spring er.

Mawdsley, E. (2009). Development update: Domestic tourism. *Geography Review, 22*(3), 32–33.

McCabe, S., & Diekmann, A. (2015). The rights to tourism: Reflections on social tourism and human rights. *Tourism Recreation Research, 40*(2), 194–204. doi:10.1080/02508281.2015.1049022

McEwan, C., Mawdsley, E., Banks, G., & Scheyvens, R. (2017). Enrolling the private sector in community development: Magic bullet or sleight of hand? *Development and Change, 48*(1), 28–53.

Mekawy, M. A. (2012). Responsible slum tourism: Egyptian experience. *Annals of Tourism Research, 39*(4), 2092–2113.

Minnaert, L., Maitland, R., & Miller, G. (2011). What is social tourism? *Current Issues in Tourism, 14*(5), 403–415. doi:10.1080/13683500.2011.568051

Mitchell, J., & Ashley, C. (2010). *Tourism and poverty reduction: Pathways to prosperity*. (1st ed.). London: Earthscan.

Monge, J., & Yagüe Perales, R., (2016). Sustainable tourism development: Tren Crucero del Ecuador. *Estudios y Perspectivas en Turismo, 25*(1), 57–72.

Morgan, N., Pritchard, A., & Sedgley, D. (2015). Social tourism and well-being in later life. *Annals of Tourism Research, 52*, 1–15. doi:10.1016/j.annals.2015.02.015

Mowforth, M., & Munt, I. (2009). *Tourism and sustainability: Development and new tourism in the third world*. London: Routledge.

Niewiadomski, P. (2014). Towards an economic-geographical approach to the globalisation of the hotel industry. *Tourism Geographies, 16*(1), 48–67.

Okazaki, E. (2008). A community-based tourism model: Its conception and use. *Journal of Sustainable Tourism, 16*(5), 511–529. doi:10.1080/09669580802159594

Pagán, R. (2012). Time allocation in tourism for people with disabilities. *Annals of Tourism Research, 39*(3), 1514–1537.

Persson, K. (2016, July 30). Kök på resa genom Europa skapar möten. *Göteborgsfria*. Retrieved from https://www.goteborgsfria.se/artikel/123903

Pingeot, L. (2014). *Corporate influence in the Post-2015 process* (Working Paper). Aachen, Berlin, Bonn: Misereor, Brot fur die Welt, Global Policy Forum. Retrieved from http://www19.iadb.org/intal/intalcdi/PE/2014/13575.pdf

Rauniyar, G., & Kanbur, R. (2010). Inclusive growth and inclusive development: A review and synthesis of Asian Development Bank literature. *Journal of the Asia Pacific Economy, 15*(4), 455–469.

Saarinen, J. (2017). Enclavic tourism spaces: Territorialization and bordering in tourism destination development and planning. *Tourism Geographies, 19*(3): 425–437. doi:10.1080/14616688.2016.1258433

Salazar, N. B. (2012). Community-based cultural tourism: Issues, threats and opportunities. *Journal of Sustainable Tourism, 20*(1), 9–22. doi:10.1080/09669582.2011.596279

Scheyvens, R. (2007). Poor cousins no more valuing the development potential of domestic and diaspora tourism. *Progress in Development Studies, 7*(4), 307–325.

Scheyvens, R. (2011). *Tourism and poverty*. New York, NY: Routledge.

Seiver, B., & Matthews, A. (2016). Beyond whiteness: A comparative analysis of representations of aboriginality in tourism destination images in New South Wales, Australia. *Journal of Sustainable Tourism, 24*(8–9), 1298–1314. doi:10.1080/09669582.2016.1182537

Selinger, E. (2009). Ethics and poverty tours. *Philosophy & Public Policy Quarterly, 29*(1/2), 2–7.

Smith, A., & Pappalepore, I. (2015). Exploring attitudes to edgy urban destinations: The case of Deptford, London. *Journal of Tourism and Cultural Change, 13*(2), 97–114. doi:10.1080/14766825.2014.896371

Sonmez, S. F., & Apostolopoulos, Y. (2000). Conflict resolution through tourism cooperation? The case of the partitioned island-state of Cyprus. *Journal of Travel & Tourism Marketing*, *9*(3), 35–48. doi:10.1300/J073v09n03_03

Sotheary, P. (2016, April 11). Eviction of beach businesses begins at Ochheuteal. *The Phnom Penh Post*. Retrieved from http://www.phnompenhpost.com/national/eviction-beach-businesses-begins-ochheuteal

Spenceley, A. (Ed.) (2012). *Responsible tourism: Critical issues for conservation and development*. London: Earthscan.

Telfer, D. J., & Wall, G. (2000). Strengthening backward economic linkages: Local food purchasing by three Indonesian hotels. *Tourism Geographies*, *2*(4), 421–447. doi:10.1080/146166800750035521

Timothy, D. (2007). Empowerment and stakeholder participation in tourism destination communities. In T. C. Andrew Church (Ed.), *Tourism, power and space* (pp. 203–216). London: Routledge.

Timur, S., & Timur, A. T. (2015). Employee ownership and sustainable development in tourism: A case in North Cyprus. *Sustainable Development*, *24* (2), 89–100.

Torres, R. (2002). Toward a better understanding of tourism and agriculture linkages in the Yucatan: Tourist food consumption and preferences. *Tourism Geographies*, *4*(3), 282–306. doi:10.1080/14616680210147436

United Nations Development Program. (2016). Inclusive Development. Retrieved from http://www.undp.org/content/undp/en/home/ourwork/povertyreduction/focus_areas/focus_inclusive_development.html

Walmsley, A. (2012). Decent work and tourism wages: An International comparison. *Progress in responsible tourism*, *2*(1), 90–99.

Wheeller, B. (1990). Responsible tourism. *Tourism Management*, *11*(3), 262–263. doi:10.1016/0261-5177(90)90050-J

Wheeller, B. (1991). Tourism's troubled times. *Tourism Management*, *12*(2), 91–96. doi:10.1016/0261-5177(91)90062-X

Wu, M. Y., & Pearce, P. L. (2016). A tale of two parks: Tibetan youths' preferences for tourism community futures. *Journal of Tourism and Cultural Change*, *15*(4), 359–379. doi:10.1080/14766825.2016.1156687

Yau, M. K.-s., McKercher, B., & Packer, T. L. (2004). Traveling with a disability: More than an access issue. *Annals of Tourism Research*, *31*(4), 946–960. doi:10.1016/j.annals.2004.03.007

Zapata, M. J., Hall, C. M., Lindo, P., & Vanderschaeghe, M. (2011). Can community-based tourism contribute to development and poverty alleviation? Lessons from Nicaragua. *Current Issues in Tourism*, *14*(8), 725–749. doi:10.1080/13683500.2011.559200

de Kadt, E. (1979). *Tourism: Passport to development?* New York, NY: Oxford University Press.

Tourism and the Millennium Development Goals: perspectives beyond 2015

Jarkko Saarinen and Christian M. Rogerson

As 2015 approaches, debates about the contribution to the United Nations Millennium Development Goals (UN MDGs) are growing in momentum. The aim of this review is to interrogate the potential contributions of tourism to the UN MDGs, specifically of poverty alleviation, and of how the relationship between tourism development and the UN MDGs has been framed in existing scholarship. It is argued that whilst the global tourism industry potentially can contribute to economic development goals in destination regions, its impacts are ambivalent so that there is a growing concern surrounding the local benefits of global tourism including support for realisation of the UN MDGs. To avert the risks in the Global South of tourism-led development, the industry needs to be clearly positioned as a potential tool *for*, not at the end of local, regional, national and global development agendas. Several promising research avenues for interrogating tourism impacts for UN MDGs are identified. Issues relating to greening of tourism, inclusive business models and backward linkages offer a powerful policy-relevant agenda for tourism scholarship to move forward our understanding of the UN MDG objectives, which were originally set down in 2000, beyond 2015.

Introduction

In 2006, Francesco Frangialli, Secretary General of the United Nations World Tourism Organisation (UNWTO), stated that the tourism industry could play a major role in the achievement of the United Nations Millennium Development Goals (UN MDGs) by 2015 (UNWTO, 2006). Likewise the World Bank (2012) recently has highlighted the transformative role that tourism might play in developing economies and societies. Thus, the potential role of tourism with respect to achieving the UN MDGs has been highlighted widely across recent policy discourses and academic literature (see Brickley, Black, & Cottrell, 2013; Saarinen, Rogerson, & Manwa, 2013), raising important questions on how and whether the tourism industry can meet these high expectations.

The UN MDGs originate from the United Nations Millennium Declaration adopted in 2000 which commits UN member states to a new global partnership and are designed to reduce extreme poverty. Nevertheless, the MDGs are not "only" focusing on poverty reduction. In addition to eradicate extreme poverty and hunger (Goal 1), there are seven other goals, viz.: achieve universal primary education (Goal 2); promote gender equality and empower women (Goal 3); reduce child mortality (Goal 4); improve maternal health

(Goal 5); combat HIV/AIDS, malaria and other diseases (Goal 6); ensure environmental sustainability (Goal 7) and develop a global partnership for development (Goal 8) (United Nations, 2000). All these goals include specific targets: for example, eradicate extreme poverty and hunger includes three targets aiming to halve the proportion of people whose income is less than $1 a day (from 1990 to 2015); achieve full and productive employment and decent work for all, including women and young people (by 2015) and halve the proportion of people who suffer from hunger (from 1990 to 2015) (United Nations, 2000).

Whilst the wider set of UN MDGs form a global landscape of development needs and targets, most tourism-related discussions and policy formulations focus on poverty (UNWTO, 2002, 2006). Tourism is increasingly seen as a force that can be used for poverty alleviation through the creation of income and employment particularly in rural areas of the developing world (Christie & Sharma, 2008). As stated by Ashley and Maxwell (2001) "Poverty is not only widespread in rural areas, but most poverty is rural" (p. 395). Accordingly, tourism's traditional connection to regional development in peripheral areas serves as the premise for the emerging linkage of tourism development and poverty alleviation. Currently, perhaps, the most contested perspective in tourism–poverty alleviation nexus is that of pro-poor tourism (PPT), which refers to a way of organising "host–guest relations" that would lead to net benefits for the poor in developing countries (Ashley & Roe, 2002; Goodwin, 2009; Pleumarom, 2012; Scheyvens, 2009, 2011).

The purpose of this review is to discuss the potential contributions of tourism to the UN MDGs, specifically of poverty alleviation, and how the relationship between tourism development and the UN MDGs has been framed in the existing literature. The review focuses on debates surrounding opportunities and constraints linked to the role of tourism in poverty alleviation within the broader mandate of the MDGs and of how the industry could be leveraged for poverty alleviation. As the basic promises and challenges of PPT have been widely scrutinised (e.g. Ashley & Roe, 2002; Hall, 2007; Scheyvens, 2009, 2011), this paper seeks to emphasise how we could potentially transcend the present barricades between PPT advocates and sceptics in future.

Tourism for poverty alleviation

Sofield (2003) estimated that developing countries enjoy a market share up to 40% of global tourism. Even if that level of share is an overestimate, the scale of tourism in developing countries is massive. In addition, given its growth potential here it is understandable why the industry has become important in the UN MDGs policy discussions on poverty alleviation (see Bolwell & Weinz, 2008; Rogerson, 2006). Indeed, several national governments (e.g. Botswana, Mozambique and South Africa) in the Global South have initiated poverty reduction strategies which are anchored on expectations for tourism-led growth (Mitchell & Ashley, 2010; Novelli & Hellwig, 2011; Scheyvens, 2011, pp. 145–170).

Overall, it is argued that there is a great potential for tourism to contribute towards the UN MDGs and specifically of targets for poverty alleviation (Meyer, 2007; Mitchell & Ashley, 2010; Spenceley & Meyer, 2012). With respect to attaining the UN MDGs PPT has attracted much scholarly debate (Scheyvens, 2011). It is stressed that PPT is not a tourism product but a wider framework to organise both host–guest relations and benefit-sharing in tourism (Ashley & Roe, 2002; Lapeyre, 2011; Rogerson, 2006). The PPT framework aims to benefit local people through tourism operations by "seeking to use mainstream tourism to achieve the objective of poverty elimination" (Goodwin, 2009,

p. 91). According to Goodwin (2009) the emphasis on making direct connections to the mainstream industry was "the radicalism" of the PPT approach which separates PPT from other approaches such as community-based tourism, which was viewed as a small-scale public-oriented development approach without sufficient capacity to contribute to the wider poverty reduction agenda (p. 91).

By utilising the principles and strategies of PPT, tourist consumption is to be harnessed to serve the poor by "unlocking opportunities" for them "at all levels and scales of operation" in tourism development (Ashley, Roe, & Goodwin, 2001, p. 3). Nevertheless, as noted by the World Bank (2012), the tourism industry, like other businesses, "comes with its own set of risks and challenges" (p. 7). Arguably, Sinclair (1988) avers that the positive economic aspects of tourism should be placed in an equation consisting of both the advantages and disadvantages of tourism-related development. Recently criticism has been directed at the reality of turning the mainstream tourism industry towards a PPT approach at a scale that might actually impact upon the UN MDGs (Scheyvens, 2009, 2011). For critics the PPT framework represents a continuation of a tourism-centric development approach which is based on neoliberal agendas and fails to question the existence, spread or legitimisation of the industry (Hall, 2007; Pleumarom, 2012).

The principal criticism of mainstream tourism's capacity and willingness to focus on the (scale of) net benefits of the poor is grounded on the essential logic of tourism as a private sector and market-driven business (Scheyvens, 2009). Tourism spaces primarily are articulated to serve the interests of non-locals (i.e. tourists, foreign investors, organisations). Especially in developing countries the imperative for external investment is recognised for initiating and boosting competitive tourism destinations and meeting the customer standards in services (Britton, 1991; Schilcher, 2007). Although local and non-local needs are not necessarily contradictory, critical questions arise concerning possible and quite common conflict situations and unequal power relationships and benefit-sharing models. Importantly, Scheyvens (2009) questions why "should we assume that they [the mainstream tourism industry] have some ethical commitment to ensuring that their businesses contribute to poverty-alleviation?" (p. 193).

Although the global tourism system has a great potential to contribute positively to the socio-economic development of destination regions, especially the peripheries of developing countries, tourism-led development is often marked by enclavisation, dependency, inequalities and revenue leakages (Britton, 1991; Brohman, 1996; Pleumarom, 2012; Scheyvens, 2011). Indeed, Britton's (1982) seminal analysis on tourism dependency in Fiji demonstrated the existence of high rates of leakages associated with foreign domination of the local tourism industry and especially the power of large multinational tourism enterprises which were drivers of international tourism expansion in developing countries. The appearance and consolidation of such leakages validate Brohman's (1996) contention that "in the absence of well-developed linkages between the external sectors and the rest of the economy, a limited and polarised form of development takes place that cannot act as a stimulus for broadly-based development" (p. 50). Thus, in many instances the growth of the globally driven tourism industry has not turned into wider economic and social development that contributes towards the MDGs in tourism destinations. On the contrary, there are mounting concerns over the local benefits of the global tourism industry, particularly with the dominant power of multinational hotel chains and of package holiday providers in global production networks of tourism (Christian, 2010). The ambivalent nature of tourism clearly underscores the need for further research to support the realisation of the UN MDGs, a point which was raised by Christie and Sharma (2008).

Beyond 2015

A broad consensus exists nowadays that tourism is not a magical cure for poverty and that the challenge of reaching the "poorest of the poor" is most problematic. The relation between tourism and poverty alleviation is observed to be "terra incognita among tourism academics" (Zhou & Richie, 2007, p. 120) and the same may apply to the identification of poverty. Questions such as what is poverty, how to measure it and who actually are the poor are still rarely elaborated in tourism scholarship (Schilcher, 2007). Whilst poverty can be framed in absolute terms it is also relative, context dependent and changing in target (Addison, Hulme, & Kanbur, 2009). The transforming characteristics of poverty problematise the identification of the "most poor" communities and community members in tourism development processes. In addition to improved contextualisation of poverty and the poor, strands of contemporary tourism scholarship are increasingly emphasising the imperative to incorporate wider socio-spatial scales, institutional arrangements and value chains in identifying bottlenecks and opportunities in the contribution of tourism development to poverty reduction (Barrett, Lee, & McPeak, 2004; Meyer, 2009).

By way of looking forward, the following discussion seeks to tease out certain existing trends which relate to the future implications of tourism for poverty alleviation and the realisation of the wider emphasis of the UN MDGs. In particular, the focus here is on the roles that different government bodies and the private sector might assume in order to strengthen tourism's contribution to poverty alleviation in a turbulent, changing and increasingly environmentally sensitive global economy which is inextricably tied both to globalisation processes and the impacts of future climate change upon destinations in the Global South.

From the perspective of national governments as well as tourism businesses, it is evident that deepening and sustaining the success of established tourism destinations require attention to an array of key policy issues and institutional arrangements surrounding local and regional sourcing and the maximisation of local linkages that add value and create local employment opportunities (Mitchell & Ashley, 2010; Spenceley & Meyer, 2012). In the context of the UN MDGs the crucial aspect is to identify and reach the poor so as to maximise tourism's potential for more broadly based patterns of economic and social development (Scheyvens, 2011). According to Ashley and Haysom (2009) opening up new "opportunities for emerging entrepreneurs to access corporate supply chains is one of the most useful ways in which mainstream business can contribute to local development" (p. 1). Accordingly, more attention must be "paid to managing their economic multipliers and impacts along local and global value chains" such that the potential of "innovative business practices that deliberately expand economic opportunities for the disadvantaged" are not fully realised (Ashley, De Brine, Lehr, & Wilde, 2007, p. 6). Several observers stress that much can be done in policy terms to boost local linkages, not least in terms of developing pro-poor impacts, such as income, employment and livelihood changes (Mitchell & Ashley, 2010; Sandbrook, 2010).

Currently, the adoption and spread of "inclusive business models" is viewed as a promising avenue for thickening poverty-reducing local linkages. Although controversial and sharing some of the problematic features of the PPT, the notion of inclusive business has attracted considerable interest among development organisations, the private sector and sections of civil society. The concept of inclusive business is defined as "profitable core business activity that also tangibly expands opportunities for the poor and disadvantaged in developing countries" (Business Innovation Facility, 2011, p. 1). The consensus at the so-called New York Dialogue in 2010 was that there is "considerable potential to accelerate progress towards the Millennium Development Goals by harnessing the power of business more creatively; by spreading the practice of inclusive business" (Business Fights Poverty, 2010, p. 3). Importantly, the context for the inclusive business model is that when the UN MDG targets were set in 2000, the private sector's contribution to meeting the targets was little understood or embraced. More recently, the private sector's role has been more widely acknowledged, not least in tourism through the scholarship and policy debates around the PPT. Ashley et al. (2007), for example, have acknowledged that tourism companies can build upon models of inclusive business in several ways, especially by increasing the quantity and quality of local procurement (p. 16). Much controversy surrounds linkages with the base of the global economic pyramid (International Finance Corporation, 2011), with supporters heralding it as "responsible capitalism", whereas detractors criticise it as "(neoliberal) business as usual" (see Business Fights Poverty, 2010).

One critical issue for developing inclusive businesses and scaling-up impacts on poverty challenges is modifying or adapting existing supply chains in order to increase the participation of disadvantaged producers and linkages between them and the industry (Business Innovation Facility, 2011, p. 2). The significance of retained tourism revenue reorients the policy gaze away from plugging leakages towards linkage analysis and greater attention on mechanisms to strengthen linkages either through national government interventions or by local-level development actions (Lacher & Nepal, 2010; Mitchell & Ashley, 2010). Undoubtedly, leveraging tourism's potential for backward linkages is critical for enhancing local impacts (Spenceley & Meyer, 2012; Torres & Momsen, 2004). Linkages can be enhanced through integrating tourism more closely into local economies and thereby to catalyse other local enterprises. Telfer and Wall (2000) assert if destination areas "are to maximise benefits from tourism development, ways must be found to increase backward economic linkages" (p. 421). This highlights the need to scrutinise these linkages or lack thereof carefully in future research. Local communities in many rural areas of the developing world "require assistance in developing the business practices and achieving the quality and dependability in delivering goods and services that are necessary to participate in tourism value chains" (Ebbe, 2010, p. 32).

Currently, perhaps the most advanced tourism research relates to issues and constraints around agriculture–tourism linkages (Torres & Momsen, 2011). In many respects this cross-cuts ongoing debates in the literature on inclusive business models (cf. Ashley et al., 2007; Torres & Momsen, 2004). The limits of evolving sustained and successful agriculture–tourism linkages in many developing tourism destinations have been recently the axis of much academic attention (Rogerson, 2011, 2012a; Torres & Momsen, 2011). Trends in existing scholarship underscore the multiple elements (e.g. quality, consistency, safety, compliance with standards, packaging, loyalty and negotiation of time and costs) which constrain tourism accommodation establishments from securing food products from groups of the "poorest of the poor" in developing countries (Rogerson, 2012b; Torres & Momsen, 2011).

Opportunities for forging future new linkages for poverty alleviation through tourism must be considered also in relation to the imperatives of the "green economy". The United Nations Environment Programme report (UNEP, 2011) flags the role of local sourcing of goods and services as a salient matter for greening the tourism sector. Specifically, the pro-poor implications in this context are made clear: "In greening the tourism sector, therefore, increasing the involvement of local communities, especially the poor, in the tourism value chain can contribute to the development of local economy and poverty reduction" (UNEP, 2011, p. 414). Shortening food supply chains offers added advantages for reducing "food miles" and the carbon footprint of tourism establishments (see Gössling, Garrod, Aall, Hille, & Peeters, 2011).

To conclude, the suite of issues as elaborated above relating to the green economy, the inclusive business model and linkage development offer potentially a powerful policy-relevant agenda for tourism scholars to take forward our understanding beyond 2015 of the UN MDGs' objectives as set forth in 2000. Whilst poverty is the overriding issue to tackle over the next decade, it is not only a cause, but also an outcome of certain other problems linked to the UN MDGs. Thus, there are emerging research needs on the wider spectrum of the UN MDGs. Working with goals such as promoting gender equity (Goal 3) (see Ferguson, 2011) and ensuring environmental sustainability (Goal 7) would be fruitful and important future research avenues for tourism geographies: gender issues are crucial in employment and in the value-chain structures of the industry, and environmental sustainability remains a key issue in tourism production and consumption. Likewise, revising global–local connections in tourism industry towards more inclusive business models and the development of the links between local agriculture and tourism industry, for example, would benefit from a deeper analysis and conceptualisation of the development of global partnerships (Goal 7) in tourism.

Overall, whilst tourism has a great potential to contribute to the UN MDGs it is clear that the positive relation between tourism and wider development is definitely not an automatic or easy outcome. To avoid risks involved with tourism industry-led development, the industry needs to be clearly positioned as a potential tool *for*, not at the end of the local, regional, national and global development agendas. For this to be realised, the inclusive business model, linkage development and the premises of evolving green economy represent promising future research and policy directions.

References

Addison, T., Hulme, D., & Kanbur, R. (2009). Poverty dynamics: Measurement and understanding from an interdisciplinary perspective. In T. Addison, D. Hulme, & R. Kanbur (Eds.), *Poverty dynamics: Interdisciplinary perspectives* (pp. 3–26). Oxford: Oxford University Press.

Ashley, C., De Brine, P., Lehr, A., & Wilde, H. (2007). *The role of the tourism sector in expanding economic opportunity* (Corporate Responsibility Initiative Report No. 23). Cambridge, MA: Kennedy School of Government, Harvard University.

Ashley, C., & Haysom, G. (2009). *Bringing local entrepreneurs into the supply chain: The experience of Spier*. London: Overseas Development Institute Project Briefing 20.

Ashley, C., & Maxwell, S. (2001). Rethinking rural development. *Development Policy Review, 19*, 395–425.

Ashley, C., & Roe, D. (2002). Making tourism work for the poor: Strategies and challenges in southern Africa. *Development Southern Africa, 19*(1), 61–82.

Ashley, C., Roe, D., & Goodwin, H. (2001). *Pro-poor tourism strategies: Making tourism work for the poor* (Pro-Poor Tourism Report 1). London: ICRT, IIED and ODI.

Barrett, C. B., Lee, D. R., & McPeak, J. G. (2004). Institutional arrangements for rural poverty reduction and resource conservation. *World Development, 33*(2), 193–197.

Bolwell, D., & Weinz, W. (2008). *Reducing poverty through tourism* (Working Paper No. 266). Geneva: International Labour Office.

Brickley, K., Black, R., & Cottrell, S. (Eds.). (2013). *Sustainable tourism and Millennium Development Goals*. Burlington, MA: Jones & Bartlett Learning.

Britton, S. (1982). The political economy of tourism in the third world. *Annals of Tourism Research, 9*, 331–358.

Britton, S. (1991). Tourism, capital and place: Towards a critical geography of tourism. *Environment and Planning D: Society and Place, 9*, 451–478.

Brohman, J. (1996). New directions in tourism for third world development. *Annals of Tourism Research, 23*, 48–70.

Business Fights Poverty. (2010). *Accelerating progress towards the Millennium Development Goals through inclusive business: Delivering results: Moving towards scale*. (Report on an Inclusive Dialogue Held on September 21 2010, During the UN Summit on the Millennium Development Goals). Retrieved from http://inclusive.businessfightspoverty.org

Business Innovation Facility. (2011). *What is inclusive business?* London: Business Innovation Facility and Innovations Against Poverty.

Christian, M. (2010, May). *Tourism scoping paper*. Paper presented at the 'Capturing the Gains' Workshop, Agra, India.

Christie, I. T., & Sharma, A. (2008). Research note: Millennium Development Goals – What is tourism's place? *Tourism Economics, 14*(2), 427–430.

Ebbe, K. (2010). *Tourism portfolio review January 2005–December 2009: Volume 1: Findings, lessons learned, recommendations*. Washington, DC: The World Bank Sub-Saharan Africa Finance and Private Sector Development.

Ferguson, L. (2011). Promoting gender equality and empowering women? Tourism and the third Millennium Development Goal. *Current Issues in Tourism, 14*(3), 235–250.

Goodwin, H. (2009). Contemporary policy debates: Reflections on 10 years of pro-poor tourism. *Journal of Policy Research in Tourism, Leisure and Events, 1*(1), 90–94.

Gössling, S., Garrod, B., Aall, C., Hille, J., & Peeters, P. (2011). Food management in tourism: Reducing tourism's carbon 'foodprint'. *Tourism Management, 32*, 534–543.

Hall, C. M. (2007). Pro-poor tourism: Do 'tourism exchanges benefit primarily the countries of the South'? *Current Issues in Tourism, 10*(2/3), 111–118.

International Finance Corporation. (2011). Inclusive business at IFC. Retrieved from http://www.ifc.org/wps/wcm/connect/AS_EXT_Content/What%20We%20Do/Advisory%20Services/Inclusive%20Business

Lacher, R. G., & Nepal, S. K. (2010). From leakages to linkages: Local-level strategies for capturing tourism revenue in northern Thailand. *Tourism Geographies, 12*, 77–99.

Lapeyre, R. (2011). The Grootberg lodge partnership in Namibia: Towards poverty alleviation and empowerment for long-term sustainability? *Current Issues in Tourism, 14*(3), 221–234.

Meyer, D. (2007). Pro-poor tourism: From leakages to linkages. A conceptual framework for creating linkages between the accommodation sector and 'poor' neighbouring communities. *Current Issues in Tourism, 10*(6), 558–583.

Meyer, D. (2009). Pro-poor tourism: Is there actually much rhetoric? And, if so, whose? *Tourism Recreation Research, 34*(2), 197–199.

Mitchell, J., & Ashley, C. (2010). *Tourism and poverty reduction: Pathways and prosperity*. London: Earthscan.

Novelli, M., & Hellwig, A. (2011). The UN Millennium Development Goals, tourism and development: The tour operators' perspective. *Current Issues in Tourism, 14*(3), 205–220.

Pleumarom, A. (2012). *The politics of tourism, poverty reduction and sustainable development*. Penang: Third World Network.

Rogerson, C. M. (2006). Pro-poor local economic development in South Africa: The role of pro-poor tourism. *Local Environment, 11*, 37–60.

Rogerson, C. M. (2011). Tourism food supply linkages in Zambia: Evidence from the African safari lodge sector. *Tourism Review International, 15*, 21–35.

Rogerson, C. M. (2012a). Tourism-agriculture linkages in rural South Africa: Evidence from the accommodation sector. *Journal of Sustainable Tourism, 20*, 477–495.

Rogerson, C. M. (2012b). Strengthening agriculture-tourism linkages in the developing world: Opportunities, barriers and current initiatives. *African Journal of Agricultural Research, 7*(4), 616–623.

Saarinen, J., Rogerson, C. M., & Manwa, H. (Eds.). (2013). *Tourism and Millennium Development Goals: Tourism, local communities and development*. London: Routledge.

Sandbrook, C. G. (2010). Putting leakage in its place: The significance of retained tourism revenue in the local context in rural Uganda. *Journal of International Development, 22*(1), 124–136.

Scheyvens, R. (2009). Pro-poor tourism: Is there value beyond the rhetoric? *Tourism Recreation Research, 34*(2), 191–196.

Scheyvens, R. (2011). *Tourism and poverty*. London: Routledge.

Schilcher, D. (2007). Growth versus equity: The continuum of pro-poor tourism and neoliberal governance. *Current Issues in Tourism, 10*(2–3), 166–193.

Sinclair, T. (1998). Tourism and economic development: A survey. *Journal of Development Studies, 34*(5), 1–51.

Sofield, T. (2003). *Empowerment for sustainable tourism development*. Oxford: Pergamon.

Spenceley, A., & Meyer, D. (2012). Tourism and poverty reduction: Theory and practice in less economically developed countries. *Journal of Sustainable Tourism, 20*, 297–317.

Telfer, D. J., & Wall, G. (2000). Strengthening backward economic linkages: Local food purchasing by three Indonesian hotels. *Tourism Geographies, 2*, 421–447.

Torres, R., & Momsen, J. H. (2004). Challenges and potential for linking tourism and agriculture to achieve pro-poor tourism objectives. *Progress in Development Studies, 4*, 294–318.

Torres, R., & Momsen, J. (Eds.). (2011). *Tourism and agriculture: New geographies of production and rural restructuring*. London: Routledge.

United Nations Environment Programme (UNEP). (2011). Towards a green economy: Pathways to sustainable development and poverty eradication. Retrieved from http://www.unep.org/greeneconomy

United Nations. (2000). *Millennium summit goals*. New York, NY: Author.

UNWTO. (2002). *Tourism and poverty alleviation*. Madrid: Author.

UNWTO. (2006). *UNWTO's declaration on tourism and the millennium goals: Harnessing tourism for the Millennium Development Goals*. Madrid: Author.

World Bank. (2012). *Transformation through tourism: Development dynamics past, present and future* (draft). Washington, DC: Author.

Zhou, W., & Richie, J. (2007). Tourism and poverty alleviation: An integrative research framework. *Current Issues in Tourism, 10*(2–3), 119–143.

Corporate social responsibility in tourism post-2015: a Development First approach

Emma Hughes and Regina Scheyvens

ABSTRACT
Most large tourism businesses have corporate social responsibility (CSR) initiatives that advance environmental, economic and social sustainability. Existing research shows that initiatives often tend to be ad hoc, however, and linked to cost-savings and the reputation of the business. We suggest that this approach equates with Tourism First planning. In response to the greater demands being placed on businesses to act responsibly in the post-2015 era, we propose a Development First framework for CSR that is adapted from Peter Burns' tourism planning model. This framework has a holistic, sustainable and people-centred focus and enables geographers and other social scientists to analyse the potential for initiatives to lead to positive, long-term development outcomes in different localities.

摘要
绝大多数大型旅游企业有企业社会责任方面的举措， 以促进环境、经济与社会可持续发展。现有研究表明， 这些举措往往比较是临时的，并且与节约成本和企业的声誉联系紧密。我们认为，目前旅游企业社会责任的方法相当于旅游第一的规划方法 。为了响应后2015年代社会对企业履行社会责任更大的需求， 我们提出了企业社会责任发展第一的框架， 这个框架由伯恩Burn的旅游规划框架 改编而来。该框架系统全面、可持续，并且强调以人为中心，促使地理学者和其他方面的社会科学家分析这些举措在不同地点促进积极、长期发展后果的潜力。

Introduction

The private sector is assuming increased prominence in development discourses with international bodies such as the United Nations and Organisation for Economic Cooperation and Development (OECD) asserting that businesses have greater responsibilities for development than ever before (OECD, 2011; United Nations, 2013). The 2030 Agenda for Sustainable Development, with the Sustainable Development Goals (SDGs) at its core, contains a 'call on all businesses to apply their creativity and innovation to solving sustainable development challenges' (United Nations, 2015, para. 67). The 17 SDGs aim to balance economic, social and environmental sustainability and focus on inclusivity, shared prosperity and shared responsibility, with businesses assuming a key role alongside governments and civil society in delivering on the targets (Scheyvens, Banks, & Hughes, 2016). Indeed, it is claimed that the SDGs provide 'an historic opportunity to scale up and align business efforts in order to contribute to United Nations priorities at unprecedented levels' (UN Global Compact, 2013, p. 2). Given that tourism is a major economic sector in many developing countries, it is important to consider whether this industry is ready to embrace such holistic goals.

Support has been built from within academia for such an approach through the concepts of ethical business and 'shared value' (Porter & Kramer, 2011), and in the private sector itself through the burgeoning corporate social responsibility (CSR) movement (see e.g. Camilleri, 2014; Idemudia, 2011; Kalisch, 2002) and aspirations for inclusive business (Saarinen & Rogerson, 2014, p. 26–27). Yet, there has been little consideration of what this means in practice for communities that are the target of development interventions, and whether this model can lead to sustainable development outcomes.

In this article, we are particularly concerned with whether the tourism industry is well placed to live up to these expectations of business. Tourism has long been touted as an 'engine of growth' which can drive economic progress and create employment in emerging economies. In 2013, the Travel and Tourism industry outperformed world gross domestic product (GDP) growth for the third consecutive year, with its contribution to GDP increasing 3% (World Travel and Tourism Council, 2014). Growth has been particularly high in emerging economies which have seen their share of international arrivals rise from 30% in 1980 to 47% by 2010, and this is projected to increase to 57% of the market share by 2030 (United Nations World Tourism Organization, 2014, p. 14–15). In 2013, the tourism industry employed over 266 million people globally, providing 1 in every 11 jobs. It also attracted investments of US$754 billion and earned US$1.3 trillion in export revenue (World Travel and Tourism Council, 2014). The existing economic contribution of tourism to development through foreign investment, job creation and tax revenue is evident, but there is greater potential for tourism to contribute more broadly to sustainable development, through mass tourism in particular.

A geographical approach drawing on development perspectives (Hall & Page, 2009) is particularly helpful in analysing whether this global growth in tourism, and the international flows of revenue associated with the industry, translates into local benefits. When assessed specifically in terms of its influence on development and poverty alleviation in different regions around the globe, the impacts of the tourism industry are ambivalent. Saarinen and Rogerson (2014, p. 23), who analysed how tourism contributed to achievement of the Millennium Development Goals, which were supposed to be achieved by 2015, noted that there was 'a growing concern surrounding the local benefits of global tourism…'. Further, they stressed that 'tourism-led development is often marked by enclavisation, dependency, inequalities and revenue leakages' (p. 25). Such concerns about the disjuncture between global economic growth and destination benefits play out strongly in the tourism industry because it is dominated by multinational companies, estimated to subsume 80% of the market (Mowforth & Munt, 2009, p. 186).

While traditionally a number of academics have been harsh critics of powerful tourism actors dominating development spaces in small emerging economies (see e.g. Britton, 1982; Pleumarom, 1994), a more balanced view has emerged. Telfer and Sharpley note the value that multinational tourism corporations can bring to development: '…these corporations also bring investment funds, know-how, expertise, managerial competence, market penetration and control, and opportunities for local entrepreneurs' (2008, p. 88), whilst Weaver contends that 'sustainable mass tourism has become the emerging and desired outcome for most destinations' (2012, p. 1030). Although scepticism remains as to the potential of tourism to lead to sustainable development (Mowforth & Munt, 2009), the role of mass tourism cannot be ignored when even '[m]arginal change across companies in a massive sector can be significant for development' (Ashley & Haysom, 2006, p. 1).

Given the expectations now placed on the private sector to deliver development outcomes, how can we determine whether tourism businesses are ready to take on the challenges of contributing holistically to destination development in line with the SDGs? This paper proposes a 'Development First' framework for CSR, adapted from Burns' model (1999, 2004) which outlined a Development First approach to tourism planning. We further develop Burns' ideas and present a framework that allows analysis of the extent to which initiatives can lead to holistic and sustainable development for destination communities. The framework could be used to support those businesses wishing to position themselves as effective development actors in the post-2015 era.

Structure and methodology

We use several methods to inform the Development First approach to tourism CSR which is introduced in this article. First, we review literature on the practice and motivation for CSR in tourism and examine how Burns' tourism planning model could be applied to common CSR approaches. Second, we analyse literature on the relationship between tourism and development to understand how tourism can contribute to destination development and third we utilise this information to develop a new framework for Development First CSR. We have drawn on both international development theory as well as empirical material from our research in Fiji to develop these ideas and construct the framework. In the final section, we argue that if the new agenda for businesses to deliver sustainable development outcomes is to be fully realised then a number of changes are required to how we approach private sector-led development.

Tourism First or Development First CSR?

CSR in the tourism industry

The growth of CSR activity in tourism responding to destination development challenges is evidenced by a multitude of company CSR reports, company websites and social media profiling social, economic and environmental initiatives. These typically include donations to schools and hospitals, water and energy saving initiatives, environmental protection, sourcing of local produce and equal opportunity recruitment and training opportunities. Academic literature provides further examples (e.g. see Ashley, de Brine, Lehr, & Wilde, 2007; Bradly, 2015; Camilleri, 2014; Dodds & Joppe, 2009; Harrison & Prasad, 2013; Kalisch, 2002; Koutra, 2013). However, much existing research on CSR in tourism primarily focuses on advanced economies (Coles, Fenclova, & Dinan, 2013, p. 129) and whilst environmental reporting is well established, research on the social impact of CSR and social reporting is either limited or absent (Coles et al., 2013, p. 136).

Ketola (2006) proposes that companies working in different contexts often exhibit different 'responsibility profiles', some weighted more towards environmental protection while others prioritise economic or social responsibilities. In a developing country context, particular challenges are presented by differing political environments, which can shape the practice of CSR (Idemudia, 2011, p. 5). Interestingly, tourism businesses located in poorer areas of emerging economies have made more direct efforts than those businesses located in advanced economies in terms of targeting social and economic sustainability. For example, an examination of 136 tourism practices who had received awards from the tourism industry revealed that it was more common for CSR practices in emerging economies to have social programmes, and these often included health or education themes and youth development (Levy & Hawkins, 2009). However, even where such initiatives exist, consideration of the social and economic value of such initiatives to host destinations remains largely absent: rather, it is assumed that they automatically add value to the community (e.g. Bohdanowicz & Zientara, 2009; Nicolau, 2008). Kalisch (2002) points out that where social and economic issues are addressed by businesses they tend to have a primary focus on charity, with little or no focus on human rights or distribution of benefits. Ashley and Haysom (2006) draw on Locke (2002) to outline a continuum of four approaches to tourism CSR from minimalist, through to philanthropic and encompassing to social activist, identifying that the majority of examples of tourism CSR are philanthropic donations. This practice is easy to administer and to profile but does not adapt business practice to bring about change

Research suggests that the key motivator is the business case for CSR: managing risk and building reputation (Kalisch, 2002). Multinational hotels and resorts in emerging economies are frequently located in poor areas with high development demands. These businesses realise that it is in their own interests to look after their neighbours, both because this enhances their reputation as an ethical business (Epler Wood & Leray, 2005, p. 4), and because it decreases the likelihood of disruptions to the business by disgruntled 'locals'. A range of studies show clear evidence of instrumental benefits motivating engagement in CSR practices for the tourist industry, for example establishing legitimacy, building reputation, attracting employees, maintaining customer satisfaction and mitigating risk (Ashley & Haysom, 2006; Ashley et al., 2007; Kalisch, 2002). Other motivating factors that encourage hotels and tour operators to embed CSR in business practices include tourist demand for ethical and sustainable practices (de Grosbois, 2012; Dodds & Joppe, 2005; Scheyvens, 2011) and the imperative to protect the local environment and culture as part of the tourism 'product' (Kalisch, 2002).

Various measurement, reporting and accreditation initiatives exist to document the CSR practices and performance of hotels including the Global Reporting Initiative, United Nations' Global Compact, World Tourism Organisation's Global Code of Ethics for Tourism, Dow Jones Sustainability Indices, FTSE-4-Good, Green Globe and International Standards Organization guidelines ISO14001 and ISO26000. However, reporting often focuses on environmental indices and satisfying legal requirements (Font, Walmsley, Cogotti, McCombes, & Häusler, 2012), and demonstrates commitment rather than compliance (Mowforth & Munt, 2009, p. 203). Furthermore, implementation can be weak (Dodds & Joppe, 2005) and selection and communication of initiatives remain at the firm's discretion (Coles et al., 2013, p. 134). de Grosbois found that the majority of 150 hotels studied documented their CSR practices; however, reporting was often 'very simplistic and superficial' (p. 904), with little evidence of performance, the extent of implementation or how the practice contributed to goals (2012, p. 904). This coincides with Holcomb, Upchurch, and Okumus' earlier findings that some CSR activities of hotels are highly publicised but do not provide evidence of performance or quality (2007). Where CSR initiatives are implemented there may also be contradictions in practice – for example making philanthropic donations to a local school while having a poor record in employment and human rights (Beddoe, 2004). Of significance for community development, the authors of this article have not been able to identify any tourism businesses which regularly and comprehensively monitor their CSR programmes to ascertain their development outcomes for destination communities. In this regard, Torres-Delgado and Saarinen make the useful suggestion that it would be effective for core global indicators to be developed along with location-specific ones (Torres-Delgado & Saarinen, 2014, p. 43).

While CSR activities have conventionally been assumed to add value by virtue of their cash or in-kind input to communities, the new agenda for business over the next 15 years suggests that a different approach is needed with a focus on sustainable outcomes. We therefore turn to Burns' tourism planning framework to draw lessons for CSR.

Burns' Tourism First, Development First framework

Burns identifies a Tourism First approach to planning as the dominant paradigm of the World Bank and aid-assisted tourism planning. Economic growth and benefits are prioritised, with development as an assumed by-product: 'the over-riding agenda is always, without exception, growth' (1999, p. 333). In contrast, Development First planning has a focus on addressing social development. Tourism is seen as a tool that can be used to achieve national social and economic development goals; such goals coincide with United Nations Development Programme (UNDP) priorities including the elimination of poverty, rural development and gender equity. A proposition for a 'Third Way' (Burns, 2004) suggests that the overarching economic development goals of mass tourism can also be consistent with development priorities, provided certain elements of planning and pre-planning are put into place to facilitate a wider spread of benefits. The Third Way envisages that '[a]t the international level, a new attitude towards planning on the part of donor agencies should define their role as human development, in essence a Third Way framed by a "Development First" approach' which could provide 'a platform for sustainable growth and human development' (Burns, 2004, p. 39–40). Stipulating that community voices and power imbalances are taken into account, it places emphasis on relationships, collaboration and the role for international players, acknowledging that the private sector is one actor among many. This has parallels with Weaver's argument for Sustainable Mass Tourism, which advances that the greatest capacity for change lies in the mass tourism market (2001, p. 167). It also suggests that application of the model in a mass tourism environment is apt.

Whilst Burns acknowledges that development itself is a contested term, a Tourism First approach is not seen as capable of fostering sustainable human development; this suggests that Tourism First CSR would similarly fail to address development concerns:

> [I]f development is taken to mean economic enlargement, then Tourism First has delivered. However, if development consists of the promises made by various aid agencies and financial institutions as they have sought to promote tourism as an agent for human development over some four decades, then it seems not to have worked (1999, p. 345).

Table 1. Tourism First CSR and Development First CSR.

Tourism planning	CSR
'Tourism First' planning	**'Tourism First' CSR**
Economic growth	Business case for participation in CSR; cost-saving initiatives
Industry focus	Industry expectations of CSR practices; obtaining social licence to operate
Consumerism and commoditisation are central	CSR used to enhance the tourism 'product'/brand and build reputation
Globalisation	Western models of CSR, developed by multinational companies responding to global issues of concern, e.g. environment, child labour
Free market will drive distribution	CSR responds to tourist demand
'Development First' planning	**'Development First' CSR**
Sustainable human development	Long-term initiatives developed to respond to a broad definition of community well-being
Holistic focus	Enhancing social, cultural and environmental well-being as well as delivering economic benefits
Culture is central	Indigenous partnerships; valuing local culture; investing in relationships
Goals defined by local people	CSR defined and developed in partnership with community
Benefits a wide range of local people	Benefits of CSR are equitably shared

Source: Authors, based on Burns (1999, 2004).

With its holistic focus and an emphasis on the importance of local knowledge, a Development First perspective allows CSR to be framed in alignment with development thinking. It has the ability to highlight key factors in an analysis of the development potential of CSR, including how initiatives are identified and developed, the distribution of benefits, the extent to which cultural, social, economic and community well-being are addressed and the capacity for sustainability.

Table 1, below, applies Burns' tourism planning spectrum to CSR by identifying corresponding examples of CSR practice for key criteria in the model, both from a Tourism First and Development First perspective.

The lack of attention to the community impact of CSR initiatives as identified earlier, along with the imperative to support a business case for CSR, is indicative of a primary focus on the industry rather than the community. This puts most CSR practices squarely at the Tourism First end of the spectrum. In fact, the nature of the private sector means it will naturally gravitate towards a Tourism First approach rather than a Development First approach (Scheyvens, 2011, p. 114). Yet, if the expectation within the SDGs is for the private sector, via industries such as tourism, to deliver development, then a Tourism First approach will clearly be inadequate.

Telfer and Sharpley assert that we need to understand 'how the industry can operate so that the destination developmental needs are taken into account and how the power that multinationals hold can be used to that end' (2008, p. 58). We, therefore, set out to develop a Development First framework for tourism with the capacity to guide and inform private sector-led development. The first step is to interrogate the wider research on tourism and development in order to consider whether there is a basis upon which CSR in the tourism sector can demonstrate a sustained Development First approach.

Tourism and development

Although there has been little analysis to date on the capacity of CSR to link tourism and development, connections can be made through analysis of the tourism and poverty and Pro-Poor Tourism (PPT) literature, which take a people-centred approach and link to the principles underpinning Burns' framework. In contrast to the niche markets targeted by alternative, community-based and ecotourism initiatives, PPT describes an approach which focuses on achieving net benefits for the poor across the industry as a whole through partnerships, policy reform and responsible consumer and business behaviour (Ashley, Boyd, & Goodwin, 2000). The focus is shifted from tourism as a means primarily towards economic growth to tourism as an enabler of poverty reduction. Key principles include the participation of the poor, a holistic livelihoods approach and attention to the distribution of benefits. Despite the focus on poverty elimination, this approach has received some criticism. Reviewing PPT a decade on, Goodwin (2009) asserted that the means to achieving PPT remained the same neoliberal business model. Schilcher (2007) challenges the PPT agenda on the basis that it fails to benefit the poor disproportionately and Higgins-Desbiolles highlights its lack of an agenda for change (2006, p. 1201). Torres and Momsen (2004) draw attention to the lack of linkages between tourism and agriculture in PPT which neglects the rural poor. As Mowforth and Munt point out, PPT is 'principally a measure for making some sections of the community "better-off" and of reducing the vulnerability of poorer groups to shocks (such as hunger)' (2009, p. 349). Furthermore, given tourism's position within a global neo-liberal market economy, Chok, Macbeth and Warren note that 'tourism policies and plans are less likely to be reflective of a community's social, cultural and environmental concerns than they are of the economic imperatives of those in power' (2007, p. 159). These outcomes are insufficient to satisfy Development First criteria.

Other tourism and poverty research points towards a number of characteristics that Development First CSR may incorporate. Spenceley and Meyer suggest that within the tourism and poverty research agenda:

> [r]ather than viewing tourism simply as an industry aligned to neo-liberal thinking, tourism [is] perceived as a powerful social force that needs to be better understood in order to connect it more effectively to development agendas that go beyond purely economic considerations (2012, p. 301).

Within this agenda, Higgins-Desbiolles underscores the 'transformative capacity' of tourism (2006, p. 1196). She recommends the use of Inayatullah's set of questions based on the values of 'distribution, growth, structural peace, personal peace, cultural pluralism and economic democracy' (Inayatullah, 1995, p. 413) as a benchmarking tool. She further calls for academics to identify 'the tangible and intangible benefits such a progressive policy could deliver the entire community (not just the business sector) through research' (Higgins-Desbiolles, 2006, p. 1206).

Scheyvens observes that neoliberalism necessitates a focus on outside (foreign) interests, for example meeting the needs of tourists and providing an 'enabling environment' for foreign investors and supranational organisations, and contends that what is needed is more of an inward focus oriented around responding to national and local development needs (2002, p. 234). In this way, tourism can be an agent for development if supported by the 'integration of local, national and international level strategies' (2002, p. 232). This might occur, for example, through greater regional and local sourcing, and linkages with local firms (Saarinen & Rogerson, 2014, p. 25). Zhao and Ritchie, with a similar inward focus, point out that the poorest of the poor should be the focus of anti-poverty tourism 'as they are least capable of directly participating in tourism enterprises' (2007, p. 349).

Others have a stronger focus on overcoming structural inequalities, with Chok et al. maintaining that '[t]he focus should be on identifying and addressing the deep-rooted structural inequities within our global development paradigm (tourism included) which exacerbate poverty and constrain pro-poor attempts' (Chok et al. 2007, p. 160). Schilcher proposes a redistributive approach rather than a growth approach, supported by a strong regulatory framework 'which gives the poor a voice, incorporates cultural as well as political and economic capital, values local knowledge and bridges micro-macro dichotomy' (2007, p. 184). Others highlight the disadvantages faced by specific societal groups: Tucker and Boonabanna, for example, stipulate that a consideration of gender inequalities is needed to avoid reproducing existing inequalities in the distribution of the benefits of tourism (2012, p. 438).

Following Burns, Telfer and Sharpley advocate for a Development First planning focus in tourism and link its capacity to enable poverty reduction as articulated in the Millennium Development Goals (2008, p. 230). They maintain that if development is the intended outcome from tourism then planning should occur in alignment with national development needs, as Burns (1999) espoused, and that the impacts of tourism must be effectively managed in order to allow this (Telfer & Sharpley, 2008, p. 179–180). They propose a framework which incorporates assessment of the influences, responses and trade-offs in tourism (2008, p. 216). There is evidence that CSR can play a role in mitigating or enhancing a number of these tourism trade-offs, for instance economic development, employment, poverty reduction, leakages, environmental protection and social empowerment. In terms of resolving the tourism-development dilemma, however, Telfer and Sharpley question whether it is possible to ensure that environment, society and economy all benefit (2008, p. 227); likewise Burns queries the capacity of master planning to achieve sustainable human development (2004, p. 40). The question can similarly be posed in relation to CSR and the potential of realising the SDGs. Constructing a framework to assess this potential can be used to examine this in greater detail.

A Development First framework for tourism and CSR

By synthesising the views above, it is possible to begin to outline the characteristics of a Development First framework for CSR. We see this as aspirational, a framework which could guide the reflection, policy and practice of tourism businesses that wish to show a strong commitment to Development First tourism. Such an approach might include the following:

- A focus on human development and community well-being
- Collaboration locally, regionally, nationally, internationally
- A focus on building capabilities
- Reducing vulnerability of the poorest
- Consideration of gender norms and inequalities
- Attention to distribution of benefits
- Valuing cultural capital
- Utilisation of local knowledge
- Acknowledgement of micro as well as macro impacts
- Monitoring and evaluation processes
- Accountability to local communities

Informed by the tourism and poverty research described above, relevant questions to be asked of the capability of CSR initiatives to deliver inclusive, sustainable and meaningful development have been formulated. These are grouped into key areas, building on the Development First planning ideas outlined in Table 1. Asking these questions of CSR initiatives can generate insight into the scope of initiatives to bring about locally meaningful development and at the same time highlight where contradictions and ambiguities may lie. The authors demonstrate this in a forthcoming article which applies the Development First framework to the hotel sector in Fiji.

A Development First approach for CSR will inevitably share some characteristics with community development projects in general which are working towards sustainable human development outcomes. Harcourt notes that uncertainty about impact applies equally to development activities as to CSR and suggests that we 'maintain a healthy skepticism that questions and "denormalizes" business practices as we would do any other development activity' (2004, p. 2). There are certainly similarities between CSR and other development activities; however, CSR must not only address community need, but also be responsive to business imperatives and we still understand very little about the social impact of CSR relative to its business impact (Hamann, 2006; Idemudia, 2011). In addition to this 'healthy skepticism', therefore, it is essential to identify specific ways to examine CSR initiatives that may differ from the ways in which other development projects are assessed. In each group of questions in Table 2 this involves examining who is setting the agenda, who benefits and what are the intended and unintended outcomes for both corporation and community. It also highlights the importance of monitoring and evaluation of CSR initiatives: as Burns (2004, p. 38) notes, there is a need for more monitoring of

Table 2. A Development First framework for CSR in tourism.

Sustainable human development	• Does CSR have a long-term or short-term focus? • Does CSR focus on building local capabilities? • Does CSR reduce vulnerabilities? • Is there evidence of collaboration with other actors, locally, regionally or nationally, and alignment with government goals for enhancing human well-being?
Holistic focus	• Does CSR contribute to social, cultural and environmental well-being, as well as contributing economic benefits to communities? • Can multiplier effects be identified?
Culture is central	• Is cultural capital valued rather than commodified or museumised? • Is local knowledge valued and respected? • How is cultural capital sustained?
Community-focused goals	• Who defines local development needs to be addressed by CSR? • How are the poorest or most marginalised sections of the community represented in decision-making? • Does CSR help the community to achieve goals that they value as a people?
Building relationships	• How are meaningful relationships between a tourism business and local communities supported? • Are initiatives developed and implemented in conjunction with communities? • Is there accountability for CSR to local communities?
Distribution of benefits	• Who benefits and how are benefits shared/distributed? • Who does not benefit or is marginalised? • Does CSR counteract or reinforce existing inequalities?
Monitoring and evaluation	• Is there evidence of monitoring and evaluation processes in place? • Who is responsible for (a) determining positive indicators of change, and (b) conducting monitoring and evaluation? • Does monitoring and evaluation lead to reflection by tourism businesses, and changes in their practices?

Source: Authors.

tourism development and '[t]he immediate community and agencies for the natural and cultural environments should be the primary stakeholders here'.

Rather than an exhaustive set of questions, this framework provides a starting point for reflection on how tourism companies can most effectively contribute to holistic development for destination communities. In an environment where terms such as 'shared value', 'win–win outcomes' and 'competitive advantage' are readily associated with community development, it is perhaps time to take a closer look at the processes and outcomes according to a people-centred perspective.

Conclusion

This article has examined the expectation that the private sector can and should lead development initiatives as we move into the post-2015 era and towards the SDGs, and has specifically considered whether tourism industry players are well placed to take on such a role. As tourism is dominated by larger players, and industry growth does not always translate into local benefits, we are particularly interested with how tourism multinationals might use the mechanism of CSR to respond to the challenge posed by the SDGs to engage in more sustainable development.

While it is pleasing to see many hotels and others applying ethical principles to their business practices, typically under the banner of CSR, the reality is that for many in the industry CSR is limited to either PR exercises, cost-saving (e.g. energy efficiency) or tokenistic sideline activities, often with direct and positive spin-offs for the company. CSR in tourism, thus, often equates with Burns' (1999) notion of Tourism First planning. Meanwhile other genuine development issues, such as building capacity, empowerment of the poor and vulnerable and protection of human rights, all of which are highly meaningful in terms of potential for a contribution to local community development, are underplayed, ignored or overlooked.

We thus proposed a Development First framework as a means of assessing tourism company efforts to support local destination development. This framework encompasses a more holistic, sustainable, people-centred approach to CSR than the norm. In reality, many tourism corporates are likely to be satisfied with a Tourism First approach to CSR: they are in business to run a business, not to contribute to holistic community development. However, where rhetoric from the development industry about the potential of partnering with the private sector to achieve development outcomes is matched by the will of tourism actors to play a more substantive role in this space, the framework proposed in Table 2 provides useful guidance for ways forward.

Beyond this voluntary commitment to destination development on the part of the tourism industry, there are indications that governments are tightening up their regulations around corporate activity and will require more stringent reporting from businesses in the future. India's Companies Act 2013, for example, involves strengthened regulation and expectations regarding reporting on non-financial performance. In the development sector reporting is gaining greater prominence; international donors entering into partnerships with businesses are asking for evidence of *impact* and *effectiveness* of their responsible business practices. Building accountability is, of course, also a key area of the SDGs: the private sector constitutes part of the revitalised and enhanced Global Partnership laid out in the 2030 Agenda with its integral expectations for ongoing engagement with the goals, tracking progress and demonstrating accountability to citizens. To fulfil these aspirations, some significant changes to practice will be needed. A Development First perspective provides the ability to assess initiatives in respect of their potential to prioritise sustainable development outcomes.

Acknowledgements

Thanks go to study participants from Fiji who inspired the creation of a Development First framework. The authors would also like to thank two anonymous reviewers for their helpful suggestions on an earlier draft.

Disclosure statement

No potential conflict of interest was reported by the authors.

Funding

This work was supported by the Royal Society of New Zealand [MAU1206].

ORCID

Emma Hughes http://orcid.org/0000-0001-9762-6074

References

Ashley, C., Boyd, C., & Goodwin, H. (2000). Pro-poor tourism: Putting poverty at the heart of the tourism agenda. *Natural Resource Perspectives*, 51, 1–12.

Ashley, C., De Brine, P., Lehr, A., & Wilde, H. (2007). *The role of the tourism sector in expanding economic opportunity.* Corporate Social Responsibility Initiative Report No. 23. Cambridge, MA: Kennedy School of Government, Harvard University.

Ashley, C., & Haysom, G. (2006). From philanthropy to a different way of doing business: Strategies & challenges in integrating pro-poor approaches into tourism business. *Development Southern Africa*, 23, 265–280.

Beddoe, C. (2004). *Labour standards, social responsibility and tourism*. London: Tourism Concern.

Bohdanowicz, P., & Zientara, P. (2009). Hotel companies' contribution to improving the quality of life of local communities and the well-being of their employees. *Tourism and Hospitality Research, 9*(2), 147−158.

Bradly, A. (2015). The business-case for community investment: Evidence from Fiji's tourism industry. *Social Responsibility, 11*(2), 242−257.

Britton, S. G. (1982). The political economy of tourism in the third world. *Annals of Tourism Research, 9*(3), 331−358.

Burns, P. (1999). Paradoxes in planning tourism elitism or brutalism? *Annals of Tourism Research, 26*(2), 329−348.

Burns, P. (2004). Tourism planning: A third way? *Annals of Tourism Research, 31*(1), 24−43.

Camilleri, M. (2014). Advancing the sustainable tourism agenda through strategic CSR perspectives. *Tourism Planning and Development, 11*(1), 42−56.

Chok, S., Macbeth, J., & Warren, C. (2007). Tourism as a tool for poverty alleviation: A critical analysis of 'pro-poor tourism' and implications for sustainability. *Current Issues in Tourism, 10*(2−3), 144−165.

Coles, T., Fenclova, E., & Dinan, C. (2013). Tourism and corporate social responsibility: A critical review and research agenda. *Tourism Management Perspectives, 6*, 122−141.

de Grosbois, D. (2012). Corporate social responsibility reporting by the global hotel industry: Commitment, initiatives and performance. *International Journal of Hospitality Management, 31*(3), 896−905.

Dodds, R., & Joppe, M. (2005). *CSR in the tourism industry? The status of and potential for certification, codes of conduct and guidelines*. Washington, DC: IFC/World Bank.

Dodds, R., & Joppe, M. (2009). The demand for, and participation in corporate social responsibility and sustainable tourism − implications for the Caribbean. *ARA Journal of Travel Research, 2*(1), 1−24.

Epler Wood, M., & Leray, T. (2005). *Corporate responsibility and the tourism sector in Cambodia*. Washington, DC: World Bank Group.

Font, X., Walmsley, A., Cogotti, S., McCombes, L., & Häusler, N. (2012). Corporate social responsibility: The disclosure−performance gap. *Tourism Management, 33*, 1544−1553.

Goodwin, H. (2009). Reflections on 10 years of pro−poor tourism. *Journal of Policy Research in Tourism, Leisure and Events, 1*(1), 90−94.

Hall, C. M., & Page, S. J. (2009). Progress in tourism management: From the geography of tourism to geographies of tourism − A review. *Tourism Management, 30*(1), 1−14.

Hamann, R. (2006). Can business make decisive contributions to development? Towards a research agenda on corporate citizenship & beyond. *Development Southern Africa, 23*, 175−195.

Harcourt, W. (2004). Editorial Is CSR rewriting development? *Development, 47*(3), 1−2.

Harrison, D., & Prasad, B. (2013). The contribution of tourism to the development of Fiji and other Pacific Island countries. In C.A. Tisdell (Ed.), *Handbook of tourism economics: Analysis, new applications and case studies* (pp. 741−761). Singapore: World Scientific.

Higgins-Desbiolles, F. (2006). More than an "industry": The forgotten power of tourism as a social force. *Tourism Management, 27*(6), 1192−1208.

Holcomb, J. L., Upchurch, R. S., & Okumus, F. (2007). Corporate social responsibility: What are top hotel companies reporting? *International Journal of Contemporary Hospitality Management, 19*(6), 461−475.

Idemudia, U. (2011). Corporate social responsibility and developing countries: Moving the critical CSR research agenda in Africa forward. *Progress in Development Studies, 11*(1), 1−18.

Inayatullah, S. (1995). Rethinking tourism: Unfamiliar histories and alternative futures. *Tourism Management, 16*(6), 411−415.

Kalisch, A. (2002). *Corporate futures: Social responsibility in the tourism industry*. London: Tourism Concern.

Ketola, T. (2006). From CR−psychopaths to responsible corporations: Waking up the inner sleeping beauty of companies. *Corporate Social Responsibility and Environmental Management, 13*(2), 98−107.

Koutra, C. (2013). *More than simply corporate social responsibility: Implications of corporate social responsibility for tourism development and poverty reduction in developing countries: A political economy perspective.* New York, NY: Nova Science.

Levy, S. E., & Hawkins, D. E. (2009, June). Peace through tourism: Commerce-based principles and practices. Paper presented at the Peace Through Commerce e-Conference, Theme 8: A Perspective from the Tourism Industry, Singapore. Retrieved from http://api.ning.com/files/kqj8PjwXzUC0*fJ JE6tpasBjQSIwiGMyReuje0glgwbc62zfLfcRGjVW3cPH-hWNkQpR*-iz8YuNrliGrXPquCDskvCYmEj-/LevyandHawkinsJBESubmission.pdf

Locke, R. M. (2002). *Note on corporate citizenship in a global economy* (Working Paper No. IPC-02-008). Cambridge, MA: Massachusetts Institute of Technology Industrial Performance Center.

Mowforth, M., & Munt, I. (2009). *Tourism and sustainability: Development, globalisation and new tourism in the third world* (3rd ed.). New York, NY: Taylor & Francis.

Nicolau, J. L. (2008). Corporate social responsibility: Worth-creating activities. *Annals of Tourism Research, 35*(4), 990−1006.

Organisation for Economic Cooperation and Development (OECD). (2011). *Busan partnership for effective development co-operation.* Busan: Fourth High Level Forum on Aid Effectiveness. (29 November−December 2011). Retrieved from http://www.oecd.org/dac/effectiveness/49650173.pdf

Pleumarom, A. (1994). The political economy of tourism. *The Ecologist, 24*(4), 142−148.

Porter, M. E., & Kramer, M. R. (2011). The big idea: Creating shared value. How to reinvent capitalism—and unleash a wave of innovation and growth. *Harvard Business Review, 89*(1−2), 62−78.

Saarinen, J., & Rogerson, C. M. (2014). Tourism and the millennium development goals: Perspectives beyond 2015. *Tourism Geographies, 16*(1), 23−30.

Scheyvens, R. (2002). *Tourism for development: Empowering communities.* Harlow: Pearson Education.

Scheyvens, R. (2011). *Tourism and poverty.* New York, NY: Routledge.

Scheyvens, R., Banks, G., & Hughes, E. (2016). The private sector and the SDGs: The need to move beyond 'business as usual'. *Sustainable Development.* Advance Online Publication. doi:10.1002/sd.1623

Schilcher, D. (2007). Growth versus equity: The continuum of pro-poor tourism and neoliberal governance. *Current Issues in Tourism, 10*(2−3), 166−193.

Spenceley, A., & Meyer, D. (2012). Tourism and poverty reduction: Theory and practice in less economically developed countries. *Journal of Sustainable Tourism, 20*(3), 297−317.

Telfer, D. J., & Sharpley, R. (2008). *Tourism and development in the developing world.* London: Routledge.

Torres, R., & Momsen, J. H. (2004). Challenges and potential for linking tourism and agriculture to achieve pro-poor tourism objectives. *Progress in Development Studies, 4*(4), 294−318.

Torres-Delgado, A., & Saarinen, J. (2014). Using indicators to assess sustainable tourism development: A review. *Tourism Geographies, 16*(1), 31−47.

Tucker, H., & Boonabaana, B. (2012). A critical analysis of tourism, gender and poverty reduction. *Journal of Sustainable Tourism, 20*(3), 437−455.

UN Global Compact. (2013). *Corporate sustainability and the United Nations post-2015 development agenda. Perspectives from UN Global Compact participants on global priorities and how to engage business towards sustainable development goals* (Report to the United Nations Secretary-General). Retrieved from http://www.unglobalcompact.org/docs/news_events/9.1_news_archives/2013_06_18/UNGC_Post2015_Report.pdf

United Nations. (2013). *A new global partnership: Eradicate poverty and transform economies through sustainable development* (The report of the high-level panel of eminent persons on the post-2015 development agenda). New York, NY: United Nations Publications. Retrieved from http://www.un.org/sg/management/pdf/HLP_P2015_Report.pdf

United Nations. (2015). *Transforming our world: The 2030 agenda for sustainable development.* Retrieved from https://sustainabledevelopment.un.org/post2015/transformingourworld

United Nations World Tourism Organization. (2014). *World Tourism Highlights* (2014 Edition). Retrieved from http://www.e-unwto.org/doi/pdf/10.18111/9789284416226).

Weaver, D. (2001). Mass tourism and alternative tourism in the Caribbean. In D. Harrison (Ed.), *Tourism and the less developed world: Issues and case studies* (pp. 161–174). Wallingford: CABI.

Weaver, D. (2012). Organic, incremental and induced paths to sustainable mass tourism convergence. *Tourism Management, 33*(5), 1030–1037.

World Travel and Tourism Council. (2014). Travel and tourism. Economic impact 2014: world. London: WTTC.

Zhao, W., & Ritchie, J. R. B. (2007). Tourism and poverty alleviation: An integrative research framework. *Current Issues in Tourism, 10*(2), 119–143.

🔓 OPEN ACCESS

Can MNCs promote more inclusive tourism? Apollo tour operator's sustainability work

María José Zapata Campos, C. Michael Hall and Sandra Backlund

ABSTRACT

Outbound tour operators are key actors in international mass tourism. However, their contribution to more sustainable and inclusive forms of tourism has been critically questioned. Drawing from new institutional theories in organization studies, and informed by the case of one of the largest Scandinavian tour operators, we examine the corporate social responsibility (CSR) and sustainability work in large tour operators and the challenges faced in being more inclusive. On the basis of in-depth interviews with corporate officers, document analysis and media reports, we show how top-down coercive and normative pressures, coming from the parent company and the host society shape the ability of the daughter corporation to elaborate a more inclusive agenda. However, daughter companies do not merely comply with these institutional pressures and policy is also developed from the 'bottom-up'. We show how the tour operator's sustainability work is also the result of organizational responses including buffering, bargaining, negotiating and influencing the parent organization. By creating intra and inter-sectoral learning and collaborative industry platforms, MNCs not only exchange and diffuse more inclusive practices among the industry, but also anticipate future normative pressures such as legislation and brand risk. Daughter organizations help shape their institutional arrangements through internal collaborative platforms and by incorporating local events and societal concerns into the multinational CSR policy, especially when flexible policy frameworks operate, and the corporate CSR agenda and organizational field are under formation. However, risks do exist, in the absence of institutional pressures, of perpetuating a superficial adoption of more inclusive practices in the mass tourism industry.

摘要：
境外旅行商是国际大众旅游的重要参与者。然而，他们对更具可持续性和包容性的旅游业的贡献备受质疑。我们从组织研究的新制度理论出发，以斯堪的纳维亚最大的一家旅行社为例，考察了大型旅行社的企业社会责任(CSR)和可持续性方面的工作，以及在发展更包容旅游方面所面临的挑战。在对公司高管深入访谈、文献分析和媒体报道的基础上，我们展示了来自母公司和东道国的自

Supplemental data for this article can be accessed https://doi.org/10.1080/14616688.2018.1457074.

This is an Open Access article distributed under the terms of the Creative Commons Attribution License (http://creativecommons.org/licenses/by/4.0/), which permits unrestricted use, distribution, and reproduction in any medium, provided the original work is properly cited.

上而下的强制性和规范性压力如何影响子公司制定包容性旅游议程的能力。然而，子公司不只是遵守这些制度压力，也"自下而上"发展包容性旅游政策。我们展示了旅行社的可持续性工作也是组织响应的结果，包括对母公司压力的缓冲、讨价还价、谈判乃至影响母公司。跨国公司通过创建内部和跨部门的学习和合作的行业平台，不仅在行业内交流和传播更包容性的实践，而且预料未来的规范性压力，如立法和品牌风险。子组织通过内部协作平台，通过将当地事件和社会问题纳入到跨国企业社会责任政策中，有助于形成组织的制度安排，特别是在灵活的政策框架运作时，企业社会责任议程和组织领域形成时期。然而，在没有制度压力的情况下，在大众旅游行业中,存在着肤浅地采用更包容做法的风险。

Introduction

Outbound tour operators are major actors in the tourism industry (Alegre & Sard, 2015; Cvelbar, Dwyer, Koman, & Mihalič, 2016; Tveteraas, Asche, & Lien, 2014). Tour operators are one of the largest facilitators of information between suppliers and customers and, consequently, are significant influencers of how the travel market can evolve towards more inclusive and responsible tourism, affecting both suppliers and demand. Inclusiveness for major operators has historically been interpreted more in terms of packages for tourists rather than considering the groups and stakeholders that are excluded from the tourism system. For the purposes of this paper, inclusive tourism is regarded as the voluntary inclusion of otherwise marginalized interests in the consumption and production of tourism (also see Scheyvens & Biddulph, 2017). From this perspective inclusivity is identified as a relative and contested, rather than an absolute, concept, the interpretation of which belongs to the involved parties. The identification of inclusivity depends on the stakeholders involved and the nature of inclusion, with inclusivity defined either by one party or by both producers and marginalized interests (Figure 1). A tourism producer may seek to include marginal interests but such interests may not recognize their inclusivity despite producer efforts, leading to a staged inclusivity or non-inclusive practices. You may even have situations where producers and marginalized interests believe that the relationship is inclusive but tourists do not recognize it as such, thereby missing the opportunity to communicate more fully inclusive tourism practices and with them the chance to show alternative practices for a more inclusive tourism. Importantly, the notion of inclusion is one that varies over socio-cultural contexts and that will change over time in response to shifts in the business,

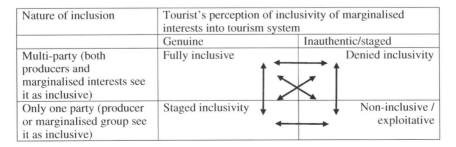

Figure 1. Types of inclusive tourism.

political and socio-economic environments; the composition of interests and stakeholders, and new interpretations of what constitutes inclusive and sustainable tourism.

Given their role in tourism, the practices of large tour operators can influence the wider industry in becoming more inclusive and sustainable (Bricker & Black, 2016; Erskine & Meyer, 2012). However, while there is significant academic interest in the role of tour operators with respect to sustainability, this has often been focussed more on niche tourism areas or specific environmental practices, such as emissions or waste reduction (Gössling, Hall, & Scott, 2015), rather than the equity and social dimensions of sustainability that may provide an operational and strategic focus for inclusive tourism (Hall, 2008).

Outbound tour operators are key actors in mass tourism and hold critical positions in the tourism value chain, especially for developing countries, where they can act as major gatekeepers of tourism flows and influence practices (de Sausmarez, 2013; Dieke, 2013). Therefore, any account of the extent to which international mass tourism can be made more inclusive must include assessment of the role of outbound tour operators and the way in which they develop particular practices that relate to inclusiveness. This paper draws from new institutional theories in organization studies to understand the practice of sustainability and social responsibility work in large tour operators. Specifically, it examines the challenges to transforming mass tourism into becoming more inclusive in terms of recognizing and incorporating new practices, as informed by the case of one of the largest Scandinavian operators, Apollo, and its corporate social responsibility (CSR) and sustainability work.

This paper draws from in-depth interviews with company officers, and document analysis of CSR and sustainability reports. In order to understand what the CSR agenda of a large tour operator looks like, how it is shaped and the challenges faced in being more inclusive, this paper is structured around two questions: how are the institutional pressures and the organizational characteristics of MNCs and subsidiaries shaping tour operators' sustainability practices? and what are the firm's organizational responses to these pressures?

In the next section, the literature on sustainability, inclusive tourism and the tour operators sector is presented, followed by the methods to collect and analyse the data. The case study of Apollo Sweden is then presented. Next, the theoretical framework used to analyse the case is explained. Thereafter, the empirical study is analysed and discussed. This paper closes with reflections on how large corporations can be encouraged to provide more inclusive tourism services.

Sustainability, inclusive tourism and the tour operator sector

The tour operator sector has become increasingly consolidated in recent decades. A few large tour operators dominate the sector and account for almost two-thirds of the European market (Schwartz, Tapper and Font, 2008). German and British large tour operators alone dominate more than 45% of the European market, with four companies estimated to control over 90% of the UK holiday market (Budeanu, 2009).

Large tour operators draw together thousands of employees in travel agencies, hotels, airlines and other tourism firms in hundreds of destinations around the world. However, inclusiveness in terms of the participation of marginalized actors in the consumption and production of tourism has not historically been a priority. The concentration of power in the hands of a few global operators has led to conflicts between operators, suppliers and destinations. Large tour operators have often been seen more as agents of exclusion than inclusion, with this often being combined with related environmental degradation, sociocultural ignorance or disruption, limited returns to local economies, human rights abuse and other negative impacts (Hall & Brown, 2006). In general, mass-market operators offering mainstream packages (i.e. all-inclusive – where a single price covers includes all charges for lodging, meals and soft drinks, most alcoholic drinks, gratuities, and possibly other services, such as sports and other activities), and have not traditionally considered sustainability in business processes in the same way as specialist operators selling 'more sustainable products' (Bricker & Black, 2016; Bruni, Cassia, & Magno, 2017; Gössling et al., 2015; Hall, Gössling & Scott, 2015). Yet, the critical role of tour operators in the mass tourism market value chain means that they must become a focal point of any initiative that seeks to make tourism more inclusive of otherwise marginalized groups and issues. For example, via their role as employers of marginalized groups in local destinations in which the notion of inclusiveness includes aspects of decent work and fair salaries as well as more socially and environmentally inclusive procurement policies (Saarinen, Rogerson, & Hall, 2017), such as purchasing from local food suppliers (Hall & Gössling, 2016).

Given how strategic priorities are set in tourism corporations, CSR and sustainability policies, codes of conduct and certification systems are likely to be the main practices through which corporations would approach inclusive tourism. Therefore, improvements in our understanding of these areas (e.g. decent work, procurement policies and monitoring strategies), and recognition of any initiatives that bear the hallmarks of inclusive tourism, can help shed light on the mechanisms by which greater inclusiveness can be encouraged and achieved.

The factors shaping the adoption of sustainability practices by tour operators show how sustainability strategies, practices and standards, to which we would potentially add inclusive tourism, are likely conceived primarily as a means of risk management (to buffer or prevent negative public image), as a competitive advantage (e.g. brand value and reputation), and as a regulation avoidance strategy (Schwartz et al., 2008), rather than as a means to provide improved services to customers, cost savings or business opportunities (Budeanu, 2007), or inclusion. Compared to other sectors, such as accommodation, the tour operator sector arguably lags behind in the integration of sustainability in business practices due to a combination of reasons: tour operators do not always take a long-term view of destination development, as their operations are more spatially flexible and easier to move between destinations compared to suppliers such as hotels; and they may claim a lack of control over impacts in destinations. Operators operate on small profit margins and the resultant pressure on suppliers to reduce prices can limit supplier capacity to invest in quality improvements (Alegre & Said, 2015) or other strategies that do not have a relatively immediate return. The industry also works with a multitude of suppliers operating under different national regulations and interests which can make it more difficult to develop consistent sustainability and CSR programs. On the demand side, customers' interest in responsible tourism services and products, and willingness to pay extra for inclusive practices in general, appears significantly lower compared to, for example, specific elements such as local food (Hall & Gössling, 2016). In relation to the regulatory environment, most of the tour package legislation is quality, health and safety related, and there is usually very little specific regulatory pressure for improved environmental or social performance in tour operator's operations. In addition, cost savings from adopting practices are not so clearly identified for tour operators as, for example, for hotels (Budeanu, 2007; Gössling et al., 2015; Tepelus, 2005).

Methods

Scandinavia is routinely cited as a global leader in CSR and sustainability (Strand, Freeman, & Hockerts, 2015). Apollo is one of the three largest tour operators in Sweden and one of the Nordic pioneers of proactively adopting CSR and sustainability practices in tourism (Schyst Resande, 2008). This paper adopts a 'critical case' approach (Flyvbjerg, 2001). Informed by this approach we have selected as favourable a setting as possible, one of the top leading Swedish tour operators working proactively with sustainability, for examining the integration of sustainability in large tour operators. A critical case approach provides the opportunity to draw valid insights from a single case that has strategic importance for a general problem, such as the challenges that large operators face in making mass tourism a more inclusive activity.

Data collection involved analysis of documents such as ethical guidelines, policies, standards, sustainability and assessment reports, voluntary performance schemes, and codes of conduct (Supplemental data). The websites of the parent (Kuoni) and daughter company (Apollo) as well as those of CSR-related stakeholders and collaboration partners were also reviewed. Semi-structured interviews were carried out with officials at Apollo and Kuoni. The interviews served to complement and triangulate the information coming from documents and electronic sources. All interviews were recorded and transcribed. The number of interviews conducted and the positions of those interviewed at Apollo and Kuoni is not stated here as this would potentially publicly identify participants.

The documents, websites and interviews were analysed through qualitative content analysis, structured by the two research questions and guided by the concepts stemming from the institutional theories used in the analysis (presented later after the case): coercive, normative and mimetic isomorphism as well as the organizational responses (strategies and tactics) of the firm to these pressures. The data coming from the personal interviews with employees at Apollo is triangulated with text documents, interview material from the parent company (Kuoni) and electronic sources. Combining methods helps to overcome the limitations of using a single case with limited interview opportunities. Interviews were conducted during spring 2015. The Apollo Nordic division was acquired by the German REWE-travel group in summer 2015. No significant changes have been observed in terms of sustainability work since then, although this new situation has not been the focus of this study.

Apollo Sweden, sustainability strategy and work

In this section we present the case of Apollo Sweden and its sustainability work, informed by corporate documents, websites, news, reports and interviews. After we present our analytical framework, the empirical data will be analysed and discussed.

Apollo Sweden

In Sweden three large tour operators (Ving, Apollo and Fritidsresor) account for 80% of the outbound tour operator market (SwedWatch and Fair Action, 2015). Apollo was founded by Fotios Costoulas in 1986 and ran as a family business providing travel from Sweden to Greece. In 2001 it was bought by Kuoni Holding Ltd, a Switzerland-based provider of services to the international travel industry and governments. Its activities are centred on global travel, travel services distribution, visa provision and tour operating, including hotel, accommodation, and land and transportation services, tours and activities. Apollo Sweden, together with its Finnish, Norwegian and Danish counterparts, and the airline Novair, belongs to the Apollo Travel Group. With approximately 900 employees and one million international travellers annually, Apollo Travel Group has an annual turnover of over US$ 590 million (Apollo, 2016a). In mid-2015 Apollo was sold to the German REWE-group and became part of the DER Touristik travel division as DER Touristik Nordic AB including Apollo Sweden, Denmark, Norway and Finland. Apollo offers travel to 20 countries in Europe, 10 in Asia, 5 in Africa, 5 in the Americas and 1 in Oceania. Among the most popular tourist destinations are Greece, Turkey, Spain, Cyprus, Thailand, Jordan, Tobago and Cuba.

Managing and strategizing sustainability at Apollo

CSR and sustainability management are integrated with the communication management department in Apollo. There were two employees working directly with sustainability at management level: one responsible for sustainability and communication; and another who worked part-time mostly on the Travelife system (a business-to-business sustainability certification program implemented by Apollo, explained below) with their suppliers. Plans, strategies, and practices that fall under the category of sustainability, CSR and ethics have existed at Apollo since it became part of the Kuoni group in 2001. However, CSR and sustainability 'was not the highest prioritized issue by the former manager of the firm' (Apollo employee).

Kuoni's Group CSR Strategy was the framework within which all work with sustainability matters at group level was assembled from 2001 until 2015. The Kuoni CSR agenda was reviewed every three years and was formulated by the central board of directors at Kuoni's headquarters in Zurich. The strategy consisted of six core areas: employees, human rights, sustainable products, natural environment, stakeholder management and sustainable supply chain management. The mapping and priority setting of sustainability topics was based on stakeholder dialogues carried out in wider and inner stakeholder consultation circles (Kuoni, 2014). Inner stakeholders were members and employees at all levels within the Kuoni Group, including the central board of directors and CSR officials from business units. Apollo participated in the stakeholder consultations for the development of Kuoni's Group CSR strategy as an internal stakeholder. External stakeholders include international, national and local non-governmental organizations (NGOs), investors, experts, suppliers, consultants, and international organizations. The strategy was also built on a range of international conventions, codes of conduct and sustainability charters including the *UN Global Compact*, the *Universal Declaration of Human Rights*, the *UN Guiding Principles on Business and Human Rights*, the OECD *Guidelines for Multinational*

Enterprises and ECPAT's *Code of Conduct*. Significantly, from an inclusive tourism perspective, even though such agreements are often held up as cornerstones of CSR practice, local communities had only a limited role in such dialogues.

Internally, Kuoni had a 'CSR steering group', in which Apollo participated, that met twice a year (Kuoni, 2016). This group consisted of representatives from Kuoni's business units, core corporate functions and external CSR specialists. The purpose of the committee was to plan CSR strategies and activities for the entire group, as well as review performance and ensure that the Group CSR strategy was aligned between business units. This was also a platform where Apollo exchanged experiences with other participants, provided inputs to the board of directors and contributed to central CSR objectives.

Apollo's sustainability strategy

Kuoni's Group CSR strategy served as the guiding framework for Apollo's work but they were encouraged to design their own corporate strategy for sustainability by taking a point of departure in the core areas of this agenda (Kuoni interview). How the Kuoni's Group CSR strategy was implemented by Apollo was neither strictly stipulated nor regulated. Apollo's CSR agenda did not need the approval of the central board of Kuoni (Kuoni Interview). Apollo's sustainability/CSR strategy has been divided into four areas: human rights, climate change, sustainable supply chain management and sustainable products (Apollo, 2016b). The following projects, dealing with the social dimension of sustainability and integrated in Apollo's human rights and supply chain areas (Table 1), are described below before subsequent analysis.

ECPAT – the code

ECPAT is an international NGO working against sexual exploitation of children since 1992 in Thailand and other South Asian countries. ECPAT Sweden was created after the World Congress against Commercial Sexual Exploitation of Children was hosted by the Swedish Government in 1996. The Code, which is a guideline consisting of six measures aimed at helping tourism businesses to protect children, was the result of this congress. Apollo states on its website that the protection of children is one of the most prioritized issues in Apollo's work with sustainability. An Apollo officer emphasizes the focus on children due to the empathy showed by travellers and employees when they come in contact with suffering children in destinations, as also observed via customer evaluation forms. Concerns raised in Sweden regarding the harmful impacts of tourism on children in South-East Asia destinations are also behind this prioritization. In the words of an Apollo official regarding ratification of the Code:

> It reaches a point where we understand that we neither can nor want to be held accountable for certain things, for which we feel that we must act and take on our responsibility (…) The

Table 1. Summary of the social components of Apollo's CSR agenda.

Human rights	Sustainable supply chain management
• Suppliers' Code of Conduct, 2008 • Statement of Commitment on Human Rights, 2012 • ECPACT – The Code, 2001 • Collaboration with SOS Children's Villages, 2004	• Suppliers' Code of Conduct, 2008 • Travelife Sustainability System, 2009

risks of not doing anything is that we acquire a bad reputation. In the end, caring for the corporate image and the reputation is a strong driving force.

In order to prevent their services being misused for exploitative purposes, Apollo joined forces with fellow signatories such as the Swedish government, ECPAT, industry partners and tour operators such as Fritidsresor and Ving. This collaborative strategy was motivated by the 'pleasant feeling of being united and not having to stand alone, and to be able to show a united front' (Apollo officer). The signatories to The Code in Sweden meet twice a year to discuss topics and strategies related to child trafficking. The Code was ratified independently by Apollo in 2001. Apollo and Nordic partners also encouraged Kuoni to ratify this policy.

SOS children's villages
Apollo's ratification of the ECPAT Code led to the collaboration in Sweden with SOS Children's Villages in 2004. SOS Children's Villages is an international organization giving family-based childcare to children without families in order to allow them to grow up in safety. Apollo donates one million SEK per year to a SOS village in Phuket. This money funds a kindergarten and three SOS families in the village. Since 2015 Apollo is partner to SOS Children's Villages at the Nordic Kuoni level, and funds an emergency help program for families in Syria. An Apollo officer states that such cooperation is a good way to show their commitment to children's right issues in a concrete way. The NGO's good reputation is also important to choosing the partner: 'Since SOS Children's Villages is a very well-known organization with a credible image it is a way for us to use their brand together with our own, which has a positive effect' (Apollo officer).

Travelife sustainability system
Travelife is a business-to-business sustainability certification programme supported by the European Union and the European Industry Association Tour Operator Initiative. It consists of an accreditation body directed towards tourism industry enterprises to make operations more sustainable. Businesses can purchase a subscription to the system and have their performance level independently assessed via an audit and the top performers in terms of these verified audits receive a Travelife award. Major UK and German tour operators, such as First Choice, Thompson, TUI, Thomas Cook, have subscribed to the Travelife Sustainability System as their preferred means of assessing their accommodation providers against environmental, social and economic criteria. Kuoni group was a founding member and has been involved in its development since 2004. Apollo achieved the status of being Travelife Certified as a tour operator in 2014 and they have been using the certification for hotel and accommodations among suppliers since 2009. Around 100 Apollo hotels are Travelife members and have achieved this certification. However, the certification, unlike the Suppliers' code of conduct, is not required of all suppliers.

The Travelife Sustainability system was one of the standards applicable to all Kuoni group members. A CSR official states that the creation of Travelife by a group of European tour operators reflected how 'the entire branch felt a need to use a standardized and simple way of ordering their hotels'. Among the many different alternatives such as ISO and other standards, the official states that 'Travelife stood out as a recognized standardized way of classifying hotels which made it possible to easily communicate to customers that this is the way we look at these questions'. Thus, the adoption of these standards was also driven by the need to promote to customers that the company had embraced sustainability practices in its operations, while their implementation has also resulted in modifications in standard operating procedures and the generation of new standards. The new owner group DER Turistik was already a member of Travelife.

Suppliers' code of conduct

The suppliers' code of conduct was first developed in 2008 by the Kuoni group in collaboration with external stakeholders such as experts, consultants and NGOs. It consists of six areas of sustainability (compliance with applicable law, environment, human rights and labour conditions, sexual exploitation of children and adolescents, local sourcing and benefiting communities, and monitoring and enforcement) and ratification of the policy was required by all Apollo's suppliers and monitored through the Travelife system. Apollo also contributed to the content of the *Suppliers' Code of Conduct* via the inner consultation circles for sustainability strategy making and, more actively, by Apollo's petition to add a clause on animals' rights issues in 2014. Apollo lobbied to include this topic as they perceived increasing customer and employee concern for animal welfare. According to Apollo officials, the concern was detected via customer feedback but it was also regarded as an issue raised by society at large in Sweden, and mobilized by NGOs. At the time of writing (February, 2017) the suppliers' code of conduct continued to operate under the new owner.

Statement of commitment on human rights

The *Statement of Commitment on Human Rights* establishes that the group will respect and promote human rights through leading by example in areas as labour rights (e.g. following international and national law, forbidding all forms of forced labour, freedom to terminate employment, freedom of association and right to collective bargaining), the rights of the child and due diligence. The standard is automatically transferred to Apollo's suppliers when a contract is confirmed and compliance is monitored with assistance from Travelife. The creation of the *Statement of Commitment on Human Rights* was an initiative of Apollo and Nordic partners. Apollo urged the creation of a policy document on human rights within Kuoni's steering committee, leading to the Statement being passed by Kuoni's board of directors in 2012.

Despite considerable progress in terms of the improvement of human and labour rights, Swedish NGOs reported during Autumn 2015 illegal labour conditions for hotel employees in properties used by the three largest Swedish tour operators (Apollo, Fritidsresor and Ving) in Dubai (SwedWatch and Fair Action, 2015) and Turkey (Fair Traveller, 2015). The report reveals how housekeepers, room attendants and other migrant workers at hotels used by the three tour operators in Dubai worked days as long as twelve hours with little or no overtime pay. Workers also stated that they paid for employment as well as employers holding their passports, which according to the International Labour Organization is a sign of forced labour. These practices violate local labour law and international conventions, as well as the human rights policies of the Swedish tour operators themselves.

The three Swedish tour operators replied in a joint communication stating they did not have knowledge about rights violations at the hotels where their customers were staying

(SwedWatch and Fair Action, 2015). Nevertheless, according to an Apollo officer, the company had performed a risk analysis regarding human rights in Dubai which shows that it is a high-risk destination, especially with regard to migrant workers (SwedWatch and Fair Action, 2015). The company also argued that the staff responsible for the contact with the hotels has instructions to report any breach of the code, and that no breach had been reported.

In a collective response to the publication of this report, the three tour operators acknowledge the violation of labour rights and communicated that together with the Travelife certification system (see below for further details about the certification system) they will start monitoring more hotels in Dubai (SwedWatch, 2015). They also argued that this is an issue affecting more than these three tour operators and it, therefore, requires a collective response. Furthermore, Apollo acknowledges that despite increasing public awareness and company concern over labour issues, consumer pressure for more sustainable and inclusive travel is not so significant (Swedish Radio A, 13/10/2015; Swedish Radio B, 13/10/2015).

Within the Kuoni Group the *Travelife Sustainability* system and *the Kuoni Suppliers Code of Conduct* were the only two standards applicable to all members and served as minimum requirements for the business units' work with sustainability issues. Apollo was encouraged by Kuoni to implement these policies, and Kuoni's CSR department regularly provide information and learning tools aiming to facilitate their implementation. However, according to Kuoni's CSR department, they struggled to achieve a 'consistent image' between members of the group in terms of sustainability. Kuoni did not monitor units such as Apollo and had no enforcement mechanism exerting punishment for non-compliance. Yet, Apollo's reliance upon Kuoni as a daughter unit means that they felt required to address these sustainability issues: 'it is not as if something would happen if we wouldn't work with sustainability and implement these standards, since they are informal requirements. However, disregarding these issues is not an alternative, it simply would not be possible' (Apollo officer).

Aware of the requirement to respond to the mother company's demands on sustainability strategy, an official stated: 'The central board of Kuoni have certain targets which they want the units to fulfil, so it is a matter of complying with their desire' (Apollo). Apollo also considered it was important to fulfil the expectations of Kuoni as Apollo also 'want to be able to impact the direction of the work that is centrally managed at Kuoni'. According to the Apollo official, the implementation of these standards has led to a steady development of awareness around issues of sustainability among Apollo employees. However, field participation of representatives from Apollo's destination areas in the strategizing of Apollo's sustainability is less visible. Local regulations as well as ideas picked up from destination personnel are mediated to Apollo's central board. Yet there are no established mechanisms to channel the flow of local demands. In the following the theoretical framework used to analyse the case is introduced.

Institutional theory

Institutional theory provides a useful framework to analyse the extent of integration of sustainability practices into corporations. While use of this theory is relatively limited in tourism (Adu-Ampong, 2017; Zapata & Hall, 2012), it has been valuable in examining sustainable practices (Van Wijk, Van der Duim, Lamers, & Sumba, 2015), including CSR reporting (de Grosbois, 2016). The following elaborates the concepts of institutional isomorphic pressures, organizational responses to institutional pressures and processes of organizational learning that are then used to frame our case under the prism of the concept of inclusive tourism.

Institutional theories focus on the pursuit of legitimacy aside from economic efficiency, with the resulting organizational conformity arising due to social norms and rituals (Meyer & Rowan, 1977). In their pursuit of legitimacy, organizations modify themselves to be compatible with the characteristics (organizational structures, beliefs and discourses) of their institutional environments. As a consequence, organizations from the same field will often be structurally similar as they respond to similar institutional pressures (cognitive, normative and coercive), resulting in a process of isomorphism (Scott, 2008).

Coercive isomorphism refers to the conformity to certain practices as a result of rules, laws or other coercive mechanisms, economic and regulatory sanctions. Yet, under conditions of uncertainty in a relatively unregulated organizational field, as in the case of sustainability in the travel industry (Gössling et al., 2015), normative and cognitive aspects of the institutional environment become more salient. Normative isomorphism comes, for example, from unquestioned adherence to industry standards but also prevalent values and preferences in a market or a community. While, cognitive isomorphism (or mimesis) refers to the unconscious reproduction of standards, practices or structures following those who appear to be successful in the organizational field.

However, organizations within the same field do not always show similar sustainability strategies and practices (Hall et al., 2016; Scott, 2008; Zapata & Hall, 2012) despite being exposed to common institutional pressures. More recent developments in institutional theory show how institutional forces can also lead to heterogeneity in a sector rather than isomorphic homogeneity, given that organizations differ in their receptivity to pressures (Hoffman, 2001). For example, the power of the department or individual promoting CSR and sustainability practices is an internal aspect that may explain different responses. Delmas and Toffel (2008) also showed how organizations channel institutional pressures through different sub-units, which frame pressures according to their routines. For example, legal departments frame them in terms of risk and liability, while financial departments do it in terms of costs and revenue. The consequence being that sustainability could be differentially framed within the same organization as a competitiveness strategy, as regulatory pressure, or as an ethical responsibility (Bansal & Roth, 2000). Other internal organizational features such as the role of leadership values (Egri & Herman, 2000), managerial attitudes (Cordano & Frieze, 2000; Sharma, 2000), and historical environmental performance can also influence how managers perceive stakeholder pressures and their response (Prakash, 2000), and the visibility of the firm. Therefore, differences in adoption of sustainability tourism practices reflect not only different levels of institutional pressures but also differences in organizational characteristics, since internal organizational dynamics act as moderating factors that magnify or diminish the influence of institutional pressures.

Oliver (1991) also suggests that organizations respond to their institutional environments in different ways, varying from compliance, compromise, avoidance, defiance and manipulation (Table 2). One of the possible responses is what has been termed as 'decoupling' (Meyer & Rowan, 1977), which refers to the process whereby

Table 2. Strategic responses to institutional pressures.

Strategies	Tactics	Examples
Acquiesce	Habit	Follow taken-for-granted institutional norms and practices
	Imitation	Copy and mimic institutional models
	Compliance	Obey rules and accept norms and practices
Compromise	Balance	Balance the expectations of multiple actors and stakeholders
	Pacification	Placate and accommodate institutional actors and elements
	Bargain	Negotiate with institutional constituents and stakeholders
Avoid	Conceal	Disguise nonconformity
	Buffer	Loosen institutional attachments
	Escape	Change goals, activities or domains
Defy	Dismiss	Ignore explicit institutional norms, mores and values
	Challenge	Contest institutional rules and requirements
	Attack	Assault the sources of institutional pressure
Manipulate	Co-option	Cooperate with influential constituents and stakeholders
	Influence	Seek to shape institutional values, rules and criteria
	Control	Seek to dominate institutional constituents and processes

Source: After Oliver (1991).

organizations 'that adopt particular structures or procedures may opt to respond in a ceremonial manner, making changes in their formal structures to signal conformity but then buffering internal units, allowing them to operate independent of these pressures' (Scott, 2008: 171). The term has been used to refer to implementation gaps in sustainability standards (Bromley & Powell, 2012; Jamali, 2010). Yet, beyond the decoupling explanation, CSR and sustainability reports and codes of conduct, although taken initially as ceremonial conformity, can turn performative and become real (Barley & Zhang, 2012). Ceremonially adopted rules can lead to change over time and recouple formal and informal structures (Egels-Zandén, 2014); as a result of reflection and negotiations that convince internal organizational actors of their appropriateness independent of instrumental considerations (Dashwood, 2012). Internal and external debates of sustainability and responsibility may, therefore, also create conditions for future change through organizational learning (Dashwood, 2012, 2014), an issue that may be critical for inclusion of inclusive tourism in CSR discourses.

Discussion

In this section, we will analyse and discuss the case of Apollo Sweden and its sustainability work informed by the theoretical framework presented above with the aim to understand what mass tourism corporations do in practice for an inclusive tourism, why their CSR and sustainability agenda is shaped as it is and the challenges they face in being more inclusive. In order to do that, we explain how institutional pressures (mimetic, coercive and normative isomorphism) shape tour operators' sustainability practices and the organizational responses to these pressures.

Institutional pressures for a more inclusive tourism

Mimetic isomorphism

In terms of mimetic isomorphism, Apollo's sustainability work follows international conventions, standards and codes of conduct promoted by international agencies such *UN Global Compact*, *Universal Declaration of Human Rights*, and the *UN Guiding Principles on*

Business and Human Rights. These standards and codes have turned into 'rational myths' (Meyer & Rowan, 1977), taken for granted and uncontested norms and solutions (Brunsson & Jacobsson, 2000) to the problem of integrating sustainability into business practices (Jamali, 2010). Unlike the diverse range of tourism industry codes and certification systems, these international standards have achieved worldwide recognition and are mimetically reproduced by large corporations. From that perspective, Travelife has turned into a norm for the certification of sustainability practices among European tour operators and their suppliers. Such initiatives help to harmonize the fragmented efforts of individual actors (Schwartz et al., 2008), and become uncontested norms as a taken for granted solution to problems of non-compliance with codes of conduct, as elaborated below.

Coercive isomorphism
Despite sustainability in tourism destinations being under-regulated (Tepelus, 2005), there are a number of coercive forces that determine Apollo's sustainability agenda. The Kuoni group has created a CSR system based on two compulsory components: the Kuoni *Suppliers Code of Conduct* and the Travelife certification system. These two components are the minimum requirement from the parent corporation, and are defined as 'recipes' by the Kuoni CSR manager with the flexibility to be translated into the different national contexts through strategies of compromise, such as negotiation (Oliver, 1991). These two components, therefore, provide consistency and cohesion to the group, helping to integrate the diversity of practices in different locations. Subsequently, the *Supplier's Code of Conduct* turned into a compulsory commitment for Apollo's suppliers. Yet in practice only 100 supplier hotels are monitored for some of the standards in the code by the Travelife certification system. In addition, these codes and conduct and certification systems rarely include local stakeholders in their design; which reflects in the poor inclusion of local voices and marginalized groups in their design.

Normative isomorphism
Apollo's sustainability agenda is also shaped by shifts in societal debate and the emergence of salient issues (Bansal & Roth, 2000), many of them promoted by NGOs, while others proceed from customer suggestions. NGOs in Sweden such as Shyst Resande (2015) or SwedWatch (Fair Trade Center and SwedWatch, 2008; SwedWatch and Fair Action, 2015) have triggered changes via publicizing research reports and conferences, and have nudged tour operators to bring new practices into their operations. This reveals that, in the absence of stronger regulations in destinations, the existence of strong pressures and/or stakeholders act as institutional factors in generating situations that encourage operators to integrate new values and norms remains crucial. Marginalized groups at destinations that are the focus of inclusive initiatives may be disadvantaged as a stakeholder in the development of company CSR agendas because they do not have a strong direct or indirect presence in the process.

The clause on animal rights in the *Suppliers' Code of Conduct*, the statement of commitment to human rights and the acknowledgement of ECPAT by the Apollo Nordic group illustrate how values and demands from stakeholders and what is perceived to exist in the generating markets travel to the daughter firm influencing the Apollo's sustainability agenda (Van Huijstee & Glasbergen, 2010). Partnering with NGOs is also an example of normative pressures. The importance of brand and legitimacy, and the potential to use this relationship to differentiate from competitors, is positively related to compliance in previous studies of CSR firms and NGOs (Hendry, 2006).

Industry associations such as the Tour Operator Initiative, to which Kuoni belongs to and which is responsible for the Travelife System; and other corporate collaborative platforms such as the one created by the three large tour operators in Sweden, also perform as a source of pressure by creating new standards, intensifying close scrutiny among competitors and transferring information about best practices. The high field cohesion (Bansal & Roth, 2000) in the tour operators' field, sometimes sparked by NGOs as explained above, also served to pressure Apollo to introduce sustainability standards and practices. Standards and norms *per se*, such as the Travelife System, are also pressing other tour operator firms to adopt them via normative isomorphism. This normative pressure turns into a coercive pressure for many hotel suppliers that have to work with the certification systems if that is stipulated in their contracts (although currently only for a few), and into a cognitive pressure prompting others to imitate the behaviour of successful pioneers.

Filtering institutional pressures

There are a number of organizational features of Apollo that further explain how the institutional pressures presented above are filtered to the organization, shaping how these pressures are internally translated. Size is one of them. Apollo's sustainability work only began after acquisition by Kuoni. Therefore, belonging to a large MNC can amplify the institutional pressures to work towards particular forms of tourism due to their visibility.

Another organizational feature is strategic positioning. In Apollo Sweden the CSR and Sustainability work is allocated within the Communication and PR department. As a result, CSR and sustainability work is often, although not only, framed in terms of brand management and risk management, reflecting Delmas and Toffel's (2008) finding that the subunit through which institutional pressures are channelled will affect the framing of CSR and sustainability issues. The department has limited human resources, as is usually the case for sustainability in firms, and competes internally for resources. One could speculate that firm crises such as the Dubai report are actually 'good' for CSR units, since they show the critical nature of this organizational function in terms of firm legitimacy, and might work to attract resources (as when Apollo decided to put more resources into monitoring hotels through the Travelife system).

Finally, a firm's historical sustainability performance influences how managers perceive stakeholders' pressures and how to respond to them. This means that managers in firms whose reputation has suffered, such as in the case of the Dubai Report in 2015, may be more sensitive to sustainability issues than those in other companies (Prakash, 2000).

Organizational responses to institutional pressures for a more inclusive tourism

Compliance with institutional pressures coming from the parent company and the travel market are not, however, the only two organizational responses shown by Apollo in its sustainability work. Apollo's sustainability work demonstrates how there is much room for buffering, bargaining, negotiation and influencing the parent organization, following Oliver's (1991) organizational responses (Table 1).

Buffering/decoupling

As shown by the Dubai scandal, suppliers' codes of conduct can be loosely coupled to changes in the hotel suppliers' employment practices. This episode reveals how codes of conduct risk becoming a form of symbolic compliance since they are not necessarily monitored through independent audits, creating the illusion of a staged inclusivity (Figure 1). In their website Apollo invites travellers interested in sustainability to choose a Travelife certified hotel transferring the responsibility for more inclusive tourism to the consumer and to the hotelier. Even if Travelife has come to unify a diverse range of certification systems in the sector, and are based on web-based self-assessments, individual audits are still necessary to monitor compliance with standards (Schwartz et al., 2008). However, the certification of a given supplier is not necessarily a guarantee of total compliance and the risk of further loosely coupled structures remains, as demonstrated by the research conducted by Fair Travel in Travelife certified hotels used by Swedish tour operators in Turkey (Schyst Resande, 2015). By revealing to the public the violation of labour rights by these suppliers, the NGOs evidenced the exploitative character (Figure 1) of the tour operator's sustainability work. Monitoring compliance with sustainability standards in order to move towards more fully inclusive practices may initially require the allocation of more resources. Yet given that the tour operator sector already operates with very low profit margins, experiences high competition, is budget oriented, and does not have customers motivated by sustainability preferences, this creates considerable challenges in absorbing the costs of monitoring performance (Schwartz et al., 2008). Business would, therefore, require a clear financial return to embark on such a course or face potential brand harm if they do not.

Since the risk for buffering is high in a lowly regulated sector with few specific resources allocated to monitoring gaps between voluntary standards and practices, the role of NGOs and the media in exposing non-implementation or fulfilment of standards is crucial. When the incongruences between the suppliers' code of conduct and the labour conditions of the hotels in Dubai were publicly revealed by the SwedWatch and Fair Travel report, the Swedish tour operators' reaction was to act together, making use of the collaborative platform they have created in Sweden to discuss issues of sustainability and social responsibility, to manage the reputation crisis collectively (Prakash & Potoski, 2007). Such an approach aims to 'pacify' (Oliver, 1991) institutional pressure and helps to manage brand crisis and regain lost legitimacy. Furthermore, as certification systems have gained credibility in the organizational field they have become a 'rational myth' (Meyer & Rowan, 1977) with respect to sustainable tourism, and recognized as the most trustful means to restate legitimacy.

Negotiating and influencing central CSR and sustainability work

Beyond decoupling, the Apollo case shows how the process of creation and implementation of CSR and sustainability is far from simple compliance to top-down policies. Negotiating, influencing, balancing, pacifying and co-opting tactics (Oliver, 1991) were displayed by Apollo and help explain why its sustainability agenda looks the way it does. Negotiations were ongoing for the design and implementation of the various components of Apollo's CSR policy. The statements on human rights and the ECPAT Code were introduced to the Kuoni group's CSR strategy via the Nordic partners (as a result of normative pressures as elaborated previously), and then turned into the norm and spread out to the rest of the group via Kuoni. Even in the case of the two components coming top-down from Kuoni (suppliers' code of conduct and Travelife) Apollo included new standards (Travelife) and added a clause on animals' rights issues in 2014 (also stemming from normative societal pressures as previously explained), which were incorporated into the general standards applied to all Kuoni daughter firms. This shows how firms in MNCs can also contribute to create new rules (Dashwood, 2012) and have the ability to influence (Oliver, 1991) the CSR agenda. CSR policy making in MNCs can, therefore, be a negotiated process influenced by subsidiaries' local practices. The case at hand represents a transition between unilateral inclusive policies towards a broader participation of stakeholders and institutional constituents. These windows of opportunity for subsidiaries to shape central CSR agendas are especially significant during agenda formation. Corporate CSR and sustainability work are the result of the history of a given organization and practices accumulate historically in layers when some of them fade away but others remain, even if the original pressure to introduce them has ceased (D'Aummno, Succi, & Alexander, 2000). However, the extent to which Apollo's CSR agenda will remain under their new owners remains to be seen.

The firm's efforts to anticipate sustainability standards and create new ones within the parent company also represent an organizational strategy to translate these standards locally (Sweden) (what Oliver (1991) refers to as balancing and pacifying the expectations of multiple constituents) by introducing measures, such as the animals' rights clause, that are perceived as relevant by the local market, but which may then be regarded as appropriate by the wider organization. Finally, partnering with NGOs with a good reputation such as SOS Children's Villages responds to a manipulative strategy whereby the firm intents to co-opt the NGO (Oliver, 1991), importing this influential constituent and thereby gaining social legitimacy; while the NGO also tries to influence and manage the firm's social responsibility agenda and gain necessary economic resources for their operations. This relationship may also offer insights as to how issues and mechanisms related to inclusivity may arise in company CSR agendas.

Organizational learning: collaborative platforms, compromise and sense-making

The creation of collaborative platforms can be interpreted in different ways. Partnership is a classical strategy to influence institutional constituents: manage crisis and reputation (Prakash & Potoski, 2007), negotiate with NGOs and governments, anticipate future regulation and influence public opinion. Yet, there is also an interesting aspect of organizational learning attached to these collaborations. These platforms turn into spaces for external dialogue and the scanning of best practices. Since Apollo is one of the largest and more visible firms in Sweden, they help define social responsibility and are a role model (Dashwood, 2014). Such firms, therefore, potentially contribute to creation and dissemination of norms, standards and rules about how a more inclusive tourism could be performed by mass tourism corporations.

Internally, debate around issues of sustainability also generates opportunities for 'sense-making' (Weick, 1995), finding a compromise between the institutional pressures and the internal practices within the firm. Apollo, by including a new clause into Kuoni's suppliers' code of conduct or modifying some of the Travelife's standards, tried to make sense and contextualize these general standards, coming from a top-down CSR policy, into Swedish society. Similarly, the creation within Kuoni of the inner CSR circles can be interpreted in terms of a strategy to enrol both external and internal actors (NGOs, governmental organizations, subsidiaries, employees, trade unions and different departments) into the sustainability work of the firm. In a context of scarce resources characteristic of the tour operator sector, internal and external collaborative strategies seem to be crucial both to convince or 'influence' (Oliver, 1991) external and internal actors of the criticality of CSR work and to gain the necessary resources and legitimacy to act. However, these collaborative networks, as often occurs with sustainability work, perform multiple roles: they can be used by NGOs and others to introduce changes in industry operations to facilitate sustainable tourism and they can also be a platform to define new norms and standards to be followed by others; but they can also be used by the industry to gain legitimacy and manage brand risk more effectively.

Operating in complex organizational fields, balancing interests
Tour operators operate in complex institutional environments, made of a multitude of constituents (parent corporations, generating markets, destination authorities, employees and NGOs) in changing, sometimes volatile, contexts with high levels of uncertainty. Apollo turned into a definer of social responsibility in tourism in Sweden. Its sustainability work reflects internal negotiations with the parent company to shape the CSR agenda and adapt it, although sometimes superficially, to the local context. It reflects how Apollo had to balance (Oliver, 1991) the interests, values and practices both in the society where its operations are embedded as a generating market, and the parent company's demands. It also shows how societal values and expectations travel from the customers to the MNC headquarters via national firms.

Yet, local voices from the destinations appear underrepresented in the internal processes for defining the CSR agenda leading towards staged inclusivity rather than fully inclusive practices, as often is the case in the planning process of certification systems (Haaland & Aas, 2010). In practice, their relative exclusion from the CSR organization charter means that there are no institutional elements for destination actors to shape a tour operator's agenda outside of the immediate local tourism industry suppliers and NGOs. Hence, other than coercive forces stemming from (often weak) regulations and laws as well as observing initiatives by destination partners, there is no formal mechanism for the flow of ideas from local actors back to Apollo. Thus, despite various sustainability measures taken by Kuoni and Apollo, these large tour operators remain far off from practicing fully inclusive tourism, since marginalized groups engaged in the production of services, as shown by the Dubai scandal, are excluded from the CSR agenda making. This latter aspect reinforces that the gap between the MNC headquarters and their shareholders and the destinations and the suppliers' employees is large since the interests of local production actors are not represented in the definition of rules that are centrally defined but locally implemented (Medina, 2005).

Certain issues are also more significant or salient than others (Bansal & Roth, 2000) for different organizational constituents. For example, as a result of the work of NGOs and government agencies, sexual and child abuse are salient issues in Swedish society, while issues relative to labour conditions, as in the case of Dubai, are not so controversial. In other words, the issues that become integrated with notions of inclusivity on CSR agendas depend on what is significant for constituents. In their specific spatial and institutional context and from the operator's perspective, the most significant constituent is the consumer.

A positive interpretation could be that not all salient issues can turn salient at once. As noted in the garment and footwear industry (Egels-Zandén, 2014), issues of child and forced labour (considered in Western societies as unacceptable) have been the first ones to be complied with. However, perhaps more realistically is the need to recognize that corporations usually interpret or argue that they have a legal responsibility to maximize returns to shareholders (Bakan, 2005; Stout, 2013), otherwise referred to as shareholder value exclusivity or primacy. While this approach does not preclude the adoption of more inclusive approaches to tourism, it does make it more difficult if such measures are not perceived as contributing towards a business bottom line. This is especially problematic for marginalized groups with tour operators who have the capacity to shift capacity between destinations when their activities are not generating sufficient return on investment or when they are subject to pressures that will affect returns in the future.

Conclusions

MNCs and daughter firms play a major role in sustainability work, as was the case of Apollo after their acquisition by Kuoni, including inclusive tourism which can be regarded as a significant element of the social and equity dimensions of sustainability. Although Apollo may be regarded as 'inclusive tourism light', it should be noted that in international terms their adoption of standards, compacts and codes with respect to human rights, children's rights and responsible business actions put them at the forefront of what many tourism corporations actually do with respect to inclusivity.

Notions of inclusive tourism are usually framed as part of CSR strategies and activities. This case study, therefore, sheds significant light on the processes by which inclusive tourism issues may become part of the CSR and sustainability agenda of large transnational tourism businesses. Critically, this research also suggests that the incorporation of inclusive tourism concerns within the CSR agenda-setting process is primarily a response to customer concerns, the activities of NGOs, or because of negative publicity. Regardless, these may affect brand reputation and consumer behaviour.

As the case illustrates, despite top-down coercive and normative pressures affecting tour operators within large international businesses, sub-units such as Apollo are not passive receivers of these pressures. Instead, issues of agency, negotiation and institutional entrepreneurship (Hardy & Maguire, 2008) have to be taken into consideration (Oliver, 1991; Suddaby, 2010), especially when flexible CSR and sustainability frameworks operate, and the agenda and organizational field is being shaped under structuration. In this vein, this paper calls attention towards the opportunities that daughter organizations within multinational corporations and their constituents have in shaping institutional arrangements through internal collaborative platforms and bringing concerns of inclusivity into the multinational CSR policy. This may be particularly significant in the absence of strong CSR regulatory frameworks in destinations. Yet, importantly, and not sufficiently recognized in the tourism literature, the complex set of transnational corporate and sub-contractual arrangements that typify large tour operators, provide substantial difficulties in achieving inclusivity given that the operational supply chain may mean contract businesses are several times removed from head office decision-making. In such situations, it is much easier for tour operators to engage with NGOs and governmental stakeholders rather than the actual communities that their customers visit. To gain further inclusivity. otherwise marginalized groups, therefore, need effective stakeholder representation so as to gain a 'voice' in the set of constituent relationships of large tourism operators. Furthermore, as possibly the case for some Apollo customers, concerns over animal rights may actually be more important than labour rights in a foreign destination. Nevertheless, suppliers' decoupling of codes of conduct from labour conditions and environmental footprints would pose a huge brand risk for tour operators given that they operate with very low profit margins, and compete in complex and price sensitive markets. A requirement for regular monitoring and increased surveillance (Lund-Thomsen & Nadvi, 2011), and the unification of disparate certification and codes of conducts are some actions that might help contribute to re-coupling sustainability policies, including inclusive tourism concerns, with tour operators and supplier practices (Egels-Zandén, 2014).

This paper highlights how sustainability policies and standards, can be loosely coupled, or decoupled, from internal practices, and have the potential to trigger further engagement with CSR (Vilanova, Lozano, & Arenas, 2009), and, therefore, potentially some aspects of inclusive tourism, by stimulating both intra- and inter-firm learning through collaborative processes among corporate competitors. These collaborative platforms are used to exchange and diffuse industry practices, and may also anticipate potential future normative pressures towards aspects of inclusive tourism through legislation, i.e. changes to corporate CSR law, or management of brand risks, i.e. breaches of human rights. Furthermore, in a context of scarce resources, internal and external collaborative arrangements serve to enrol, co-opt and influence both internal (employees, management boards, subsidiaries and different departments), and external stakeholders to access necessary knowledge, resources and legitimacy. The gaining of access to such arrangements by marginalized groups, for example via NGO activities, would greatly increase the likelihood of the adoption of inclusive tourism measures. Similarly, more collaborative relationships between tour operators and their suppliers could also potentially contribute to couple tighter sustainability policies and suppliers' practices (Egels-Zandén, 2014; Locke, Kochan, Romis, & Qin, 2007), for example by working together in the local translation of global standards and their application (Haaland & Aas, 2010).

Yet, none of these efforts can lead to profound changes in the sustainability practices of the mass tourism industry, including inclusive tourism, if the field remains underinstitutionalized. Previous research has shown how sustainability standards compliance is improved in countries with strong labour regulation (Locke et al., 2007; Toffel, Short, & Ouellet, 2015). Powerful players in the industry, such as large tour operators, have the ability to enable greater sustainability and more inclusive forms of tourism. But if more coercive institutional pressures, in the form of laws, regulations and incentives, are not enacted to accelerate this process, it risks perpetuating a limited adoption of inclusive practices in the mass tourism industry.

Disclosure statement

No potential conflict of interest was reported by the authors.

References

Adu-Ampong, E. A. (2017). Divided we stand: Institutional collaboration in tourism planning and development in the central region of Ghana. *Current Issues in Tourism, 20*, 295–314.
Alegre, J., & Sard, M. (2015). When demand drops and prices rise. Tourist packages in the Balearic Islands during the economic crisis. *Tourism Management, 46*, 375–385.
Apollo (2016a). Financial information. Retrieved October 28, 2016, from http://www.apollo.se/om-apollo/om-foretaget/finansiell-information
Apollo (2016b). En bättre resa [A better travelling]. Retrieved October 29, 2016, from http://www.apollo.se/om-apollo/en-battre-resa
Bakan, J. (2005). *The corporation; the pathological pursuit of profit and power*. London: Constable and Robinson.
Bansal, P., & Roth, K. (2000). Why companies go green: A model of ecological responsiveness. *Academy of Management Journal, 43*(4), 717–736.
Bartley, T., & Zhang, L. (2012). *Opening the 'black box': Transnational private certification of labor standards in China* (RCCPB Working Paper No. 18). Bloomington, IN: Research Center for Chinese Politics and Business, Indiana University.
Bricker, K., & Black, R. (2016). Framework for understanding sustainability in the context of tourism operators. In S. McCool & K. Bosak (Eds.), *Reframing sustainable tourism* (pp. 81–99). Dordrecht: Springer.
Bromley, P., & Powell, W. W. (2012). From smoke and mirrors to walking the talk: Decoupling in the contemporary world. *The Academy of Management Annals, 6*, 483–530.
Bruni, A., Cassia, F., & Magno, F. (2017). Marketing performance measurement in hotels, travel agencies and tour operators: A study of current practices. *Current Issues in Tourism, 20*(4), 339–345.
Brunsson, N. & Jacobsson, B. (2000). *A world of standards*. Oxford: Oxford University Press.
Budeanu, A. (2007). *Facilitating transitions to sustainable tourism. The role of the tour operator*. Lund: International Institute for Industrial Environmental Economics, Lund University.
Budeanu, A. (2009). Environmental supply chain management in tourism: The case of large tour operators. *Journal of Cleaner Production, 17*(16), 1385–1392.
Cordano, M., & Frieze, I. H. (2000). Pollution reduction preferences of US environmental managers: Applying Ajzen's theory of planned behaviour. *Academy of Management Journal, 43*, 627–641.
Cvelbar, L. K., Dwyer, L., Koman, M., & Mihalič, T. (2016). Drivers of destination competitiveness in tourism a global investigation. *Journal of Travel Research, 55*, 1041–1050.
D'Aummno, T., Succi, M., & Alexander, J. A. (2000). The role of institutional and market forces in divergent organizational change. *Administrative Science Quarterly, 45*, 679–703.

Dashwood, H. S. (2012). CSR norms and organizational learning in the mining sector. *Corporate Governance, 12*(1), 118–138.

Dashwood, H. S. (2014). Sustainable development and industry self-regulation: Developments in the global mining sector. *Business & Society, 53*(4), 551–582.

de Grosbois, D. (2016). Corporate social responsibility reporting in the cruise tourism industry: A performance evaluation using a new institutional theory based model. *Journal of Sustainable Tourism, 24*(2), 245–269.

de Sausmarez, N. (2013). Challenges to Kenyan tourism since 2008: Crisis management from the Kenyan tour operator perspective. *Current Issues in Tourism, 16*, 792–809.

Delmas, M. A., & Toffel, W. M. (2008). Organizational responses to environmental demands: Opening the black box. *Strategic Management Journal, 29*, 1027–1055.

Dieke, P. U. (2013). Tourism in sub-Saharan Africa: Production–consumption nexus. *Current Issues in Tourism, 16*, 623–626.

Egels-Zandén, N. (2014). Revisiting supplier compliance with MNC Codes of Conduct: Recoupling policy and practice at Chinese toy suppliers. *Journal of Business Ethics, 119*, 59–75

Egri, C., & Herman, S. (2000). Leadership in the North American environmental sector: Values, leadership styles and contexts of environmental leaders and their organizations. *Academy of Management Journal, 43*, 44–63.

Erskine, L. M., & Meyer, D. (2012). Influenced and influential: The role of tour operators and development organisations in tourism and poverty reduction in Ecuador. *Journal of Sustainable Tourism, 20*(3), 339–357.

Fair Trade Center & Swed Watch (2008). *En exkluderande resa. En granskning av turismens effecter I Thailand och Brasilien* [An exclusive travel. An evaluation of the tourism's effects in Thailand and Brazil] (SwedWatch Report 24). Retrieved from http://www.fairtradecenter.se/sites/default/files/FTC%20och%20SW%20rapport%20om%20turism%20081029.pdf

Fair Traveller (2015). *Travelife's broken promises to hotel workers. A study of labour rights at hotels in Turkey contracted by Apollo (Kuoni), Fritidsresor (TUI) and Ving (Thomas Cook)*. Retrieved from http://www.schystresande.se/schyst-resandes-material

Flyvbjerg, B. (2001). *Making social science matter: Why social inquiry fails and how it can succeed again*. Cambridge: Cambridge University Press.

Gössling, S., Hall, C. M., & Scott, D. (2015). *Tourism and water*. Bristol: Channel View.

Haaland, H., & Aas, Ø. (2010). Eco-tourism certification - Does it make a difference? A comparison of systems from Australia, Costa Rica and Sweden. *Scandinavian Journal of Hospitality and Tourism. Journal of Sustainable Tourism, 10*(3), 375–385.

Hall, C. M. (2008). *Tourism planning*. Harlow: Pearson.

Hall, C. M., Dayal, N., Majstorović, D., Mills, H., Paul-Andrews, L., Wallace, C., & Truong, V. D. (2016). Accommodation consumers and providers' attitudes, behaviours and practices for sustainability: A systematic review. *Sustainability, 8*(7), 625.

Hall, C. M., & Gössling, S. (Eds.). (2016). *Food tourism and regional development: Networks, products and trajectories*, Abingdon: Routledge.

Hall, C. M., Gössling S., & Scott, D. (Eds.) (2015). *The Routledge handbook of tourism and sustainability*. Abingdon: Routledge.

Hall, D. R., & Brown, F. (2006). *Tourism and welfare: Ethics, responsibility and sustained well-being*. Wallingford: CABI.

Hendry, J. (2006). Taking aim at business: What factors lead environmental non-governmental organizations to target particular firms?. *Business and Society, 45*, 47–85.

Hardy, C., & Maguire, S. (2008). Institutional entrepreneurship. In R., Greenwood, C., Oliver, R. Suddaby, & K. Sahlin-Andersson (Eds.), *The SAGE handbook of organizational institutionalism* (pp. 198–217). Thousand Oaks, CA: Sage.

Hoffman, A. J. (2001). Linking organizational and field-level analyses – The diffusion of corporate environmental practice. *Organization and Environment, 14*, 133–156.

Jamali, D. (2010). MNCs and international accountability standards through an institutional lens: Evidence of symbolic conformity or decoupling. *Journal of Business Ethics, 95*, 617–640.

Kuoni (2014). *The Kuoni Travel holding Ltd. corporate responsibility charter*. Kuoni Travel Holding Ltd.
Kuoni (2016). *Corporate social responsibility at Kuoni*. Retrieved October 29, 2016, from http://cr.kuoni.com/corp-responsibility/sustainability-at-kuoni/organisation
Locke, R., Kochan, T., Romis, M., & Qin, F. (2007). Beyond corporate codes of conduct: Work organization and labour standards at Nike's suppliers. *International Labour Review, 146*(1–2), 21–40.
Lund-Thomsen, P., & Nadvi, K. (2011). Clusters, chains and compliance: Corporate social responsibility and governance in football manufacturing in South Asia. *Journal of Business Ethics, 93*, 201–222.
Medina, L. K. (2005). Ecotourism and certification: Confronting the principles and pragmatics of socially responsible tourism. *Journal of Sustainable Tourism, 13*, 281–295
Meyer, J. W., & Rowan, B. (1977). Institutionalized organization: Formal structure as myth and ceremony. *American Journal of Sociology, 83*, 340–363.
Oliver, C. (1991). Strategic responses to institutional processes, *The Academy of Management Review, 16*(1), 145–179.
Prakash, A. (2000). Responsible care: An assessment. *Business and Society, 39*, 183–209.
Prakash, A., & Potoski, M. (2007). Collective action through voluntary environmental programs: A club theory perspective. *Policy Studies Journal, 35*, 773–792.
Saarinen, J., Rogerson, C. M., & Hall, C. M. (2017). Geographies of tourism development and planning. *Tourism Geographies, 19*(3), 307–317
Scheyvens, R., & Biddulph, R. (2017). Inclusive tourism development, *Tourism Geographies*. doi:10.1080/14616688.2017.1381985
Schwartz, K., Tapper, R., & Font, X. (2008). A sustainable supply chain management framework for tour operators, *Journal of Sustainable Tourism, 16*(3), 298–314.
Schyst Resande. (2008). *Kartläggning av Sveriges Researrangörer* [Mapping Swedish tour operators]. Stockholm: Schyst Resande.
Scott, R. W. (2008). *Institutions and organizations: Ideas and interests*. Thousand Oaks, CA: Sage.
Sharma, S. (2000). Managerial interpretations and organizational context as predictors of corporate choice of environmental strategy. *Academy of Management Journal, 43*, 681–697.
Shyst Resande. (2015). Travelifes broken promises to hotel workers. A study of labour rights at hotels in Turkey contracted by Apollo (Kuoni), Fritidsresor (TUI) and Ving (Thomas Cook). Retrieved from http://www.schystresande.se/schyst-resandes-material
Stout, L. A. (2013). The toxic side effects of shareholder primacy. *University of Pennsylvania Law Review, 161*(7), 2003–2023.
Strand, R., Freeman, R. E., & Hockerts, K. (2015). Corporate social responsibility and sustainability in Scandinavia: An overview. *Journal of Business Ethics, 127*, 1–15.
Suddaby, R. (2010). Challenges for institutional theory, *Journal of Management Inquiry, 19*(1), 14–20.
Swedish Radio. (2015a, October 13). A. 'Vi har brustit' [We have failed]. Retrieved from http://sverigesradio.se/sida/artikel.aspx?programid=83&artikel=6277270
Swedish Radio. (2015b, October 13). B 'Kan inte byta job eftersom laggen i Dubai inte tillåter det' [I can't change job since law in Dubai does not allow it]. Retrieved from http://sverigesradio.se/sida/artikel.aspx?programid=83&artikel=6277144
SwedWatch and Fair Action (2015). *Shattered dreams. Migrant workers and rights violations in the Dubai tourism sector* (Report No. 75). Stockholm: SwedWatch. Retrieved from http://www.swedwatch.org/sites/default/files/tmp/75_dubai_lowres_new.pdf
Tepelus, C. (2005). Aiming for sustainability in the tour operating business. *Journal of Cleaner Production, 13*, 99–107.
Toffel, M. W., Short, J. L., & Ouellet, M. (2015). Codes in context: How states, markets, and civil society shape adherence to global labor standards. *Regulation & Governance, 9*(3), 205–223.
Tveteraas, S., Asche, F., & Lien, K. (2014). European tour operators' market power when renting hotel rooms in Northern Norway. *Tourism Economics, 20*(3), 579–594.
Van Huijstee, M., & Glasbergen, P. (2010). NGOs moving business: An analysis of contrasting strategies. *Business & Society, 49*(4), 591–618.
Van Wijk, J., Van der Duim, R., Lamers, M., & Sumba, D. (2015). The emergence of institutional innovations in tourism: The evolution of the African Wildlife Foundation's tourism conservation enterprises. *Journal of Sustainable Tourism, 23*(1), 104–125.

Vilanova, M., Lozano, J. M., & Arenas, D. (2009). Exploring the nature of the relationship between CSR and competitiveness. *Journal of Business Ethics, 87*(1), 57–69.

Weick, K. E. (1995). *Sensemaking in organizations*. London: Sage.

Zapata, M. J., & Hall, C. M. (2012). Public–private collaboration in the tourism sector: Balancing legitimacy and effectiveness in local tourism partnerships. The Spanish case. *Journal of Policy Research in Tourism, Leisure and Events, 4*(1), 61–83.

Tourism and Poverty Reduction: Issues for Small Island States

REGINA SCHEYVENS & JANET H. MOMSEN

ABSTRACT *The notion that tourism can contribute significantly to poverty reduction strategies is attracting great interest from multilateral institutions, tourism bodies, donors and other organizations around the globe. Tourism is certainly a major contributor to economic development in many small island developing states (SIDS) and often it is the only industry in these countries to consistently demonstrate growth in recent years. However, the growth of tourism in SIDS is by no means synonymous with poverty reduction, in fact, in some cases it entrenches existing inequalities. If tourism is to contribute significantly to the reduction of poverty in SIDS, a broad approach that values social sustainability as well as the more popular environmental sustainability and economic growth will be necessary. In addition, governments need to establish an effective policy environment and play a stronger regulatory role if sustainable, equity-enhancing tourism is to emerge. The paper suggests effective ways in which national planning can both encourage private sector actors to support poverty reduction and facilitate the involvement of wider sectors of society in tourism development. It is not sufficient for governments to simply promote tourism development in line with neoliberal growth-orientated policies.*

Introduction

Tourism is the world's largest industry and has been an integral component of economic development strategies in developing nations for over half a century: 'The industry's potential to generate foreign exchange earnings, attract international investment, increase tax revenues and create new jobs has served as an incentive for developing countries to promote tourism as an engine for macro-economic growth' (Torres and Momsen 2004: 294–5). In many small island developing states (SIDS), tourism is the only sector to have seen growth over recent years as the real value of traditional primary export products has been declining or they are losing their preferential markets, as for example among the banana and sugar exporters of the Caribbean.

Recent World Bank figures show that of the ten most tourism-dependent countries in terms of tourism receipts as a percentage of GDP, nine are SIDS, with six in the Caribbean, two in the Indian Ocean, plus the island state of São Tomé and Principe off West Africa. In terms of the top ten performers measured by International Tourism Receipts (ITR) per capita in 2002, only Croatia is not a SIDS. All are lower or upper middle income countries. The island city-state of Singapore earns more from tourism than most SIDS but is not dependent on these earnings because of its broad-based economic structure (Ashe 2005: 3). These figures appear to indicate that those SIDS with a high economic dependency on tourism are among the richest of such states (McElroy 2006). Thus, it has been asserted that 'tourism is an essential component for both economic development and poverty reduction in SIDS' (Ashe 2005: 5). However, this macro-level analysis does not consider the distribution of the benefits of tourism within national populations, which is the focus in this paper.

Despite tourism's potential to generate wealth, many SIDS face enormous challenges in overcoming poverty and inequality often because of their colonial heritage, ethnic diversity, postcolonial economic dominance of foreign tourism multinational corporations, and low levels of education. Tourism can be seen as an exploitative form of neocolonialism (Britton 1982; Brohman 1996) but, with the inexorable growth of transnationalism and globalization, it appears that nothing can deter the spread of tourism and its penetration into the world's poorest nations. Hence, critics argue that tourism can perpetuate unequal relations of dependency as well as encourage uneven and inequitable socio-economic and spatial development (Milne 1997). As Oppermann (1993) warned, however, such dependency-style critiques of tourism in small island states suffer from a major shortcoming in that they fail to identify effective strategies whereby these states could work to secure greater benefits from tourism. Thus, it would seem judicious that the notion of 'pro-poor tourism' (PPT), an approach which aims to ensure that tourism delivers more net benefits to the poor, should be applied to those island states that are currently heavily reliant on tourism revenues. This approach certainly encompasses much that is of merit. Examples are utilized from the Caribbean, the Pacific and the Indian Ocean to demonstrate that despite the hopeful rhetoric of PPT, there are significant problems to be faced to ensure that tourism benefits a wide range of people in these island groups.

This article begins by documenting the growth of interest in PPT and what it might mean for SIDS, before outlining key issues concerning the sustainability of tourism in SIDS. To date, tourism scholars have been concerned primarily with environmental and economic sustainability, yet it is issues of social sustainability that must also be prioritized if tourism is to make a serious contribution to poverty reduction in

SIDS. The article discusses why island governments should put in place an appropriate policy and regulatory framework to support PPT, and attention is drawn to a number of the strengths of SIDS, which advocates of PPT may draw upon when devising strategies to ensure that tourism becomes more 'pro-poor' in its application. In conclusion, approaches to support poverty reduction through tourism in SIDS are recommended.

The Pro-Poor Tourism Approach

Views on the relationship between poverty and tourism have varied widely over the past half-century. In the 1950s and 1960s tourism was identified as a modernization strategy that could help newly-independent Third World countries earn foreign exchange (de Kadt 1979). By the 1970s and through the 1980s many social scientists were arguing that poor countries are typically excluded from or disadvantaged by what tourism can offer (Britton 1983; Scheyvens 2007). There has now been a concerted push towards a reversal of this thinking in the 1990s, coinciding with the development industry's global focus on poverty alleviation, as epitomized by the Millennium Development Goals. The poverty alleviation thrust is founded on a consensus among donors that globalization offers a path out of poverty (Storey *et al.* 2005) and tourism is one of the main industries that globalization can bring to SIDS. It is within this context that 'tourism' and 'poverty alleviation' are being linked increasingly.

The term 'pro-poor tourism' was coined in 1999 and, in the short period since then, it has been adopted rapidly by a wide range of agencies in the development industry, from bilateral donors to multilateral institutions and international non-governmental organizations (NGOs). PPT is an enticing concept as it promises that tourism can play a significant role in reducing poverty, indeed it is defined as 'tourism that generates net benefits for the poor' (Ashley and Roe 2002: 62). PPT emerged out of UK-sponsored research on sustainable livelihoods conducted in southern Africa, as well as a comparative study of tourism, conservation and sustainability issues in protected areas of Indonesia, India and Zimbabwe (see, for example, Ashley and Roe 1998; Goodwin 1998; Deloitte and Touche 1999). Much of this work has been conducted through the Pro Poor Tourism Partnership which involves the collaboration of Harold Goodwin (International Centre for Responsible Tourism), Dilys Roe (International Institute for Environment and Development) and Caroline Ashley (Overseas Development Institute) (see www.propoortourism.org.uk). Recently, the PPT Partnership has focused some research on SIDS, specifically the Dominican Republic, although ecotourism in St Lucia had been studied earlier (Ashley *et al.* 2005).

Interest in tourism as a mechanism for poverty reduction has since been taken up by a wide range of interest groups. A 1999 meeting of the UN Commission on Sustainable Development urged governments to 'maximise the potential of tourism for eradicating poverty by developing appropriate strategies in cooperation with all major groups, indigenous and local communities' (IIED 2001: 41). Meanwhile, the World Tourism Organization initiated the ST~EP Project: 'Sustainable Tourism – Eliminating Poverty' (see http://www.unwto.org/step/index.php; Sofield *et al.* 2004). The UK Tour Operators have produced a Preferred Code for their overseas suppliers which includes community partnerships and linkages (www.propoortourism.org.uk/caribbean/Caribbean_Background.pdf accessed 29/12/05). Elsewhere donors (such as the Dutch bilateral aid agency, SNV) multilateral organizations (e.g. the Asian Development Bank, World Bank and World Trade Organization), and tourism organizations (e.g. the Pacific and Asia Travel Association) have expressed support for strategies whereby tourism can lead to poverty reduction (Ashe 2005; Christie 2002; PPT Partnership 2005). While PPT has generated much interest, few geographers have incorporated this approach into their research (Torres and Momsen 2004).

The PPT Partnership stresses that PPT is not a product or a niche sector of tourism but is an *approach* to tourism that seeks to bring a wide range of benefits to the poor, including social, environmental and cultural benefits in addition to economic benefits. PPT does not aim to expand the size of the sector, but to 'unlock opportunities for the poor within tourism, at all levels and scales of operation' (Ashley *et al.* 2001: 13). Thus, it extends beyond community-based tourism where, for example, villagers might be encouraged to establish cultural tourism homestay or craft ventures, to an approach suggesting that a wide range of stakeholders, from local entrepreneurs to government officials, resort managers and international tour companies, will need to make concerted efforts if poverty reduction is to occur. The three main strategies of PPT focus on increasing economic and non-cash livelihood benefits, improving policy and reducing negative impacts such as cultural intrusion, or lost access to land or coastal areas (IIED 2001). Specific tactics include enhancing backward and forward linkages, provision of training, marketing, credit and technical support for local entrepreneurs, development of collective community income through tourism-based activities, and improving access to services and infrastructure (Momsen 2003). The policy-orientated strategies can create a more supportive planning framework, increase participation by the poor in decision making and facilitate PPT partnerships with the private sector (IIED 2001).

Proponents of PPT argue that there is significant potential to deliver more benefits from tourism to the poor, as tourism is a significant or growing economic sector in most developing countries with high levels of poverty. At present, tourism receipts from the 49 least developed countries add up to less than 0.5 percent of the world total, so there is presumably capacity for further growth (UNCTAD 2004). Furthermore, UNCTAD (1998) referred to tourism as the 'only major sector in international trade in services in which developing countries have consistently had surpluses'. The tourism industry already employs over 200 million people worldwide, and there has been a 9.5 percent annual growth in arrivals to developing countries since 1990, compared to 4.6 percent world-wide (IIED 2001). It is argued that tourism as a sector 'fits' nicely with pro-poor growth because 'it can be labour-intensive, inclusive of women and the informal sector; based on natural and cultural assets of the poor; and suitable for poor rural areas with few other growth options' (Ashley and Roe 2002: 61).

For 50 of the world's poorest countries, tourism is one of the top three contributors to economic development (World Tourism Organization 2000, cited in Sofield 2003: 350). In fact, tourism enabled the Maldives to move out of the group of the world's 49 least developed countries just six days before they were hit by the tsunami of 26 December 2004. Connell (1993: 128) asserted that the handful of SIDS for whom tourism is not an important economic sector are among the poorest island states in the world.

The rhetoric and statistics supporting the notion of poverty reduction through tourism are convincing. The question remains, however, as to how this might be operationalized and made meaningful particularly, from the perspective of this article, in the context of small island states.

Tourism in Small Island Developing States

Interest in the phenomenon of tourism in SIDS is not new. According to Wilkinson's calculations some 18 years ago, there were over six hundred articles either directly or indirectly addressing concerns of tourism in island microstates (Wilkinson 1988, cited in Butler 1993: 73; Duval and Wilkinson 2004). This interest has not waned over time. Common themes are the heavy dependence of many SIDS on the tourism sector, and concerns about the environmental sustainability of tourism development.

Simultaneously a number of major meetings pertaining to the well-being of SIDS has been held around the globe. From the Earth Summit in Rio (1992), to the United Nations Global Conference on the Sustainable Development of Small Island Developing States in Barbados (1994), the International Conference on Sustainable Tourism in Small Island Developing States and Other Islands in Spain (1998), and the World Summit on Sustainable Development in Johannesburg (2002), as well as at a number of regional meetings, small islands have been identified as being particularly fragile in both an economic and environmental sense. While some papers emerging from these meetings identify sustainability of the tourism industry as a major concern, in more recent meetings it is noticeable that the interests of the countries themselves, rather than just growth of an industry, have been prioritized. Below are summarized some key points from the literature on tourism in SIDS, together with a demonstration of why more attention needs to be paid to issues of social sustainability.

Heavy Dependence on the Tourism Sector

Tourism is of vital importance to the economies of many small island states. Around 65 percent of the small island tourism market is captured by Caribbean islands, followed by Europe (16%), East Asia and the Pacific (11%), Africa (5%) and South Asia (3%) (WTO 2002: 14). Tourism is the single largest foreign exchange earner in over half the countries in the Caribbean (Croes 2006), where it was expected to generate $US45.5 billion in 2005 and over two million jobs, which constitute 15.1 percent of total employment. In 2005 tourism in the Caribbean grew by 5 percent, with Cuba showing a gain of 13 percent, despite the devastating hurricanes experienced. In Oceania tourism grew by 4 percent (Travel Wire News 2006). Demand for tourism in the Caribbean region is expected to grow by 3.4 percent per annum between 2006 and 2015 and, in Oceania, growth is expected to be even higher, at around 5 percent per annum for this same period (Ashe 2005).

These small islands rely for the majority of their earnings on tourists from post-industrial and industrializing countries around the world whose fascination with island holidays fuels a multimillion dollar industry (King 1993; Baum 1997). Isolation is often considered a disbenefit to those trading products around the globe, but – for tourism – it may be a benefit in that it tends to make the destination more attractive, exotic and enticing, especially in the case of small islands. According to Gartázar and Marin (1999, cited in d'Hauteserre 2003: 49), 'islands are the second most important holiday destination after the category of historic cities'. This huge tourism demand must be understood in terms of the small land size and populations of many small island states, which intensifies the impacts that tourism may have: '...tourism is ...more pervasive in its impact on the small island community than it is on larger mainland resort destinations' (MacNaulty 2002: 38). The WTO (2002: 17) noted that 24 SIDS receive more tourists per year than their population, with the British Virgin Islands and Cayman Islands exhibiting a particularly extreme case: foreign tourists numbers here are ten times those of local residents.

For many SIDS the significance of tourism revenues is of increasing importance due to declines in other parts of their economies. Colonial and post-colonial governments in SIDS have typically pursued export agriculture as the major economic development sector yet, with continuing reduction in the real value of commodity exports, many island states are being forced to look elsewhere to earn foreign exchange. For example, comparing the value of crops such as coconuts, bananas, cocoa and coffee with tourism receipts for South Pacific countries over a twenty-year period, it has been found that '*in every case* the value of these primary products in real terms has declined and the only sector to demonstrate a continuous upward trend has been tourism' (Sofield *et al.* 2004: 25–6). Other authors also identified tourism as being the industry offering greatest potential to SIDS (Kakazu 1994; Chand 2003; Ashe 2005). One reason that tourism is said to offer great potential for small islands is that foreign exchange comes to the producer rather than having to incur the high transportation costs that make many products of small islands non-competitive on the world market.

However, there are concerns that tourism as a form of globalization does not necessarily provide answers to the development woes of impoverished nations, and that the heavy dependence on tourism revenues leads to vulnerability and associated problems.

Economic and Environmental Vulnerabilities

SIDS are seen as economically vulnerable for a number of reasons. They have small economies which leads to diseconomies of scale, their resources are limited, their economic base is generally quite narrow (perhaps relying on a few primary product exports and tourism) and they are isolated from major markets, have small populations and thus a small domestic market (Britton 1983; Pearce 1987; Milne 1997). Furthermore, economic development within SIDS is often impeded by inadequate transportation links, lack of accessibility to remote locations, lack of appropriate skills among the local population and inadequate amounts of local capital (Harrison 2003: 7).

Such factors combine to mean that SIDS have low resistance to external shocks, including natural disasters, political upheavals and terrorism (Hoti *et al.* 2005). Commenting specifically on the Pacific Islands, Harrison (2003: 7) noted, '... tourism is seen to be crucially, even cruelly, influenced by external factors far beyond local control'. As many SIDS constitute 'long-haul' destinations, they tend to suffer significant declines during periods of international or regional terrorism (for example, 9/11 and the Bali bombings), and when there are health threats (such as SARS and bird flu) in their broader regions. Some 5,000 tourism employees were made redundant on Bali in 2002/3 as a direct result of the first Bali bombings followed by the SARS epidemic (James 2004: 13), and it is still unclear whether the industry here will ever fully recover after the second bombings in 2005. Similarly, countries often have little control over the rise or decline in their popularity as they are reliant on the whims of international tourists.

The tourism industry can also have direct negative economic impacts through its influences on other economic sectors within a country. Thus, for example, primary production may suffer as a result of land, labour and capital being invested in tourism, significantly threatening the livelihoods of some groups of people (Mowforth and Munt 2003: 273). In some islands competition for beach space has undermined the fishing industry and, in other cases, agriculture has suffered because the needs of tourism enterprises for large amounts of water have received priority over farmers' requirements for water to irrigate their crops. Competition for labour also impinges on local agriculture, especially if the high season for tourism coincides with the busy season in agriculture. Loss of agricultural labour may result in sub-optimal production levels. Strategies for development of international tourism require governments to invest in infrastructure to meet the needs of tourists, while local people often have to live without the basics (Richter 2001). Such problems are particularly acute in small coral islands, such as Barbados, dependent on limited supplies of groundwater. Tourists are thought to consume three times the amount of water per person per day that locals use, while golf courses in the tropics need constant watering.

The small economies of SIDS mean that it can be difficult to raise capital for investment in tourism locally, thus control over tourism and its benefits can end up in the hands of outsiders who do not have local or national interests at heart. Overseas companies and investors that come into a country under pro-globalization policies (e.g. tax breaks and other investment incentives) can push out small, local entrepreneurs who find they cannot compete. And, when multinational companies and international agencies loan funds for infrastructure development for tourism, they gain increasing control over the industry in the destination area (Telfer 2003: 100). The airlines that deliver the tourists to isolated islands are also generally foreign owned so that tourist travel expenditure does not stay in the tourist destination. In the Caribbean, which has high levels of foreign ownership of hotels, up to 70 percent of tourist expenditure is repatriated (Potter 1993: 102). In addition, a significant proportion of the foreign exchange earned from tourism is needed to import goods and services required by the tourism industry so that the tourism multiplier in SIDS tends to be low (Hoti *et al.* 2005). This is particularly problematic in the case of SIDS catering for 'higher end', luxury tourists. Thus, noted Harrison (2003: 7), 'In the Pacific, the more developed the tourism industry, and the more it caters for high-spending tourists or for tourists in great numbers, the more likely it will be owned and operated by overseas interests'. Hotels and bungalows owned by local people tend to use more local products and services as they have the contacts and direct interest in doing so (Momsen 1998; Scheyvens 2005).

With the prominence accorded to environmental issues on the global stage, it is not surprising that a great deal of attention has also been devoted to environmental sustainability in SIDS (Gössling 2003). The focus here has been on issues of small, dispersed areas of land and a lack of rich natural resources, two factors directly associated with the narrow economic base of many island nations, and their often heavy dependence on aid and on international trade. Other areas of concern include the threat of sea-level rise, the location of small islands in relation to phenomena such as cyclones, hurricanes and seismic activity and, in many cases, their limited natural resource base with, for example, topsoil and fresh water being in short supply (Briguglio *et al.* 1996). It has thus been suggested that 'the environmental effects of tourism in small countries will be more pronounced and severe than that in large countries' (Liu and Jenkins 1996: 113). Tourism-based construction has been identified as a major cause of beach erosion, siltation of lagoons and reef damage (McElroy and Albuquerque 2002). In addition, the creation of Marine Protected Areas in places that are attractive to tourists can actually undermine local well-being and impoverish sectors of the population as they lose entitlements to resources important for maintaining their livelihoods (Stonich 2003). On the other hand, successful participatory planning in such areas can be beneficial to both fisherpeople and hoteliers (Pugh in press).

The Need for Greater Attention to Issues of Social Sustainability

It is clear from the discussion above that the environmental vulnerabilities and economic constraints of SIDS with relation to tourism development have been well documented. In many cases the close relationship between an intact, resilient environment and economic well-being are highlighted. In fact, to some it appears that the main goal in protecting the environment is sustainability of the tourism industry itself: 'The vulnerability that many islands have may put at risk the long-term sustainability of tourism-based economic development of the islands' (WTO 2002: 12). Of less interest, apparently, to most writers making this connection between tourism in SIDS and sustainable development, are issues of social sustainability such as inequalities between the rich and poor.

In many cases poverty levels are high in SIDS. Material poverty can be seen in terms of poor quality housing and a lack of adequate nutrition, while poverty of opportunity also exists due to a range of factors such as a lack of educational facilities, poorly developed rural infrastructure and inadequate health care facilities. Indeed, the demonstration effect of the presence of wealthy tourists may make local perceptions of relative poverty more keenly felt. In addition, social problems which are often exacerbated by poverty, including domestic violence and youth suicide, are a growing concern in many island states. This does not accord with the picture of an island paradise, which tourists pay to experience, so usually it is hidden away from them. Of interest in this article is whether, as the pro-poor tourism literature asserts, the tourism industry can contribute to reducing poverty and so contribute to a solution to some of these problems.

The neglect of social issues in much of the sustainable tourism literature led Filho (1996) to suggest that it has not kept pace with the sustainable development literature in terms of dealing with the 'social'. In *Sustainable Tourism in Islands and Small States: Issues and Policies* (Briguglio *et al.* 1996), for example, all but one chapter focus only on environmental and economic aspects of sustainability. Berno (2003) also noted that discussions concerning the sustainability of tourism rarely consider social, psychological or cultural dimensions. Neto (2003) squarely criticized the sustainable tourism literature's overemphasis on environmental issues. By failing to highlight social issues, a partial picture is presented and thus 'solutions' which may be posed are unlikely to deal adequately with various development challenges. Thus, for example, Ghosh *et al.* (2003), writing with reference to islands in the Indian Ocean, argued that ecotourism is the answer because they believe the key issue in the region is environmental sustainability. The power of elites over the means of production for tourism and the growing gap between the rich and the poor are social and political issues that are apparently not deemed worthy of attention.

Those who do draw attention to social sustainability tend to focus almost exclusively on concerns about social impacts of tourists, such as inappropriate dress or behaviour and the demonstration effect, and cross-cultural conflict or cultural erosion, rather than suggesting that overcoming poverty and reducing inequality should be goals of tourism development in SIDS. Carbone's (2005) approach is refreshing, calling for comprehensive tourism strategies that embrace issues of environmental and economic sustainability as well as social, cultural, ethical and participatory sustainability. In addition, the increasing application of political ecology perspectives to tourism studies holds promise for encouraging more in-depth social analysis (see Gössling 2003).

In some ways the Maldives epitomize the dilemmas of SIDS engaging in tourism as a means to achieve development. The government restricts tourism to uninhabited islands, and the natural environment has been protected through regulations requiring, for example, that all resorts treat their own wastes, that coastal development must not unduly disturb coastal ecology, and that indigenous vegetation may not be removed (Firaag 1996; Domroes 2001: 129–30; Ghina 2003). Presumably this is an excellent example of sustainable tourism in practice and, as such, the Maldives has been lauded by the World Tourism Organization (Lyon 2003: 15). However, tourism revenues do not benefit those who need them most. Thus, while a large percentage of GDP is made up of income from tourism (tourism accounted for 93% of GNP in 2000, making it the least developed country (LDC) most dependent on international tourism (WTO 2002, cited in Abdulsamad 2004: 12)), there are heavy leakages (Tourism Concern 2004). The resorts cater largely for higher-spending, luxury tourists, and most of the provisions on the resort islands need to be imported, as there is little arable land in the Maldives. Tourism has certainly generated employment, around 14,000 formal positions, however 6,000 of these jobs are filled by foreigners. This includes both highly skilled positions and more menial positions. In the case of the latter, there is no minimum wage or agreement on labour rights, thus Maldivians often choose to stay on their home islands rather than residing for eleven months of the year hundreds of kilometres away from their families on a resort island where they are required to work 12 hours a day, six and a half days of the week (Maldivian waiter, pers. comm.: August 2005). While generating essential revenue for the government and for a small number of the elite, tourism has exaggerated existing inequalities between Maldivians. The average annual income is approximately $US5,000, which seems good compared to other countries in the region, yet many outer islanders live on $US365 per annum and around 40 percent of the population survive on less than $US1.17 a day. While fruit and vegetables are flown in to the resort islands, non-tourist islands receive few fresh foods leading to a situation where thirty percent of children under the age of five are undernourished and one quarter of them have experienced stunted growth (Tourism Concern 2004).

One reason why issues of social sustainability are often not accorded priority is that focusing on the environment and economic development is a more politically safe path to take. Thus, for example, most tour operators, government organizations and conservation agencies would probably see the creation of a marine protected area and an associated ecolodge near a turtle nesting area as a 'good thing', worthy of support, but they may be less willing to support an initiative that seeks to challenge the control elites have over tourism enterprises, or to ensure a fairer distribution of the benefits of tourism. Similarly, hoteliers and resort owners may not be willing to support implementation of effective labour rights legislation. Instead, in order to remain competitive in relation to other sand, sea and sun destinations, pay rates and labour conditions of tourism workers may be compromised (James 2004). Essentially, it requires significant power to challenge the rights of certain groups to direct tourism development or control the benefits of tourism and, in reality, most SIDS do not have the power to bargain effectively with foreign investors in order to support more enlightened labour force policies (Richter 2001: 49).

Discussion: Strategies to Reduce Poverty Through Tourism in SIDS

If tourism is to be considered a legitimate avenue for addressing social concerns and especially reducing poverty in SIDS, specific strategies will need to be put in place. If they are to be effective, these strategies require direction from the state in terms of appropriate policies, plans and a regulatory framework, and the support of private sector and community stakeholders.

First, governments will need to play a guiding role if PPT is to offer more than simply another way of expanding tourism with benefits for the major players in this sector. Even an author such as Harrison who draws attention to the many constraints and vulnerabilities of SIDS, acknowledges that 'properly planned and managed, tourism can conserve natural resources and bring widespread benefits to local communities' (Harrison 2003: 17). Thus, contrary to Liu and Jenkins (1996: 101), who seem to suggest that there is a need for governments to take a strong role in the tourism sector only in those places that are at an early stage of development, this article argues that the government's role is important in both new and more mature small island destinations. There is a need for comprehensive involvement of governments in tourism (Wilkinson 1989). Too often governments of SIDS focus narrowly on earning more tourism revenues and increasing tourist arrivals, rather than being concerned with the impacts of tourism, socially, environmentally and economically (Harrison 2003: 17). Thus, for example, while Siddique and Ghosh (2003) suggested that the role of governments is to promote tourism, provide appropriate infrastructure, research the market and provide financial incentives for investors, it is argued here that if sustainable, equity-enhancing tourism is to emerge, governments need to play a stronger regulatory role and to develop strategies to direct benefits of tourism to the poor. As Potter (1993: 113) observed, 'In the past, states have all too often abdicated their responsibility to help the people in their efforts to help themselves'.

It should be noted, however, that in more recent times the actions of states have often been heavily influenced by the neoliberal agendas of multilateral institutions to which they are indebted and thus their decisions can conflict with those of local communities (Carbone 2005). Arguing that 'externally-oriented, growth-maximising' paths to development have resulted in increasing levels of inequality among local populations in many Eastern Caribbean states, Potter (1993: 103) went against dominant neoliberal discourse and instead asserted that 'the needs of the poor should be met in priority to externally-oriented growth imperatives' (Potter 1993: 97 – emphasis added). In this regard it is interesting that Bonaire's tourism policy clearly tries to balance the needs of tourists with the interests of local communities and protection of the environment, and in one place it states that no permits will be given for 'American style fast-food restaurants' (MacNaulty 2002: 41).

SIDS may also be influenced by their metropolitan ties. It has been suggested that the most successful tourism-driven SIDS are those that are still politically dependent (McElroy 2006). Thomas *et al.* (2006) showed that the dependent territories of Cayman and the British Virgin Islands grew faster than other Caribbean SIDS in the 1990s. Foreign investors may feel more secure in such islands because of the protection of metropolitan nations. While a lack of sovereignty may contribute to their economic success at a macro level, it could impede these SIDS from implementing policies that are directed at poverty reduction, such as some of the measures suggested below.

The onus is nevertheless on the governments of SIDS to step forward and develop appropriate policies and plans for tourism development if the needs of the poor are to receive priority. They can take practical steps to reduce poverty by ensuring that when costly infrastructural projects are undertaken to support growth in tourism, the needs of the poor are not overlooked (MacNaulty 2002; Ashe 2005). For example, if new roads or water systems are to be built, the former should provide local access to markets as well as tourist access to resorts and the latter should be connected to local houses as well as to hotels. Reducing leakages and maximizing multiplier effects should perhaps be the major goal of governments of SIDS with an important tourism sector. To do this it is thus important that they ensure that national development plans highlight linkages between tourism and other economic sectors such as agriculture, fisheries and transportation (Ashe 2005). In many cases economic opportunities for small farmers are being lost because of inadequate linkages between them, agricultural extension officers and hoteliers (see Momsen 1998; Torres and Momsen 2004). By encouraging the use of local supplies and ensuring provision of training and credit to small-scale entrepreneurs, such as producers of souvenirs, governments can assist even small businesses to make a significant contribution to the economies of SIDS (Ashley *et al.* 2005).

Milne suggests that where there are high levels of local ownership of businesses and strong economic linkages between tourism and other local industries, the benefits can be great:

> ... while tourist development in South Pacific microstates is undoubtedly influenced by broader global processes, these nations cannot simply be viewed

as victims of change. With careful management and improved levels of local participation, these nations have the potential to develop tourism in a way that offers long-term economic growth without sacrificing the cultural and environmental inheritance of future generations (Milne 1997: 283).

Private sector tourism operators have also developed strategies that support poverty reduction. This has occurred both in small-scale family ventures and large-scale resorts based on the understanding that it is both socially and politically savvy to contribute to the development of local communities. In some cases, external pressure from governments and others has spurred on such initiatives. A small but growing number of businesses contribute actively to poverty reduction by, for example, providing in-house training to people from poorer backgrounds, implementing procurement practices which prioritize locally produced goods and services, or by encouraging the philanthropy of guests and establishing a community development fund in conjunction with local actors. Thus, for example, some tour operators and NGOs are now beginning to work together to develop a 'Travelers' Philanthropy' approach, which directly links tourists and local communities through involving the tourist in the economies of communities that they visit while on holiday and they can continue to support financially (Duim *et al.* 2005). In Trinidad a local guesthouse owner has trained people to be local guides for nature walks and bird watching (Oda van der Heijden, manager of Pax Guesthouse, pers. comm., 17 December 2005), while in Samoa owners of beach *fale* (basic beach huts) make a conscious attempt to support the wider community by hiring youth groups, church groups and the like to perform at their weekly *fiafia* cultural nights (Scheyvens 2005). In Jamaica and in St Lucia, the Sandals all-inclusive resorts owned by local entrepreneur Gordon 'Butch' Stewart buy produce from local farmers, thus countering the assumption that such resorts offer few benefits to local communities. In Negril, Jamaica, Sandals operates a local elementary school, offers scholarships for local students, provides seeds and technical support for local farmers, and purchases their produce at guaranteed market-value prices (Kingsbury 2006). Sandals encourages its guests to establish off-property contacts with local people, it hires local entertainers and guides for a variety of cultural and educational programmes and provides space on its property for local craftworkers to display their wares. In addition, Sandals (Negril) incorporates local community based organizations in the corporation's decision making (Kingsbury 2006). In St Lucia, since 2002, Sandals' chefs and other food service personnel have had regular exchange visits with farmer suppliers, 75 per cent of whom are women (IICA 2006: 11). In Nevis, when the Four Seasons Resort opened in 1990 it implemented a market-led production system among farmers, which now supplies over 40 commodities to the Resort (IICA 2006). Similarly, staff of the exclusive Turtle Island Resort in Fiji have worked hard to ensure residents of nearby islands benefit from tourism development, both by providing schooling facilities and by assisting an association of backpacker tourism providers with assistance in marketing, administration, service and quality control (Harrison and Brandt 2003: 155).

Governments can also introduce initiatives that encourage private sector actors to support poverty reduction goals. Thus, for example, they can provide tax breaks to tour operators, hoteliers or other industry players who are actively working to direct more of their benefits to the poor. In some cases governments have provided 100 percent tax relief schemes for families who wish to upgrade their bed-and-breakfast style accommodation, and a 50 percent subsidy for training costs (MacNaulty 2002: 35). Other initiatives the private sector may adopt, given a supportive taxation regime, include using a share of their profits to improve community well-being by funding a new well irrigation system, or sewage treatment plant (Ashe 2005). In Barbados, external pressure from hoteliers led to the InterAmerican Institute for Agricultural Cooperation (IICA) instituting culinary festivals and training support for local farmers (Ena Harvey, pers. comm., July 2005).

Another area of concern in attempting to ensure that tourism contributes to poverty reduction is that of local participation and agency. PPT is supposed to engage a wide range of stakeholders, but the biggest challenge to this occurring in practice is often the relative lack of power of those stakeholders who are most likely to experience negative effects of tourism: local communities. Governments can, to some extent, facilitate a stronger role for communities in planning for tourism development by actively seeking out their voices on tourism planning matters and responding to their concerns through appropriate processes (Scheyvens 2002). In addition, there needs to be adequate awareness raising among the local population in tourism destination areas, both about the benefits of tourism as well as potential problems that they may need to anticipate and seek to control. Residents cannot go on to contribute to community tourism monitoring forums, planning committees or the like without such information.

Thus, as Carbone (2005: 562) argued, 'tourism planning should be based on "bottom-up globalization", which engages in distributive justice by entrusting more decision making power in local communities'. Similarly, Dann (1996: 116) called for the 'democratization of tourism', including 'resident responsive tourism'. This may require enhanced community awareness of tourism and natural resource issues, development of grassroots institutions, conflict-resolution forums led by local people, and other means to facilitate 'the institutionalization of community participation in actual tourism-related natural-resource decision making' (McElroy and de Alburquerque 2002: 26).

Such awareness raising and participation in planning by communities can seriously challenge the balance of power in areas popular with tourists. In French Polynesia, for example, residents from the island of Moorea managed to stop the development of a foreign-owned luxury resort, which had been approved by a corrupt official, who has since been sent to jail (d'Hauteserre 2003). In the Caribbean, a hotel development was stopped because of local protests, even though permission had been given by the government (Pugh in press). Also, where tourism development does go ahead, there are some very good examples of local communities exerting considerable power over this process and consequently gaining a number of benefits, as with traditional landowners living near to Mana Island resort, Fiji (Sofield 2003: Chapter 9).

Conclusions

Notions of PPT, which have emerged in the last few years, appear to suggest that there is a simple win–win scenario between tourism growth, development and reduction of poverty. This article has attempted to reflect on how meaningful the PPT concept might be when applied to the particular situation of small island states, destinations highly sought after by international tourists, but which experiences huge barriers to sustainable development. One major concern that arose from an examination of the literature on tourism in SIDS is the fact that while the environmental and economic vulnerabilities of island states that engage heavily in tourism enterprises are well recognized, there has been a certain disregard for the importance of social sustainability issues, notably, concerning poverty, inequality and social problems. If the PPT ideal is to offer any hope to SIDS, these social issues will need to be addressed directly rather than included as an add-on to strategies emphasizing a clean environment, intact natural resources and economic growth.

Empowerment of local residents to encourage greater participation in planning and decision-making regarding tourism development could help them to corner the benefits of tourism, however, governments also need to play a strong role if tourism is to become more pro-poor. It may be vital, for example, for states to intervene to provide appropriate legislation (e.g. to protect local rights to land and to encourage joint venture arrangements, as well as ensuring that adequate environmental standards are adhered to) and support in the way of information, credit and training, and incentives to the private sector. It is fitting that the size of SIDS encourages widespread knowledge of planned tourism projects, as this can help the public to keep investors and the government in check.

Clearly, therefore, tourism in SIDS need not lead to wide-ranging negative impacts. Rather, it can lead to genuine improvements in the spread of benefits to the poor, particularly if governments in SIDS are willing to direct tourism development in ways that reflect both local and national interests.

References

Abdulsamad, A. (2004) Maldives, *Just Change*, Issue 1, p. 12 (Wellington: Dev-Zone, International Development Studies Network of Aotearoa New Zealand).

Ashe, J. W. (2005) Tourism investment as a tool for development and poverty reduction: the experience in Small Island Developing States (SIDS). The Commonwealth Finance Ministers Meeting, 18–20 September, Barbados.

Ashley, C., Goodwin, H. & McNab, D. (2005) *Making Tourism Count for the Local Economy in Dominican Republic: Ideas for Good Practice* (London: Pro Poor Tourism Partnership).

Ashley, C. & Roe, D. (1998) *Enhancing Community Involvement in Wildlife Tourism: Issues and Challenges,* IIED Wildlife and Development Series No. 11 (London: International Institute for Environment and Development).
Ashley, C. & Roe, D. (2002) Making tourism work for the poor: strategies and challenges in southern Africa, *Development Southern Africa*, 19(1), pp. 61–82.
Ashley, C., Roe, D. & Goodwin, H. (2001) *Pro-Poor Tourism Strategies: Making Tourism Work for the Poor. A Review of Experience* (London: Overseas Development Institute).
Baum, T. (1997) The fascination of islands: a tourist perspective, in: D. G. Lockhart & D. Drakakis-Smith (Eds) *Island Tourism: Trends and Prospects*, pp. 21–35 (London: Pinter).
Berno, T. (2003) Local control and the sustainability of tourism in the Cook Islands, in: D. Harrison (Ed.) *Pacific Island Tourism*, pp. 94–109 (New York: Cognizant Communication).
Briguglio, L., Archer, B., Jafari, J. & Wall, G. (1996) *Sustainable Tourism in Islands and Small States: Issues and Policies* (London: Pinter).
Britton, S. G. (1982) The political economy of tourism in the third world, *Annals of Tourism Research*, 9(3), pp. 331–358.
Britton, S. G. (1983) *Tourism and Underdevelopment in Fiji*, Monograph 31 (Canberra: Development Studies Centre, Australian National University).
Brohman, J. (1996) New directions in tourism for the Third World, *Annals of Tourism Research*, 23(1), pp. 48–70.
Butler, R. W. (1993) Tourism development in small islands: past influences and future directions, in: D. G. Lockhart, D. Drakakis-Smith & J. Schembri (Eds) *The Development Process in Small Island States*, pp. 71–91 (London: Routledge).
Carbone, M. (2005) Sustainable tourism in developing countries: poverty alleviation, participatory planning, and ethical issues, *The European Journal of Development Research*, 17(3), pp. 559–565.
Chand, S. (2003) Economic trends in the Pacific island countries, *Pacific Economic Bulletin*, 18(1), pp. 1–15.
Christie, I. (2002) Tourism, growth and poverty: framework conditions for tourism in developing countries, *Tourism Review*, 57(1&2), pp. 35–41.
Connell, J. (1993) Island microstates: development, autonomy and the ties that bind, in: D. G. Lockhart, D. Drakakis-Smith & J. Schembri (Eds) *The Development Process in Small Island States*, pp. 117–147 (London: Routledge).
Croes, R. R. (2006) A paradigm shift to a new strategy for small island economies: embracing demand side economics for value enhancement and long term economic stability, *Tourism Management*, 27, pp. 453–465.
d'Hauteserre, A. (2003) A response to 'Misguided policy initiatives in small-island desintations: why do up-market tourism policies fail?' by Dimitri Ioannides and Briavel Holcomb, *Tourism Geographies*, 5(1), pp. 49–53.
Dann, G. (1996) Socio-cultural issues in St Lucia's tourism, in: L. Briguglio, R. Butler, D. Harrison & W. L. Filho (Eds) *Sustainable Tourism in Islands and Small States: Case Studies* pp. 103–121 (London: Pinter)
de Kadt, E. (Ed.) (1979) *Tourism: Passport to Development?* (New York: Oxford University Press).
Deloitte & Touche (1999) *Sustainable Tourism and Poverty Elimination: A Report for the Department of International Development* (London: International Institute for Environment and Development, and the Overseas Development Institute).
Domroes, M. (2001) Conceptualising state-controlled *resort islands* for an environment-friendly development of tourism: the Maldivian experience, *Singapore Journal of Tropic Geography*, 22(2), pp. 122–137.
Duim, R., Peters, K. & Wearing, S. (2005) Planning host and guest interactions: moving beyond the empty meeting ground in African encounters, *Current Issues in Tourism*, 8(4), pp. 286–305.

Duval, D. T. & Wilkinson, P. F. (2004) Tourism development in the Caribbean: meaning and influences, in: D. T. Duval (Ed.) *Tourism in the Caribbean: Trends, Development, Prospects*, pp. 59–80 (London: Routledge).

Filho, W. L. (1996) Putting principles into practices: sustainable tourism in small island states, in: L. Briguglio, B. Archer, J. Jafari, & G. Wall (Eds) *Sustainable Tourism in Islands and Small States: Issues and Policies*, pp. 61–68 (London: Pinter)

Firaag, I. (1996) Tourism and the environment: current issues for management (Republic of Male: Ministry of Tourism). Available at www.fao.org/docrep/X5623E/x5623e0p.htm (accessed 23 May 2005).

Ghina, F. (2003) Sustainable development in small island developing states: the case of the Maldives, *Environment, Development and Sustainability*, 5, pp. 139–165.

Ghosh, R. N., Siddique, M. & Gabbay, R. (Eds) (2003) *Tourism and Economic Development: Case Studies from the Indian Ocean Region* (Aldershot: Ashgate).

Goodwin, H. (1998) *Sustainable Tourism and Poverty Elimination* DFID/DETR Workshop on Sustainable Tourism and Poverty, 13 October 1998 (London: Department for International Development).

Gössling, S. (2003) *Tourism and Development in Tropical Islands: Political Ecology Perspectives* (Cheltenham: Edward Elgar)

Harrison, D. (2003) Themes in Pacific Island tourism, in: D. Harrison (Ed.) *Pacific Island Tourism*, pp. 1–23 (New York: Cognizant Communication Corporation).

Harrison, D. & Brandt, J. (2003) Ecotourism in Fiji, in: D. Harrison (Ed.) *Pacific Island Tourism*, pp. 139–156 (New York: Cognizant Communication Corporation).

Hoti, S., McAleer, M. & Shareef, R. (2005) Modelling country risk and uncertainty in small island tourism economies, *Tourism Economics*, 11(2), pp. 159–183.

IICA (2006) *Agriculture and Tourism Partners in Development* Report on the Agro-Tourism workshop, St Kitts & Nevis, 3–5 October, 2005, Bridgetown, Barbados.

International Institute for Environment and Development (IIED) (2001) Pro-poor tourism: harnessing the world's largest industry for the world's poor. Available at http://www.iied.org/docs/wssd/bp_tourism_eng.pdf (accessed 23 May 2004).

James, G. (2004) Riding the wave: working within a globalised tourism economy, *In Focus*, 52, pp. 12–13.

Kakazu, H. (1994) *Sustainable Development of Small Island Economies* (Boulder: Westview).

King, R. (1993) The geographical fascination of Islands, in: D. G. Lockhart, D. Drakakis-Smith & J. Schembri (Eds) *The Development Process in Small Island States*, pp. 13–37 (London: Routledge).

Kingsbury, R. (2006) Corporate environmental sustainability: Sandals Resorts International in Jamaica, in: J. Pugh & J. H. Momsen (Eds) *Environmental Planning in the Caribbean*, pp.111–128 (Aldershot: Ashgate).

Liu, Z.-H. & Jenkins, C. L. (1996) Country size and tourism development: a cross-nation analysis, in: L. Briguglio, B. Archer, J. Jafari, & G. Wall (Eds) *Sustainable Tourism in Islands and Small States: Issues and Policies*, pp. 90–117 (London: Pinter).

Lyon, J. (2003) *Maldives* (Melbourne: Lonely Planet).

MacNaulty, M. (2002) The role of government in successful island tourism, in: *The Economic Impact of Tourism in the Islands of Asia and the Pacific: A Report on the WTO International Conference on Tourism and Island Economies*, pp. 28–41 (Madrid: World Tourism Organization).

McElroy, J. L. (2006) Small island tourist economies across the life cycle, *Asia Pacific Viewpoint*, 47(1), pp.61–77.

McElroy, J. L. & de Albuquerque, K. (2002) Problems for managing sustainable tourism in small islands, in: Y. Apostolopoulos & D. J. Gayle (Eds) *Island Tourism and Sustainable Development: Caribbean, Pacific, and Mediterranean Experiences*, pp. 15–31 (Westport, Connecticut: Praeger).

Milne, S. (1997) Tourism, dependency and South Pacific microstates: beyond the vicious cycle?, in: D. G. Lockhart & D. Drakakis-Smith (Eds) *Island Tourism: Trends and Prospects*, pp. 281–301 (London: Pinter)

Momsen, J. H. (1998) Caribbean tourism and agriculture: new linkages in the global era?, in: T. Klak (Ed.) *Globalization and Neoliberalism: The Caribbean Context*, pp. 115–134 (Lanham: Rowman and Littlefield).

Momsen, J. H. (2003) Participatory development and indigenous communities in the Mexican Caribbean, in: J. Pugh & R. Potter (Eds) *Participatory and Communicative Planning in the Caribbean*, pp. 155–172 (Aldershot: Ashgate).

Mowforth, M. & Munt, I. (2003) *Tourism and Sustainability: Development and New Tourism in the Third World* (London: Routledge).

Neto, F. (2003) A new approach to sustainable tourism development: moving beyond environmental protection, *Natural Resources Forum*, 27(3), pp. 212–222.

Oppermann, M. (1993) Tourism space in developing countries, *Annals of Tourism, Research*, 20(3), pp. 535–556.

Pearce, D. (1987) *Tourism Today: A Geographical Analysis* (New York: Longman).

Potter, R. (1993) Basic needs and development in the small island states of the Eastern Caribbean, in: D. G. Lockhart, D. Drakakis-Smith & J. Schembri (Eds) *The Development Process in Small Island States*, pp. 92–116 (London: Routledge).

Pro-Poor Tourism Partnership (2005) *Pro-Poor Tourism: Annual Register 2005* (London: Pro-Poor Tourism Partnership).

Pugh, J. (in press) The participation paradox: stories from St Lucia, in: J. Besson & J. H. Momsen (Eds) *Land and Development Revisited*, pp. 00–01 (New York: Palgrave).

Richter, L. K. (2001) Tourism challenges in developing nations: continuity and change at the millennium, in: D. Harrison (Ed.) *Tourism and the Less Developed World: Issues and Case Studies* pp. 47–59 (New York: CABI Publishing).

Scheyvens, R. (2002) *Tourism for Development: Empowering Communities* (Harlow: Prentice Hall).

Scheyvens, R. (2005) Growth of beach *fale* tourism in Samoa: the high value of low-cost tourism, in: C. M. Hall & S. Boyd (Eds) *Nature-based Tourism in Peripheral Areas: Development or Disaster?*, pp. 188–202 (Clevedon: Channelview Publications).

Scheyvens, R. (2007) Exploring the poverty-tourism nexus, *Current Issues in Tourism*, 10, pp. 231–254.

Siddique, M. & Ghosh, R. N. (2003) Tourism in the Indian Ocean region, in: R. N. Ghosh, M. Siddique & R. Gabbay (Eds) *Tourism and Economic Development: Case Studies from the Indian Ocean Region*, pp. 8–18 (Aldershot: Ashgate).

Sofield, T. (2003) *Empowerment for Sustainable Tourism Development* (Oxford: Pergamon).

Sofield, T., Bauer, J., De Lacy, T., Lipman, G. & Daugherty, S. (2004) *Sustainable Tourism – Eliminating Poverty: An Overview* (Australia: Cooperative Research Centre for Sustainable Tourism).

Stonich, S. (2003) The political ecology of Marine Protected Areas: the case of the Bay Islands, in: S. Gössling (Ed.) *Tourism and Development in Tropical Islands: Political Ecology Perspectives*, pp. 121–147 (Cheltenham: Edward Elgar).

Storey, D., Bulloch, H. & Overton, J. (2005) The poverty consensus: some limitations of the 'popular agenda', *Progress in Development Studies*, 5(1), pp. 30–44.

Telfer, D. J. (2003) Development issues in destination communities, in: S. Singh, D. J. Timothy & R. K. Dowling (Eds) *Tourism in Destination Communities*, pp.155–180 (New York: CABI Publishing).

Thomas, R. N., Pigozzi, B. W. and Sambrook, R. A. (2005) Tourist Carrying Capacity Measures: Crowding Syndrome in the Caribbean, *The Professional Geographer*, 57(1), pp. 13–20.

Torres, R. M. & Momsen, J. H. (2004) Challenges and potential for linking tourism and agriculture to achieve PPT objectives, *Progress in Development Studies*, 4(4), pp. 294–318.

Tourism Concern (2004) The Maldives: the lost paradise,*In Focus*, 51, insert.

Travel Wire News (2006) International tourism up by 5.5% to 808 million arrivals in 2005. Available at http://www.travelwirenews.com/cgi-script/csArticles/articles/000074/007417-p.htm (accessed 27 January 2006).

UNCTAD (1998) Developing countries could target tourism to boost economic growth. Press Release 9/6/98. Available at http://www.unctad.org/templates/Webflyer.asp?docID=3243&intItemID=2024&lang=1 (accessed 3 September 2005).

UNCTAD (2004) UNCTAD activities on sustainable tourism for development to be discussed in Lisbon. Press Release 03/03/04. Available at http://www.unctad.org/Templates/webflyer.asp?docid=4491&intItemID=1634&lang=1 (accessed 3 September 2005).

Wilkinson, P. F. (1989) Strategies for tourism in island microstates, *Annals of Tourism Research*, 16, pp. 153–177.

WTO (World Tourism Organization) (2002) *The Economic Impact of Tourism in the Islands of Asia and the Pacific: A Report on the WTO International Conference on Tourism and Island Economies* (Madrid: World Tourism Organization).

Résumé: Le tourisme et la lutte contre la pauvreté: difficultés pour les petits états insulaires

La notion que le tourisme puisse contribuer de façon importante aux stratégies de lutte contre la pauvreté attire l'attention d'institutions multilatérales, d'organismes de tourisme, de donneurs et d'autres organizations à travers le monde. Le tourisme contribue effectivement au développement de nombreux petits états insulaires en voie de développement (SIDS dans le texte) et est souvent la seule activité économique dans ces pays à faire la preuve d'une croissance continue. La croissance du tourisme dans les SIDS n'est cependant pas du tout synonyme de réduction de la pauvreté et, en fait, dans certains cas, entérine les inégalités qui existent. Nous affirmons que pour contribuer à une véritable réduction de la pauvreté dans les SIDS, il faudra adopter une approche compréhensive qui tienne compte de la durabilité sociale ainsi que des notions plus populaires de durabilité de l'environnement et de croissance économique. Qui plus est, nous suggérons que les gouvernements doivent établir un environnement de prise de décisions efficace et renforcer leur rôle réglementaire pour permettre à un tourisme durable et égalitaire d'émerger. L'article suggère des modes efficaces pour que la planification au niveau national à la fois encourage les acteurs du secteur privé à soutenir l'action pour lutter contre la pauvreté et facilite l'implication de plus de secteurs de l'économie dans le tourisme et l'emploi. Les gouvernements ne peuvent pas se contenter de promouvoir le développement du tourisme d'après les directives néolibérales de croissance économique.

Mots-clés: Lutte contre la pauvreté, tourisme en faveur des pauvres, petits états insulaires en voie de développement (SIDS)

Zusammenfassung: Tourismus und Armutsminderung: Themen für kleine Inselstaaten

Der Satz, dass der Tourismus erheblich zu Armutsminderungsstrategien beitragen kann, zieht großes Interesse von multilateralen Institutionen, Tourismusgremien, Spendern und anderen Organisationen des Erdballs auf sich. Der Tourismus ist zweifellos ein Hauptagent der ökonomischen Entwicklung in vielen kleinen Inselentwicklungsstaaten (small island developing states, SIDS) und häufig ist er die einzige Industrie in diesen Inselstaaten, die in den letzten Jahren kontinuierliches Wachstum gezeigt hat. Jedoch ist das Wachstum von Tourismus in SIDS auf keinen Fall ein Synonym für Armutsminderung, tatsächlich verstärkt dieser in einigen Fällen vorhandene Ungleichheiten. Es ist unsere Argument, dass der Tourismus nur dann erheblich zur Armutsreduzierung in SIDS beiträgt, wenn notwendiger Weise ein breiter Ansatz verfolgt wird, der auch Werte wie soziale Nachhaltigkeit als auch die populäreren Werte wie ökologische Nachhaltigkeit und ökonomisches Wachstum einbindet. Zusätzlich schlagen wir vor, dass Regierungen ein wirkungsvolles Politikklima herstellen und eine strenger regulierende Rolle spielen müssen, sofern ein nachhaltiger und gleichheitsfördernder Tourismus entstehen soll. Der Beitrag schlägt wirkungsvolle Wege vor, auf denen nationale Planung sowohl Akteure der Privatwirtschaft zur Unterstützung der Armutsminderung ermutigen als auch Einbeziehung breiterer Schichten der Gesellschaft in den Tourismus und die Beschäftigung erleichtern kann. Es ist nicht genügend für Regierungen, einfach Tourismusentwicklung in Übereinstimmung mit neoliberalen Wachstumspolitiken zu fördern.

Stichwörter: Armutsminderung, Pro-Poor-Tourismus, Small Island Developing States (SIDS)

Using indicators to assess sustainable tourism development: a review

Anna Torres-Delgado and Jarkko Saarinen

The aim of this paper is to examine the role of indicators in the transition to sustainability in tourism development and planning, identifying their main characteristics and summarising the challenges posed by their use in tourism development and in the research field. Indicators today constitute significant elements in sustainability programmes, but their use has been hampered by technical and conceptual difficulties. Furthermore, given that specific socio-spatial contexts and scales are highly influential in their application in the field, there is a need to identify the nature and characteristics of these indicators of sustainable tourism. After the in-depth development of a theoretical and phenomenological framework for indicators in tourism sector based on literature review, some interesting findings were identified. Indicators of sustainability have been widely adopted in tourism planning and management, and the indicator type (set or index) is selected depending on the situation under analysis and the purpose underpinning the study. In general, a set of indicators may prove more useful and accurate for assessing sustainability in one tourism destination, while an index may be better suited for comparing different spatial units. However, indicator effectiveness to achieve the ideals of sustainable tourism development is affected by the ambiguity in the definition of the concept of sustainable tourism and problems associated with data availability and baseline knowledge. The main challenge is to overcome strategic guidelines and political and theoretical proposals of indicators and achieve practical applications for the sustainable development of tourism. It is in this regard that innovations and knowledge transfer have been stressed, albeit that the nature of this knowledge remains the key.

Introduction

Since the early 1990s sustainable development has established itself as the prevailing paradigm of tourism policies, planning, management and research (Bianchi, 2004; Bramwell & Lane, 1993). Although demands for more environmentally sensitive practices in the sector were first expressed in the 1960s and 1970s (see Hall & Lew, 1998; Saarinen, 2006), sustainability is concerned with the guidance and control of broader impacts and processes of tourism development than those simply affecting the physical environment (Bramwell & Lane, 2008; Holden, 2003). However, after two decades of research, sustainable tourism is still a controversial concept (see Liu, 2003; Sharpley, 2009; Wheeller,

1993). The main criticism concerns the difficulties of transposing the principles of sustainable development onto a single sector, in this instance tourism (Sharpley, 2000). In spite of these challenges, here we understand the term sustainable tourism to mean a sector that operates and is operated in line with the principles of sustainable development, that seeks inter- and intra-generational equity and that adopts a holistic and ethical approach to development based on sound ecological, sociocultural and economic principles (Butler, 1999, 2011). Clearly, such aims represent a considerable challenge to this, or any other sector, operating at the global–local nexus.

Since the emergence of sustainability as a target for tourism development, the need has arisen to introduce parameters, that is, indicators that can measure the impact of tourism (Butler, 1993; Wheeller, 1993). As Hunter (1997) and Wheeller (1993) note, sustainable tourism as a concept is meaningless without indicators and other monitoring tools that can inform us about the impacts of tourism and determine whether they are acceptable or not (see McCool, Moisey, & Nickerson, 2001). As such, the development of indicators is fundamental to both the research and practices of sustainable tourism development.

The methodologies for identifying and quantifying the impact of tourist practices comprise, in the main, statistical compilations that supply numerical data (see McElroy, 1998; Spanish Ministry for the Environment [SME], 2003; White, McCrum, Blackstock, & Scott, 2006a; World Tourism Organization [WTO], 2005). In discussing these methodologies, we are in fact referring to indicators in their broadest sense. Thus, while indicators of sustainable tourism should serve to provide essential information, they must also serve to manage the development of a particular activity and guide it towards sustainability. In this way, they provide an operative framework with policy relevance for tourism managers to incorporate sustainability within their planning and decision processes (see Hezri & Dovers, 2006). This paper aims to provide a review of the application of indicators to the sustainable tourism development. In addition, the purpose is to assess their potential contribution to sustainable tourism practices in a local level and discuss the specific challenges related to the use of indicators, namely set of indicators and indices, in tourism development operating in the local–global nexus.

Indicators of transition to sustainability in tourism

At the 1992 United Nations Earth Summit the need for an international set of indicators to assess the transition to sustainability was stressed. Subsequently, numerous international and national organisations, including non-governmental organisations, have proposed indicators of sustainability (Vera & Ivars, 2003), and the need to quantify sustainable development has spread to all economic sectors, including the tourism industry. Thus, for example, at the Rio +10 Summit, sustainable tourism development was incorporated into its Plan of Implementation (World Summit on Sustainable Development, 2002).

Sustainable tourism has been widely debated in the literature, and numerous theoretical frameworks, models and approaches have been forwarded reflecting these principles (see Hunter, 1997; Saarinen, 2006; Sharpley, 2009). One of the main challenges to have emerged from these discussions has been the fixing and monitoring of the limits to growth in tourism (see Holden, 2007; Hunter, 1995). Here, indicators serve as an essential tool for sustainability by (1) monitoring sectoral development so as to facilitate the assessment of tourism policies and practices, measuring sectoral performance and developing suitable strategies for a preferred future (Castellani & Sala, 2010; Crabtree & Bayfield, 1998;

Dahl, 1995; Gahin, Veleva, & Hart, 2003; Smeets & Weterings, 1999; Valentin & Spangenberg, 2000) and (2) communicating the knowledge via the generation of quantitative and objective data that provide a fuller understanding of tourist phenomena in their spatial context (Blackstock, McCrum, Scott, & White, 2006; Blancas, González, Lozano-Oyola, & Pérez, 2010; Roberts & Tribe, 2008; Sánchez & Pulido, 2008; WTO, 1996).

The European Community Models of Sustainable Tourism project was one of the first studies of tourism to be conducted from a sustainable perspective and to include indicators. Published in 1994 by the International Federation of Tour Operators, it drew up a list of indicators of the local environment and the long-term sustainability of the profitability of a tourist activity. It included such factors as safeguarding economic effectiveness, the prosperity of local residents, cultural identity and the upgrading of accommodation. Its aim was to detect critical features affecting the island of Majorca as a tourist destination by applying indicators and by comparing results with those obtained for the island of Rhodes (Hughes, 1994). Later, in 1995, the WTO published the guide that has probably oriented most recent indicators – What Tourism Managers Need to Know: A Practical Guide to the Development and Use of Indicators of Sustainable Tourism (WTO, 1995) – which was updated in 2005 as the Guidebook on Indicators of Sustainable Development for Tourism Destinations (WTO, 2005).

The design of sustainable tourism indicators has become a common working strategy for many institutions. In 2001, the German Federal Environment Agency, for example, published a report on such indicators in the Baltic Sea Region. A year later, the English Tourism Council presented a set of headline indicators based on three objectives for the management of sustainable tourism: (1) to protect and enhance the built and natural environment; (2) to support local communities and their culture; and (3) to benefit the economies of tourism destinations (White et al., 2006a). Likewise, the French Institute for the Environment has created a set of national indicators, organised according to destination type (coast, mountain, rural or urban space), so as to enhance the integration of the environment within national tourism policy (Céron & Dubois, 2000). Similarly, the SME published its own set of environmental indicators for tourism in Spain (SME, 2003).

In addition to these specific cases, many institutional papers addressing issues of tourism management call for indicators to evaluate sustainability in the sector. In 1996, Agenda 21 for the travel and tourism industry made it its priority "to fix realistic indicators, applied at the local and national levels, for assessing and monitoring progress in sustainable tourism development" (WTO, 1996, p. 15). At a later date, the European Commission's (EC) communication – Basic Orientations for the Sustainability of European Tourism – reiterated the "urgent need for reliable carrying capacity analysis techniques, development of user-friendly sustainability reporting mechanisms, and better statistical monitoring and indicator systems to provide information for managing tourism supply and demand" (EC, 2003, p. 13).

The same need has also been identified by many academics. Thus, Butler (1999) wrote that "the greatest research need is to develop measures of sustainability and to apply these to existing and new forms of tourism development to help determine what affects sustainability and how it can be achieved" (p. 20). In addition, Ko (2005) stressed that "if sustainable development is one of the tourism industry's major contemporary objectives, then the industry needs to be able to measure its performance and impacts" (p. 432). Hence, indicators are being increasingly called upon to guide the tourism sector to sustainability, but they are not without their problems. Below, we discuss the ideal characteristics that these indicators should adopt.

Nature of indicators

Indicators: definition and characterisation

The WTO (1995) defines indicators of sustainability as quantitative tools that facilitate the analysis and assessment of information so that managers can take sound decisions. This definition emphasises the importance of indicators for public management, as well as the precautionary principle. James (2004) argues that indicators help to evaluate the sustainability of a destination by identifying the key factors of change, their evolution and potential threats. However, in the tourism sector various characteristics need to be taken into account when defining indicators of sustainability. Schianetz, Kavanagh, and Lockington (2007, p. 1) list three key factors: (1) destinations are often located in or close to ecologically fragile and/or culturally sensitive areas; (2) destinations are characterised by highly dynamic processes and tourism development is inherently unstable and often unpredictable; and (3) destinations constitute a conglomerate of many small independent but interacting businesses which are also directly and/or indirectly dependent on each other.

Thus, given their crucial role in planning and management processes, indicators need to be capable of supplying information, while at the same time being methodologically and scientifically valid. They must also be easily applied and their results readily disseminated. In general, indicators need to be simple and directionally clear (Valentin & Spangenberg, 2000) so as to maintain clear channels of communication between the various actors involved in planning programmes. Smeets and Weterings (1999) stress the importance of communication on the grounds that indicators must promote information exchange. White et al. (2006a) add that, despite their complexity and the need for accuracy and transparency in their construction, indicators must be simple enough to be understood and used by the layperson, not just the expert. In spite of the variety of opinions expressed, Table 1 seeks to summarise the general criteria and conditions that a good indicator should satisfy.

One of the main conditions is measurability since the practical application of an indicator depends on the availability and reliability of the data used in its measurement. This

Table 1. Conditions of a good indicator.

Condition	Meaning
Relevance	Relevant to the research programme
Scientific precision	Scientifically well founded
Measurability	Containing the necessary and reliable data to proceed to its calculation
Transparency	Clear as regards its methodology and the selection of parameters
Adaptability	Adaptable to specific characteristics of the territory
Comparability	Producing comparable results
Updating	Using updated data
Cost efficiency well balanced	Efforts expended in data collection well balanced with information ultimately obtained
Territorial representation	Possibility of mapping using georeferenced data
Temporal representation	Showing trends over time
Sensitivity	Sensitive to spatial and temporal changes
Communication	Results easily communicated and understandable to all
Participation	Meeting the needs and interests of target audience

Source: Based on Bell and Morse (2003), Ivars (2001) and White et al. (2006b).

also means that limits of sustainability have to be fixed so as to evaluate the levels of sustainability provided by the indicator. However, any objective or precise definition of these thresholds is not straightforward, principally because of the inherent vagueness of the concept of sustainability and the overall paucity of baseline information (Butler, 1999; Ivars, 2001). Indeed, the ambiguity of the concept has often resulted in actions that offer little more than empty rhetoric and which contribute nothing to the sustainable development of tourism or societies in general (Hunter, 1995; Wheeller, 1993). As McCool et al. (2001) state, sustainability does not readily translate into specific policies, actions or indicators, and their application depends on the system of reasoning underpinning their use.

Establishing thresholds of sustainability is further complicated by differences in real and perceived conditions (Ivars, 2001). Furthermore, when clear and effective thresholds are not established by legislative bodies, researchers are left to create them in accordance with the specific characteristics of each specific case (i.e., context), which can often be a highly subjective process (White, McCrum, Blackstock, & Scott, 2006b). In an attempt at overcoming this, or at least minimising the problem, Bell and Morse (2003, p. 47) propose four methods for establishing a reference condition for indicators: (1) using historical trends or data, assuming that a sustainable state prevailed in the past; (2) using a current system, comparing levels of sustainability in different territories; (3) using a theoretical approach, constructing a reference condition based on conceptual principles; or (4) consulting stakeholders to establish "best" and "worst" case scenarios (see also Roberts & Tribe, 2008). Clearly, while none of these approaches is fully objective, they are helpful in that they can be used to fix the limits of acceptable change in tourist settings (see Choi & Sirakaya, 2006).

There are basically two types of indicators: simple and complex indicators (or indices), the choice of which depends on the quality of the information available. While simple indicators provide statistics directly from the field or involve a simple data treatment, complex indicators are adimensional measures resulting from the combination of several simple indicators through a weighting system that organises components into a hierarchy (Sánchez & Pulido, 2008). The information associated with each type of indicator clearly differs, and its usefulness depends on the working scale and the assessment that is required. Simple indicators can be most useful for detecting specific impacts and for applying partial solutions, whereas indices provide a broader, integrated overview. Lying at a point between these two types of indicators, we can locate sets of indicators, which are able to combine several simple indicators and provide joint interpretations.

In attempting to evaluate sustainability holistically, sets of indicators and the aggregation of these into indices are increasingly being used to make policy and management decisions (Hezri & Dovers, 2006). Despite procedural and interpretative differences, the two can be considered complementary with complex indicators providing a broader, holistic view and sets of indicators providing more specific information, thereby overcoming any possible bias introduced by index methodology and data inclusion (Mayer, 2008).

Sets of indicators

A set of indicators is a compilation of simple indicators organised to meet certain research goals and offer a new perspective on a particular phenomenon. Thus, it is more than the sum of individual indicators and can provide a more spatially oriented interpretation of the whole data set (Castro, 2005). In this sense, Blackstock et al. (2006) claim that an individual indicator has to be seen as a component of a wider group of indicators possessing a distinct identity. As such, the organisation of information is an essential characteristic of any set of indicators, since this facilitates the identification of causal relationships between variables and the interpretation and dissemination of results. However, the initial selection of relevant indicators is also a crucial step in avoiding any potential misunderstanding of the phenomenon. While many models have been accepted for organising the indicators, there is no consensus as to the minimum number of indicators needed to constitute a set.

What is required is a framework for organising indicators in a coherent structure and for providing guidelines for data collection, communication with stakeholders and report production. In seeking to systematise such organisational models, Sureda and Felipe (2010) describe six frameworks typically adopted in structuring indicators of sustainable development: physical environments, economic sectors, dimensions, themes, systems and causes. Each of these models fulfils a distinct purpose and establishes different relationships between the chosen variables; however, they are not exclusive and can be combined if necessary. In fact, Bofill, Felipe, and Barrado (2009) recommend combining them at the outset research so as to obtain complementary perspectives on any given phenomenon.

The number of simple indicators constituting a set is determined by the need to assess all the dimensions of sustainability while guaranteeing simplicity of application (Bossel, 1999; Schianetz & Kavanagh, 2008; Sirakaya, Jamal, & Choi, 2001; White et al., 2006b). Thus, each researcher faces the challenge of devising a set of indicators, which while clearly subjective, is also conditioned by the characteristics of a given context.

Addressing the issue of subjectivity, Manning (1999) claims that there is no single "perfect" set of indicators as each user will develop their own ideal depending on the specific case and the purposes of their study (see Roberts & Tribe, 2008). Inevitably, the criteria applied in selecting indicators will depend also on an individual researcher's academic background, knowledge and experience. For this reason, a participatory process is commonly adopted in evaluating a potential set of indicators, thereby ensuring that it is suitable for a case and satisfies the aims of stakeholders. The Delphi method is one such method commonly adopted (Miller, 2001; Choi & Sirakaya, 2006) as it enables experts to reach a consensus in the selection process, while public forums ensure stakeholder participation.

Indices

Having built a set of indicators, these can then be aggregated to constitute an index of sustainability. Mayer (2008) defines such an index as "a quantitative aggregation of many indicators that can provide a simplified, coherent, multidimensional view of a system" (p. 279). Thus, the main goals of a composite indicator are to summarise complex issues, provide a general overview, attract public interest and reduce the overall size of a list of indicators (Saltelli, 2007).

However, the excessive simplification of information entailed by the building of indices is also criticised since the process might fail to reveal issues or changes of significance and, moreover, it involves considerable subjectivity in determining the weighting to be assigned to each component (Céron & Dubois, 2003; Mayer, 2008; Singh, Murty, Gupta, & Dikshit, 2009). Opinion is therefore divided on the use of indices between (1) those who believe that indices as a statistic summary are needed to capture situations more holistically, helping to garner media interest and, hence, the attention of policy makers and (2) those who claim that efforts should focus on creating an appropriate set of indicators rather than on producing a composite index, because of the arbitrary nature of aggregate indicators (Sharpe, 2004).

Should a researcher choose to build an index, the first step is to define what issue(s) requires measuring as this needs to be clearly understood in order to provide a solid conceptual framework and in ensuring that the necessary information is available (Schuschny & Soto, 2009). The next step is to draw up a set of indicators, which requires selecting appropriate simple indicators and organising them into a set. The simple indicators are then standardised, by creating adimensional values that are weighted and aggregated. The Organisation for Economic Co-operation and Development (OECD, 2008) reports this approach in a 10-step procedure, which outlines the ideal sequence from the development of a theoretical framework to the presentation and dissemination of a composite indicator (see Table 2).

In general, the majority of sustainability indices are built following the key steps discussed above (OECD, 2008), and many incorporate the same data given the paucity of "global" sustainability data-sets (Mayer, 2008).

Use of indicators in sustainable tourism

Various sets of indicators have been developed in tourism research. Miller (2001), for example, conducts a Delphi survey among experts to construct indicators of sustainable tourism in the context of how best to encourage consumers to choose their holiday destinations. Choi and Sirakaya (2006) also adopt a modified Delphi technique in proposing indicators for measuring community tourism development within a sustainable framework (see Table 3). Bossel (1999) criticises indicators based solely on expert opinion,

Table 2. Key steps for building a composite indicator.

Step	Meaning and rationale
(1) Theoretical framework	Provides the basis for the selection and combination of variables into a meaningful index under a fitness-for-purpose principle
(2) Data selection	Should be based on the analytical soundness, measurability, country coverage and relevance of the indicators to the phenomenon being measured and relationship to each other
(3) Imputation of missing data	Is needed in order to provide a complete data-set
(4) Multivariate analysis	Should be used to study the overall structure of the data-set, assess its suitability and guide subsequent methodological choices (e.g., weighting, aggregation)
(5) Normalisation	Should be carried out to render the variables comparable
(6) Weighting and aggregation	Should be carried out according to the theoretical framework
(7) Uncertainty and sensitivity analysis	Should be undertaken to assess the robustness of the composite indicator
(8) Back to the data	Is needed to reveal the main drivers for an overall good or bad performance. Transparency is primordial to good analysis and policy-making
(9) Links to other indicators	Should be made to correlate the composite indicator (or its dimensions) with existing (simple or composite) indicators
(10) Visualisation of the results	Should receive proper attention, given that the visualisation can influence or help interpretability

Source: Based on Organisation for Economic Co-operation and Development (2008, p. 20).

Table 3. Examples of proposed indicator sets and indices.

Set of indicators	
Chris and Sirakaya (2006)	Top three indicators in each dimension (18 of 125): **Economic dimension** • Availability of local credit to local business • Employment growth in tourism • Percent of income leakage out of the community **Social dimension** • Resident involvement in tourism industry • Visitor satisfaction/attitude towards tourist destinations • Litter/pollution **Cultural dimension** • Availability of cultural site maintenance fund and resources • Type and amount of training given to tourism employees • Types of building material and decor **Ecological dimension** • Air quality index • Amount of erosion on the natural site • Frequency of environmental accidents related to tourism **Political dimension** • Availability and level of land zoning policy • Availability of air, water pollution, waste management and policy • Availability of development control policy **Technological dimension** • Accurate data collection • Use of low-impact technology • Benchmarking
McCool et al. (2001)	Twenty-six indicators evaluated at three levels (state, region, and local): • Visits to parks, recreation areas and historic sites • No. of non-resident visitors • Tourism promotion budget • Hotel occupancy rate • Per capita tourist expenditures • Presence of a sustainable tourism plan • Lodging revenues • Inquiries from promotions • Highway traffic count • Resident attitudes towards tourism • No. of non-resident fishing and hunting licenses • No. of tourism employees • Percentage of labour force in tourism • Annual no. of new tourism businesses • Labour income from tourism • Airline deplanements • Resident perceptions of quality of life • No. of state parks • Gasoline tax revenue • State park management budget • Crime rate • Water pollution from sewage • Per capita water consumption • Building permits • Per capita energy consumption • Real estate sales

(continued)

Table 3. (*Continued*)

Set of indicators	
Moore and Polley (2007)	Six potential indicators according to visitors' experience: • No. of parking bays • No. of camping bays • No. of signs • Percentage of area of erosion • Area of vegetation loss • Pieces of litter

Indices	
McElroy (1998)	Three indicators combined using an unweighted average: • Visitor spending per capita • Daily visitor densities per 1000 population • Hotel rooms per square kilometre
Sánchez and Pulido (2008)	Fourteen indicators weighted according to the confirmatory factor analysis model: **Driving forces indicators** • Annual tourist spending • Percentage of employees in hotels and restaurants • Percentage of tourist population • No. of hospitality structures per 100 inhabitants **Pressure indicators** • Potential pressure on natural spaces • Density of tourists in urban environment • Tourism and sport interventions in natural spaces • Production of waste attributed to tourism • Electric energy consumption attributed to tourism • Water consumption attributed to tourism **State indicators** • Naturalisation level of environment • Quality of swim water **Response indicators** • No. of hotels with environmental certificate • Separate tourism waste collection
Castellani and Sala (2010)	Twenty indicators weighted according to the priority of action emerging from the analysis and the consultation of local stakeholders: **Population** • Net migration • Old-age index • Level of education **Housing** • Rate of houses not owned by resident people • Services • No. of local unit in services sector • Voluntary work • No. of daily routes of public transport **Economy and labour** • Employment rate • No. of enterprises with ISO 14001 or Environmental Management and Audit Scheme (EMAS) certificate • Rate of new enterprises survived after 18 months

(*continued*)

Table 3. (*Continued*)

Set of indicators		
		• Female entrepreneurship • Rate of commuting population • Per capita value added **Environment** • Urbanisation • Production of energy from renewable sources • Ecological state of fresh water • Percentage of separate waste collection • Percentage of farming area occupied by organic farming **Tourism** • Overnights • No. of bed and breakfast and agritourism/total no. of hospitality structures
Blancas et al. (2010)		Thirty-two indicators weighted by variance and absolute value of the correlation: **Social dimension** • Ratio of tourists to locals • Ratio of peak season tourists to locals • Sports facilities per inhabitant available to the community • Health centres per inhabitant available to the community • Public transport vehicles for travellers and merchandise per inhabitant • Ratio of peak-season tourism employment to low-season tourism employment • Percentage of beach area without security devices in coastal zone • No. of crimes and misdemeanours made at provincial level **Economic dimension** • Total no. of tourist arrivals in coastal zone • Daily average expenditures of sun and beach tourists • Ratio of peak-month tourists to low-month tourists • Occupancy rate for official accommodations • Ratio of average peak-season occupancy rate to average low-season occupancy rate for official accommodations • Percentage of official tourism accommodation establishments which open all year • Ratio of tourism employment to total employment • Public investments in coastal issues **Environmental dimension** • No. of tourists per square metre of beaches in coastal zone • No. of peak-season tourists per square metre of beaches • Waste volume produced by destinations • Volume of glass recycled • Percentage of energy consumption attributed to tourism • Percentage of renewable energy consumption attributed to tourism • Consumption of urban supplying water attributed to tourism • Volume of water reused • Volume of sewage receiving treatment • Percentage of coastal zone considered to be in eroded state • Percentage of beach area considered to be in high-urbanisation state • Percentage of sampling points with good sanitary qualification • Percentage of beach area with Blue Flag status • Percentage of beach area with cleaning services • Percentage of beach area considered to be protected natural area • Percentage of beach area considered to be in high-occupation state

arguing that the development of indicators should encompass the opinions of people of different social and scientific backgrounds and political persuasion. Failure to do so means that the indicators developed might neglect certain views that may have a significant impact on the day-to-day systems of local people. In this sense, McCool et al. (2001) attach considerable importance to the opinions of stakeholders in the tourist sector, including members of the lodging, restaurant and resort sectors, when defining their indicators. In addition, Moore and Polley (2007) develop their set of indicators and standards by asking visitors to describe the conditions that contributed to their tourism experience (see Table 3). Clearly, the outcomes of these distinct methodologies are uncertain, but they highlight the fact that participatory approaches are commonly used in building sets of indicators. Indeed, it has been claimed that a bottom-up approach is useful in creating indicators that more closely resemble the contextual situation (Roberts & Tribe, 2008).

One of the first sustainable tourism indices to be designed was the tourism penetration index (see Table 3). It was proposed by McElroy (1998) on realising that mass tourism was threatening the sustainability of small Caribbean islands. Based on perceptions of the situation, he sought to build a composite indicator that might measure the economic, social and environmental impact of the tourism industry. Due in the main to a paucity of data, his index was based on just three indicators (visitor spending per capita, daily visitor densities per 1000 population and hotel rooms per square kilometre). Sánchez and Pulido (2008) developed the sustainable tourism index, which they then calculated for several Spanish autonomous communities using the weighted sum of 14 simple indicators (see Table 3). Similarly, Castellani and Sala (2010) produced a sustainable performance index (SPI) for tourism policy development based on 20 indicators concerned with demographic dynamics, economic and social conditions of local communities, environmental factors and tourism characteristics of the region under investigation. The SPI was used to assess the implementation of the European Charter for Sustainable Tourism by the Alpi Lepontine Mountain Community (Italy). Blancas et al. (2010) have assessed sustainable tourism by developing and applying a multidimensional index that comprised 32 simple indicators (see Table 3). They applied their index to Spanish coastal destinations and their results served as a guideline for tourism planning. In addition, other well-known environmental indices have been applied to tourism, for example, the carrying capacity (see Cocossis & Mexa, 2004; Garrigós, Narangajavana, & Palacios, 2004) and the ecological footprint (see Hunter & Shaw, 2007).

Initially indicators were applied to areas in which the boundaries of the destination were relatively easy to define and where the range of stakeholders was relatively small (Manning, 1999). Municipalities, or similar administrative regions, have typically been regarded as constituting a suitable level of analysis (see Blancas et al., 2010; Torres-Delgado, 2010; Vera & Ivars, 2003), given that larger spatial scales (e.g., country or state level) might be problematic due to the availability of space–time information and the fact that the issues and impacts they involve are too diverse and complex to manage (Lee, 2001). On the other hand, overly small spatial units, such as resorts or individual hotels, do not allow a meaningful or comprehensive analysis of sustainability based on the broader tourist sector and its impacts (see Gössling, 2000; Saarinen, 2006).

Although administrative boundaries may not always be the most appropriate for applying the sustainability indicators or determining tourist impacts, policy decisions and related activities and resources are often the responsibility of a local authority or municipality, through which regional planning, management and regulation are often conducted (Schianetz et al., 2007). As a result, most of the research on tourism and sustainability has focused on local-scale issues in administratively defined units. This is also understandable in terms of the fact that local changes represent perhaps the most visible and concrete processes and impacts of global tourism and sustainability (Vera & Ivars, 2003).

Although problematic in relation to global and holistic sustainability, this focus on the local scale can be justified in terms of governance and ensuring broader participation, since monitoring the impact of tourism at the local level can be more useful because communities are where tourism takes place (Choi & Sirakaya, 2006, p. 1296; see Valentin & Spangenberg, 2000). Indeed, numerous articles and projects have focused on monitoring tourism sustainability at the local scale (see James, 2004; Logar, 2010; Torres-Delgado, 2010; Vera & Ivars, 2003; Vila, Costa, & Rovira, 2010). In addition, the experience of public administrations is that indicators serve to support local sustainable tourism planning, especially as part of Agenda 21, for example, the municipality of Calvià (Balearic Island) and Lloret de Mar (Catalonia) where indicators have been developed to lead mass tourism in a more sustainable direction. Local-scale analyses using sets of sustainable tourism indicators have also been undertaken on small islands and in nature protection areas (see Balearic Islands Centre for Research of Tourist Technologies, 2000; Blackstock, White, McCrum, Scott, & Hunter, 2008; Sancho & Ruíz, 2004; Twining-Ward & Butler, 2002).

Monitoring tourist sustainability also implies to consider the historical axis, which enables to identify tendencies as well as to test the success of specific actions and strategies. Being aware about this important indicator function, The EC has developed a European Tourism Indicators System (ETIS) for Sustainable Management at Destination Level, which is a comprehensive and flexible system relatively to use and is suitable for a wide scale of tourism destinations. The ETIS is currently in a testing period and it has three pilot phases starting on 15 July 2013, 1 December 2013 and 1 February 2015. The proposal has been successful as approximately 100 tourism destinations across Europe have expressed their interest to participate in the first period. Other observatories and similar initiatives have been developed with the aim of collecting regular and systematic gathering, analysis and communication of data. For example, in China five observatories are currently in operation (Yangshuo, Huangshan, Zhangjiajie, Chengdu and Kanas) as a result of the Global Observatory on Sustainable Tourism Initiative.

Discussion and conclusion

The ability to characterise the prevailing situation and to monitor change are the main virtues of indicators of sustainability, and as a result they have been widely adopted in tourism planning and management.

In particular, sets of indicators have typically been adopted, given that their methodological simplicity enables specific impacts to be detected and practical (albeit partial) solutions to be applied. However, there is no consensus as to the minimum number of indicators needed to quantify sustainability, and so more often than not sets become long lists of statistics that are not easily handled. Indices have also become increasingly popular, as they provide a global, integrated understanding of the tourist activity, its impacts and level of sustainability. An index is also easier to interpret since it expresses sustainability in a single value that is readily comparable between areas and points in time (Schuschny & Soto, 2009). However, this simplification may conceal problems owing to the standardisation and aggregation of impacts presenting different qualities. Thus, it would appear that the indicator type (set or index) needs to be carefully selected depending on the situation under analysis and the purpose underpinning the study. For instance, a set of indicators may prove more useful and accurate for assessing sustainability in one tourism destination, while an index may be better suited for comparing different spatial units.

However, their use has been hampered by technical and conceptual difficulties in their application, which also reduce the capacity to integrate them in joint analyses (see Céron & Dubois, 2003; Vila et al., 2010). Arguably, the greatest shortcomings affecting indicators are limited data availability and subjectivity in their building and interpretation. Additionally, given the conceptual ambiguity surrounding sustainable tourism many interpretations may be drawn. This absence of consensus as to the meaning of sustainability, combined with a paucity of data, has undermined the effectiveness of the indicators to achieve the ideals of sustainable tourism development (Wilson, Tyedmers, & Pelot, 2007). However, Miller (2001) remains optimistic when claiming that "the process of developing indicators does help in determining the important tenets of the concept" (p. 361).

Although sets of indicators and indices are often seen as serving different purposes, they can also complement each other so that general tendencies can be identified without their causal factors being overlooked. As there is no consensus about how to quantify tourism sustainability, nor a universal methodology accepted, a practical proposal could be to combine a set of indicators with a complementary index. Using these two tools, a progressive approach to tourism sustainability could be reached, overcoming weaknesses of each individual tool. The first step would be to build a set of indicators based on a theoretical framework as well as scientific consensus. This proposal should compile social, economic and environmental indicators and be applied to several case analyses ensuring the data availability and its functionality for tourism managers. Based on this empirical analysis, key variables of tourism sustainability would be identified and then aggregated into a complementary index. This index would enable to extrapolate thresholds of tourism sustainability that could then be used to define the degree of tourism sustainability for a destination. This process would define a formula to translate tourism sustainability into quantifiable ratings, providing a tool for tourist destinations to assess and define their tourism strategies for the future with sustainability in mind.

Undoubtedly, working with indicators is challenging, as the processes involved are by no means straightforward. In order to overcome these difficulties there is a need for transparent methods and fully participatory processes which should ensure the application of the same indicators in different locations, thereby meeting the stakeholders' aims. However, the frameworks developed to date are not easily transposed from one place to another. Indeed, Twining-Ward and Butler (2002) stress that when thinking about sustainable tourism we should not necessarily assume that the issues are the same in different destinations or in different tourist activities, thereby highlighting the importance of context for the design and use of sustainable tourism indicators. Thus, calls for universal indicators may serve little purpose in practice, and what we have seen in part is a shift towards the development of local-scale analyses in sustainable tourism.

However, the perspectives afforded by local- and community-scale studies (often centred on administrative units) may exclude some of the broader regional and especially global issues of sustainability. This is important to tote but in spite of this the site-specific focus does not necessarily reduce the possibilities of developing "core indicators" for different destinations (Roberts & Tribe, 2008) that reflect the goals of sustainable development at a more holistic or global scale. Proposals need to strike a balance between their contextual specificity and their global relevance. Thus, the challenge in developing sustainable tourism indicators is achieving coverage not only of local impacts but also of global issues, such as climate change and the way in which the expanding sector and increased tourist mobility impact on it.

In addition to this question of placing programmes on a different scale and analysing the impact of tourism at the global–local nexus, a further challenge facing the development of indicators of sustainable tourism is the need to overcome strategic guidelines and political and theoretical proposals and, thereby, achieve practical applications for the sustainable development of tourism. It is in this regard that innovations and knowledge transfer have been stressed (see Blackstock et al., 2006; Blancas et al., 2010; Sánchez & Pulido, 2008; WTO, 1996), albeit that the nature of this knowledge (e.g., how we might determine the limits to growth and monitor the changes) remains the key. In order to meet this challenge, there is a growing need for multidisciplinary approaches to the study of sustainable tourism involving not only experts and scholars in the field of tourism but also those working in environmental, economic and sociocultural studies.

References

Balearic Islands Centre for Research of Tourist Technologies. (2000). *Indicadors de sostenibilitat del turisme a les Illes Balears* [Sustainable tourism indicators in the Balearic Islands]. Majorca: Govern de les Illes Balears, Conselleria de Turisme.

Bell, S., & Morse, S. (2003). *Measuring sustainability: Learning from doing*. London: Earthscan Publications.

Bianchi, R. (2004). Tourism restructuring and the politics of sustainability: A critical view from the European periphery (the Canary Islands). *Journal of Sustainable Tourism, 12*(6), 495–529.

Blackstock, K., McCrum, G., Scott, A., & White, V. (Eds.). (2006). *A framework for developing indicators of sustainable tourism*. CNPA and Macaulay Institute Sustainable Tourism Indicator Framework Project. Retrieved from http://www.macaulay.ac.uk/ruralsustainability/FrameworkReport.pdf

Blackstock, K. L., White, V., McCrum, G., Scott, A., & Hunter, C. (2008). Measuring responsibility: An appraisal of a Scottish national park's sustainable tourism indicators. *Journal of Sustainable Tourism, 16*(3), 276–297.

Blancas, F. J., González, M., Lozano-Oyola, M., & Pérez, F. (2010). The assessment of sustainable tourism: Application to Spanish coastal destinations. *Ecological Indicators, 10*(2), 484–492.

Bofill, J., Felipe, J. C., & Barrado, C. (2009). Model conceptual d'un sistema d'informació per estudis de sostenibilitat d'un territori [Conceptual model of an information system for studying the territory sustainability]. In *Meeting of II International Conference on Sustainability Measurement and Modelling*. Terrassa: International Center for Numerical Methods in Engineering.

Bossel, H. (1999). *Indicators for sustainable development: Theory, methods, applications*. Winnipeg: International Institute for Sustainable Development.

Bramwell, B., & Lane, B. (1993). Sustaining tourism: An evolving global approach. *Journal of Sustainable Tourism, 1*(1), 1–5.
Bramwell, B., & Lane, B. (2008). Priorities in sustainable tourism research. *Journal of Sustainable Tourism, 16*(1), 1–4.
Butler, R. W. (1993). Tourism – an evolutionary perspective. In J. G. Nelson, R. Butler, & G. Wall (Eds.), *Tourism and sustainable development: Monitoring, planning, managing* (pp. 26–43). Waterloo: University of Waterloo.
Butler, R. W. (1999). Sustainable tourism: A state-of-the-art review. *Tourism Geographies, 1*(1), 7–25.
Butler, R. W. (2011). Sustainable tourism and the changing rural scene in Europe. In D. V. L. Macleod & S. A. Gillespie (Eds.), *Sustainable tourism in rural Europe* (pp. 15–27). London: Routledge.
Castellani, V., & Sala, S. (2010). Sustainable performance index for tourism policy development. *Tourism Management, 31*(6), 871–880.
Castro, J. M. (2005). *Indicadores de desarrollo sostenible urbano. Una aplicación para Andalucía* [Indicators of urban sustainable development. An application for Andalucía]. Sevilla: Instituto de Estadística de Andalucía.
Céron, J. P., & Dubois, G. (2000). Les indicateurs du tourisme durable. Un outil à manier avec discernement [Sustainable tourism indicators. A discernment tool]. *Tourisme Durable-Cahiers Espaces, 67,* 30–46. Retrieved from http://www.revue-espaces.com/librairie/940/tourisme-durable.html
Céron, J. P., & Dubois, G. (2003). Tourism and sustainable development indicators: The gap between theoretical demands and practical achievements. *Current Issues in Tourism, 6*(1), 54–75.
Chris, H., & Sirakaya, E. (2006). Sustainability indicators for managing community tourism. *Tourism Management, 27*(6), 1274–1289.
Cocossis, H., & Mexa, A. (2004). *The challenge of tourism carrying capacity assessment: Theory and practice.* Aldershot: Ashgate.
Crabtree, B., & Bayfield, N. (1998). Developing sustainability indicators for mountain ecosystems: A study of the Cairngorms, Scotland. *Journal of Environmental Management, 52*(1), 1–14.
Dahl, A. L. (1995). Towards indicators of sustainability. In *Meeting of SCOPE Scientific Workshop on Indicators of Sustainable Development.* Wuppertal: United Nations.
Gahin, R., Veleva, V., & Hart, M. (2003). Do indicators help create sustainable communities? *Local Environment, 8*(6), 661–666.
Garrigós, F. J., Narangajavana, Y., & Palacios, D. (2004). Carrying capacity in the tourism industry: A case study of Hengistbury Head. *Tourism Management, 25*(2), 275–283.
Gössling, S. (2000). Sustainable tourism development in developing countries: Some aspects of energy use. *Journal of Sustainable Tourism, 8*(5), 410–425.
Hall, C. M., & Lew, A. A. (1998). The geography of sustainable tourism: Lessons and prospects. In C. M. Hall & A. A. Lew (Eds.), *Sustainable tourism: A geographical perspective* (pp. 199–203). New York, NY: Longman.
Hezri, A. A., & Dovers, S. R. (2006). Sustainability indicators, policy and governance: Issues for ecological economics. *Ecological Economics, 60*(1), 86–99.
Holden, A. (2003). In need of new environmental ethics for tourism? *Annals of Tourism Research, 30*(1), 94–108.
Holden, A. (2007). *Environment and tourism.* London: Routledge.
Hughes, P. (1994). *La planificación del turismo sostenible. El proyecto Ecomost* [Sustainable tourism planning. The Ecomost project]. Lewes: Federación Internacional de Tour Operadores (IFTO).
Hunter, C. J. (1995). On the need to re-conceptualise sustainable tourism development. *Journal of Sustainable Tourism, 3*(3), 155–165.
Hunter, C. J. (1997). Sustainable tourism as an adaptive paradigm. *Annals of Tourism Research, 24*(4), 850–867.
Hunter, C., & Shaw, J. (2007). The ecological footprint as a key indicator of sustainable tourism. *Tourism Management, 28*(1), 46–57.
Ivars, J. A. (Ed.). (2001). *Planificación y gestión del desarrollo turístico sostenible: Propuestas para la creación de un sistema de indicadores* [Planning and management of sustainable

tourism development: Proposal for producing a set of indicators]. Alicante: University of Alicante, Geographical University Institute.

James, D. (2004). Local sustainable tourism indicator. *Estudios Turísticos, 161–162*, 219–232.

Ko, T. G. (2005). Development of a tourism sustainability assessment procedure: A conceptual approach. *Tourism Management, 26*(3), 431–445.

Lee, K. F. (2001). Sustainable tourism destination: The importance of cleaner production. *Journal of Cleaner Production, 9*(4), 313–323.

Liu, Z. (2003). Sustainable tourism development: A critique. *Journal of Sustainable Tourism, 11*(6), 459–475.

Logar, I. (2010). Sustainable tourism management in Crikvenica, Croatia: An assessment of policy instruments. *Tourism Management, 31*(1), 125–135.

Manning, T. (1999). Indicators of tourism sustainability. *Tourism Management, 20*(2), 179–181.

Mayer, A. L. (2008). Strengths and weaknesses of common sustainability indices for multidimensional systems. *Environment International, 34*(2), 277–291.

McCool, S. F., Moisey, R. N., & Nickerson, N. P. (2001). What should tourism sustain? The disconnect with industry perceptions of useful indicators. *Journal of Travel Research, 40*(2), 124–131.

McElroy, J. L. (1998). Tourism penetration index in small Caribbean islands. *Annals of Tourism Research, 25*(1), 145–168.

Miller, G. (2001). The development of indicators for sustainable tourism: Results of a Delphi survey of tourism researchers. *Tourism Management, 22*(4), 351–362.

Moore, S. A., & Polley, A. (2007). Defining indicators and standards for tourism impacts in protected areas: Cape Range National Park, Australia. *Environmental Management, 39*(3), 291–300. Retrieved from http://www.springerlink.com/content/0364-152X

Organisation for Economic Co-operation and Development. (2008). *Handbook on constructing composite indicators. Methodology and user guide.* Retrieved form http://browse.oecdbookshop.org/oecd/pdfs/free/3008251e.pdf

Roberts, S., & Tribe, J. (2008). Sustainability indicators for small tourism enterprises – an exploratory perspective. *Journal of Sustainable Tourism, 16*(5), 575–594.

Saarinen, J. (2006). Traditions of sustainability in tourism studies. *Annals of Tourism Research, 33*(4), 1121–1140.

Saltelli, A. (2007). Composite indicators between analysis and advocacy. *Social Indicators Research, 81*(1), 65–77.

Sánchez, M., & Pulido, J. I. (2008) *Medida de la sostenibilidad turística. Propuesta de un índice sintético* [Measuring the tourism sustainability. Proposal of a synthetic index]. Madrid: Editorial Universitaria Ramón Areces.

Sancho, A., & Ruíz, P. (2004). Planteamiento metodológico para el uso de indicadores en la gestión turística de espacios naturales protegidos [Methodological approach for using indicators in tourism management of natural reserves]. In *Meeting of IX Congreso AECIT. El Uso Turístico de los Espacios Naturales* [IX AECIT Congress. Tourist Use of Natural Spaces]. Logroño: AECIT.

Schianetz, K., & Kavanagh, L. (2008). Sustainability indicators for tourism destinations: A complex adaptive systems approach using systemic indicator systems. *Journal of Sustainable Tourism, 16*(6), 601–628.

Schianetz, K., Kavanagh, L., & Lockington, D. (2007). Concepts and tools for comprehensive sustainability assessments for tourism destinations: A comparative review. *Journal of Sustainable Tourism, 15*(4), 369–389.

Schuschny, A., & Soto, H. (Eds.). (2009). *Guía metodológica. Diseño de indicadores compuestos de desarrollo sostenible* [Methodological guide. Design of composite indicators of sustainable development]. Santiago de Chile: United Nations. Retrieved from http://www.eclac.org/publicaciones/xml/7/36127/W255-2.pdf

Sharpe, A. (Ed.). (2004). *Literature review of frameworks for macro-indicators.* Ottawa: Centre for the Study of Living Standards. Retrieved form http://www.csls.ca/reports/LitRevMacro-indicators.pdf

Sharpley, R. (2000). Tourism and sustainable development: Exploring the theoretical divide. *Journal of Sustainable Tourism, 8*(1), 1–19.

Sharpley, R. (2009). *Tourism development and the environment: Beyond sustainability?* London: Earthscan.

Singh, R. K., Murty, H. R., Gupta, S. K., & Dikshit, A. K. (2009). An overview of sustainability assessment methodologies. *Ecological Indicators, 9*(2), 189–212.

Sirakaya, E., Jamal, T., & Choi, H. S. (2001). Developing indicators for destination sustainability. In D. B. Weaver (Ed.), *The encyclopedia of ecotourism* (pp. 411–432). New York, NY: CAB International.

Smeets, E., & Weterings, R. (Eds.). (1999). *Environmental indicators: Typology and overview.* Copenhagen: European Environment Agency. Retrieved from http://www.eea.europa.eu/publications/TEC25

Spanish Ministry for the Environment. (2003). *Sistema español de indicadores ambientales de turismo* [Spanish set of environmental indicators for tourism]. Madrid: Ministerio de Medio Ambiente.

Sureda, B., & Felipe, J. J. (2010). Avaluació de la sostenibilitat [Sustainability assessment]. In E. Carrera & J. Segalàs (Eds.), *Tecnologia i sostenibilitat* [Technology and sustainability]. Terrassa: Universitat Politècnica de Catalunya. Retrieved from http://tecnologiaisostenibilitat.cus.upc.edu

Torres-Delgado, A. (2010). Sostenibilitat i modalitats turístiques: Una anàlisi de casos a Catalunya [Sustainability and tourist modalities: Case studies in Catalonia]. *Documents d'Anàlisi Geogràfica, 56*(3), 479–502. Retrieved from http://ddd.uab.es/record/14

Twining-Ward, L., & Butler, R. (2002). Implementing STD on a small island: Development and use of sustainable tourism development indicators in Samoa. *Journal of Sustainable Tourism, 10*(5), 363–387.

Valentin, A., & Spangenberg, J. H. (2000). A guide to community sustainability indicators. *Environmental Impact Assessment Review, 20*(3), 381–392.

Vera, J. F., & Ivars, J. A. (2003). Measuring sustainability in a mass tourist destination: Pressures, perceptions and policy responses in Torrevieja, Spain. *Journal of Sustainable Tourism, 11*(2–3), 181–203.

Vila, M., Costa, G., & Rovira, X. (2010). The creation and use of scorecards in tourism planning: A Spanish example. *Tourism Management, 31*(2), 232–239.

Wheeller, B. (1993). Sustaining the ego. *Journal of Sustainable Tourism, 1*(2), 121–129.

White, V., McCrum, G., Blackstock, K. L., & Scott, A. (Eds.). (2006a). *Indicators of sustainability and sustainable tourism: Some examples sets.* Aberdeen: The Macaulay Institute.

White, V., McCrum, G., Blackstock, K. L., & Scott, A. (Eds.). (2006b). *Indicators and sustainable tourism: Literature review.* Aberdeen: The Macaulay Institute.

Wilson, J., Tyedmers, P., & Pelot, R. (2007). Contrasting and comparing sustainable development indicator metrics. *Ecological Indicators, 7*(2), 299–314.

World Summit on Sustainable Development. (2002). *Report of the World Summit on sustainable development.* New York, NY: United Nations.

World Tourism Organization. (1995). *What tourism managers need to know: A practical guide to the development and use of indicators of sustainable tourism.* Madrid: Author.

World Tourism Organization. (1996). *Agenda 21 for the travel and tourism industry.* Madrid: World Travel Tourism Council and Earth Council.

World Tourism Organization. (2005). *Guidebook on indicators of sustainable development for tourism destinations.* Madrid: Author.

Sustainability indicators of rural tourism from the perspective of the residents

Mercedes Marzo-Navarro, Marta Pedraja-Iglesias and Lucia Vinzón

In tourism, sustainable development represents a way to exercise a business activity such that the needs of both the tourists and the receiving regions are satisfied, while at the same time protecting and fostering future opportunities by preserving essential ecological processes, biological diversity and cultural integrity. There is broad scientific consensus about the need to consolidate an ethical paradigm that combines economic objectives with the principles of ecology, sustainable development and citizen participation. In view of this situation, it has become necessary to identify how to measure compliance with these principles, identify what indicators must be used and determine what perspective must be adopted. Therefore, the objective of this work was to develop measurement models of the sustainability concepts associated with rural tourism from the residents' perspective. Using data from a survey, the results obtained have led to the development and validation of instruments that reliably measure the sustainability dimensions from the residents' perspective. As a result, tourism managers have access to an instrument that allows them to analyse the opinions of the residents of an area regarding the tourism development that takes place there.

在旅游,可持续发展是一种方式来行使商业活动,例如,无论是游客和接收地区的需求得到满足,而在同一时间的保护和维护所必需的生态过程,生物多样性和文化的完整性促进未来的机会。有大约需要巩固,结合经济目标与生态,可持续发展和公民参与的原则的道德范式广泛的科学共识。鉴于这种情况,它已成为必要确定如何衡量遵守这些原则,确定指标必须使用什么,决定什么角度来看,必须通过。因此,这项工作的目的是开发与居民乡村旅游相关的可持续发展概念的计量模型观点。从调查所用数据, 得到的结果也导致了可靠地测量从居民的角度来看,可持续性方面的仪器的开发和验证。因此,旅游经营者有机会获得一个工具,使他们能够分析一个地区的居民就旅游业发展,发生在那里的意见。

Introduction

The approaches used as the basis for economic growth in the twentieth century began to be questioned at the time of the serious international economic crises of the seventies. These approaches were characterised by the complete absence of any relationship between the economic system and the environmental system, given that they were based on mass production and mass consumption and considered resources to be unlimited. The economic crises resulted in the appearance of a new form of understanding economic development at the end of the eighties, in which not only was the environmental variable included, but also a social variable.

Tourism was one of the fields in which this new paradigm of sustainable development soon began to be applied (Saarinen, 2006; Valdés, 2001). Ever since the initial studies conducted by the International Union of Official Travel Organizations during the 70's tourism's dependence on the conservation of natural resources has been emphasised, and studies have consistently highlighted the fact that the risks of tourism's impacts would become worse with an increase in tourism (Flores, 2007). Currently, there is broad scientific consensus about the need to consolidate an ethical paradigm that combines economic objectives with the principles of ecology, sustainable development and citizen participation.

Sustainability involves reconciling economic interests with natural resources and local cultures so that these resources and cultures can be preserved in benefit to future generations. Thus, sustainability in relation to tourism should be understood as a strategic decision that contributes to local development based on ecological, sociocultural and economic principles (Butler, 1999, 2011; Flores, 2007; Sánchez, 2009).

But, how can compliance with these principles be measured? What indicators should be used? What perspective should be adopted? Despite the years that have gone by, there are still no clear answers to these questions. Recently, Torres-Delgado and Saarinen (2014) have conducted a major review of the main indicators used to measure the impacts of tourism. These authors reveal the problems that exist, both conceptual and technical, and the absence of a consensus regarding the possible solutions. In addition, impacts can be different depending on the destination, the business activity and/or the analysed stakeholder (Nunkoo & Ramkissoon, 2011; Twining-Ward & Butler, 2002), wherefore it is clearly necessary to apply multidisciplinary approaches to the study of sustainable tourism (Torres-Delgado & Saarinen, 2014).

The objective of this work has been to develop measurement models of the sustainability concepts associated with rural tourism from the residents' perspective. This approach, centred on the residents, is due to the fact that they represent the central stakeholder of a tourism destination, given that the tourism development of a destination is only justified if the quality of life of the residents improves, or at least it does not deteriorate (Andriotis & Vaughan, 2003; Ap, 1992; Jurowski & Gursoy, 2004; Jurowski, Uysal, & Williams, 1997). Moreover, in rural areas, tourism constitutes an important tool for development (Briedenhann & Wickens, 2004; Millán & Pérez, 2014), given that it is an activity that generates wealth for local communities and is a determining factor in the conservation of the natural and sociocultural resources (Reyna, 1992). Therefore, it is hereby endeavoured to provide measurement instruments of the economic, sociocultural and environmental sustainability of rural tourism from the point of view of the residents in an area.

To do so, a review of the concept of sustainable tourism is conducted, thereby establishing its dimensions and emphasising the importance of having subjective indicators. Subsequently, reliable measurement instruments of the sustainability dimensions from the residents' perspective are developed and validated. An instrument is thus provided so that tourism managers can analyse the opinions of the residents of an area regarding the tourism development that is taking place there. And even though quantitative objective indicators may not be used, these opinions are vitally important, given that the attitude of the residents is key to the success of a tourism destination (Ap, 1992; Choi & Murray, 2010; Lee, 2013; Lindberg & Johnson, 1997; McGehee & Anderek, 2004; Ramseook & Naidoo, 2011; Stylidis, Biran, Sit, & Szivas, 2014).

Sustainable tourism

Sustainable development attempts to reconcile the interests of economic growth with better living conditions. In tourism, this development represents a way to exercise a business activity such that the needs of both the tourists and the receiving regions are satisfied, while at the same time protecting and fostering future opportunities by preserving essential ecological processes, biological diversity and cultural integrity (Bosch, 1998; Zeballos, 2003).

This sustainable tourism development requires political will and the participation of the local population to achieve a balance between preserving the natural and cultural heritage, the economic viability of tourism and the social equity of development (Ivars, 2001; Farmaki, Altinay, Botterill, & Hilke, 2015). Therefore, all the social players must be involved in the search for sustainability, which is why tourism development models must be defined from a comprehensive perspective and a holistic view (Sánchez, 2009).

Dimensions of sustainable tourism

The World Tourism Organization (WTO) and the United Nations Environment Programme (UNEP) (2006) define sustainable tourism as tourism that takes full account of its current and future economic, social and environmental impacts, addressing the needs of visitors, the industry, the environment and host communities. Therefore, the concept of sustainability is multidimensional, given that it has economic, sociocultural and environmental dimensions. Thus, sustainable results must be reached, which balance the social, economic and environmental aspirations of the communities, as well as the costs and benefits of the key stakeholders, and which do not deteriorate the quality of the existing resources (United Nations Development Programme [PNUD], 2008; Saxena, Clark, Oliver, & Ilbery, 2007). The implicit attempt is to reach harmony between modernness and tradition (Tracey & Clark, 2003).

The *economic dimension* is fundamentally related to satisfying human material needs and objectives. It refers to the fact that the level of economic gain from an activity should be sufficient to cover the costs of all actions taken to take care of tourists, to mitigate the effects caused by their presence and to offer adequate income to pay for the inconveniences caused to the visited community, all without violating any of the other dimensions (Mowforth & Munt, 2003). Moreover, it refers to the capacity to promote a dynamic competitiveness of tourism products and destinations that allows an advantage to continue to be generated for the inhabitants of an area. This is where macro- and micro-economic policies that generate income, currencies, investment, employment and high added value for the country or region, companies and persons in both the tourism sector and in related support sectors should be included, thereby seeking an optimum balance, in each place and at each moment, between national production and the input of imported goods and services (Carner, 2001).

The *sociocultural dimension* is related to questions of equity, fairness and social development. It refers to the ability of a community to absorb the tourism inputs and to continue functioning without rupturing social harmony or the ability to adapt the functioning and relations of a community so that the disharmony that is created can be mitigated (Mowforth & Munt, 2003). It also takes into account the ability of the people to retain or adapt elements of their culture. Culture is as dynamic as society or the economy, although the process of cultural change and adaptation does not necessarily have to be negative. Thus, controlling harmful effects, emphasising the responsible behaviour of visitors and preventing the distortion of local culture could be considered essential elements of cultural sustainability (Mowforth & Munt, 2003). This sustainability is based on a series of strategies that include the use of tourism to effectively develop people in terms of access to basic infrastructure services, in addition to effectively preserving and extolling cultural identity.

The *environmental dimension* is what studies related to sustainable tourism development initially focussed on (Gössling, 1999; Gössling, Borgström, Hörstmeier, & Saggel, 2002; Maldonado, Hurtado, & Saborio, 1992). This dimension refers to protecting natural varieties and preserving the cycles of the environment. Thus, management and control of the impacts to the environment caused by the production and consumption of tourism services are the principal themes that have been analysed (Carner, 2001; Mowforth & Munt, 2003; Saxena et al., 2007).

To promote the sustainability of tourism in rural areas, certain requisites must be met, which include support for economic aspects and, in turn, protection of the characteristics inherent in the local culture and the quality of the environment (Northcote & Macbeth, 2006; Pigram, 1994). The activities and objectives of the industrial sector can enter into conflict with the priorities of sustainability, yet they must not receive preference and must meet the aforesaid requisites (Cawley & Gillmor, 2008). The sustainable use of resources and activities tends towards economic viability and towards the sociocultural conservation of resources, but non-sustainable use tends to generate high rates of business failure and sociocultural deterioration (Saxena et al., 2007). Moreover, an analysis of the environmental dimension is critical in rural tourism, since rural territories are characterised by being fragile; yet at the same time, enjoying the environment is one of the main motivations, if not the main motivation, for the demand (Flores, 2007).

Sustainability indicators from a subjective perspective

In order to be able to manage the previously established sustainability dimensions, they must be made operational. To do so, a series of observable indicators that include the most important aspects of each dimension must be determined (Churchill, 1979).

The studies that have been conducted, regardless of the tourism destination, focus on trying to establish indicators of the previously established dimensions. These indicators can be established from an objective perspective (Blancas, González, Lozano-Oyola, & Pérez, 2010; Castellani & Sala, 2010; McCool, Moisey, & Nickerson, 2001; Chris & Sirakaya, 2006; Sánchez & Pulido, 2008) and/or from a subjective perspective (Andereck & Vogt, 2000; Byrd, Bosley, & Dronberger, 2009; Clark & Chabrel, 2007; Ilbery, Saxena, & Kneafsey, 2007; Tsaur, Lin, & Lin, 2006).

The problems that are derived from the search for objective indicators (Torres-Delgado & Saarinen, 2014), in conjunction with the need to know the opinions of certain stakeholders, reveal the importance of the subjective perspective. Thus, the reality is that matters related to the nature and extent of tourism development must be supported by the community as a whole. This means that, regardless of the direction taken by tourism development in a community, it must be supported by the citizens who are affected by it (Goeldner & Ritchie, 2006). Given that the residents are a fundamental part of the tourism product, their attitudes and behaviours have a considerable impact on the success of the destination (Deery, Jago, & Fredline, 2012; Lee, 2013; Liu & Var, 1986), considering that, for example, they affect visitor satisfaction (Andriotis & Vaughan, 2003; Díaz & Gutiérrez, 2010).

Specialised literature shows that residents represent the central stakeholder of a tourism destination, and implementing specific tourism development is only justified if it improves the quality of life of the residents or at least does not cause their quality of life to deteriorate

(Allen, Hafer, Long, & Perdue, 1993; Andriotis & Vaughan, 2003; Fredline & Faulkner, 2000; Jurowski et al., 1997; Jurowski & Gursoy, 2004; Sheldon & Abenoja, 2001; Sirakaya, Teye, & Sonmez, 2002). Thus, the residents are ultimately those who decide which impacts by tourism are acceptable and which impacts are not. As it was established by Andriotis and Vaughan (2003), the balance between the costs and benefits that residents perceive to be associated with tourism development constitutes the main determining factor of tourist satisfaction, wherefore it is essential for the success of the tourism industry.

Therefore, a study of the residents' attitudes is key (Kim, Uysal, & Sirgy, 2013), because their attitudes must necessarily form a part of the planning processes of destinations. And as a result, the perceived impact of tourism is one of the main predictors of stakeholder support for the development of sustainable tourism in a community (Alector, Oom, & Albino, 2013; Kayat, Mohd, & Karnchanan, 2013; Lee, 2013; Sharpley, 2014; Stylidis et al., 2014).

Methodology

In order to be able to advance in a field of knowledge, the concepts of that field must be suitably measured through empirical indicators (Carmines & Zeller, 1994). Therefore, it is essential to correctly define these concepts, considering both the content and how they are worded. These concepts are operationalised through variables, which generally cannot be directly observed or for which a direct assessment cannot be assigned. In these cases, a measurement instrument that allows measuring the variable and reliably and validly estimating the nature of the concept must be created. The processes used most often for developing measurement instruments are those proposed by Churchill (1979), DeVellis (1991) and Lazarsfeld (1985).

These processes start with a definition of the concept or domain under study. A sample of items for each domain is subsequently generated, for which it is necessary to review relevant literature, interview experts, interview subjects, etc. (Escrig & Bou, 2002; Ortega, Jiménez, Palao, & Sainz, 2008). Then information from the selected sample is gathered through a pre-test. The objective is to conduct an initial filter of the created measurement instrument by assessing its reliability (Cronbach's alpha) and validity. After filtering the scale, new field work is conducted using different samples. The reliability and validity of the scale is assessed in depth, and finally it is necessary to define how the obtained values are interpreted. This process therefore allows us to propose standardised measures to assess variables that are not directly observable.

A review of specialised literature (Andereck & Vogt, 2000; Ap, 1992; Ap & Crompton, 1998; Byrd et al., 2009; Clark & Chabrel, 2007; Ilbery et al., 2007; Lankford & Howard, 1994; Lindberg & Johnson, 1997; Liu & Var, 1986; Tsaur et al., 2006) allowed us to propose a conceptual definition for each one of the domains, which would allow operationalising those elements through a series of observable indicators that include the most important aspects of each concept (Churchill, 1979). Specifically, the definitions and indicators were proposed, as shown in Chart 1.

A group of 89 international experts were selected and contacted. The experts on the panel conduct their academic and/or professional activities in Argentina, Australia, Bolivia, Spain and Portugal. This panel included academics and researchers specialising in sustainable tourism, rural development, tourism and environmental management, territorial studies and tourism, rural community development, tourism marketing, tourism planning and rural entrepreneurship. The panel also included consultants on sustainable tourism projects, consultants on the development of tourism destinations and municipal

Chart 1. Proposed indicators.

Economic Sustainability	
Referring to the economic effects caused by the development of tourism.	The rural tourism activities that exist in the region generate employment opportunities for the community.
	The rural tourism activities that exist in the region provide benefits to the companies involved.
	The rural tourism activities that exist in the region generate benefits for the entire community.
	The rural tourism activities that exist in the region allow improvement of the existing infrastructures.
	The rural tourism activities that exist in the region improve the quality of life.
Sociocultural Sustainability	
Referring to the sociocultural effects caused by the development of tourism.	The rural tourism activities that exist in the region help to preserve the culture and identity of the region.
	The rural tourism activities that exist in the region maintain the traditional culture.
	The rural tourism activities that exist in the region improve the look of the cities and towns.
	The rural tourism activities that exist in the region help to preserve the social welfare (health, safety, etc.) of the region.
	The rural tourism activities that exist in the region increase leisure opportunities.
	The rural tourism activities that exist in the region improve public services and infrastructures (transport, roads, water services, electric power, etc.).
Environmental Sustainability	
Referring to the environmental effects caused by the development of tourism.	The rural tourism activities that exist in the region favour the conservation of natural resources.
	The rural tourism activities that exist in the region increase the ecological awareness of society.
	The rural tourism activities that exist in the region favour the development of policies directed at maintaining the environment.

directors of tourism. Responses were obtained from 34 of them, out of which 26 were valid for this study since they provided all the requested information. Thus, the minimum of 10 experts recommended for this type of study was exceeded (Dunn, Bouffard, & Rogers, 1999). These experts were asked to fill out a questionnaire in which the definitions included in Chart 1 and a list of the potential indicators thereof was provided. Using an agreement scale ranging from 0 for 'Completely Disagree' to 10 for 'Completely Agree', the experts were requested to assess two aspects: (1) the suitability of each proposed indicator for building a valid measurement of the analysed dimension and (2) the ease of comprehension of each indicator by potential respondents. This procedure took place during the months of September and October 2011. An analysis of the experts' responses did not reveal the existence of any major problems regarding comprehension of the proposed indicators. Thus, all the average values and the corresponding medians of

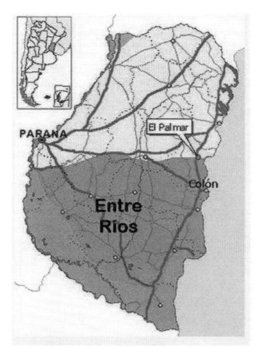

Figure 1. Map of El Palmar.

the proposed items were greater than 8, wherefore, following Bulger and Housner (2007), it was not necessary to modify and/or eliminate any item.

After the experts' assessment of content validity, the proposed instruments were then tested in a representative sample of the population under study. The analysed information was obtained from a personal survey, face to face, targeted at residents of the locales and towns of the districts of Colón and San Salvador (Argentina). Questionnaires were handed out to residents by one of the researchers. These areas offer rural tourism activities, and they are characterised by the richness and variety of their natural and cultural resources. Their main tourism attractions are river beaches, hot springs and one of the main natural reserves of Argentina, 'El Palmar' National Park (see Figure 1). Moreover, many of the locales in this area are agricultural colonies founded by European immigrants, whose historical and cultural legacy holds importance to tourism. There are also small rural towns that offer the charm of their local culture and identity. These locales have been collaborating since 2007 on the development of a joint tourism destination, called 'Tierra de Palmares'. One of its objectives is sustainable development.

The field work was conducted during January and February 2012, when 377 usable questionnaires were obtained.[1]

All the variables were measured through 11-point Likert scales, from 0 for 'Completely Disagree' to 10 for 'Completely Agree'.

There is a predominance of women (64.51%) and 58.4% of the sample is under the age of 35. Nearly half the sample (43%) have completed secondary education, and 17.1% have taken university studies. Regarding the place of residence, 42.7% reside in Colón, the main city in the area, and 12.9% reside in the smallest communities (9.6% in towns with fewer than 1000 inhabitants). Regarding the years of residence in the area, it can be observed that over half of the sample (56.7%) are long-term residents (over 25 years).

Analysis and results

Table 1 shows the main descriptive of the items used, and it can observe that all the mean values obtained are above the mid-point of the scale used. Thus, looking at economic sustainability, it can be observed how the highest assessments correspond to the perceptions of benefits being obtained by the companies involved in tourism development (8.01) and of generating employment opportunities (7.09). The remaining indicators have mean values of close to 7. Regarding Sociocultural Sustainability, the values obtained show the belief that tourism development improves the look of towns and cities (7.54) and helps to preserve local culture and identity (7.53). Lower average assessments correspond to the improvement of public infrastructures (5.75) and social welfare (6.17). Finally, the Environmental Sustainability indicators show mean values of close to 6.5, wherefore it could be deduced that there is a good impact by tourism on the conservation of natural resources (6.77), on increasing ecological awareness (6.49) and on developing actions to maintain the natural environment (6.45).

In this research content validity and construct validity are used to assess the validity of the proposed instruments. For content validity, the 'expert judges' technique is used (Nunnally, 1987; Wieserma, 2001), while for construct validity, an exploratory factor analysis with principal components is performed (Martínez, 1996), which is validated through a confirmatory analysis. This allows us to determine whether the proposed measurement instrument can be reproduced (Thomas & Nelson, 2007), thus providing evidence of reliability. In other words, it is possible to know the extent to which the

Table 1. Sustainability descriptives.

The rural tourism activities that exist in the region ...		Mean		Mode	SD
Economic sustainability					
P1	... generate employment opportunities for the community	7.09	↑	10.00	2.71
P2	... provide benefits to the companies involved	8.01	↑	8.00	1.90
P3	... generate benefits for the entire community	6.94	↑	8.00	2.56
P4	... allow improvement of the existing infrastructures	6.99	↑	7.00	2.46
P5	... improve the quality of life	6.65	↑	8.00	2.46
Sociocultural sustainability					
P6	... help to preserve the culture and identity of the region	7.53	↑	8.00	2.13
P7	... maintain the traditional culture.	7.30	↑	8.00	2.18
P8	... improve the look of the cities and towns.	7.54	↑	8.00	2.00
P9	... help to preserve the social welfare (health, safety, etc.) of the region	6.17	↑	5.00	2.53
P10	... increase leisure opportunities.	6.76	↑	8.00	2.44
P11	... improve public services and infrastructures (transport, roads, water services, electric power, etc.).	5.75	↑	7.00	2.76
Environmental sustainability					
P12	... favour the conservation of natural resources	6.77	↑	8.00	2.32
P13	... increase the ecological awareness of society	6.49	↑	7.00	2.42
P14	... favour the development of policies directed at maintaining the environment	6.45	↑	8.00	2.54

Note: ↓ Statistically below the mid-point of the scale (5) (with a 95% confidence interval); ↑ Statistically above the mid-point of the scale (5) (with a 95% confidence interval)

Table 2. Communalities and percentage of variance explained by the economic sustainability component.

The rural tourism activities that exist in the region …	F1
P1 … generate employment opportunities for the community	0.863
P2 … provide benefits to the companies involved	0.764
P3 … generate benefits for the entire community	0.881
P4 … allow improvement of the existing infrastructures	0.865
P5 … improve the quality of life	0.791
Factor variance %	69.569
Cronbach's alpha	0.889

proposed indicators reflect the theoretical latent constructs that those indicators are designed to measure (Hair, Black, Babin, & Anderson, 2010).

The Principal Components Analysis with varimax rotation conducted to determine the underlying dimensional structure in the representative variables of economic sustainability led to the results shown in Table 2. These results clearly show the existence of a component (F1) that explains 69.569% of the variance. This component groups together the five items that reflect the economic effects that are derived from the tourism development (mainly rural) that exists in the analysed region. Moreover, the reliability of the proposed scale is supported by the value of Cronbach's alpha coefficient, 0.889 (Nunnally, 1987).

To judge the suitability of the identified structure, the confirmatory factor analysis model was estimated (Model 1). This model presents the overall goodness-of-fit statistics and indexes shown in Table 3. As it can be observed, the proposed model (Model 1) must be rejected in view of the values of the p-value statistic. Moreover, the reliability of the observed variables is not suitable, given that the R^2 of the P2 variable ('The rural tourism activities that exist in the region provide benefits to the companies involved') takes a value of <0.5, so this indicator should not be considered.

A new measurement model is therefore given, which has one factor and four items (Model 2). The goodness-of-fit statistics and indexes of the proposed model, shown in Table 3, demonstrate the suitability of the structure. Regarding the estimated parameters of the economic sustainability component (F1) and observing Figure 2, it should be pointed out that the reliability coefficients of the observed variables (R^2) exceed 0.7. In addition, the reliability coefficients (CF1 and CF2) of the latent variable are indicative of the reliability according to which the latent variable is inferred. Thus, the economic sustainability structure is confirmed in terms of internal validity.

Therefore, the existence of the economic sustainability dimension is confirmed, as well as its unidimensional structure. Its main indicators are the improvement of infrastructures (P4) and the generation of benefits for the entire community (P3).

The same procedure was followed for the two remaining types of sustainability. Thus, the Principal Components analysis with varimax rotation conducted with the set of

Table 3. Goodness-of-fit statistics and indexes, economic sustainability models.

	DF	χ^2S-B	p	R-RMSEA	SRMR	GFI	AGFI	R-BBN	R-CFI
Model 1	5	20.5033	0.00101	0.097	0.045	0.941	0.822	0.953	0.928
Model 2	2	6.2745	0.04340	0.080	0.019	0.986	0.930	0.983	0.966

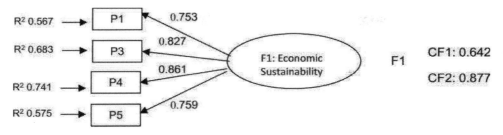

Figure 2. Reliability parameters and coefficients of Model 2, economic sustainability.

variables representing Sociocultural Sustainability shows the existence of a component that explains 54.933% of the variance (see Table 4).

The reliability analysis of the scale by calculating Cronbach's alpha coefficient, which takes a value of 0.820, allows accepting the scale (Nunnally, 1987). However, this reliability is increased if item P11, 'The rural tourism activities that exist in the region improve public services and infrastructures (transport, roads, water services, electric power, etc.)', and item P10, 'The rural tourism activities that exist in the region increase leisure opportunities', are eliminated. After eliminating these indicators, the final reliability of the proposed scale is increased and takes a value of 0.841.

To judge the suitability of the identified structure, the confirmatory factor analysis model was estimated (Model 3). This model presents the overall goodness-of-fit statistics and indexes shown in Table 5. As it can be observed, the proposed model (Model 3) must be rejected in view of the values of the *p*-value statistic. Moreover, the reliability of two observed variables is not suitable, given that the R^2 of variable P9, 'The rural tourism activities that exist in the region help to preserve the social welfare (health, safety, etc.)

Table 4. Communalities and percentage of variance explained by the sociocultural sustainability component.

The rural tourism activities that exist in the region …	F2
P6 … help to preserve the culture and identity of the region	0.815
P7 … maintain the traditional culture	0.806
P8 … improve the look of the cities and towns	0.809
P9 … help to preserve the social welfare (health, safety, etc.) of the region	0.793
P10 … increase leisure opportunities	0.612
P11 … improve public services and infrastructures (transport, roads, water services, electric power, etc.)	0.569
Factor variance %	54.933
Cronbach's alpha	0.820

Table 5. Goodness-of-fit statistics and indexes, sociocultural sustainability models.

	DF	χ^2S-B	*p*	R-RMSEA	SRMR	GFI	AGFI	R-BBN	R-CFI
Model 3	2	19.5986	0.00006	0.165	0.060	0.952	0.759	0.944	0.949
Model 4	1	0.0039	0.94993	0.000	.002	.0000	1.000	1.000	1.000

Figure 3. Reliability parameters and coefficients of Model 4, sociocultural sustainability.

of the region', and variable P8, 'The rural tourism activities that exist in the region improve the look of the cities and towns', end with values of <0.5 (0.297 and 0.420), wherefore said items should not be considered.

Therefore, a new measurement model is given, with one factor and two items (Model 4), and this model shows negative degrees of freedom. In order to be able to estimate this model, two restrictions have to be established: (1) equality of errors and (2) equality of factor loadings, which imply that the measurements are parallel. By establishing these restrictions, one degree of freedom can be obtained, and it is therefore possible to obtain the goodness-of-fit statistics and indexes of the model.

The goodness-of-fit statistics and indexes of the proposed model (Model 4), shown in Table 5, demonstrate the suitability of the structure. Regarding the estimated parameters of Sociocultural Sustainability (F2) and observing Figure 3, it should be pointed out that the reliability coefficients of the observed variables (R^2) exceed 0.7. In addition, the reliability coefficients (CF1 and CF2) of the latent variable are indicative of the reliability according to which the latent variable is inferred. Thus, the structure of the Sociocultural Sustainability construct is confirmed in terms of internal validity.

Finally, the Principal Components analysis with varimax rotation conducted with the set of variables representing Environmental Sustainability shows the existence of a component (F3) that explains 84.788% of the variance (see Table 6).

This component groups together three items that are indicators of the environmental effects that can be exercised by tourism development in the area. The reliability analysis conducted by calculating Cronbach's alpha coefficient, which takes a value of 0.910, allows accepting the reliability of the scale (Nunnally, 1987), and it is not necessary to eliminate any indicator.

To judge the suitability of the identified structure, the confirmatory factor analysis model was estimated with one dimension and three items (Model 5). This model shows no degrees of freedom, and therefore, to obtain the goodness-of-fit statistics and indexes in the confirmatory factor analysis, it was necessary to establish the equality of errors as a restriction, thereby allowing us to obtain two degrees of freedom of the model.

Table 6. Communalities and percentage of variance explained by the environmental sustainability component.

The rural tourism activities that exist in the region ...	F3
P12 ... favour the conservation of natural resources	0.900
P13 ... increase the ecological awareness of society	0.948
P14 ... favour the development of policies directed at maintaining the environment	0.913
Factor variance %	84.788
Cronbach's alpha	0.910

Table 7. Goodness-of-fit statistics and indexes, environmental sustainability models.

	DF	χ^2S-B	p	R-RMSEA	SRMR	GFI	AGFI	R-BBN	R-CFI
Model 5	2	11.3852	0.00337	0.116	0.032	0.945	0.835	0.984	0.986

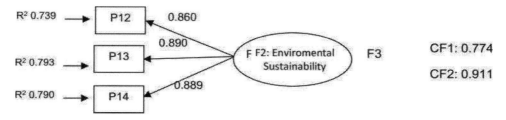

Figure 4. Reliability parameters and coefficients of Model 5, environmental sustainability.

The estimate of the model presents the overall goodness-of-fit statistics and indexes shown in Table 7. As it can be observed, the proposed model (Model 5) must be rejected in view of the values of the p-value statistic. However, the values taken by the robust-root mean square error of approximation (R-RMSEA) statistic and the goodness-of-fit indexes are adequate. Moreover, and as it can be observed in Figure 4, the reliability of the three observed variables is adequate, given that all the R^2 take on values that exceed 0.5.

Conclusions

In rural environments, due to the restructuring of the agricultural sector and the emigration of young people to cities, tourism is contemplated as a possible tool for the socio-economic reactivation of these areas. The development potential of tourism in certain rural areas is high, given the existence of natural landscapes, the existence of rural cultures and traditions, the possibility of participating in outdoor activities, the gastronomy, etc. Therefore the industries that exist in these areas could see tourism as a complement to their business activities, thereby forming an attractive tourism product that responds to the demands for new experiences by tourists. Tourism could thus constitute an alternative for diversifying and reconverting rural areas.

However, tourism development does not always generate only benefits that contribute to the development of regions. It must be kept in mind that a wide variety of players, facilities and resources participate in rural tourism, among which there are a multitude of relationships and interactions. If these elements are not considered and managed correctly, they could hinder the path towards sustainable development. Therefore, in order to manage this complex reality, it is necessary to use a comprehensive framework of analysis and a holistic model of tourism development.

The organisational structure of a tourism destination is perceived as a network of interdependent and multiple stakeholders. Therefore and in order to more sustainably manage tourism, it is imperative to both acknowledge the stakeholders and take into account their different perspectives on the issues. However, the multiplicity and heterogeneity of tourism stakeholders (residents, entrepreneurs, tourists, etc.) makes it a complex structure. Thus, different stakeholder groups can have different perceptions about tourism development, although the residents' perceptions are a key factor. Residents are the core stakeholder group of a tourist destination. The development of sustainable tourism is difficult if the residents of a community do not provide support and participate. Residents can halt the tourism efforts in their community if they do not see the benefits. Rural tourism development can only be justified if it serves to improve the quality of life of the residents or, at least, if it does not deteriorate their quality of life. Thus, as Sharpley states (2014, p. 43), 'from a planning perspective, understanding residents' perceptions of tourism impacts is as important, if not more so, than understanding the impacts themselves'.

In order to learn what opinions exist and therefore be able to adequately manage tourism, it is necessary to have an instrument that measures the main dimensions that determine sustainable development. Existing literature, despite providing different indicators, has not empirically covered this question and does not provide valid measurement instruments. Therefore, the structured procedure followed in this research allows transferring the theoretical concepts of the sustainability dimensions to empirical indicators, thereby guaranteeing validity.

The results obtained in this research increase our knowledge about the three main variables on which sustainable rural tourism is based, from the residents' point of view. Reliable and valid measures of economic, sociocultural and environmental sustainability are proposed. These measures are obtained by following a rigorous process that ranges from a detailed review of the literature used to generate the indicators to validation of the construct. Development of the scale is an integral part of advancing in our understanding of tourism. As Churchill (1979, p. 64) says 'scale development is a critical element in the evolution of a fundamental body of knowledge'.

The proposed measures are based on the opinions of the residents in a rural area of Argentina. This area is immersed in a process of tourism development, called 'Tierra de Palmares'. Its objective is to succeed with micro, regional tourism development based on sustained, sustainable and harmonic development of the tourism activity, with the guiding principles of respect for the common aspirations of the residents and visitor satisfaction.

Therefore, when planning and managing the development of a certain destination, the opinions of the residents must be taken into account and be adequately managed. Understanding the residents' perspective can facilitate policies that minimise the potential negative impacts of tourism development and maximise the benefits, thereby leading to community development and greater support for tourism. The ability to measure these opinions is as important as finding ways to increase residents' support for tourism. The results obtained have empirically verified the unidimensional structure of each one of the analysed concepts. It was subsequently possible to establish the main indicators from the point of view of the residents. Specifically, in order to determine the opinions of residents about the economic effects of rural tourism, the main indicator is their perception of the improvements to existing infrastructures and how the economic benefits are distributed to the entire community. Moreover, the notion that employment is generated and that quality of life is improved also constitute relevant indicators. If these perceptions are positive, the attitude and involvement of residents with respect to tourism development will be greater.

The same thing happens with sociocultural sustainability and environmental sustainability, which constitute key objectives for sustainable tourism development. Being able to maintain the culture and identity of a tourism destination, as well as maintain environmental resources and increase the ecological awareness of society, emerge as the fundamental aspects for guaranteeing the future of sustainable tourism development.

Therefore, it is not important for residents to have objective information about the indicators of sustainability. What is important are their beliefs. Thus, more than knowing the number of jobs that are created, they must believe that employment is actually being generated. This fact is very important if there are discrepancies between reality and beliefs. Thus, if employment is actually being created, but the residents do not perceive it, managers must make it known and modify that perception to get residents involved. Conversely, if actions are carried out and they achieve positive perceptions of the proposed indicators, then the residents' involvement in development is being fostered, and therefore favourable conditions for reaching success will be established.

This study has several limitations that provide opportunities for further research. Among the limitations, the proposed measures were only tested in relation to one recently developed destination. The perceptions of residents will be different according to the level of development of a destination. Therefore, the proposed scales must be tested in more mature destinations. Moreover, the moment in time and the circumstances (especially economic) in which the study was conducted could also have affected the results obtained. A longitudinal approach would also be adequate. Finally, it would be recommendable to analyse the points of view of the remaining stakeholders in order to study any existing discrepancies.

Disclosure statement

No potential conflict of interest was reported by the authors.

Funding

This work was supported by MICINN-FEDER [grant number ECO2010-20880] and by DGA-FSE through IMPORVE research group (S-106).

Note

1. The population of the analysed tourism area is approximately 80,000 people, so the sample obtained is representative with a confidence level of 94.4%, an error margin of 5% and a heterogeneity level of 50%.

References

Alector, M., Oom, P., & Albino, J. (2013). Residents' attitudes towards tourism development in Cape Verde Islands. *Tourism Geographies, 15*(4), 654−679.

Allen, L., Hafer, H., Long, P., & Perdue, R. (1993). Rural residents' attitudes toward recreation and tourism development. *Journal of Travel Research, 31*(4), 27−33.

Andereck, K. L., & Vogt, C. A. (2000). The relationship between residents' attitudes toward tourism and tourism development options. *Journal of Travel Research, 39,* 27−36.

Andriotis, K., & Vaughan, R. D. (2003). Urban residents' attitudes toward tourism development: The case of Crete. *Journal of Travel Research, 42*(2), 172−185.

Ap, J. (1992). Residents' perceptions on tourism impacts. *Annals of Tourism Research, 19,* 665−690.

Ap, J., & Crompton, J. L. (1998). Developing and testing a tourism impact scale. *Journal of Travel Research, 37*(November), 120−130.

Blancas, F. J., González, M., Lozano-Oyola, M., & Pérez, F. (2010). The assessment of sustainable tourism: Application to Spanish coastal destinations. *Ecological Indicators, 10*(2), 484−492.

Bosch, R. (1998). *Turismo y Medio Ambiente* [Tourism and environment]. Madrid: Centro de Estudios Ramón Arces.

Briedenhann, J., & Wickens, E. (2004). Tourism routes as a tool for the economic development of rural areas − vibrant hope or impossible dream? *Tourism Management, 25,* 71−79.

Bulger, S. M., & Housner, L. D. (2007). Modified Delphi investigation of exercise science in physical education teacher education. *Journal of Teaching in Physical Education, 26,* 57−80.

Butler, R. W. (1999). Sustainable tourism: A state-of-the-art review. *Tourism Geographies, 1*(1), 7−25.

Butler, R. W. (2011). Sustainable tourism and the changing rural scene in Europe. In D. V. L. Macleod & S. A. Gillespie (Eds.), *Sustainable tourism in rural Europe* (pp. 15−27). London: Routledge.

Byrd, E., Bosley, H., & Dronberger, M. (2009). Comparisons of stakeholder perceptions of tourism impacts in Rural Eastern North Carolina. *Tourism Management, 30,* 693−703.

Carmines, E. G., & Zeller, R. A. (1994). Reliability and validity assessment. In M. S. Lewis-Beck (Ed.), *Basic measurement* (pp. 1−58). London: Sage.

Carner, F. (2001). *Encadenamientos Generados por el Sector Turismo* [Chains from tourism sector]. México: CEPAL, Reunión de Expertos sobre el turismo en Centroamérica y el Caribe: Una visión Conceptual.

Castellani, V., & Sala, S. (2010). Sustainable performance index for tourism policy development. *Tourism Management, 31*(6), 871−880.

Cawley, M., & Gillmor, D. (2008). Integrated rural tourism: Concepts and practice. *Annals of Tourism Research, 35*(2), 316−337.

Clark, G., & Chabrel, M. (2007). Measuring integrated rural tourism. *Tourism Geographies, 9,* 371−386.

Choi, C., & Murray, I. (2010). Resident attitudes towards sustainable community tourism. *Journal of Sustainable Tourism, 18*(4), 575−594.

Chris, H., & Sirakaya, E. (2006). Sustainability indicators for managing community tourism. *Tourism Management, 27*(6), 1274−1289.

Churchill, G. A. (1979). A paradigm for developing better measures of marketing constructs. *Journal of Marketing Research, 16*(February), 64−73.

Deery, M., Jago, L., & Fredline L. (2012). Rethinking social impacts of tourism research: A new research agenda. *Tourism Management, 33*(1), 64−73.

DeVellis, R. F. (1991). *Scale development: Theory and applications*. Newbury Park, CA: Sage Publications, Inc.

Díaz, R., & Gutiérrez, G. (2010). La Actitud del Residente en el Destino Turístico de Tenerife: Evaluación y Tendencia. *Pasos, 8*(4), 431−444.

Dunn, J. L., Bouffard, M., & Rogers, W. T. (1999). Assessing item content-relevance in sport psychology scale-construction research: Issues and recommendations, measurement. *Physical Education and Exercise Science, 3*(1), 15−36.

Escrig, A. B., & Bou, J. C. (2002). Desarrollo y Validación de un Instrumento de Medida de la Dirección de la Calidad: Una Propuesta de Mejora. *Investigaciones Europeas de Dirección y Economía de la Empresa, 8*(1), 151−176.

Farmaki, A., Altinay, L., Botterill, D., & Hilke, S. (2015). Politics and sustainable tourism: the case of Cyprus. *Tourism Management, 47,* 178−190.

Flores, D. (2007). *Competitividad Sostenible de los Espacios Naturales Protegidos como Destinos Turísticos: un Análisis comparativo de los Parques Naturales Sierra de Aracena y Picos de*

Aroche y Sierras de Cazorla, Segura y las Villas (Tesis de Doctorado) [Sustainable competitiveness of protected natural areas as destinations tourist: A comparative an parsing of Natural Parks Sierra de Aracena and Picos de Aroche and Cazorla, Segura and Las Villas (Unpublished doctoral dissertation)]. Universidad de Huelva, Huelva.

Fredline, E., & Faulkner, B. (2000). Host community reactions: A cluster analysis. *Annals of Tourism Research, 27*(3), 763–784.

Goeldner, C. R., & Ritchie, J. R. B. (2006). *Tourism: Principles, practices, philosophies.* Hoboken, NJ: John Wiley.

Gössling, S. (1999). Ecotourism: A means to safeguard biodiversity and ecosystem functions? *Ecological Economics, 29*(2), 303–320.

Gössling, S., Borgström, C., Hörstmeier, O., & Saggel S. (2002). Ecological footprint analysis as a tool to assess tourism sustainability. *Ecological Economics, 43,* 199–211.

Hair, J., Black, W. C., Babin, B. J., & Anderson, R. E. (2010). *Multivariate data analysis: A global perspective.* Upper Saddle River: New Jersey-Pearson.

Ilbery, B., Saxena, G., & Kneafsey, M. (2007). Exploring tourists and gatekeepers' attitudes towards integrated rural tourism in the England-Wales border region. *Tourism Geographies, 9* (4), 441–468.

Ivars, J. A. (2001). *Planificación y Gestión del Desarrollo Turístico Sostenible: Propuesta para la Creación de un Sistema de Indicadores* [Planning and management of sustainable tourism development proposal for the creation of a system of indicators]. Alicante: Instituto Universitario de Geografía, Universidad de Alicante.

Jurowski, C., & Gursoy, D. (2004). Distance effects on residents' attitudes toward tourism. *Annals of Tourism Research, 31*(2), 296–312.

Jurowski, C., Uysal, M., & Williams, R. (1997). A theoretical analysis of host community resident reactions to tourism. *Journal of Travel Research, 36*(2), 3–11.

Kayat, K., Mohd, N., & Karnchanan, P. (2013). Individual and collective impacts and residents' perceptions of tourism. *Tourism Geographies, 15*(4), 640–653.

Kim, K., Uysal, M., & Sirgy, M. (2013). How does tourism in a community impact the quality of life of community residents? *Tourism Management, 36,* 527–540.

Lazarsfeld, P. (1985). De los Conceptos a los Índices Empíricos [From concepts to the Empirical Indices]. In P. Lazarsfeld & R. Boston (Ed.), *Metodología de las Ciencias Sociales* (Vol. 1, pp. 35–62). Barcelona: Laia.

Lankford, S. V., & Howard, D. R. (1994). Developing a tourism impact attitude scale. *Annals of Tourism Research, 21,* 121–139.

Lee, T (2013). Influence analysis of community resident support for sustainable tourism development. *Tourism Management, 34*(1), 37–46.

Lindberg, K., & Johnson, R. (1997). Modeling resident attitudes toward tourism. *Annals of Tourism Research, 24*(2), 402–424.

Liu, J. C., & Var, T. (1986). Resident attitudes toward tourism impacts in Hawaii. *Annals of Tourism Research, 13,* 193–124.

Maldonado, T., Hurtado, L., & Saborio, O. (1992). *Análisis de Capacidad de Carga para Visitación en las Áreas Silvestres de Costa Rica* [Load capacity analysis for visitation in the wilderness of Costa Rica]. San José: Fundación Neotrópica.

Martínez, R. (1996). *Psicometría: Teoría de los Tests Psicológicos y Educativos* [Psychometrics: Psychological theory and educational tests]. Madrid: Editorial Síntesis Educativa.

McCool, S. F., Moisey, R. N., & Nickerson, N. P. (2001). What should tourism sustain? The disconnect with industry perceptions of useful indicators. *Journal of Travel Research, 40*(2), 124–131.

McGehee, N., & Anderek, K. (2004). Factors predicting rural residents' support for tourism. *Journal of Travel Research, 43*(2), 131–140.

Millán, G., & Pérez, L. M. (2014). Comparación del Perfil de Enoturistas y Oleoturistas en España. Un Estudio de Caso [Comparison of wine tourists and Oleoturistas profile in Spain. A case study]. *Cuadernos de Desarrollo Rural, 11*(74), 167–188.

Mowforth, M., & Munt, I. (2003). *Tourism and sustainability: Development and new tourism in the Thir World* (2nd ed.). London: Routledge.

Northcote, J., & Macbeth, J. (2006). Conceptualizing yield: Sustainable tourism management. *Annals of Tourism Research, 33,* 199–220.

Nunkoo, R., & Ramkissoon, H. (2011). Developing a community support model for tourism. *Annals of Tourism Research, 38*(3), 964–988.

Nunnally, J. (1987). *Teoría Psicométrica* [Psychometric theory]. México: Trillas.
Ortega, E., Jiménez, J. M., Palao, J. M., & Sainz, P. (2008). Diseño y Validación de un Cuestionario para Valorar las Preferencias y Satisfacciones en Jóvenes Jugadores de Baloncesto [Design and validation of a questionnaire to assess the preferences and satisfaction in young basketball players]. *Cuadernos de Psicología del Deporte, 8*(2), 39–58.
Pigram, J. (1994). Alternative tourism: Tourism and sustainable resource management. In V. Smith & W. Eadington (Eds.), *Tourism alternatives* (pp. 76–87). Chichester: Wiley.
Ramseook, P., & Naidoo, P. (2011). Residents' attitudes towards perceived tourism benefits. *International Journal of Management and Marketing Research, 4*(3), 45–56.
Reyna, S. (1992). El Turismo Rural como Factor Determinante en la Conservación de los Recursos Naturales y Socioculturales en el Desarrollo Local [Rural tourism as a factor in the conservation of natural resources and local development in sociocultural]. In Actas de El Turismo Rural en el Desarrollo Local, Laredo (Cantabria). Madrid: Ministerio de Agricultura, Pesca y Alimentación de España.
Saarinen, J. (2006). Traditions of sustainability in tourism studies. *Annals of Tourism Research, 33*(4), 1121–1140.
Sánchez, D. C. (2009). Un Sistema de Indicadores Turísticos Básicos: Primera Aproximación [Basic system of tourism indicators: First approach]. In Actas *II Congreso Nacional de Calidad Turística*. Argentina: Mar del Plata.
Sánchez, M., & Pulido, J. I. (2008). *Medida de la sostenibilidad turística. Propuesta de un índice sintético* [Measurement of sustainable tourism. Proposal for a synthetic index]. Madrid: Editorial Universitaria Ramón Areces.
Saxena, G., Clark, G., Oliver, T., & Ilbery, B. (2007). Conceptualizing integrated rural tourism. *Tourism Geographies, 9*(4), 347–370.
Sharpley, R. (2014). Host perceptions of tourism: A review of the research. *Tourism Management, 42*, 37–49.
Sheldon, P., & Abenoja, T. (2001). Resident attitudes in a mature destination: The case of Waikiki. *Tourism Management, 22*, 435–443.
Sirakaya, E., Teye, V., & Sonmez, S. (2002). Understanding residents' support for tourism development in the central region of Ghana. *Journal of Travel Research, 41*(1), 57–67.
Stylidis, D., Biran, A., Sit, J., & Szivas, E. D. (2014). Residents' support for tourism development: The role of residents' place image and perceived tourism impacts. *Tourism Management, 45*, 260–274.
Thomas, J. R., & Nelson, J. K. (2007). *Métodos de Investigación en Actividad Física* [Research methods in physical activity]. Barcelona: Paiddotribo.
Torres-Delgado, A., & Saarinen, J. (2014). Using indicators to assess sustainable tourism development: A review. *Tourism Geographies, 16*(1), 31–47.
Tracey, P., & Clark, G. (2003). Alliances, networks and competitive strategy: Rethinking clusters of innovation. *Growth and Change, 34*(1), 1–16.
Tsaur, S. H., Lin, C. H., & Lin, J. H. (2006). Evaluating ecotourism sustainability from the integrated perspective of resource, community and tourism. *Tourism Management, 27*, 640–653.
Twining-Ward, L., & Butler, R. (2002). Implementing STD on a small island: development and use of sustainable tourism development indicators in Samoa. *Journal of Sustainable Tourism, 10*(5), 363–387.
United Nations Development Programme (PNUD). (2008). *Estrategia de Turismo Sustentable en Reservas de Biosfera y Sitios Ramasar de Argentina* [Strategy of sustainable tourism in biosphere reserves and sites Ramasar of Argentina]. Unidad de Turismo Sustentable y Ambiente de la SAyDS.
Valdés, L. (2001). Turismo, Desarrollo y Sostenibilidad [Tourism, development and sustainability]. In J. D. Buendía Azorín & J. Colino Suerias (Eds.), *Turismo y Medioambiente* (pp. 19–49). Madrid: Civitas.
World Tourism Organization (WTO) & United Nations Environment Programme (UNEP). (2006). *Making tourism more sustainable: A guide for policy makers*. Retrieved from http://www.unep.fr/shared/publications/pdf/DTIx0884xPA-TourismPolicyES.pdf
Wieserma, L. D. (2001). Conceptualization and development of the sources of enjoyment in youth sport questionnaire. *Measurement in Physical Education and Exercise Science, 5*(3), 153–157.
Zeballos, P. (2003). *Turismo Sustentable ¿Es posible en Argentina?* [Sustainable Tourism. Is it possible in Argentina?]. Buenos Aires: Ediciones Turísticas (Colección Temas de Turismo).

Requirements for Sustainable Nature-based Tourism in Transfrontier Conservation Areas: a Southern African Delphi Consultation

ANNA SPENCELEY

ABSTRACT *Over the years a plethora of factors have been associated with sustainable tourism in the literature, but little has been done to prioritize those that are most important to stakeholders in destinations. In particular, this research aimed to identify factors perceived as essential for sustainable nature-based tourism operating in transfrontier conservation areas (TFCAs) in southern Africa. A Delphi consultation was conducted in which 518 southern African experts from government, academia, non-governmental organizations, the private sector and consultancies were invited to contribute. Participants rated the relative importance of 502 policy, planning, economic, environmental and social factors drawn from the literature, and additional factors suggested by regional consultees. A statistically significant level of consensus was achieved on 159 multidisciplinary factors considered to be 'essential' or 'incompatible' with sustainable nature-based tourism in TFCAs. The implications for the assessment of sustainable nature-based tourism in southern African TFCAs are discussed, with a review of how they relate to tourism in the Great Limpopo TFCA: a transboundary protected area that incorporates protected areas in Mozambique, South Africa and Zimbabwe.*

Introduction

The volume of research literature focusing on sustainable tourism development has grown since the Rio Earth Summit in 1992 (e.g. see reviews by Bramwell and Lane 1993; Owen *et al.* 1993; Archer and Cooper 1994; Murphy 1994; Harris and Leiper 1995; Mowforth and Munt 1998; Eagles *et al.* 2002).

Definitions for sustainable tourism vary, as an industry standard the United Nations World Tourism Organization (1998: 21) stated that:

sustainable tourism development meets the needs of present tourists and host regions while protecting and enhancing opportunities for the future. It is envisaged as leading to management of all resources in such a way that economic, social, and aesthetic needs can be fulfilled while maintaining cultural integrity, essential ecological processes, biological diversity, and life support systems.

Robinson (2005) acknowledged that of the most striking characteristics of the term sustainable development is that it means so many different things to so many different people and organizations. He stated that the literature is 'rife' with different attempts to define the term and that debates have ensued between parties that prefer the three pillars approach (emphasizing the social, ecological and economic dimensions of sustainable development) or a more dualistic typology (emphasizing the relationship between humanity and nature). Neto (2003) stressed that there needs to be more focus on the use of tourism to alleviate poverty: essentially to use pro-poor tourism as an integral factor of sustainable tourism (Ashley *et al.* 2001), rather than focusing narrowly on ecological aspects. Traditionally, sustainable tourism research tends to be dominated by concerns for the environment and community involvement (Roe and Urquhart 2002) rather than addressing sustainability across Elkington's (1997) triple bottom line. Echtner and Jamal (1997) suggested that this may be a consequence of researchers approaching tourism studies from the main discipline in which they are trained, rather than using holistic approaches. Liu (2003) explored six key weaknesses of sustainable tourism development: the lack of attention to tourism demand; limited appreciation of the complexity of natural tourism resources; fairness of the distribution of benefits and costs between stakeholders; the presiding view that communities should accrue economic benefits of tourism but retain their culture; the limited success in measuring sustainable tourism using indicators and carrying capacities; and the limited realistic potential for 'sustainable' forms of tourism such as ecotourism and community tourism. The interdisciplinary research presented here addresses the factors highlighted by Liu (2003), the economic, environmental and social facets of sustainable tourism, and also considers the policy and planning context.

Nature-based tourism is described as all forms of tourism that use undeveloped natural resources, including landscape, habitats, water features and species for the purpose of enjoying natural areas or wildlife (Goodwin 1996). Nature-based tourism often takes place within protected areas: areas dedicated primarily to the protection and enjoyment of natural or cultural heritage, the maintenance of biodiversity and the maintenance of ecological life-support services (World Conservation Union [IUCN] 1991). At the Vth World Parks Congress, the World Conservation Union reported that in 2003 there were 102 protected areas conserving over 18.8 million km^2 (12.65% of the Earth's surface: Chape *et al.* 2003). However, fragmentation has effectively created 'islands' of biodiversity, which are prone to problems of inbreeding depression, genetic heterozygosity and localized extinctions due to environmental fluctuations (Caldecott *et al.* 1996). These problems have been addressed partially by linking protected areas through wildlife corridors, which allow species to migrate and recolonize areas to reduce the likelihood of extinction (Newark *et al*. 1993). Protected areas have also been amalgamated within Transfrontier Conservation Areas (TFCAs).

The 1990s were characterized by an increasing international interest among conservationists in transboundary areas (e.g. Thorsell 1990; Westing 1993; Hanks 1998; BSP 1999). TFCAs are characterized as relatively large areas encompassing one or more protected areas that straddle frontiers between two or more countries (World Bank 1996). When compared with national parks, TFCAs have the potential to conserve a greater diversity of species within larger geographical areas and promote co-operative wildlife management between nations (BSP 1999). TFCAs may also improve opportunities for tourism, allowing visitors to disperse over greater areas and obtain better quality experiences (Singh 1999) with more diverse attractions (van der Linde *et al*. 2001).

Systematic evaluations determining whether the purported conservation and development advantages of TFCAs are realistic, or simply rhetoric, have not been undertaken previously. The consultation initiative described here explicitly explored regional stakeholders' perceptions of the implications of TFCAs for sustainable tourism.

This paper describes how the Delphi technique was used to determine factors critical to the sustainable development of nature-based tourism in TFCAs. The consultation formed part of a process to develop a Sustainable Nature-based Tourism Assessment Toolkit (Spenceley 2003). The objectives of the consultation were to: (1) identify factors relevant to the development of sustainable tourism that had not been described previously within the literature; (2) list political, planning, economic, environmental, social and cultural factors that were linked with sustainable tourism; (3) determine the relative importance of these factors in generating sustainable nature-based tourism to southern African stakeholders; (4) evaluate the degree of consensus on the relative importance of individual sustainability factors among the regional consultees.

This research is important for five main reasons. First, although the literature describes a plethora of issues, factors and impacts linked to tourism development (e.g. de Kadt 1979; Mathieson and Wall 1982; Allen *et al*. 1988; Inskeep 1991; Archer and Cooper 1994; Ashley 1998), there has been no systematic identification of individual factors, or combinations of factors, which promote sustainable nature-based tourism and are relevant to the value systems of stakeholders within destinations (Butler 1998). Secondly, little work has been done to evaluate sustainable tourism issues in developing countries (Tosun 2001), despite the fundamental implications of nature-based tourism for biodiversity conservation in the tropics. Swarbrooke (1999) reflected that most of the current thinking and ideas in sustainable tourism are based on Western perceptions of the impacts of tourism in developing countries, rather than based on the perceptions of people living in developing countries. Thirdly, there is increasing interest among conservationists and politicians regarding the potential for TFCAs to contribute towards sustainable development, but the characteristics of sustainable nature-based tourism in transboundary areas have not been explored previously. Fourthly, this paper supports previous research on the value of the Delphi technique in exploring complex issues (e.g. Seely *et al.* 1980; Kaynak and Macauley 1984; Miller 2001) and, in particular, defining tourism themes (Garrod and Fyall 2005), but suggests a novel approach for determining consensus. Finally, the paper describes how researchers working within unfamiliar environments may use the Delphi technique as a tool to ascertain locally relevant issues, develop stakeholder ownership over research and use appropriate approaches to investigate sustainable tourism.

The results of this consultation are important for people working in southern Africa on sustainable nature-based tourism and TFCAs. Practical information is presented regarding the planning, implementation and analysis phases of Delphi consultations. The advantages and limitations of the Delphi technique are presented to aid researchers considering different options for stakeholder engagement. Stakeholders working at the macro-level to design viable policies and plans for transboundary conservation and tourism will benefit from the results of this consultation process, by improving their understanding of the policy, planning, economic, environmental and social factors southern African stakeholders concur are most important to the sustainable development of tourism.

The Delphi Consultation

The Delphi technique is a widely accepted consultation method that provides a rapid, effective way of collecting expert opinion and gaining consensus from a group of knowledgeable people on various unknown factors, subjective issues or complex problems (Pill 1971; Linstone and Turoff 1975; Green *et al.* 1990; Garrod and Fyall 2005). The technique was developed by the RAND Corporation for use as a tool in technological forecasting (Dalkey and Helmer 1963). The technique works on group communication to systematically elicit and 'pool' judgements from a panel of experts without their communicating with each other, while ensuring that they collaborate anonymously (Barrow 1997: 18).

The Delphi process is initiated with an anonymous survey of selected individuals who have an interest in the subject or possess relevant skills. The individuals form a panel, and an initial scoping round is undertaken to solicit opinions from panel members with respect to certain issues. A second round provides the participants with information, and they are asked to rate the value of certain factors. These responses are then combined and circulated to panel members, who are asked if they wish to revise their valuations in light of the group's responses. The controlled feedback process continues until there is some convergence of views between the experts (Sinclair and Stabler 1997). Delphi processes undertaken in the past predominantly evaluated consensus through the calculation of the mean or median score, while the degree of convergence has been reflected in the standard deviation (e.g. Seely *et al.* 1980; Kaynak and Macauley 1984; Miller 2001).

As applied to tourism, the Delphi technique has been used to define other tourism issues, such as 'marine ecotourism' (Garrod and Fyall 2005); to identify and rank events that would influence international tourism business (Kibedi 1981); to forecast tourism demand in particular tourism destinations (Lui 1998); and how best to market those locations (Pan *et al.* 1995); how and when future developments might affect the world tourism industry (Moutinho and Witt 1995); to develop indicators for sustainable tourism (Miller 2001); develop evaluation frameworks for tourism projects (Bridenhann and Butts 2006); and also to predict changes in the tourism industry relating to political change (Lloyd *et al.* 2000).

A three-round Delphi consultation process undertaken between September 1999 and March 2000 is described below in relation to the sampling process, materials and analysis.

Survey Materials

Delphi questionnaires were written in English, which was deemed appropriate given the educational status of panel members and the prevalence of the language's use in southern Africa. The survey materials were introduced with a covering letter inviting the addressee to participate in the consultation. The letter described the purpose of the study, its context, and highlighted the particular importance of their contribution. In return for their confidential participation in the study, the letter offered to provide participants with the results of the consultation and a copy of the final assessment toolkit (after Richey *et al.* 1985). An instruction sheet detailed the Delphi consultation approach, and definitions of both 'sustainable tourism' and 'nature-based tourism' were provided for consistency (after Butler 1993; WTTERC 1993).

During Round 1, panel members were asked to 'suggest factors that they considered crucial in achieving sustainable nature-based tourism'. This scoping exercise aimed to identify regionally relevant factors that were not illustrated in the literature. Similarly to Miller's (2001) method, after Seely *et al.* (1980), the questionnaires used in Round 2 required panel members to rate the relative importance of factors identified in the literature and during Round 1 on a Likert (1967) scale. Rating factors provided a mechanism by which consensus could be gauged within the group by tallying ratings of importance. Of 871 factors related to sustainable tourism identified during the literature review, and 392 additional factors identified by panel members during Round 1, 502 discrete factors across four themes (policy and planning, economics, environment and social issues) were applied in Round 2.

The number of factors was condensed through two pilot studies. In the first pilot study a sample of ten science undergraduates from the University of KwaZulu-Natal were asked to complete the questionnaires to check their validity. In the second pilot study a group of seven lecturers and researchers at the university working in the fields of policy, planning, tourism, business management, environment and sociology were asked to review the factors for any internal inconsistencies or areas of overlap.

During Round 3, panel members who had responded to the second round received a unique questionnaire. Their own responses were reported for each factor, and they were asked if they wanted to change their response in light of the group's mode response. Non-respondents to the second round also received a questionnaire and were given the opportunity to rate the factors in light of the mode response (e.g. either agreeing with the mode rating or providing an alternative rating).

All materials were reviewed for clarity and errors by third parties before distribution. Questionnaires were dispatched by email (preferentially), post or fax. At each stage of the process, attempts were made to obtain confirmation by telephone or email that participants had received their consultation invitations, and also to encourage their participation once deadlines had passed.

Study Sample

Although 'balanced' panels of experts from different backgrounds are recommended (Wheeller *et al.* 1990), criteria can be set for the types of skills required from stakeholders in relation to the objectives of particular Delphi studies (Richey *et al.* 1985). Individuals had to meet four criteria to be considered for inclusion in this Delphi panel:

1. experience in policy and planning, tourism and business management, environmental and conservation management or social and cultural issues;
2. employment within government, a conservation organization, academia, a consultancy, a non-governmental organization (NGO), an international NGO or private sector tourism organization;
3. experience within southern Africa;
4. a high level of professional productivity as evidenced by publications; involvement in significant relevant projects or institutions; or a senior employment position within a relevant institution.

The undemocratic nature of selecting participants (as critiqued by Sinclair and Stabler 1997) was an inevitable trade-off with the overriding objective of anonymous participation required in a Delphi consultation. Stakeholders were identified from sources including peer-reviewed journal articles, grey literature (including conference and workshop proceedings), directories of institutions, institutional databases, websites, peer recommendation, and the media. Where populations of particular stakeholders in the region were small (e.g. conservation parastatals, government officials) all of the individuals identified were invited to participate. Where stakeholder groups had larger populations (e.g. academics and private sector enterprises), random sampling was applied.

As Table 1 indicates, the number of people invited to participate in each round varied, and panel sizes were within accepted limits (Sinclair and Stabler 1997). Not

Table 1. Field of expertise of participants included within the Delphi consultation

	Policy/planning	Economics/tourism	Environment	Social/cultural	Totals
Round 1					
Invitees	8	42	9	6	75
Respondents	4	25	6	7	42 (56%)
Round 2					
Invitees	100	190	129	99	518
Respondents	28	72	46	38	184 (36%)
Round 3					
Invitees	41	107	74	58	280
Respondents	12	42	31	19	104 (37%)

all potential panel members drawn from different stakeholder groups were placed easily within one 'category' of expertise, given the diversity of their work, but they were placed in the cell that fitted their experience and current employment most closely.

Round 1 included panel members from 45 organizations drawn from five southern African countries: South Africa, Zimbabwe, Mozambique, Botswana and Namibia. Panel members from the first round were invited subsequently to participate in Round 2. Additional individuals were also invited into the Delphi consultation to increase the reliability and validity of the process, by engaging with greater numbers of representatives of different institutions and countries across southern Africa. Since it was only during Round 2 that consensus was sought, the increase in the sample size between Rounds 1 and 2 did not undermine the validity of the approach. During the second round 516 individuals drawn from 356 southern African organizations in nine southern African countries (Botswana, Lesotho, Malawi, Mozambique, Namibia, South Africa, Swaziland, Zambia and Zimbabwe) were invited to participate. Two panel members from Uganda and Tanzania were also invited to participate because of their expertise in southern Africa. The final round consisted of all the respondents to Rounds 1 and 2 and non-respondents to Round 2 with whom contact had been acknowledged. This approach allowed the sample size to be strengthened by providing a final opportunity for non-respondents to consolidate or disagree with the consensus from Round 2, by submitting their own ratings. Green *et al* (1990) stated that three rounds are sufficient to achieve group consensus in Delphi consultations against declining response rates, which was the approach adopted here.

Although not illustrated in Table 1, during all three rounds, the 'government' and 'private sector tourism' stakeholders were under-represented. This was due partly to the low numbers of individuals identified in government with specific expertise in policy, planning and the environment. There was also a bias towards South African stakeholders, which may be a reflection of the availability of information regarding potential participants from the different countries, and also of the underlying dominance of South African expertise in the region. Small sample sizes obtained from certain countries meant that responses from stakeholders in different nations could not be statistically analysed validly.

Analysis

Tallies and modes were calculated for responses made during Round 3. Round 2 responses that had not been altered in Round 3 were retained. The level of significance of agreement between panel members on the mode rating was determined using Chi-square analysis (Aron and Aron 1997) when scale items had received ≥ 5 scores from respondents (after Brink 1987). This approach contrasted with previous Delphi consultations, which predominantly use mean or median scores, coupled with the standard deviations to reflect concurrence on ratings and the degree of convergence (e.g. Seely *et al*. 1980; Kaynak and Macauley 1984; Miller 2001). Some researchers suggest that agreement amongst 60 percent of a panel can be viewed as group consensus (Hill and Fowles 1975), while others note that the inter-quartile range should not be move more than ten percent away from the median (Frechtling 1996). The statistical approach taken in this research avoided potential problems where frequencies of different ratings were very similar. For example, if 51 percent of panel members rated a particular factor as 'essential' and 49 percent of respondents scored it as 'desirable', Chi-square analysis could determine whether the difference was at least statistically significant (i.e. $p < 0.05$).

To address the sampling constraint of differences in the number of panel members representing different fields of expertise, the analysis was repeated for sub-sets of panel members from different fields of expertise. For example, in addition to recording the mode from the Policy and Planning questionnaire for all panel members, the responses from the sub-set of panel members who had expertise in policy and planning were evaluated and recorded separately. The sub-set results were compared consequently with responses from the entire panel (which incorporated the sub-set responses) to determine whether the sampling constraints had influenced the results.

One weakness of the consultation process was inherent to the Delphi technique: consultees rated the relative importance of individual factors presented by the researcher, but the Delphi process did not permit any combination of factors to be considered simultaneously. However, the Delphi consultation reported here formed part of a wider research initiative to develop a Sustainable Nature-based Tourism Assessment Toolkit (SUNTAT) and field tests of the toolkit enabled a combination of the factors to be evaluated practically (see Spenceley 2003). Other researchers may also find value in applying complementary research methods following Delphi consultations, in order to improve the validity and reliability of their work.

Factors Critical to Sustainable Nature-based Tourism in Transfrontier Conservation Areas

Table 2 summarizes the number of factors from the four themes that the Delphi panel concurred (to at least a significant degree [$p < 0.05$]) were 'essential' or 'incompatible' with the development of sustainable nature-based tourism. These frequencies have been corrected for different responses by the sub-groups of experts, as described above. For example, in cases where the whole panel had deemed a factor 'desirable' but the sub-group of experts in that field considered it to be 'essential', the expert rating took precedence. Of 502 factors presented to the Delphi panel, 159 (32%) were agreed to be 'essential' and 24 (5%) were deemed 'incompatible' with the development of sustainable nature-based tourism in TFCAs. Of these, 47 related to policy and planning, 46 addressed tourism and business management, 47 concerned environmental and conservation management, and 43 were social and cultural factors.

Policy and Planning Factors

The policy and planning factors rated as 'essential' to sustainable nature-based tourism with a statistically significant level of consensus within the sample are described in Table 3.

Economic Factors

The economic factors rated as 'essential' to sustainable nature-based tourism with a statistically significant level of consensus within the sample are described in Table 4.

Table 2. Summary of factors rated 'Essential' and 'Incompatible' to the development of sustainable nature-based tourism in transfrontier conservation areas

	Net essential ** & *	Net incompatible ** & *	Net % change caused by sub-group of experts	Total factors
Policy and planning	47	0	−13	99
Tourism and business management	46	0	15	142
Environmental and conservation management	28	19	11	146
Social and cultural issues	38	5	13	115
Totals	159	24		502

*$p < 0.05$; **$p < 0.1$.

Table 3. Policy and planning factors that are essential to sustainable nature-based tourism in southern Africa

Policy process factors
1. Political stability within and between the TFCA nations
2. Strong, sustained political support for the TFCA
3. A policy framework that supports transboundary co-operation
4. Established dispute settlement guidelines
5. Policies to monitor and deal with corruption at all levels
6. Transparency of policy development and implementation processes
7. Agreed protocols for the TFCA during times of conflict between or within the participating nations
8. Multi-lateral policy to monitor environmental, social, cultural and economic impacts

Legal factors
9. A multi-lateral agreement regarding the existence and geographical boundaries of the TFCA
10. Recognition of the sovereign integrity of each country land within the TFCA
11. Awareness of law enforcement agents of their jurisdictions to deal with cross-border, TFCA issues

Environmental policy factors
12. Multi-lateral management policies regarding natural resources within the TFCA (e.g. policies on wildlife management; sustainable utilization of resources; human–wildlife conflict; and integrated disease control)
13. Clear and secure land tenure policies for owners and tenants

Socio-cultural policy factors
14. Effective linkages and communication between stakeholder groups
15. Clear responsibilities for the institutions and stakeholders involved in TFCA processes
16. That stakeholders accept the need for good management and control of TFCA processes
17. Awareness of the context and constraints of local communities (e.g. poverty and public health) within TFCA policy

Economic policy factors
18. A multi-lateral TFCA strategic tourism development policy
19. Policy mechanisms that facilitate good business management in the TFCA tourism industry
20. Policies that allow clear and strong property rights for investors, developers and local communities
21. Policy designed to improve employment opportunities for local communities
22. Policies that require fair distribution of benefits from TFCA tourism to affected local communities

Planning strategy
23. Utilization of a strategic planning framework
24. Integrated and holistic planning processes
25. That developments authorized are consistent with strategic land-use plans
26. Comprehensive impact studies for each tourist development project in the TFCA before permitting development
27. Avoidance of overcapitalization (the development of tourism infrastructure and services that exceeds demand)

Table 3. Policy and planning factors that are essential to sustainable nature-based tourism in southern Africa *(Continued)*

28 Planned response mechanisms to crises posed by war, insecurity, kidnappings and conflicting international policy
29 Design and construction standards for tourism development projects

Planning for sustainability
30 Planning guidelines designed for sustainable TFCA development
31 Strategic plans that state explicitly what natural and cultural resources are to be sustained
32 That the objectives for sustainable tourism planning are feasible
33 Strategic planning of the number and type of tourism development projects within the TFCA
34 Planning of developments that are to be sustained in the long term
35 An appreciation that what is sustainable in one area, context, development stage and time period may not be sustainable in another
36 Specific planning goals for sustainability of TFCA tourism with measurable indicators

Planning with participation
37 Collaboration between TFCA countries at all stages, and in all sectors of planning
38 Participation of all relevant stakeholders from early stages and throughout the TFCA planning process
39 TFCA planning that incorporates local community factors such as increasing human populations, poverty and lack of food security
40 Planning of TFCA developments sensitive to the attitudes of local communities to wildlife and protected areas
41 Plans to enhance educational opportunities of the local community regarding TFCA tourism and business management

Plan content factors
42 Strategic and co-ordinated planning of appropriate tourism infrastructure development
43 Planning of developments appropriate to the availability of water
44 Planning control of development within environmentally and culturally important or sensitive areas
45 Zonation of TFCA tourism development with respect to environmentally and socially acceptable conditions
46 Planning frameworks that facilitate joint tourism ventures between local communities and the private sector
47 Planning of developments with respect to the availability of public services (e.g. transport, medical facilities, waste disposal)

The issue of employment, with regard to seasonal and part-time jobs was of particular interest in light of the wider literature, which generally cites seasonal, part-time labour in the tourism industry as undesirable (e.g. Oppermann and Chon 1997). The economic experts concurred that creating seasonal and part-time jobs was essential to sustainability. The contrast between the panel's perceptions and the literature may reflect the geographical context of this research in development countries and the predominance of regional private sector experts on the panel.

Table 4. Economic factors that are essential to sustainable nature-based tourism in southern Africa

Economic and tourism management
1. Institutional stability and capacity
2. Clear business strategies
3. Mechanisms to feedback information regarding tourism trends, impacts and needs to planners and policy makers
4. Ethical business management
5. Good working relationships and communication between TFCA tourism managers and other stakeholders
6. Establishing long-term management objectives to achieve environmental sustainability of TFCAs

Business and investment
7. Transparent and accountable criteria for granting tourism concessions within the TFCA
8. Consideration of the bidder's ability and willingness to deliver a sustainable enterprise
9. Consultation and participation of local communities affected by potential tourism development
10. That commercially viable returns can be generated by private sector investment and enterprises
11. Length of concession tenure appropriate to the type of infrastructural and business development required

Sales and pricing
12. Tourism projects that are self-financing in the long term (e.g. do not run at a loss)
13. That funds generated are sufficient to manage the TFCA
14. Revenue that covers construction/establishment costs of tourism enterprises
15. Revenue that covers operating and maintenance costs of tourism enterprises
16. Mechanisms to sell the TFCA tourism product overseas

Market and marketing
17. Stable or increasing demand for nature-based tourism
18. Market research to establish the most effective TFCA marketing strategies for the target visitors
19. Information regarding access to the TFCA and its attractions is easily available to potential visitors
20. A strategic, co-ordinated approach to TFCA marketing

Product and service
21. Tourism infrastructure that is appropriate to the level and type of demand
22. Tourism product and service development based on the type of market demand

Access
23. Easy access to the TFCA (e.g. by air, private and public transport)
24. Graded roads in the TFCA allowing access to caravans and coaches

Regulation and control
25. Specific regulations for impacts on the natural environment (e.g. waste disposal and water consumption)
26. Monitoring of compliance with basic development standards
27. Licensing of hotels, lodges, camps, safari operators and tour operators working in the TFCA

Table 4. Economic factors that are essential to sustainable nature-based tourism in southern Africa *(Continued)*

    28. Clear delineation of responsibilities for stakeholders utilizing the TFCA
    29. Limits on tourist numbers and tourist density in the TFCA based on ecological and social principles
    30. Codes of conduct for tourists and operators for environmentally and socio-culturally appropriate behaviour in the TFCA
    31. Rules and restrictions enforced with appropriate enforced punishments (e.g. fines)
    32. Incentives for tourists and tour operators to moderate damaging behaviour
    33. Avoidance of tourism in areas that are undermanaged or fragile

Monitoring and auditing
    34. Development of effective environmental, social and economic monitoring programme for tourism enterprises
    35. Recording of an environmental baseline from which to monitor change
    36. Mechanisms to feedback monitoring results to management and policy planning

Sustainability
    37. Sharing of expertise and experience in dealing with wildlife, tourism and local communities between TFCA countries
    38. That employees and tourists know and understand the company environmental policy
    39. Capacity by government to fulfil obligations and responsibilities with respect to TFCA

Employment factors
    40. Creation of seasonal, part-time jobs

Hospitality
    41. Management that aims to satisfy the needs and desires of tourists
    42. Provision for guests to state any complaints about the operation of the tourism development
    43. Active responses to complaints from tourists
    44. Provision for tourists to purchase goods and spend currency at the destination

Security
    45. Safety and security for visitors and staff
    46. Perception of security and safety by visitors

Environmental Factors

Environmental factors rated as 'essential' or 'incompatible' with sustainable nature-based tourism with a statistically significant level of consensus within the sample are described in Table 5. Regarding stocking alien species, some comments from participants indicated that this was possible if the integrity of local species was not compromised, and alien species were not invasive. For example, one participant indicated that cattle and plantations might be compatible with TFCAs if planned and managed appropriately. Participants also recognized that ecological systems were poorly understood, and therefore management activities would be reliant on contemporary and locally appropriate best practice. In addition, some forms of sustainable

Table 5. Environmental factors that are essential and incompatible with sustainable nature-based tourism in southern Africa

ESSENTIAL FACTORS

Management plan and process factors
1. Mechanisms to finance integrated management schemes that are agreed by TFCA nations
2. Effective, appropriate and simple management procedures
3. A multidisciplinary approach to TFCA management
4. Long-term management objectives
5. Management processes that can adapt to avoid or mitigate negative impacts
6. Integrated multi-lateral TFCA management design and implementation
7. Strategic adaptive management processes
8. Key champions that oversee development, co-ordination and implementation of management plans

Monitoring and auditing factors
9. Monitoring of the impacts of policy, planning and implementation on the TFCA
10. Monitoring that is planned strategically and scientifically
11. Feedback of monitoring results into the planning and policy process
12. Monitoring and auditing mechanisms that are integrated between TFCA countries

Conservation management
13. Management that incorporates ecological and conservation principles
14. Adaptive management strategies to cope with unpredictable ecosystems
15. Management programmes designed to enhance the long-term conservation of natural resources in the TFCA
16. Sustainable levels of natural resource use within the TFCA
17. Strategic, integrated poaching control within the TFCA
18. Control of invasive species in the TFCA
19. Conservation management plans with standardized, measurable conservation objectives

Tourism development
20. A balance between the need for conservation and the economic need for tourism development
21. Environmental mitigation plans designed to deal with negative environmental impacts from tourist developments
22. Tourist resorts that discourage sales of rare natural products (e.g. animals, plants, and their products)

Landscape factors
23. A landscape management approach

Faunal factors
24. A transparent and accountable hunting system
25. Regulation and policing of a licensed hunting system

Waste
26. Remediation of contaminated watercourses and water bodies polluted by tourism
27. That organic waste disposal does not exceed the assimilative capacity of natural sinks
28. Monitoring of waste water quality by tourism developments

Table 5. Environmental factors that are essential and incompatible with sustainable nature-based tourism in southern Africa *(Continued)*

INCOMPATIBLE FACTORS

Conservation management
1. Stocking of non-indigenous species in the TFCA
2. Use of non-renewable resources that exceeds the rate at which replacement resources can be created
3. That renewable resources are used at a rate higher than their regeneration rates

Tourism development
4. The use of invasive plant species in tourist resort landscaping schemes

Landscape
5. Irrigation (or filling in) of wetland areas to develop resorts on dry land
6. Vandalism in the TFCA
7. Damage to natural landmarks or heritage sites by tourists or developers

Ecosystem and vegetation
8. Reduction in plant species diversity and composition due to tourism disturbance
9. Disappearance of fragile species due to tourism disturbance
10. Negative impacts on plant germination, establishment and growth due to tourism disturbance
11. Fire caused by tourists

Faunal factors
12. Changes in wildlife species composition due to disturbance by tourists
13. Changes in diversity of wildlife species in tourist areas
14. Decreased survivorship of young due to disturbance or destruction by tourism
15. Selling more hunting quotas than is appropriate for the population size and regeneration rate of wildlife
16. Poaching wildlife for trophies
17. Changes in community structures of wildlife due to tourism disturbance

Water
18. Consumption that exceeds the recharge rate of reservoirs and aquifers from rainfall

Waste
19. Harmful impacts of waste disposal on the environment

consumptive use might not be compatible with non-consumptive tourism (e.g. hunting versus photographic tourism).

Social Factors

Social factors rated as 'essential' or 'incompatible' with sustainable nature-based tourism with a statistically significant level of consensus within the sample are described in Table 6.

Some panel members commented that democracy was not always present in community groups and that external stakeholders did not have the right to alter the way in which communities traditionally worked. Participants noted that the extent to which

Table 6. Social factors that are essential and incompatible with sustainable nature-based tourism in southern Africa

ESSENTIAL FACTORS

Context factors
1. An awareness of historical impacts of wildlife and the protected area on communities (e.g. displacement, conflict, resource use)
2. An appreciation of the socio-economic context of local communities (e.g. level of poverty)
3. Evaluation of whether tourism development is an appropriate industry for the communities concerned
4. Evaluation of whether tourism development is desired by the communities concerned
5. That the good and bad social, economic and environmental implications of tourism development are understood by local communities
6. Local community support for conservation
7. An awareness of historical relationships between stakeholders (e.g. government, tour operators, communities, parks boards, tourists)

Community group factors
8. That community groups/forums within communities affected by the TFCA are considered stakeholders
9. That stakeholder community groups include representatives who have standing and respect from the community
10. An appreciation that communities are not homogeneous, simple entities
11. That conflicts of interest are dealt with within and between stakeholder groups
12. Conflict resolution processes within and between stakeholder groups
13. Accountability of community group activities
14. Democratic processes within community groups
15. Understanding that traditional authorities are not representative of whole communities

Capacity building
16. That TFCA processes involve the participation of all stakeholders
17. Active participation of local communities in TFCA processes (e.g. planning, policy making, and decision making)
18. Empowerment of local communities with the knowledge and skills to participate effectively
19. Active participation of local communities in natural resource management
20. That communities are treated as partners, not just beneficiaries
21. Transparency regarding power relations of different stakeholders
22. Effective communication processes within and between stakeholder groups
23. Active participation of local communities in tourism development and implementation

Training
24. Education of all stakeholders (e.g. the public, government, NGOs, private sector, tourists) on the principles of sustainable development
25. Education of local communities regarding the nature of the TFCA, the environment, tourism and business management
26. Preparation of local communities for the likely behaviour and needs of tourists

Socioeconomics
27. That local communities affected by the presence of the TFCA benefit from tourism in it
28. That benefits off-set opportunity costs (e.g. not hunting wildlife in the TFCA)
29. Benefits that provide incentives for conservation

Table 6. Social factors that are essential and incompatible with sustainable nature-based tourism in southern Africa *(Continued)*

30. Regulators that impose sanctions on those that default on their responsibilities (e.g. cause crime; poach wildlife)
31. Improvement of communities' standard of living through tourism
32. Benefits that are linked to responsibilities
33. Access to seed credits/micro-financing schemes for local people to develop tourism and related enterprises

Employment:
34. Fair and equitable contracts that formalize joint community–private sector tourism enterprise agreements

Social and cultural factors
35. Improved quality of life for communities
36. Appreciation of the environment by communities
37. Tolerance of tourists by local communities
38. That cultural rights to utilize natural resources critical to livelihoods continue despite the presence of the TFCA

INCOMPATIBLE FACTORS

Social and cultural factors
1. Hostility, tension and conflict between communities and tourists
2. Increased antisocial and criminal activities (e.g. prostitution, begging, alcohol, vandalism, gambling, adultery and drugs)
3. Degradation of traditional or sacred sites
4. Relocation of communities against their will to make way for tourism development
5. Degradation of language and artefacts

---

traditional authorities represented local communities varied widely, and that an appreciation of this diversity was very important.

So, in reality, are the multidisciplinary factors that southern African stakeholders considered critical to sustainable tourism in TFCAs actually being applied? To illustrate, it is useful to consider the presence of sustainability factors relating to one tourism niche (community-based tourism development) within a particular TFCA in southern Africa: the Great Limpopo TFCA.

Relevance of Critical Delphi Consultation Factors to the Great Limpopo Transfrontier Conservation Area

The Great Limpopo TFCA links core protected areas of Kruger National Park in South Africa, Gonarezhou National Park in Zimbabwe and Limpopo National Park in Mozambique and interstitial areas of communal and private land (Figure 1).

In a review of responsible tourism investment in the Great Limpopo TFCA, Spenceley (2006) highlighted tourism enterprises that promoted residents' active involvement in the industry and, in particular, joint-ventures between the Makuleke people and private sector operators in Kruger National Park. During South Africa's apartheid

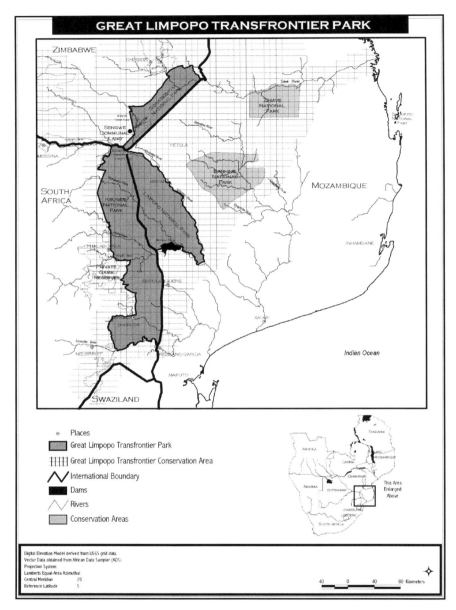

Figure 1. Great Limpopo Transfrontier Park and Transfrontier Conservation Area. *Source*: GoM *et al.* (2002).

period, the Makuleke people were forcibly removed by the state from 24,000 hectares of land in the north of Kruger National Park. Through the land restitution process, they were compensated in 1998 with the return of their land and the creation of a contractual park (Elliffe 1999). A 25-year agreement was established between the Makuleke people and South African National Parks, specifying that the land may be used only for wildlife conservation (Steenkamp 1998; Steenkamp and Grossman 2001). The contract enables the Makuleke to make sustainable use of specified natural resources, with the option of developing six small camps with a cumulative occupancy of 224 beds (Grossman and van Riet 1999). The Makuleke currently have contracts with two private sector operators: Matswani Safaris and Wilderness Safaris. Key elements of both tourism partnerships are that the community (Collins 2003, cited in Spenceley 2006; Maluleke 2003):

- receives 8–10 percent of turnover, as negotiated during the tender process;
- capital investment on their land;
- is guaranteed a high proportion of the jobs and skills training to be able to take up the long-term employment and short-term construction jobs; and
- will eventually own the infrastructure, as the arrangements are for built–operate–transfer. Therefore, their private sector partners will build and operate for a specific number of years and then they will transfer the ownership of the lodge to the community.
- These agreements illustrate a number of the Delphi consultations' 'essential' factors for sustainability, including the following:
- transparent and accountable criteria for granting tourism concessions within the TFCA;
- consideration of the bidders' ability and willingness to deliver a sustainable enterprises
- consultation and participation of local communities affected by tourism development;
- length of concession tenure that is appropriate to the type of infrastructural and business development required.
- tourism infrastructure that is appropriate to the level and type of demand;
- creation of seasonal, part-time jobs;
- that benefits off-set opportunity costs (e.g. not hunting wildlife in the TFCA).
- fair and equitable contracts that formalize joint community–private sector tourism enterprise agreements; and
- benefits that provide incentives for conservation.

Ferreira (2004) reviewed tourism development in the Gonarezhou portion of the Great Limpopo TFCA, located in Zimbabwe. Ferreira (2004) highlighted that severe socio-economic challenges faced by Zimbabwe have been compounded by national and international hostility towards the government's 'Land and Agrarian Reform

Program'. In this programme, people were paid to occupy white commercial forms under police supervision (Willemese 2002). With regards to Gonarezhou, local Shangaan people had been forced to re-settle outside the parks' boundaries in 1975 and, since 2000, people (including previous inhabitants and opportunistic war veterans) have entered the park to occupy, clear and burn sections of the land (Sharman 2001) and to graze their cattle. Although the incursions have taken place only in some areas of the park, poaching and a decline in tourism numbers have affected the Great Limpopo TFCA (Ferreira 2004). Ferreira (2004) suggested that the political problems could lead to 'cracks' in the Communal Areas Management Programme for Indigenous Resources (CAMPFIRE), which has been a pioneering programme in community-based natural resource management in Zimbabwe that has often used trophy hunting tourism to generate revenue from wildlife. The problems led for calls for the TFCA project to be halted until the situation had stabilized (Molefe 2002).

With regard to the Delphi consultation factors, several 'essential' factors are relevant to the situation in Zimbabwe, in so far that they are not currently observed. Their absence could be contributing to undermining the sustainability of tourism in the area:

- political stability within and between TFCA nations;
- policies that allow clear and strong property rights for investors, developers and local communities;
- clear and secure land tenure policies for owners and tenants;
- planned response mechanisms to crises posed by war, insecurity, kidnappings and conflicting international policy;
- planning control of development within environmentally and culturally important or sensitive areas; and
- transparent and accountable criteria for granting tourism concessions within the TFCA.

In Mozambique, the World Bank has been working since 1998 to strengthen the management of TFCAs, including around the Great Limpopo TFCA. The projects key activities include the development of environmentally sound and socially inclusive nature tourism (emphasizing community/private sector partnership), and directly related economic activities, in areas with high tourism potential (World Bank 2005). As part of this initiative, a Community Environment Fund has been established, which will allows NGO brokers to secure funding for rural communities living with the TFCAs. The funding is geared primarily for community-based ecotourism projects that secure tangible community benefits through private sector-led initiatives (Anon. 2006). This initiative addresses at least two of the Delphi consultation's 'essential' factors:

- that local communities affected by the presence of the TFCA benefit from tourism in it; and
- access to seed credits/micro-financing schemes for local people to develop tourism and related enterprises.

Overall, however, Spenceley (2006) concluded that is too early to establish if tourism development in the Great Limpopo TFCA will be cumulatively sustainable. The – as yet – limited level of tourism infrastructure development in Mozambican regions of the TFCA and the political unrest and land invasions in Zimbabwe are in stark contrast to the generally well-established and developed tourism in South Africa. Therefore, there are currently only spatially fragmented evidence of endeavours in sustainable tourism.

Conclusion

The contribution of this research lies in answering a question that researchers have struggled with over recent years: what is sustainable tourism? Rather than assuming that perceptions of sustainability are uniform globally, factors identified within the literature relevant to sustainable tourism have been through a systematic process to establish consensus to provide a definitive picture of what sustainable nature-based tourism in TFCAs means to southern African stakeholders. By inviting stakeholders with experience in policy, planning, economic, environmental and social issues to participate, it was possible to address cumulatively Echtner and Jamal's (1997) concern that holistic approaches are used rarely in tourism studies. This work also contributes to the literature through the application of the Delphi technique in a novel way, as consensus was determined by establishing the statistical significance of the mode response, using Chi-square analysis, rather than using the mean and standard deviation (Kaynak and Macauley 1984; Seely et al. 1980; Miller 2001).

Areas where the consultation panel's opinions supported the literature included the importance of using local knowledge and participation by local people in tourism and conservation. This supports literature indicating that local knowledge is valuable and may support sustainable development (Chimbuya 1996) and enhance tourism services, given the implications of local conditions for the development of practical and appropriate infrastructure (Hawkins et al. 1995). Delphi panel members also noted that communities bordering protected areas should participate as actively as possible in decision-making processes in those areas. This supports Kiss (1990), who reported that the extent of local participation in decision making is related directly to the tendency of local people to support conservation policies. Similarly, the consultees indicated that communities would only appreciate the environment if they had somewhere to live and sufficient food (e.g. supporting Clark 1991; Redclift 1992; Akama 1996).

Areas of difference between the consultation panel's responses and the literature included issues of employment and energy use. The panel did not consider that the prevalence of seasonal, part-time and menial labour was an adverse characteristic of the tourism industry, as had been indicated elsewhere (de Kadt 1979), but instead consistently stated that any employment was beneficial. This difference in perception may reflect the geographical context of the consultees (i.e. within developing countries) in contrast with authors of the literature (i.e. who predominantly originate in industrialized nations). In addition, energy conservation factors were consistently given a low rating of importance by the Delphi consultees, despite the growing international concern of the linkages between energy use and global climate change (Adams 1990). In their analysis of climate change and nature tourism in southern Africa, Preston-Whyte and Watson (2005) concluded that transboundary areas will substantially enhance the chance of biota adapting to climate change.

Not only did the consultation provide data that supported and contradicted existing knowledge, but it also generated new debate regarding the specific characteristics of nature-based tourism and TFCAs. Neither this form of tourism nor this type of protected area had been systematically evaluated previously with regard to sustainable development. Additional comments made by consultees illustrated how the Delphi technique may be used to obtain valuable information regarding the practicality of achieving sustainability factors. For example, however statistically significant the agreement on factors considered 'essential' or 'incompatible' with sustainability might be, the reality of implementing them is more complex.

The application of the Delphi technique in other regions in the future may be useful in ascertaining the similarity of factors relevant to sustainable nature-based tourism in southern Africa with other regions of the globe. If perceptions of the 'essential' and 'incompatible' factors are consistent, and value systems are similar (Butler 1998), this would have important implications for the transferability of international efforts to promote sustainable tourism development.

Consideration of the relevance of the critical sustainable tourism factors from the Delphi factors to a particular TFCA in southern Africa (the Great Limpopo TFCA) reveals that they are highly relevant. This implies that if the factors were applied systematically, they could provide practical guidance to policy makers and practitioners in interventions to promote stability and sustainability of transboundary protected areas.

In the future, researchers selecting the Delphi technique as a consultation tool should be aware that it is demanding with respect to both time and persistence if viable return rates from geographically dispersed participants are to be obtained. For example, the consultation process undertaken within this research was structured around three rounds, invited over five hundred stakeholders to participate, and took six months to complete. Other researchers have also found the technique to be lengthy, but that this time is required to ensure reliability (Garrod and Fyall 2005). In this case the use of the Delphi technique as a consultation approach was advantageous because it ensured that regional stakeholders had the opportunity to participate anonymously, and also engaged debate around sustainable nature-based tourism and TFCAs in southern Africa.

Acknowledgement

The author wishes to thank Professor Harold Goodwin of the International Centre for Responsible Tourism and Professor Charles Breen and Dr Trevor Hill of the University of KwaZulu-Natal for their advice; The Leverhulme Trust for their financial support; and all of the Delphi consultees in southern Africa who participated anonymously in this research. Thanks also to anonymous reviewers from *Tourism Geographies* who provided constructive comments that were used to strengthen this paper.

References

Adams, W. M. (1990) *Green development: environment and sustainability in the Third World*, 2nd edn (London and New York: Routledge).

Akama, J. S. (1996) *Wildlife Conservation in Kenya: A Political Ecological Analysis of Nairobi and Tsavo Regions* (Washington, DC: African Development Foundation).

Allen, L., Long, R., Perdue, R. & Kieselbach, S. (1988) The impact of tourism development on resident's perceptions of community life, *Journal of Travel Research*, 27, pp. 16–21.

Anon. (2006) A Community Enterprise Fund Manual (CEF), The Transfrontier conservation area tourism development project, Version # 1, February 2006.

Archer, B. & Cooper, C. (1994) The positive and negative impacts of tourism, in: W. Theobald (Ed.) *Global tourism: The next decade*, pp. 73–91 (Oxford: Butterworth Heinneman).

Aron, A. & Aron, E. N. (1997) *Statistics for the behavioral and social sciences: A brief course* (New Jersey: Prentice Hall International Inc).

Ashley, C. (1998) The impact of tourism on rural livelihoods: Namibia's Experience. Paper presented to the SADC–NRMP Workshop on Community Tourism in Southern Africa, Namibia, Windhoek, 27–29 January.

Ashley, C., Roe, D. & Goodwin, H. 2001. *Pro-poor tourism strategies: making tourism work for the poor: A review of experience*, Pro-poor tourism report No. 1, April 2001 (London: Overseas Development Institute/International Institute for Environment and Development/Centre for Responsible Tourism, The Russell Press).

Barrow, C. J. (1997) *Environmental and social impact assessment: an introduction* (London: Arnold).

Biodiversity Support Program [BSP] (1999) *Study on the development of Transboundary Natural Resource Management Areas in Southern Africa: highlights and findings* (Washington DC: World Wildlife Fund, Biodiversity Support Program).

Bramwell, B. & Lane, B. (1993) Sustainable tourism: An evolving global approach, *Journal of Sustainable Tourism*, 1(1), pp. 6–16.

Bridenhann, J. & Butts, S. (2006) Application of the Delphi technique to rural tourism project evaluation, *Current Issues in Tourism*, 9(2), pp. 171–190.

Brink, H. I. L. (1987) *Statistics for nurses* (Pretoria and Cape Town: Academica).

Butler, R. W. (1993) Tourism – an evolutionary perspective, in: J. G. Nelson, R. Butler & G. Wall (Eds) *Tourism and sustainable development: piloting, planning, managing*, pp. 27–43 (Ontario: University of Waterloo, Department of Geography Publication Series No. 37).

Butler, R. W. (1998) Sustainable tourism – looking backwards in order to progress?, in: M. Hall & A. A. Lew (Eds) *Sustainable tourism: a geographical perspective*, pp. 25–34 (Harlow and New York: Addison-Wesley Longman).

Caldecott, J. O., Jenkins, M. D., Johnson, T. H. & Groombridge, B. (1996) Priorities for global species richness and endemism, *Biodiversity and Conservation*, 5, pp. 699–727.

Chape, S., Blyth, S., Fish, L., Fox, P. & Spalding, M. (compilers) (2003) *United Nations list of protected areas* (Gland, Switzerland and Cambridge, UK: IUCN and Cambridge, UK: UNEP–WCMC).

Chimbuya, S. (1996) The District Environmental Action Planning Process. Paper presented at the OECD/DAC workshop on Capacity Development in Environment, Rome (Government of Zimbabwe: Department of Natural Resources).

Clark, C. W. (1991) Economic biases against sustainable development, in: R. Costanza (Ed.) *Ecological economics*, pp. 319–330 (New York: Columbia).

Dalkey, N. C. & Helmer, O. (1963) An experimental application of the Delphi method to the use of experts, *Management Science*, 9, pp. 458–467.

de Kadt, E. (1979) *Tourism: passport to development* (London: Oxford University Press).

Eagles, P. F. J., McCool, S. F. & Haynes, C. D. A. (2002) *Sustainable tourism in protected areas: guidelines for planning and management* (Gland, Switzerland and Cambridge, UK: IUCN).

Echtner, C. M. & Jamal, T. B. (1997) The disciplinary dilemma of tourism studies, *Annals of Tourism Research*, 24(4), pp. 868–883.

Elkington, J. (1997) *Cannibals with forks: the triple bottom line of 21st century business* (Oxford: Capstone Publishing Ltd).

Elliffe, S. (1999) Guidelines for the Release/development of Dormant state or community assets for ecotourism development in the context of community involvement, land issues and environmental requirements. Paper presented at the Community Public Private Partnerships Conference, Johannesburg, 16–18 November.

Ferreira, S. (2004) Problems associated with tourism development in Southern Africa: the case of Transfrontier Conservation Areas, *GeoJournal*, 60(3), pp. 301–310.

Frechtling, D. (1996) *Practical tourism forecasting* (Oxford: Butterworth Heinemann).

Garrod, B. & Fyall, A. (2005) Revisiting Delphi: the Delphi technique in tourism research, in: B. Ritchie, P. Burns, & C. Palmer (Eds) *Tourism research methods: integrating theory with practice*, pp. 85–98 (Wallingford: CABI Publishing).

Goodwin, H. (1996) In pursuit of ecotourism, *Biodiversity and Conservation*, 5, pp. 277–292.

Green, H., Hunter, R. & Moore, B. (1990) Assessing the environmental impact of tourism development: using the Delphi technique, *Tourism Management*, 11(2), pp. 111–120.

Grossman, D. & van Riet, W. (1999) Makuleke tourism development, Report to Mafisa, January.

Government of Moazmbique (GOM), Government of South Africa (GOS) and Government of Zimbabwe (GOZ) (2002) *Treaty between the Government of the Republic of Mozambique, the Government of the Republic of South Africa and the Government of the Republic of Zimbabwe on the establishment of the Great Limpopo Transfrontier Park*, 1 December.

Hanks, J. (1998) The role of transfrontier conservation areas in Southern Africa in the conservation of mammalian biodiversity. International symposium on wildlife utilization.

Harris, R. & Leiper, N. (1995) *Sustainable tourism: an Australian perspective* (Australia: Butterworth Heinneman).

Hawkins, D. E., Epler Wood, M. & Bittman, S. (1995) *The ecolodge sourcebook* (North Bennington: Ecotourism Society).

Hill, K. Q. & Fowles, J. (1975) The methodological worth of the Delphi technique, *Technological Forecasting and Social Change*, 7, pp. 179–192.

Inskeep, E. (1991) *Tourism planning: An integrated and sustainable development approach* (New York: Van Nostrand Reinhold).

Kaynak, E. & Macauley, J. A. (1984) The Delphi technique in the measurement of tourism market potential: the case of Nova Scotia, *Tourism Management*, 5(2), pp. 87–101.

Kibedi, G. (1981) Future trends in international tourism, *Revue de Tourism*, 36, pp. 3–6.

Kiss, A. (Ed.) (1990) *Living with wildlife: wildlife resource management with local participation in Africa* (Washington, D.C: World Bank, Africa Technical Department Series, Technical Paper No. 130).

Likert, R. (1967) The method of constructing an attitude scale, in: M. Fishbein (Ed.) *Readings in attitude theory and measurement*, pp.90–95 (New York: Wiley).

Linstone, H. A. & Turoff, M. (Eds) (1975) *The Delphi method: techniques and applications* (London and Reading, MA: Addison-Wesley).

Liu, Z. (2003) Sustainable tourism development: a critique, *Journal of Sustainable Tourism*, 11(6), pp. 459–475.

Lloyd, J., La Lopa, J. M. & Braunlich, C. G. (2000) Predicting changes in Hong Kong's hotel industry given the change in sovereignty from Britain to China in 1997, *Journal of Travel Research*, 38, pp. 405–410.

Lui, J. C. (1998) Hawaii tourism to the year 2000: a Delphi forecast, *Tourism Management*, 9, pp. 279–290.

Maluleke, M. L. (2003) Presentation by Mashangu Livingston Maluleke on behalf of the Makuleke Community to the World Parks Congress, Durban, 8–17 September.

Mathieson, A. & Wall, G. (1982) *Tourism: economic, physical and social impacts* (New York: Longman).

Miller, G. (2001) The development of indicators for the promotion of sustainable tourism, PhD Dissertation, Management Studies, University of Surrey.

Molefe, R. (2002) Zim crisis won't effect new park, *Sowetan*, 17 September, p. 8.

Moutinho, L. & Witt, S. F. (1995) Forecasting the tourism environment using a consensus approach, *Journal of Travel Research*, 33, pp. 46–50.

Mowforth, M. & Munt, I. (1998) *Tourism and sustainability: new tourism in the Third World* (London: Routledge).

Murphy, P. (1994) Tourism and sustainable development, in: W. Theobald (Ed.) *Global tourism: the next decade*, pp. 274–290 (Oxford: Butterworth Heinneman).

Neto, F. (2003) A new approach to sustainable tourism development: moving beyond environmental protection, *Natural Resources Forum*, 27, pp. 212–222.

Newark, W. D., Leonard, N. L., Sariko, H. I. & Gamassa, D. G. M. (1993) Conservation attitudes of local people living adjacent to five protected areas in Tanzania, *Biological Conservation*, 63, pp. 177–183.

Oppermann, M. & Chon, K-S. (1997) *Tourism in developing countries* (UK: ITBP).

Owen, R.E., Witt, S. F. & Susan, G. (1993) Sustainable tourism development in Wales, *Tourism Management*, 14(6), pp. 463–474.

Pan, S. Q., Vega, M., Vella, A. J., Archer, B. H. & Parlett, G. (1995) A mini-Delphi approach: an improvement on single round techniques, *Progress in Tourism and Hospitality Research*, 2, pp. 27–39.

Pill, J. (1971) The Delphi method: substance, context, a critique and an annotated bibliography, *Socio-economic Planning*, 5(1), pp. 57–71.

Preston-Whyte, R. A. & Watson, H. K. (2005) Nature tourism and climatic change in Southern Africa, in: C. M. Hall & J. Higham (Eds) *Tourism, recreation and climate change*, pp. 130–142 (London: Channel View Publications: London).

Redclift, M. (1992) The meaning of sustainable development, *Geoforum*, 23, pp. 395–403.

Richey, J. S., Mar, B. W. & Horner, R. R. (1985) The Delphi technique in environmental assessment, *Journal of Environmental Management*, 21(2), pp. 135–146.

Robinson, J. (2005) Squaring the circle? Some thoughts on the idea of sustainable development, *Ecological Economics*, 48, pp. 369–384.

Roe, D. & Urquhart, P. (2002) *Pro-poor tourism: harnessing the world's largest industry for the world's poor* (London: International Institute for Environment and Development, World Summit on Sustainable Development Opinion).

Seely, R. L., Iglarsh, H. & Edgell, D. (1980) Utilising the Delphi technique at international conferences: a method for forecasting international tourism conditions, *Travel Research Journal*, 1(1), pp. 30–35.

Sharman, J. (2001) Invasions threaten peace park, *Weekly Mail and Guardian*, October 26 to November 1, p. 17.

Sinclair, M. T. & Stabler, M. (1997) *The economics of tourism* (London and New York: Routledge).

Singh, J. (1999) *Study on the development of Transboundary Natural Resource Management Areas in Southern Africa – global review: lessons learned* (Washington D.C.: Biodiversity Support Program).

Spenceley, A. (2003) Managing sustainable nature-based tourism in Southern Africa: a practical assessment tool, PhD Dissertation, University of Greenwich.

Spenceley, A. (2006) Tourism in the Great Limpopo Transfrontier Park, *Development Southern Africa*, 23(5), pp. 649–667.

Steenkamp, C. (1998) The Makuleke Land Claim signing ceremony: harnessing social justice and conservation, *African Wildlife*, 52(4), July/August. Available at http://wildnetafrica.co.za/wildlifearticles/africanwildlife/1998/julaugust_makuleke.html (accessed 8 April 2002).

Steenkamp, C. & Grossman, D. (2001) *People and parks: cracks in the paradigm* (Gland, Switzerland?: IUCN?, IUCN Policy Think Tank Series, No. 10, May).

Swarbrooke, J. (1999) *Sustainable tourism management* (Wallingford: CABI Publishing).

Thorsell, J. (Ed.) (1990) *Parks on the borderline: experience in transfrontier conservation* (Gland, Switzerland: IUCN).

Tosun, C. (2001) Challenges of sustainable tourism development in the developing world: the case of Turkey, *Tourism Management*, 22, pp. 289–303.

van der Linde, H., Oglethorpe, J., Sandwith, T., Snelson, D. & Tessema, Y. (with contributions from Tiega, A. & Price, T.) (2001) *Beyond boundaries: transboundary natural resource management in Sub-Saharan Africa* (Washington D.C.: Biodiversity Support Program).

Westing. A. H. (Ed.) (1993) *Transfrontier reserves for peace and nature: a contribution to human security* (Nairobi: UNEP).

Wheeller, B., Hart, T. & Whysall, P. (1990) Application of the Delphi technique: a reply to Green, Hunter and Moore, *Tourism Management*, 11(2), pp. 121–122.

Willemese, J. (2002) Chaos in Zimbabwe raak SA regstreeks, *Landbou weekblad*, 30 (August), pp. 10–11.

World Bank (1996) Mozambique, Transfrontier conservation areas pilot and institutional strengthening project (Washington, D.C: World Bank, Global Environment Facility Project Document).

World Bank (2005) Project appraisal document on a proposed credit in the amount of SDR13,90 millions (USD 20 millions equivalent) and proposed grant from the Global Environment Facility Trust Fund in the amount of USD 10 millions to the Republic of Mozambique for a Transfrontier Conservation Areas and tourism development project, Project September 6 (Washington, D.C: World Bank, Report No. 32148-MZ).

World Conservation Union [IUCN] (1991) *Parks*, 2(3) (Gland, Switzerland: IUCN).

World Tourism Organization (1998) *Guide for local authorities on developing sustainable tourism* (Madrid: World Tourism Organization).

World Travel and Tourism Environment Research Centre [WTTERC] (1993) *World travel and tourism environment review* (Oxford: World Travel and Tourism Environment Research Centre).

Résumé : **Exigences du tourisme de nature durable dans les zones transfrontalières de conservation : une consultation Delphi en Afrique du Sud**

Il y a pléthore de facteurs invoqués dans la littérature au sujet du tourisme durable mais on n'a guère donné priorité à ceux qui importent aux résidents désireux de développer de telles destinations. Cette recherche vise plus particulièrement à identifier les facteurs qui sont perçus comme essentiels pour l'opération d'un tourisme de nature durable en zones de conservation transfrontalières (TFCA dans le texte) en Afrique du Sud. On a mené une consultation Delphi avec 518 experts sud-africains (agents du gouvernement, académiques, et membres d'ONGs, du secteur privé et d'agences d'expertise). Les participants ont hiérarchisé l'importance relative de 502 facteurs (décisions politiques, économiques et de planification, facteurs environnementaux et sociaux) tirés de la littérature ainsi que d'autres facteurs suggérés par les personnes consultées. On a obtenu un consensus statistiquement significatif pour 159 facteurs multidisciplinaires, considérés comme 'essentiels' ou 'incompatibles' pour le développement d'un tourisme de nature durable en TFCA. On discute des conséquences pour l'évaluation du tourisme de nature durable en TFCA d'Afrique du Sud, en examinant comment elle s'applique au tourisme dans la TFCA du Grand Limpopo : une zone protégée transfrontalière qui recouvre une partie du Mozambique, de l'Afrique du Sud et du Zimbabwe.

Mots-clés: Consultation Delphi, durable, tourisme de nature, zone de conservation transfrontalière du Limpopo, le sud de l'Afrique

Zusammenfassung: Anforderungen an den nachhaltigen Naturtourismus in grenzüberschreitenden Naturschutzgebieten: Ein südafrikanische Delphi-Befragung

Über die die Jahre sind in der Literatur eine Fülle von Faktoren mit dem nachhaltigen Tourismus verbunden worden, aber nur wenig ist unternommen worden, um jene herauszuheben, welche für die Interessenten vor Ort am wichtigsten sind. Diese Untersuchung zielt insbesondere darauf ab, diejenigen Faktoren zu identifizieren, welche als grundlegend erfahren werden für einen nachhaltigen Naturtourismus in Transfrontier Conservation Areas (TFCA) im Südlichen Afrika. Hierfür wurde eine Delphi-Befragung durchgeführt, zu der 518 südafrikanische Experten aus Regierung, Wissenschaft, NGO's, Privatwirtschaft und Consulting-Firmen eingeladen wurden. Die Teilnehmer bewerteten die relative Wichtigkeit von 502 politischen, wirtschaftlichen, ökologischen und sozialen Faktoren, welche aus der Literatur abgeleitet worden waren, sowie weiterer Faktoren, die regionale Konsultanten vorgeschlagen hatten. Ein statistisch signifikantes Niveau der Übereinstimmung wurde bei 159 multidisziplinären Faktoren erzielt, welche die as 'essentiell' oder 'unvereinbar' mit nachhaltigem Natuttourismus in grenzüberschreitenden Naturschutzgebieten angesehen werden. Die Implikationen für die Einschätzung des nachhaltigen Naturtourismus in südafrikanischen TFCA's werden besprochen im Hinblick darauf, wie sich diese verhalten zum Tourismus im Great Limpopo TFCA, einem grenzüberschreitenden Schutzgebiet, welches Schutzgebiete im Mocambique, Südafrika und Simbabwe beinhaltet.

Stichwörter: Delphi-Befragung, nachhaltig, Naturtourismus, Great Limpopo Transfrontier Conservation Area, Südliches Afrika.

Regional network governance and sustainable tourism

Anna Farmaki

Effective governance has been identified as one of the most important factors in sustainable tourism implementation. As governance structures are increasingly becoming network-based, attention needs to be diverted to the effectiveness of partnerships in achieving sustainability in tourism. Evaluating the effectiveness of regional tourism governance in Cyprus by considering regional tourism organisations' (RTOs) public–private network involved exploratory research whereby semi-structured interviews with key tourism stakeholders were performed. Findings reveal that network governance-related challenges interact with region-specific characteristics, inhibiting the effectiveness of regional tourism governance in implementing sustainable tourism. Specifically, RTOs represent a weak form of governance and their effectiveness in implementing sustainable tourism is limited by the continuing dependence on foreign tour operators, a system of mutual favours which complexifies the nature of tourism planning and a growing emphasis on economic interests further fuelled by recent austerity measures imposed in Cyprus. The paper concludes that network governance cannot be considered separately from the socio-cultural, economic and environmental factors of the context in which it is studied and proposes that further research reflects the horizontal relations across regional, national and global networks.

Introduction

The tourism-sustainability nexus has preoccupied academics, governments and practitioners alike. Over the years, the adoption of sustainability principles in tourism development received extensive attention and a fair share of criticism. On one hand, the importance of the application of sustainability in creating a favourable policy landscape, where the negative outcomes of tourism development can be better managed, is increasingly recognised. Joint initiatives of intergovernmental (i.e. World Tourism Organisation) and private sector organisations (i.e. World Travel and Tourism Council) demonstrate the convergence of views on the importance of the concept. On the other, arguments have been put forward highlighting the inability of destinations to apply the rhetoric of sustainability into practice. Several authors argued that the problem of sustainable tourism implementation lies in its practical application, with stakeholder relations being identified as a barrier to sustainable tourism development (Bianchi, 2004; Daphnet, Scott, & Ruhanen, 2012; Dewhurst and Thomas, 2003; Dodds, 2007; Hardy, Beeton, & Pearson, 2002; Logar, 2010; Waligo, Clarke, & Hawkins, 2013; Yasarata Altinay, Burns, & Okumus, 2010).

Researchers have recognised that the success of sustainable tourism development is largely dependent on the policies, planning and management tools used (Mowforth & Munt, 2009; Ritchie & Crouch, 2003). Effective tourism planning (i.e. a systemised approach that does not simply let market forces prevail) is a prerequisite for destination resources to be sustainably managed and to ensure that inclusive decision-making takes place. Indeed, integrated comprehensive planning has been recognised as the most appropriate form of planning for sustainable tourism development. Milne and Ateljevic (2001) emphasised the need for localised cooperation and networking for successful tourism development outcomes. Consequently, tourism governance is widely considered as a determinant of successful sustainable tourism development. Governance is seen as a participatory process which 'embraces a variety of ideas that encompass intergovernmental relations and imply bottom-up decision making by having all concerned people at every level of government and nongovernmental organisations participate' (Organisation for Economic Cooperation and Development [OECD], 1995, p. 26). Thus, governance proposes collective action and coordination in realising effective destination management and planning (Bramwell, 2011). As changes in decision-making, planning and management processes are required for the sustainable development of tourism, governance becomes pertinent to discussion on sustainability in tourism. Bramwell and Lane (2011) stated that sustainable tourism development requires effective governance processes, if the goals of sustainability are to be realised.

Ayikoru, Tribe, and Airey (2009) posit that as destinations attempt to respond to competitive pressures, improve the coordination of activities and find more effective planning strategies, a decentralisation process with regards to tourism administrative structures and processes arose. The process of decentralisation of authority involves two aspects: (1) territorial delegation of power through the creation of regional institutional arrangements and (2) the transition of governance from formal government structures to network-based partnerships. The rationale behind the delegation of authority is two-fold. First, the creation of tourism organisations at the regional level represents a synergistic viewpoint of tourism governance, which fosters regional development and supports the principles of sustainability. Second, the departure from centralised governance structures to horizontal governance systems, demonstrating the interrelations among tourism stakeholders, encourages a holistic approach to tourism decision-making and development.

The shift toward governance fostered interest in the concept of networks spanning public and private sectors (Dredge, 2006), with networks being considered as channels for managing social relations between tourism stakeholders. Networks are assumed to bring several benefits to destinations through the promotion of an integrated planning process, inclusive decision-making and increased synergies and thus support the notion of sustainability (Bell, 2004; Dredge, 2006; Moscardo, 2011; Nordin & Svensson, 2007). Public–private partnership (PPPs) networks in particular have become popular within tourism as they represent the mutual dependency between the government and the private sector and therefore provide a bridging ground, which encourages integrated decision-making and effective planning. According to de Bruyn and Alonso (2012), PPPs represent a good governance model by ensuring a balance in decision-making and management. Nonetheless, the interplay between government, industry and civil society and the increasingly blurred roles of public and private sectors in policy-making has been scrutinised. Previous studies highlight the difficulty of balancing public and private interests (Hall, 2007; Mowforth & Munt, 2009; Pechlaner, Volgger, & Herntrei, 2012; Timur & Getz, 2008; Wray, 2011) and acknowledging public and private sector responsibilities (Beaumont & Dredge, 2010). Within the context of sustainable tourism the variety of stakeholder interests, the numerous policy domains affiliated to sustainable tourism development, the poor coordination of activities and the failure to include local communities in policymaking have been identified as inhibiting factors to its implementation (Bramwell, 2011; Dodds & Butler, 2010; Ghina, 2003; Reid & Schwab, 2006).

Existing literature informs us is that the social context in which policymaking takes place and institutional arrangements pertaining tourism planning are influential on sustainable tourism development and implementation. Thus, research on tourism governance is pivotal if insights are to be gained with regard to sustainable tourism development (Bramwell & Lane, 2011). Beritelli (2011) agreed that as governance research receives increasing scientific significance and practical value, understanding into effective planning and management of destinations may be enhanced. The link of policy implementation with societal processes and social relations merits the need for further research into the dialectical associations between policymaking, governance and by extent the political, socio-economic and cultural sphere (Krutwaysho & Bramwell, 2010). Additionally, as collaborative working has become a pressing matter in sustainable tourism discourse, the need to study regional tourism partnerships is imminent if insights are to be gained with respect to cooperation and coordination in planning at the national, regional and local level (Araujo & Bramwell, 2002).

Therefore, the aim of this paper is to examine the effectiveness of regional tourism governance in implementing sustainable tourism. In particular, the paper attempts to explore the effectiveness of regional tourism governance in Cyprus by considering regional tourism organisations (RTOs) as a form of network promoting sustainability in tourism. It must be highlighted that the intent of this research is to examine the effectiveness of the governance and management of the RTO network rather than the regional institutional structure. While several case studies have been performed on regional tourism governance (Araujo & Bramwell, 2002; Beaumont & Dredge, 2010; Dredge & Jamal, 2013; Wesley & Pforr, 2010; Zahra, 2011) with some linking governance to sustainability (Bramwell, 2011; Bramwell & Lane, 2011; Dinica, 2009; Higgins-Desbiolles, 2011; Sofield & Li, 2011), further research on the topic can enhance existing knowledge by underlying the social phenomena that underpin governance structures and the way they influence policy implementation. The similarity and/or difference of causes leading to failure in sustainable tourism implementation between destinations can elucidate planning practice.

The paper begins by examining the concept of sustainability in tourism before moving on to discussing governance and its changing nature within destination contexts. Then, the dimensions of effective governance are discussed before the case study is presented. The methodology section covers the strategy for data collection and analysis and the resulting findings are presented. The paper identifies challenges in relation to sustainable tourism development, arising from network-based and regional factors.

Literature review

Sustainable tourism development

Sustainability is widely regarded as a vehicle for addressing negative tourism impacts, by addressing issues of resource maintenance, ecosystem conservation and physical capacity. Initial attempts to conceptualise the term placed emphasis on the environmental aspects of tourism development (Gössling, Hansson, Hörstmeier, & Saggel, 2002; Hunter,

2002), with alternative tourism forms (such as ecotourism) being closely associated with sustainability (Oriade & Evans, 2011). Over the years, the definition of sustainable tourism moved away from an ecological to a cultural orientation while recently economic and managerial perspectives have been added in the explanation of the concept (Hall & Brown, 2008; Ko, 2005; Neto, 2003; Tyrrell & Johnston, 2008). According to Jayawardena, Patterson, Choi, and Brain (2008) sustainability as a notion has been reshaped becoming a more practical consideration embracing socio-cultural and economic perspectives. Scheyvens (2011) stipulated that tourism policies must echo the economic, social and environmental principles of sustainability, as the application of the concept requires a holistic approach to tourism development. Defined as 'the forms of tourism which meet the needs of tourists, the tourist industry and host communities today without compromising the ability of future generations to meet their own needs' (Swarbrooke, 1999, p. 13), sustainable tourism has often been presented as the antidote to mass tourism problems. Nonetheless, while sustainability is a state-focused goal to maintain the quality of life, sustainable development is process-oriented as it is associated with managed change towards improvement. Consequently, sustainable tourism represents all forms of tourism (conventional and alternative) that need to be compatible with the economic, social and environmental principles of sustainability.

Acknowledged as a critical success factor for both governments and the industry (Kuosmanen & Kuosmanen, 2009), sustainability in tourism has been related to destinations' competitiveness as a number of benefits may be gained including conservation of nature, preservation of traditional culture, destination self-sufficiency and a more balanced distribution of costs and benefits. Sustainability has become pivotal particularly to mature Mediterranean destinations suffering from the negative impacts of unplanned mass tourism growth (Yüksel, Bramwell, & Yüksel, 2005). Specifically, sustainable tourism development in small island states which are characterised by fragile eco-environments has been recognised as a practical necessity. The inclusion of sustainability principles in national plans is supported by scholars as a prerequisite for effective planning, with literature documenting the relationship between planning and sustainable tourism (Berno & Bricker, 2001; Ruhanen, 2013).

Recognised as a process of change which requires a balance between resource exploitation, the direction of investments and institutional change, sustainable development in tourism is inherently linked to the concept of governance. Bramwell (2011) argued that effective governance can enhance the objectives of sustainable tourism in two ways. First, the inclusion of a range of stakeholders in decision-making can strengthen the democratic processes and responsibility associated with sustainable development. Second, tourism development can achieve the economic, social and environmental goals of sustainability through effective governance if suitable institutional arrangements and instruments are adopted.

The changing nature of tourism governance

Following public sector reforms in the USA and UK in the 1980s, deregulation of government activities through networks and partnerships including the public and private sectors lend prominence to the notion of governance. Initial attempts to conceptualise governance drew from corporate management and political economy, with literature reporting a perplexed landscape with regard to the term's definition and dimensions (Windsor, 2009). Defined as the sum of the ways in which individuals and institutions (public and private) manage their common affairs and take cooperative action (Commission on Global Governance, 1995), governance is inherently linked to the exercise of power. According to Bulkeley (2005) governance refers to the way societies are 'steered'. Therefore, a governing system is the tool in which resources are allocated and control is exercised (Rhodes, 1996). Hall (2011) suggested that the conceptualisation of governance involves first a description of the government's adaptability to economic and political reforms and second a description of governing activities that include various actors and reflect new modes of governance. Similarly, Atkinson (2003, p. 103) argued that governance involves processes 'whereby some degree of societal order is achieved, goals decided on, policies elaborated and services delivered'. Hence, governance as a concept is broader than that of the government as it recognises that formal and informal agencies are involved in decision-making and planning (Goodwin & Painter, 1996). Therefore, governance implies less government control and no given hierarchy (Breda, Costa and Costa, 2006) and involves multiple stakeholders (Beritelli, Bieger, & Laesser, 2007; Kjaer, 2004).

In tourism, governance has become an increasingly significant area of study as the industry exemplifies the interplay of the public, private and community sectors. As a result of socio-political requirements, which saw a progression from a centralised 'top down' approach to tourism planning to a decentralised, inclusive 'bottom up' managerial trend, the changing nature of tourism governance has received extensive attention. Studies examine tourism governance in relation to policymaking (Dredge & Pforr, 2008; Hall, 2011; Moscardo, 2011), within different geographical scales (Beaumont & Dredge, 2010; Yüksel et al., 2005; Zahra, 2011) and from a sustainability perspective (Bramwell, 2011; Bramwell & Lane, 2011; Pavlovich, 2001; Sofield & Li, 2011). Similarly, governance has been examined from different standpoints. For instance, Beritelli et al. (2007) combined the corporate-based and the political sciences perspectives arguing that governance is a set of rules and mechanisms used for policymaking as well as business strategies, involving all the related institutions and stakeholders. While various theories (i.e. transaction cost theory, principal agency theory, etc.) have been used to explain governance in destinations, network theory remains dominant. As the increasing participation of multiple stakeholders in tourism planning and development gives relevance to network theory, several scholars adopted the network analytical approach in tourism governance studies (Beritelli et al., 2007; D'Angella & Go, 2009; Dredge, 2006; Novelli, Schmitz, & Spencer, 2006; Saxena, 2005; Scott, Cooper, & Baggio, 2008; Wang & Xiang, 2007). Defined as types of relations (ties) linking defined sets of persons or objects (nodes), networks have been largely examined intrinsically by considering network structural characteristics including centrality and density. Research on governance networks has examined institutional structures and processes in an attempt to evaluate the effectiveness of destination management organisations (Sainaghi, 2006; Scott et al., 2008; Svensson, Nordin, & Flagestad, 2005). However, as Provan and Kenis (2008) highlight in this type of research it is the relations within a network that are studied rather that the network itself. Lewis (2011) suggested the term 'network governance' as more appropriate to highlight the focus on the changing relationship between the government and society, arguing that while there is an overlap between policy networks and network governance, the first deals with a way of organising stakeholders and the second refers to a horizontal form of governing. The author further argued that network governance is the right metaphor to describe the proliferation of governance arrangements such as partnerships.

Literature highlights the increasing importance placed on sustainable tourism and the influence governance exerts on its implementation. Indeed, the topic deserves further attention given the rise in popularity of partnerships as a form of governance in tourism. Thus, this paper considers the RTO network as effective governance with regard to sustainable tourism development. In doing so, the paper focuses on network governance rather than network structural characteristics.

Effective tourism governance

According to the UN (2002) a healthy governance environment is one of the most important factors in achieving sustainable tourism development. Nonetheless, there is no defined concept of governance for sustainability (Bosselmann, Engel, & Taylor, 2008). It is generally agreed that 'good' governance, exemplified through economic, political and administrative dimensions, is a prerequisite for achieving sustainability. With effective governance acquiring an imminent position in international organisations' agenda, attempts to define 'good' governance dimensions have been made. The principles for good governance as derived from leading organisations such as the European Union, the United Nations and the Organisation for Economic and Cooperative Development can be summarised in five categories: (1) openness and transparency, (2) participation and equity in common affairs, (3) accountability, (4) effectiveness in delivering services and (5) consistency in the rule of law and policy formulation.

Similarly, Ruhanen, Scott, Ritchie and Tkaczynski (2010) argued that governance is multi-dimensional and identified six variables as most predominant in literature: accountability, transparency, involvement, structure, effectiveness and power. Good governance aims at the best use of tourism space, resources, human capital, facilities and services in a sustainable way (Ritchie & Crouch, 2003) and is assumed to yield less conflicts, greater effectiveness in decision-making, innovation and empowerment of actors. An effective governance model for sustainability implies holistic awareness, benign empowerment, social equality and responsibility in values and actions. Kemp, Parto, and Gibson (2005) identified policy integration, common objectives, information for implementation and frameworks for innovation as the four components of governance required for sustainable development. Additional requirements for achieving sustainable development governance include the existence of an institution facilitating sustainable development, the availability of quality information and knowledge, the intergovernmental coordination on the local–global scale, the coordination among policies in different sectors other than tourism, the implementation of innovative policy instruments, an effective bureaucratic quality, a participatory culture and the agreement over sustainability as well as the strengthening of social capital (United Nations, 2002).

PPPs are considered a good governance model, addressing the above mentioned requirements with regard to sustainable development. It is widely advocated that networks based on PPPs represent a holistic governance form which is in line with sustainability principles. For instance, PPPs foster entrepreneurship and innovation due to the sharing of resources between the government and the private sector (Pike, May, & Bolton, 2011), thus promoting stronger governance systems through more efficient management and advanced technologies. PPPs are also considered as representative of an integrated framework which embraces local interests and increases coordination among tourism actors. According to Morisson, Lynch, and Johns (2004) public–private networks may be perceived as a tool of regional economic development and a means of redirecting public sector resources. While the role of the government in adopting sustainable development principles in national tourism plans is undoubted, discourse on sustainable tourism highlights the importance of an interactional model in decision-making and planning, in which the public and private sectors as well as the society cooperate. Nevertheless, evidence showed that tourism governance is challenged by the complex nature of the industry, where the multiplicity of different interests impedes consensus and policy implementation (Bruyn & Alonso, 2012; Von Malmborg, 2003; Wray, 2011). The extent to which networks act on self-interest opposed to collective wellbeing has been highlighted as a key influencer in sustainable tourism development (Dredge, 2006b; Erkus-Ozturk & Eraydin, 2010). Pierre and Peters (2000, p. 20) summarised the problematic nature of networks arguing that while 'it needs networks to bring societal actors into joint projects, it tends to see its policies obstructed by those networks'. Such dilemmatic opinions reinforce the belief that network governance studies should focus on the process rather than the outcome. According to Wilkinson (2005), governance is outcome-focused with Zahra (2011) agreeing that governance is not only about the process. While the dynamic environment of networks is undoubtedly influential on the outcome of sustainable tourism development, acknowledgement of other factors that might be potentially powerful on the implementation of policies is required.

The alignment of sustainability principles at the national, regional and local levels has been highlighted as a key element of implementation success and an enormous challenge. An inclusive process of decision-making, whereby local communities participate in public policy, is seen as effective governance. However, this represents a simplistic notion that fails to identify regional tourism governance linkages and exchange networks (Lynch & Morrison, 2007). Beaumont and Dredge (2010) found that local tourism organisations tend to demonstrate high levels of transparency and accountability primarily to their members, excluding other stakeholders. Moreover, the public funding several local tourism organisations receive limits their ability to implement tourism initiatives due to disagreement with national tourism authorities (Beaumont & Dredge, 2010). Similarly, external factors such as political ideology, funding flows and spatial scale have been known to contribute to regional governance effectiveness (Dredge, 2006). Zapata and Hall (2012) agreed that local tourism organisations are highly dependent on public subsidies and the minimisation of these funds leads to inefficiency. Indeed, critics have questioned the ability of regionally diffused tourism authorities to bypass bureaucracy, secure funds, integrate conflicting interests and manage narrow regional strategies under national priorities (Yüksel et al., 2005). Ruhanen (2013) concluded that local governments can act as both facilitators and inhibitors of sustainable tourism development and emphasised the need for further academic attention on the subject of regional governance.

Hence, this study is directed by the need to illuminate current literature on regional tourism governance and broaden knowledge on the effectiveness of RTOs in achieving sustainable tourism development. The paper focuses on Cyprus and aspires to contribute insights to the increasing pool of case studies available on regional tourism governance and to the on-going debate on sustainable tourism. In doing so, this study considers the characteristics of efficient networks, as proposed by Morrison et al. (2004), in conjunction to the dimensions of effective governance as identified by Ruhanen et al. (2010) (Figure 1).

By looking at the factors that influence the effectiveness of networks it is possible to evaluate the success of RTOs in meeting the requirements for effective governance. Consequently, it can be determined if RTOs constitute effective network governance with regard to sustainable tourism development.

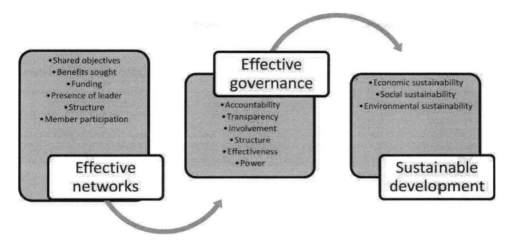

Figure 1. Governance networks/sustainability nexus.

Methodology

The case study context

Cyprus is a well-known sea and sun Mediterranean destination whose economy relies heavily on tourism (Figure 2). Primarily appealing to Northern European markets, tourism development in Cyprus coincided with the mass coastal tourism explosion in the 1970s. Over the years, the island saw its tourist arrivals increase significantly and by the

Figure 2. Map of Cyprus.
Source: Map Data @2015 Basarsoft, Google, Mapa GISrael.

end of the 1990s, 2.5 million tourists were arriving annually on the island yielding almost €1927.7 million in tourism revenue.

The rapid growth of tourism resulted in several negative outcomes including environmental degradation, unskilled foreign labour, perishing cultural identity and a persistent sea and sun image (Clerides & Pashourtidou, 2007). By the 2000s, it was clear that the tourism product of Cyprus had reached stagnation and was being further threatened by emerging competition and changing tourist needs. With tourist arrivals fluctuating throughout the last decade, the tourism authorities in Cyprus highlighted the need to adopt a more sustainable developmental approach in tourism and initiated a repositioning strategy by focusing primarily on targeted marketing, the distribution of benefits to local communities and new product development, with a primary focus on culture and nature. The development of sustainable tourism also aimed at de- seasonalising the main 'sea and sun' product, minimising environmental pressures on the coastline and preserving traditional culture.

The pressure to adopt a sustainability approach led to the regional delegation of power. In 2009 the national tourism authority – the Cyprus Tourism Organisation (CTO) – established six regional tourism boards based on a PPP structure (four RTOs located in the southern coastal areas of Pafos, Limassol, Larnaca and Famagusta and two representing the inland regions of Troodos mountains and Nicosia). Each regional tourism board was set up as an independent private company and until self-sustainability is achieved through membership, the CTO remains their primary subsidiser. The notion behind the establishment of the RTOs was to reflect the network-based structure of the tourism industry and improve decision-making by allowing the participation of all stakeholders involved. According to the CTO (2010) through the establishment of the RTOs each region is encouraged to develop a regional tourism development strategy, envisaging regional strengths and which supports the repositioning of the island. With the CTO providing financial and technical assistance, the RTOs aim at improving cooperation and ensuring the active participation of local/regional public and private stakeholders in tourism so that the RTOs can acquire the capacity to tackle regional problems and resolve them with flexibility. The Strategic Plan of the CTO (2010, p. 4) outlines that the PPP framework in which RTOs were established represents 'the horizontal aspect of intervention in the Tourism Strategy 2011–2015. It is proposed that their actions are extended horizontally in significant programmes of the Strategy such as in marketing, the environment, extending the tourist period, coastal development . . .' The RTOs consist of 13 public and private sector members including hoteliers, travel agent association members, municipality officers and CTO officers, and their activities span across lobbying, promoting tourism developmental plans and the creation of a regional brand. The RTOs are also responsible for coordinating tourism development efforts by communicating with the respective ministries involved and the CTO. Hence, the role of the RTOs goes beyond development and marketing as they act as a liaison between the public and the private sector and constitute an umbrella under which public and private stakeholders and local authorities interact. In order to understand the characteristics of each region, the following section presents their main product offering as well as key tourism facts.

Tourism development policies

Nicosia is the capital of Cyprus and the main governmental and economic centre. While Nicosia has adequate cultural resources and its dividing line attracts tourists curious of the political status quo, it is not a tourism-oriented region and focuses primarily on business tourism. Similarly, Troodos with its amble byzantine churches and natural resources lacks the infrastructural development necessary to support a growing tourism market. Thus, Cyprus' tourism relies mostly on its coastal regions which offer a similar 'sea and sun' product. In recent years, additional tourism products have been developed as part of the island's repositioning attempt including sports tourism, weddings and honeymoons, nature trails, cultural routes and spa tourism. Events and festivals have also been increasingly promoted in order to extend the tourist season. Nevertheless, 80% of arrivals to Cyprus are between April-October, confirming the appeal of Cyprus as a summer destination. Table 1 shows the key tourism indicators by region.

Research methods

Exploratory research has been commonly used in previous studies of tourism governance (Araujo & Bramwell, 2002; Moscardo, 2011; Wan & King, 2013; Yüksel et al., 2005; Zahra, 2011). With several studies on network governance adopting a quantitative approach, the need for qualitative research in addressing the 'softer' elements of networks is considered an effective strategy (Dredge, 2006). Therefore, exploratory semi-structured interviews were undertaken with key stakeholders identified by the researcher as being directly and indirectly related to the tourism sector of Cyprus. Purposive sampling technique was utilised to select the informants for the investigation. Purposive sampling enables researchers to use their judgement to select people that will best enable them to answer their research questions and to meet their objectives and so informants were chosen based on their position in the organisation and experience in tourism. Care was taken to select interviewees which represented different sectors of the tourism industry including the state, the private sector as well as non-governmental institutions and academia, consequently enlarging the perspective and adding richness to the research.

Data collection was conducted in two phases. A preliminary phase of 16 interviews took place from March 2012 to March 2013. Additional interviews were performed throughout May and June 2013. Overall, 24 interviews were conducted with stakeholders from different groups including CTO officers (4), regional tourism board officers (6), local authority administrators (4), private sector members (4), non-profit organisations (2), associations (2) and academics (2). The interviewees were selected carefully to represent different sectors of the industry as well as academia in order to

Table 1. Key tourism indicators by region (2011).

Region	Tourist arrivals in 000s	%	Bed units in 000s	%
Pafos	829,338	*34.7*	27,837	*32*
Famagusta	748,000	*31.3*	34,893	*40.1*
Limassol	310,808	*13*	13,193	*15.2*
Larnaca	251,911	*10.5*	6,367	*7.3*
Nicosia	134,727	*5.6*	2,467	*2.8*
Troodos	4,760	*0.2*	2,325	*2.7*

Source: CTO (2012).

allow for enriched views to be gained. The interviews lasted between 30 and 45 minutes and were recorded with the permission of the interviewees. Literature reports that the examination of governance structures requires the observation of stakeholder relations as these may influence decision-making and policy outcomes. Hence, understanding of the influential role of stakeholder relations was sought, even though structural characteristics of the RTO network were not considered in this study. This study adopted a deductive and inductive approach. First, it considers the dimensions of effective governance as well as the characteristics of effective networks as identified by existing literature. Second, it aims to contribute to the theoretical background surrounding the subject by allowing new themes to emerge to acquire deeper meaning with regard to the development of sustainable tourism. Thus, the interviews included a consistent set of open-ended questions that were designed to elicit discussions about the tourism development of regions, sustainable tourism implementation, decision-making processes, stakeholder relations and constraints faced by RTOs among others. The following questions as shown in Table 2 directed the data collection process although it must be noted that additional questions were probed:

Data were analysed thematically whereby emerging topics were grouped into interrelated themes, following a coding scheme. According to Miles and Huberman (1994) there is no right way to analyse voluminous qualitative data. They can be interpretative and eclectic in nature and researchers can employ a 'tight', more theoretically driven approach, or a 'loose', inductively oriented approach (Yin, 2003). For the purposes of this study both inductive and deductive data analysis modes were employed. First, a broad coding scheme was derived from literature review. Transcripts and notes from the interviews were then read several times in order to identify key themes according to the coding scheme. Subsequently, blocks of verbatim text were copied, re-organised and cross-referenced to allow the identification of thematic categories. Additionally, an inductive analysis approach was adopted whereby data

Table 2. Interview questions.

Questions	Governance dimensions	Network characteristics
Who are the stakeholders participating in the RTO? Who are the stakeholders involved in tourism development?	Structure involvement	Structure
How is sustainable tourism perceived by participants in both the public and private sector?	Accountability	Shared objective benefit sought
How is information on sustainable tourism policies communicated?	Transparency	Participation
Who is responsible for sustainable tourism policy implementation?	Accountability	Participation
Which stakeholders in the RTOs are more powerful in terms of decision-making and policy implementation?	Power involvement	Presence of leader
What are the structural constraints and opportunities that RTOs face with regard to sustainable tourism implementation, operation and management?	Structure efficiency	Funding structure

were analysed freely without a framework or coding scheme. Instead, new insights were sought from data, which combined with the pre-identified themes provided in-depth meaning into the development of tourism at the regional level. This was undertaken by re-reading transcripts and related documents, identifying emerging themes and incorporated them into the research findings. Overall, findings were grouped into themes related to the dimensions of effective governance.

Findings

The findings of the study are presented in two sections. In the first section, the key stakeholders of the Cyprus tourism industry are identified and their knowledge of sustainable tourism is discussed. In the second section, the effectiveness of network governance is examined in terms of sustainable tourism implementation.

Stakeholder identification and sustainable tourism awareness

The role of the public sector in tourism development was highlighted by informants. The main tourism authority in Cyprus is the CTO, which is accountable to the Ministry of Energy, Industry, Commerce and Tourism. While the responsibilities of the Ministry include the enactment of laws, regulations and policies, the coordination of all governmental departments engaged in tourism development, the approval of tourism plans and the allocation of budgets, the CTO (a quasi-governmental organisation) remains the primary department solely engaged with tourism. Although in its mission statement the CTO's tasks include tourism planning, product development, marketing and licensing of accommodation, respondents from both the public and private sectors agreed that the organisation has no power in decision-making or policymaking. As one officer from the CTO put it, 'we are only able to influence the development of sustainable tourism indirectly' in a process of suggesting ideas, policies and regulations to the Ministry.

Similarly, the private sector was recognised as another important stakeholder group, as tourism development is dependent on private investment. Possessing significant financial and land resources, the private sector is regarded as a catalyst for the growth of the industry, with evidence suggesting that the accumulative power of industry associations (primarily hoteliers and tourism entrepreneurs) is such that they are frequently consulted in terms of tourism planning. Informants from both the public and private sector stated that following the bank crisis on the island in March 2013, the government consulted members of the private sector regarding the future of tourism, elevating its role into one of great prominence. Despite the influence of the private sector on the tourism industry in Cyprus, it was generally agreed amongst informants that the government remains the ultimate decision-maker. Hence, the development of a harmonious relationship between the two sectors and the alignment of interests was considered essential for the development of sustainable tourism. Other important stakeholders identified include the six regional tourism boards established by the CTO as well as non-profit organisations such as the Cyprus Sustainable Tourism Initiative (CSTI). Despite the efforts of such organisations to raise awareness on sustainability in tourism, they remain powerless in terms of decision-making. Lastly, the civic societies of Cyprus were identified as a stakeholder. While community involvement is a prerequisite for sustainable tourism, informants highlighted the lack of awareness in relation to sustainability and environmental consciousness among the members of the civic society, signalling the weak position of sustainable tourism policy implementation. Sustainability, being a new term, has not penetrated the Cyprus society's culture.

All interviewees were aware of the term of sustainability, albeit in different extents. While sustainable tourism development in Cyprus is an aspiration, dominating much of the strategic plan of the CTO it was agreed among informants that its implementation remain problematic. As informants argued the lack of awareness of the importance and the benefits of sustainability on the part of policymakers within the public sector is a primary factor in sustainable tourism development failure.

> The political ideology guiding tourism development supports large-scale tourism projects ... sustaining resources or protecting the fragile environment of the island was never a primary goal of any government ... The words 'development' and 'sustainability' appear together on paper but in reality [tourism] development moves to a completely opposite direction than that suggested by the principles of sustainability approach. (Academic)

Informants seemed to agree that the sustainable tourism approach largely promoted by the CTO's strategic plan is an appropriate concept theoretically, yet concluded that the necessity to reinforce the island's damaged economy through a pro-growth approach in tourism prevails.

> After the recent events [bank crisis] numerous meetings were undertaken between the government and the representatives of associations like the hoteliers' association ... we had meeting after meeting in order to come up with ideas and suggestions regarding the way to overcome difficulties. It is not easy but our country's economy relies on tourism ... of course we acknowledge the importance of sustainability but when your country is in trouble you need to take the less risky solution ... investing on tourism projects that will attract large numbers of tourists is of key priority at the moment. (Hoteliers' association)

Being a full member of the European Union entails that Cyprus is obliged to follow EU regulations of sustainability. Nevertheless, informants from NGOs and the private sector argued that the lack of governmental support for sustainable tourism initiatives and the absence of appropriate infrastructure for the development of sustainable tourism weakens the process of adopting sustainability principles in tourism. As an interviewee from an NGO stated 'Cyprus is a small island suffering from the lack of natural resources, urbanism, lack of environmental culture and lack of education regarding responsible practices'. With the recovery of the economy being currently a pressing issue, the concept of sustainable tourism has been pushed further down the agenda and the pro-growth developmental approach became a justifiable strategy.

Effective governance dimensions
Accountability and transparency

Most of the informants acknowledged the role of collaboration in tourism, highlighting that in order for the industry to be developed sustainably coordination and a shared vision is required. 'We need to be on the same page' said one CTO officer who further argued that sustainable tourism requires commitment from everyone involved in the industry. Several RTO officers supported this view, stating that the RTOs are required to adhere to the regulations set by the CTO. However, two officers highlighted the limited power of RTOs saying that their primary task is to promote the region and to propose projects to the national tourism authorities, rather than influence decision-making. 'We make propositions to the CTO but we are not alone ... the board relies on the municipality which is not tourism-oriented and consequently there are delays which impact tourism negatively' said one RTO officer. Another RTO officer agreed stating that:

> We are eager to progress with upgrading of facilities, cleaning of beaches and construction of projects but local authorities are very late in implementing the activities we request from them. They don't understand that clean beaches are a selling point for the region! We could utilise beaches for instance for events but again they are reluctant to approve the organisation of themed events.

Consequently, the role of the RTOs in tourism development was questioned by several interviewees. When asked about the availability of information on sustainability schemes, interviewees highlighted that the RTOs officially communicate information to their members yet the small size of Cyprus was found to contribute to the spread of information among non-members also. As a regional tourism officer argued:

> The way stakeholders in the region utilise the information or regard it as important is determined by their ties to foreign networks and past experience. Small businesses are successful if they know how the industry operates or if they have worked in the industry before. Entering into alternative tourism forms such as agrotourism is something that we support, and we have a good relationship with some of the small establishments in the area, but the success of the business is ultimately determined by the knowledge and understanding of the owner ... so they may not see membership as a necessity.

Also, duplication of activities between the CTO and RTOs, primarily in the area of marketing and promotion, was identified by both private and public sector interviewees. In particular, interviewees suggested that while theoretically the RTOs act as a tool towards a sustainable developmental approach, practically they are impaired in their ability to implement activities that will benefit the local community.

> The RTOs are basically the same thing like the CTO. So all of the problems the CTO has are now transferred at the regional level ... how do the RTOs support the local community? Who is the local community and how are its interests promoted? Instead we are lost in a labyrinth of bureaucracy, where more people are involved in tourism. (Private sector informant)

Private and public sector informants argued that the role of each tourism stakeholder is ambiguous. On one hand, the government's role in directing tourism development and providing tourism infrastructure was acknowledged. On the other, the significance of the private sector in providing investment capital and funds was emphasised. Evidently, the complex nature of the industry requires the cooperation of all stakeholders. Nevertheless, as several informants claimed conflicts arise as various groups of stakeholders attempt to satisfy different sets of goals. The creation of the RTOs has led to more actors being involved in decision-making, which informants highlighted as an antecedent to the current complicated nature of administration and decision-making. The view of the necessity for RTOs was in fact questioned with a public sector interviewee stating:

> I don't see the point of having RTOs in a small place like Cyprus. Tourists don't think of us in terms of regions anyway, we are too small. The establishment of RTOs appears as a sustainable tourism approach but I don't see how they support sustainable tourism development.

Structure and effectiveness

The antagonistic behaviour of RTOs in terms of tourism development was highlighted by several informants as an unsustainable practice with serious environmental, social and economic implications. Favouritism, for instance, on behalf of the government towards certain regions was mentioned by an interviewee. 'The CTO continues to promote coastal regions, not offering support to Nicosia or Troodos which try to develop agrotourism or conference tourism' said one RTO officer. The lack of private funding was identified by informants as an impeding factor to RTOs' ability to compete efficiently. 'Development is left to the private sector' claimed one RTO officer whereas a local authority officer stated that the lack of investment interest impedes the development of regions and widens the economic inequality gap among them. Thus, the presence of investment interest in a region influences tourism development and verifies the importance of the private sector. As a local authority officer highlighted 'regions are competitive when there are entrepreneurs in the locality'. The absence of entrepreneurship and/or investment capital in a region was recognised by informants as a key factor forcing RTOs to turn to foreign investors. However, as one interviewee noted 'foreign investment will not necessarily benefit the locals . . . instead it strengthens the dependence on foreign stakeholders'.

The dependence of RTOs on public subsidies further impedes the situation. Specifically, all RTO officers stated that the CTO does not provide sufficient funds for their effective operation and management, with almost all highlighting the budgetary restrictions imposed following the economic crisis on the island as an influencer on RTO efficiency. The importance of funding was underlined by a regional tourism officer who argued that 'a lack of funds translates into a lack of action'. The support of the CTO in regional tourism development is fundamental due to the limited access to funds, which problematises the viability of the RTOs. The RTOs were established as private companies with the aim of becoming self-sustained within the first five years of operation. Self-sustainability is yet to be achieved and was recurrently mentioned by interviewees from both the public and private sector as a major obstacle in achieving autonomy.

> Self-sustainability has not been achieved and I don't think it is possible. When the CTO established the RTOs the aim was to initially finance these for about 5 years and then allow them to become self-financed through membership. But there is limited interest from the private sector to participate in the RTOs due to the membership fees . . . the question that many potential members ask . . . what's in it for me? Why should I pay to become a member? (Public sector informant)

Indeed, the viability of the RTOs becomes questionable considering that not all regions are equally tourism oriented. As the Nicosia tourism board officer argued its ability to become self-sustained is limited due to the low number of tourists the city accepts and the few hotels and tourism facilities available. The Troodos regional tourism board officer agreed stating that the region has a small number of tourist establishments; therefore, the availability of potential members is restricted. The officer further highlighted the unwillingness of several tourism businesses to participate in the Troodos RTO as the owners of tourism companies reside and possibly work in other regions. Reliance on funding also problematises the legitimacy that stakeholders attach to the RTOs. While nearly all informants regarded the boards as a legitimate organisation, supported by the national tourism authorities, the unwillingness of stakeholders to join as members in the RTOs can be indicative of mistrust. As a regional tourist officer put it:

We are an official organisation representing regional tourism ... not everyone wishes to join as members and I think the membership fee might be a deterring factor but it is not that high considering the benefits these businesses will receive. I think that some people have not understood the purpose of the RTO and perhaps see us [RTO] as another CTO which serves political aspirations and so have lost faith ...

Power and involvement

Informants commented on the multiplicity of stakeholders involved in the RTO structure which was characterised as problematic with regards to the implementation of tourism policies. The varying interests pursued by multiple stakeholders were deemed by interviewees as influential on the actions of different actors. Also, ignorance of sustainable tourism principles and lack of knowledge on tourism were recognised as an inhibiting factor which complicates the implementation of policies. The government was recognised as a catalyst to sustainable tourism development, as per the requirements of the EU, yet the private sector was accused by several informants of failure to comply with sustainability practices. Specifically, one interviewee from an NGO stated:

The CTO and the RTOs might say they are aware of the importance of sustainability but in reality the situation is different ... behind the wheel, driving the decisions are businessmen who have economic interests ... [they] don't care about the social or environmental benefits of tourism as their primary aim is to make profits.

The issue of conflicting interests among the various members of the RTOs prompted interviewees to question the role of the government, arguing that higher levels of authority do not necessarily safeguard societal benefits or promote sustainability. Specifically, interviewees highlighted the role of the CTO in decision-making claiming that currently the national tourism authority remains powerless.

The problem with the CTO is that they are not making the policies. Policymaking is in the hands of the ministries and the government ... but there are so many different public sector departments and agencies involved in a project that delays are common. (Local authority officer)

Informants also emphasised the underrepresentation of certain groups of stakeholders in the RTO structure. Specifically, small-medium-sized enterprises (SMEs), academics and NGOs such as environmental groups were identified as being marginalised from decision-making processes. Therefore, the public–private structure of the RTOs is not necessarily inclusive or participatory in nature. Rather the dominance of key players in regional governance impairs sustainable tourism development. It was suggested by informants that the exclusion of local businesses from tourism policymaking as well as of key stakeholders (i.e. NGOs) mirrors the approach followed in tourism development. An academic argued that 'a vicious cycle is created in which tourism development in Cyprus became supply-driven and centred on the economic interests of powerful stakeholders'. The informant further suggested that 'the line between the public and private sector in terms of objectives and benefits sought in tourism development is thin in practice'.

Interviewees suggested that following the exposure of Cyprus' banks in March 2013, the role of tourism on the island was heightened. Indeed, the need to boost the economy through tourism development has been advocated by the newly-appointed government, who claimed that a pro-growth approach is the only economic viable solution to Cyprus' financial problems. Consequently, the development of large-scale luxury projects initiated several years ago (such as the Limassol marina and golf course resorts) has been justified. As a private sector informant stated:

> In the difficult economic era we live in, the importance of mass tourism cannot be ignored ... but tour operators take advantage of this and pressurise for further price cuts. Hoteliers are forced to offer all-inclusive packages to target tourists despite the CTO's effort to reposition the island away from mass tourism. The CTO is aware of this problem but they are not doing anything to support hoteliers and hoteliers are businessmen who must comply with market forces.

Indeed, the developmental approach favoured by the government has been questioned by NGO informants as a flawed practice in terms of sustainability, as the main recipients of economic benefits are foreign tour operators. Therefore, despite the objective of the CTO to minimise dependency on foreign tour operators and to distribute economic benefits to the local community, tourism development remains largely directed by external powerful forces. Several interviewees suggested that the private sector steers public policy accordingly to serve personal interests. Indeed, several examples exist in Cyprus indicating that dominance of private interests directs decision-making. For instance, it is not unusual for projects (i.e. Limassol marina) to be cancelled and re-announced with the project being given to a different bidder than initially agreed. Similarly, the development of the luxury Limnis project in an environmentally protected area raised concerns, primarily from NGOs, about the influence some private stakeholders have on policymaking.

> Many of the key stakeholders directing the development of tourism on the island have no understanding of the concept of sustainability, and if they do they ignore it for the sake of economic interests ... the government doesn't do anything to correct the problem. (Academic informant)

An interviewee argued that public and private interaction is shaped by a highly developed system of mutual favours, in which the right financial background and good interpersonal relations are dominant factors in tourism planning and development. The informant further argued that the executive power of politicians is frequently used to favour their private financial supporters resulting in a dominance of personal interests over societal welfare. Several interviewees suggested that the majority of politicians abuse their positions to enrich themselves and their acquaintances. 'It is not surprising to find owners of hotels acting as mayors of a municipality while holding a position in the board of the RTOs' argued an NGO member. Consequently, decision-making is directed by short-term economic benefits whereas a system is fostered, in which people with inadequate qualifications or knowledge of sustainable tourism are in power.

Tourism development at the regional level follows a parallel path as the objective to invest on large-scale projects is shared among private stakeholders in primarily coastal regions. Public sector interviewees stated that with four golf courses being developed in the region of Pafos, petitions to construct similar projects have been filed by RTOs in other regions. 'A golf course in Famagusta will boost the regional economy and allow us to target tourists off season' said the regional board's officer. While RTOs welcome such large-scale projects enthusiastically, concerns have been raised over the adherence of such developmental projects to sustainability principles. As one interviewee from the public sector concluded:

For a small island like Cyprus there is no need to have so many golf courses and marinas. We have limited resources, we have a persistent water shortage problem yet all the regions try to imitate each other. Such a strategy will cause problems in the future as each region will keep target tourists in one periphery rather than encourage them to travel around, as all the regions will be offering the same product.

Discussion and conclusion

The influence of governance on sustainable tourism development is well documented. With decentralised tourism administration being increasingly regarded as a way towards achieving sustainability in tourism, through the promotion of inclusive decision-making and integrated planning, regional tourism governance provides an interesting context for research. This study aimed at examining the effectiveness of regional tourism governance in implementing sustainable tourism by considering network governance of RTOs in Cyprus. Unsurprisingly, and in support of previous studies' findings (Beaumont & Dredge, 2010; Dredge, 2006; Hall, 2007), this research reveals that RTOs represent a weak form of governance with regard to sustainable tourism implementation. Several factors inhibit the effectiveness of regional network governance.

First, it becomes apparent that what limits accountability and effectiveness of RTOs is the nature of the tourism industry, which requires the interplay of multiple actors. Although the public–private structure of RTOs in Cyprus aims at counteracting tourism problems and aligning the industry with sustainability principles, this study highlights the difficulty of such an aspiration. The multiplicity of stakeholders involved in regional tourism governance has been previously acknowledged as an impeding factor with regards to policy implementation, with Dredge (2006) and Hall (2007) suggesting that it is the diversity in objectives as well as conflicting interests of each group of stakeholders that impede implementation. Von Malmborg (2003) stated that different actors in the public–private network strive for different goals; some are interested in ecological sustainability, others for social or economic sustainability with some members' interests being based on organisational development. In the case of Cyprus, findings report that a dominance of private interests drives decision-making at the expense of sustainable tourism. For instance, powerful private stakeholders may hold multiple positions (i.e. mayors in municipalities) while also finding their way in RTOs' boards of directors. Accountability, legitimacy and transparency of RTOs are thus dubious due to the multiple positions held by powerful stakeholders, actively involved in both the private and public sector. Indeed, scholars have previously questioned PPPs as being fixed within a centralised political system or public programmes being anchored in private investment (Zapata & Hall, 2012).

Second, while the role of each sector is clear among the informants, findings reveal that when it comes to decision-making and implementation of sustainable tourism policies responsibility is not assumed by the respective stakeholders. Specifically, an apathetic behaviour towards sustainability is evident, particularly among local authorities. Consequently, policy implementation remains in the hands of actors who often lack adequate knowledge on sustainability or are uninterested in implementing sustainable tourism practices.

Additionally, findings indicate that certain important stakeholders such as NGOs are marginalised from decision-making. As the scale of power in Cyprus tourism leans towards private influential stakeholders, the local community remains the weaker participant in decision-making. Thus, sustainable tourism remains a malingering concept in the Cyprus tourism industry and civic society. As findings highlight understanding of the concept of sustainability relies on individual actors and in the case of Cyprus it is past experience or ties with foreign stakeholders (such as tour operators) that contribute to the success of regional businesses promoting sustainable tourism development. The support provided by the RTOs to small businesses may be perceived by actors as less important, leading to a widespread belief that membership is not a prerequisite for the successful development of the business. Nonetheless, lack of participation translates into lack of funding and further dilutes the legitimacy of RTOs.

With the absence of a strong regulatory framework, sustainability in Cyprus remains a contested paradigm with little support from both the national and regional authorities. Bramwell (2011) highlighted the challenge of adopting sustainability in tourism due to policies often being made in domains outside tourism. Therefore, an examination of governance effectiveness cannot be considered separately from external forces. For instance, the structure of the RTOs is not only influenced by the relations between the participants of the network but is also largely shaped by other networks in the industry. As this study demonstrates, the RTOs echo national tourism authorities' priorities which encourage economic growth through large-scale tourism development. The pursuit for economic benefits has been justified in recent years due to the financial problems Cyprus is facing at the expense of sustainability in tourism. Indeed, Gill and Williams (2014) suggest that political support of economic development compromises sustainability goals, as the power of entrepreneurs leads to a short-lived commitment towards sustainability.

Furthermore, findings emphasise the influence of regional characteristics on RTO's effectiveness in implementing sustainable tourism. The tourism orientation of regions, the type of tourism activity present and the availability of funds shape up the context in which the development of sustainable tourism is to occur as evidenced by Dredge (2006) and Bruyn and Alonso (2012). For instance, the effective performance of RTOs is largely influenced by their linkages to local investors, or in the absence of these, foreign investors. The presence of entrepreneurs in a region can facilitate development, yet the type of developmental approach followed is further encouraged by economic goals. Similarly, the economic inequality gap among regions may widen if entrepreneurship in a region is absent. The pursuit for economic sustainability, therefore, runs the risk of social exclusion, environmental pressures and further dependence on foreign networks such as tour operators. In addition, a form of isophormism arises whereby the development of similar projects across the coastal regions in particular leads to an undifferentiated tourism product that is largely based on large-scale tourism development and therefore reinforces the current mass tourism status quo. Similarly non-coastal regions remain marginalised, receiving minimal support from the government in terms of infrastructural provision and funding. Therefore, the goal for economic benefit fosters a competitive behaviour among RTOs which may lead to significant environmental disadvantages (such as ecological degradation and the over-utilisation of resources) in the near future.

Evidently, as the study concludes what should drive discussion on governance is not only the longstanding question of who governs in tourism planning but attention should also be diverted on the factors shaping policy outcomes. As this study concludes while the dimensions of effective governance serve a rightful purpose in understanding network performance, they cannot be considered separately from factors stemming from the regional sociocultural and economic environment. The outcome of sustainable tourism development in destinations may be largely influenced by the power certain stakeholders possess, yet the power of actors is regulated by their relations to other stakeholders. Similarly, RTOs should not be seen as a distinct form of network governance as they are interlinked with tourism networks at the regional, national and global level. Discussion on whether a 'bottom up' approach in tourism planning is a prerequisite for sustainable tourism is futile if the horizontal relations across regional, national and global networks are not recognised.

Torres-Delgado and Saarinen (2014) posited that indicators for successful sustainable tourism implementation cannot be easily transposed from one place to another. As this paper illustrated although networks have been advocated as an appropriate form of governance, supporting inclusive and participatory decision-making, there is no ideal recipe for effective regional tourism governance as contextual factors interact with network characteristics. Governance evolves and as Provan and Kenis (2008) suggested one form of governance may produce positive outcomes for some planning elements but not others. Originating from similar ancestry, governance and sustainability are contested concepts with different meanings to various people. The contextual application of the terms requires appreciation of the empirical knowledge researchers will produce. Further research on governance and sustainability is thus required. It is advised that researchers incorporate a multiplicity of methods and perspectives in the study of governance and sustainable tourism, if understanding of their character is to be gained.

Disclosure statement

No potential conflict of interest was reported by the author.

References

Atkinson, R. (2003). Addressing urban social exclusion through community involvement in urban regeneration. In R. Imrie, & M. Raco (Eds.), *Urban renaissance? New Labour, community and urban policy* (pp. 101–119). Bristol: Policy Press.

Ayikoru, M., Tribe, J., & Airey, D. (2009). Reading tourism education: Neoliberalism unveiled. *Annals of Tourism Research, 36*(2), 191–221.

Beaumont, N., & Dredge, D. (2010). Local tourism governance: A comparison of three network approaches. *Journal of Sustainable Tourism, 18*(1), 7–28.

Bell, S. (2004). Appropriate policy knowledge, and institutional and governance implications. *Australian Journal of Public Administration, 63*(1), 22–28.

Beritelli, P. (2011). Tourist destination governance through local elites-Looking beyond the stakeholder level. In *Kumulative Habilitationsschrift* (pp. 1–43). St. Gallen: Institute for Systemic Management and Public Governance, University of St. Gallen.

Beritelli, P., Bieger, T., & Laesser, C. (2007). Destination governance: using corporate governance theories as a foundation for effective destination management. *Journal of Travel Research, 46*, 96–107.

Berno, T., & Bricker, K. (2001). Sustainable Tourism Development: The Long Road From Theory To Practice. *International Journal of Economic Development, 3*(3), 1–18.

Bianchi, R. V. (2004). Tourism restructuring and the politics of sustainability: A critical view from the European periphery (The Canary Islands). *Journal of Sustainable Tourism, 12*(6), 495–529.

Bosselmann, K., Engel, R., & Taylor, P. (2008). *Governance for sustainability*. The World Conservation Union, Environmental Law and Policy Series, Switzerland: IUCN.

Bramwell, B. (2011). Governance, the state and sustainable tourism: A political economy approach. *Journal of Sustainable Tourism, 19*(4–5), 459–477.

Bramwell, B., & Lane, B. (2011). Critical research on the governance of tourism and sustainability. *Journal of Sustainable Tourism, 19*(4&5), 411−421.

Breda, Z., Costa, R., & Costa, C. (2006). Do clusters and networks make small places beautiful? The case of Caramulo (Portugal). In L. Lazzeretti & C. S. Petrillo (Eds.), *Tourism Local Systems and Networking* (pp. 67−82). Oxford: Elsevier.

de Bruyn, C., & Alonso, A. F. (2012). Tourism Destination Governance. *Bridging Tourism Theory and Practice, 4*, 221−242.

Bulkeley, H. (2005). Reconfiguring environmental governance: Towards a politics of scales and networks. *Political Geography, 24*(8), 875−902.

Clerides, S., & Pashourtidou, N. (2007). Tourism in Cyprus: Recent trends and lessons from the tourist satisfaction survey. *Cyprus Economic Policy Review, 1*(2), 51−72.

Commission on Global Governance. (1995). *Our global neighbourhood: The Report of the commission on global governance*. Oxford: Oxford University Press.

Cyprus Tourism Organisation. (2010), *Strategic Plan* [accessed 14 March 2014]. Retrieved from http://www.visitcyprus.com/media/Downloads/Strategy/Executive_Summary_Tourism_Strategy_2011_2015.pdf

d'Angella, F. and Go, F. (2009). Tale of two cities' collaborative tourism marketing: Towards a theory of destination stakeholder assessment. *Tourism Management, 30*(3), 429−440.

Daphnet, S., Scott, N., & Ruhanen, L. (2012). Applying diffusion theory to destination stakeholder understanding of sustainable tourism development: A case from Thailand. *Journal of Sustainable Tourism, 20*(8), 1107−1124.

de Araujo, L. M., & Bramwell, B. (2002). Partnership and regional tourism in Brazil. *Annals of Tourism Research, 29*(4), 1138−1164.

Dewhurst, H., & Thomas, R. (2003). Encouraging sustainable business practices in a non-regulatory environment: A case study of small tourism firms in a UK National Park. *Journal of Sustainable Tourism, 11*(5), 383−403.

Dinica, V. (2009). Governance for sustainable tourism: A comparison of international and Dutch visions. *Journal of Sustainable Tourism, 17*(5), 583−603.

Dodds, R. (2007). Sustainable tourism and Policy Implementation: Lessons from the Case of Calviá, Spain. *Current Issues in Tourism, 10*(4), 296−322.

Dodds, R., & Butler, B. (2010). Barriers to implementing sustainable tourism policy in mass tourism destinations. *Tourismos: An International Multidisciplinary Journal of Tourism, 5*(1), 35−53.

Dredge, D. (2006). Networks, conflict and collaborative communities. *Journal of Sustainable Tourism, 14*(6), 562.

Dredge, D., & Jamal, T. (2013). Mobilities on the Gold Coast, Australia: Implications for destination governance and sustainable tourism. *Journal of Sustainable Tourism, 21*(4), 557−579.

Dredge, D., & Pforr, C. (2008). Policy networks and tourism governance. In N. Scott, R. Baggio, & C. Cooper (Eds.), *Network analysis and tourism: From theory to practice* (pp. 58−78). Clevedon: Channel View Publications.

Erkus-Ozturk, H., & Eraydin, A. (2010). Environmental governance for sustainable tourism development: Collaborative networks and organisation building in the Antalya tourism region. *Tourism Management, 31*(1), 113−124.

Ghina, F. (2003). Sustainable development in small island developing states. *Environment, Development and Sustainability, 5*(1−2), 139−165.

Gill, A. M., & Williams, P. W. (2014). Mindful deviation in creating a governance path towards sustainability in resort destinations, *Tourism Geographies, 16*(4), 546−562.

Goodwin, M., & Painter, J. (1996). Local governance, the crises of Fordism and the changing geographies of regulation. *Transactions of the Institute of British Geographers, 21*, 635−648.

Gössling, S., Hansson, C. B., Hörstmeier, O., & Saggel, S. (2002). Ecological footprint analysis as a tool to assess tourism sustainability. *Ecological Economics, 43*(2), 199−211.

Hall, C. M. (2007). *Pro-poor tourism: who benefits?: Perspectives on tourism and poverty reduction* (Vol. 3). UK: Channel View Publications.

Hall, C. M. (2011). Policy learning and policy failure in sustainable tourism governance: From first- and second-order to third-order change?. *Journal of Sustainable Tourism, 19*(4−5), 649−671.

Hall, D., & Brown, F. (2008). Finding a way forward: an agenda for research. *Third World Quarterly, 29*(5), 1021−1032.

Hardy, A., Beeton, R., & Pearson, L. (2002). Sustainable tourism: An overview of the concept and its position in relation to conceptualisations of tourism. *Journal of Sustainable Tourism, 10*(6), 475–496.

Higgins-Desbiolles, F. (2011). Death by a thousand cuts: Governance and environmental trade-offs in ecotourism development at Kangaroo Island, South Australia. *Journal of Sustainable Tourism, 19*(4–5), 553–570.

Hunter, C. (2002). Sustainable tourism and the touristic ecological footprint. *Environment, Development and Sustainability, 4*(1), 7–20.

Jayawardena, C., Patterson, D. J., Choi, C., & Brain, R. (2008). Sustainable tourism development in Niagara: Discussions, theories, projects and insights. *International Journal of Contemporary Hospitality Management, 20*(3), 258–277.

Kemp, R., Parto, S., & Gibson, R. B. (2005). Governance for sustainable development: Moving from theory to practice. *International Journal of Sustainable Development, 8*(1), 12–30.

Kjaer, A. M. (2004). *Governance*. Cambridge: Polity Press.

Ko, T. G. (2005). Development of a tourism sustainability assessment procedure: A conceptual approach. *Tourism Management, 26*(3), 431–445.

Krutwaysho, O., & Bramwell, B. (2010). Tourism policy implementation and society. *Annals of Tourism Research*, 37 (3), 670–691.

Kuosmanen, T., & Kuosmanen, N. (2009). How not to measure sustainable value (and how one might). *Ecological Economics, 69*(2), 235–243.

Lewis, J. M. (2011). The future of network governance research: strength in diversity and synthesis. *Public Administration, 89*(4), 1221–1234.

Logar, I. (2010). Sustainable tourism management in Crkvenica, Croatia: An assessment of policy instruments. *Tourism Management, 31*, 125–135.

Lynch, P., & Morrison, A. (2007). The role of networks. In E.J. Michael (Ed.), *Micro-clusters and networks: The growth of tourism* (pp. 43–60). Amsterdam: Elsevier.

Miles, B., & Huberman, M. (1994). *Qualitative data analysis*. Beverly Hills: Sage.

Milne, S., & Ateljevic, I. (2001). Tourism, economic development and the global-local nexus: Theory embracing complexity, *Tourism Geographies, 3*(4), 369–393.

Morrison, A., Lynch, P., & Johns, N. (2004). International tourism networks. *International Journal of Contemporary Hospitality Management, 16*(3), 197–202.

Moscardo, G. (2011). The role of knowledge in good governance for tourism. In Laws E., Richins H., Agrusa J.F. & Scott N. (Eds.), *Tourist destination governance: Practice, theory and issues* (pp. 67–80). Oxfordshire: CABI.

Mowforth, M., & Munt, I. (2009). *Tourism and sustainability: Development, globalisation and new tourism in the third world*. Oxford: Routledge.

Neto, F. (2003). A new approach to sustainable tourism development: Moving beyond environmental protection. In *Natural Resources Forum* (pp. 212–222). Oxford: Blackwell Publishing Ltd.

Nordin, S., & Svensson, B. (2007). Innovative destination governance: The Swedish ski resort of Åre. *The International Journal of Entrepreneurship and Innovation, 8*(1), 53–66.

Novelli, M., Schmitz, B., & Spencer, T. (2006). Networks, clusters and innovation in tourism: A UK experience. *Tourism Management, 27*(6), 1141–1152.

Organisation for Economic Cooperation and Development (OECD). (1995). *Governance in transition: Public management in OECD countries*. Paris: OECD/PUMA.

Oriade, A., & Evans, M. (2011). Sustainable and Alternative Tourism. In Robinson, P., Heitmann, S. & Dieke, P. (Eds.), Research Themes for Tourism (pp. 69–86). Oxfordshire: CABI.

Pavlovich, K. (2001). The twin landscapes of Waitomo: Tourism network and sustainability through the Landcare Group. *Journal of Sustainable Tourism, 9*(6), 491–504.

Pechlaner, H., Volgger, M., & Herntrei, M. (2012). Destination management organizations as interface between destination governance and corporate governance. *Anatolia, 23*(2), 151–168.

Pierre, J. and Peters, B. (2000). *Governance, politics and the state*. London: Macmillan Press Ltd.

Pike, S. D., May, T., & Bolton, R. (2011). DMO governance: Reflections from a former marketing team. *Journal of Travel and Tourism Research, Fall,* 117–133.

Provan, K. G., & Kenis, P. (2008). Modes of network governance: Structure, management, and effectiveness. *Journal of Public Administration Research and Theory, 18*(2), 229–252.

Reid, M., & Schwab, W. (2006). Barriers to Sustainable development Jordan's sustainable tourism strategy. *Journal of Asian and African Studies, 41*(5–6), 439–457.

Rhodes, R. A. W. (1996). The new governance: Governing without government1. *Political Studies, 44*(4), 652–667.

Ritchie, J. B., & Crouch, G. I. (2003). *The competitive destination: A sustainable tourism perspective.* Wallingford, Oxon: CABI.

Ruhanen, L. (2013). Local government: Facilitator or inhibitor of sustainable tourism development?. *Journal of Sustainable Tourism, 21*(1), 80–98.

Ruhanen, L., Scott, N., Ritchie, B., & Tkaczynski, A. (2010). Governance: A review and synthesis of the literature. *Tourism Review, 65*(4), 4–16.

Sainaghi, R. (2006). From contents to processes: Versus a dynamic destination management model (DDMM). *Tourism Management, 27*(5), 1053–1063.

Saxena, G. (2005). Relationships, networks and the learning regions: Case evidence from the Peak District National Park. *Tourism Management, 26*(2), 277–289.

Scheyvens, R. (2011). The challenge of sustainable tourism development in the Maldives: Understanding the social and political dimensions of sustainability. *Asia Pacific Viewpoint, 52*(2), 148–164.

Scott, N., Cooper, C., & Baggio, R. (2008). Destination networks: Four Australian cases. *Annals of Tourism Research, 35*(1), 169–188.

Sofield, T., & Li, S. (2011). Tourism governance and sustainable national development in China: A macro-level synthesis. *Journal of Sustainable Tourism, 19*(4–5), 501–534.

Svensson, B., Nordin, S., & Flagestad, A. (2005). A governance perspective on destination development-exploring partnerships, clusters and innovation systems. *Tourism Review, 60*(2), 32–37.

Swarbrooke, J. (1999). *Sustainable tourism management.* Cabi.

Timur, S., & Getz, D. (2008). A network perspective on managing stakeholders for sustainable urban tourism. *International Journal of Contemporary Hospitality Management, 20*(4), 445–461.

Torres-Delgado, A., & Saarinen, J. (2014). Using indicators to assess sustainable tourism development: A review. *Tourism Geographies, 16*(1), 31–47

Tyrrell, T. J., & Johnston, R. J. (2008). Tourism sustainability, resiliency and dynamics: Towards a more comprehensive perspective. *Tourism and Hospitality Research, 8*(1), 14–24.

United Nations. (2002). *Report of the international colloquium on regional governance and sustainable development in tourism-driven economies,* Department of Economic and Social Affairs: Division for Public Economics and Public Administration, New York: UN.

von Malmborg, F. (2003). Conditions for regional public–private partnerships for sustainable development – Swedish perspectives. *European Environment, 13*(3), 133–149.

Waligo, V.M., Clarke, J., & Hawkins, R. (2013). Implementing sustainable tourism: A multi-stakeholder involvement management framework. *Tourism Management, 36*, 342–353.

Wan, P., & King, Y. (2013). A comparison of the governance of tourism planning in the two Special Administrative Regions (SARs) of China–Hong\sKong and Macao. *Tourism Management, 36*, 164–177.

Wang, Y., & Xiang, Z. (2007). Toward a theoretical framework of collaborative destination marketing. *Journal of Travel Research, 46*(1), 75–85.

Wesley, A., & Pforr, C. (2010). The governance of coastal tourism: Unravelling the layers of complexity at Smiths Beach, Western Australia. *Journal of Sustainable Tourism,* 18(6), 773–792.

Wilkinson, R. (2005). *The global governance reader.* London: Routledge.

Windsor, D. (2009). Tightening corporate governance. *Journal of International Management, 15*(3), 306–316.

Wray, M. (2011). Adopting and implementing a transactive approach to sustainable tourism planning: Translating theory into practice. *Journal of Sustainable Tourism, 19*(4–5), 605–627.

Yasarata, M., Altinay, L., Burns, P., & Okumus, F. (2010). Politics and sustainable tourism development – Can they co-exist? Voices from Cyprus. *Tourism Management, 31*, 345–356.

Yin, R. K. (2003). Case study research: Design and methods. Thousand Oaks, CA: Sage.

Yüksel, F., Bramwell, B., & Yüksel, A. (2005). Centralized and decentralized tourism governance in Turkey. *Annals of Tourism Research, 32*(4), 859–886.

Zahra, A. L. (2011). Rethinking regional tourism governance: The principle of subsidiarity. *Journal of Sustainable Tourism, 19*(4–5), 535–552.

Zapata, M. J., & Hall, C. M. (2012). Public–private collaboration in the tourism sector: balancing legitimacy and effectiveness in local tourism partnerships: The Spanish case. *Journal of Policy Research in Tourism, Leisure and Events, 4*(1), 61–83.

Mindful deviation in creating a governance path towards sustainability in resort destinations

Alison M. Gill and Peter W. Williams

Drawing on recent work in evolutionary economic geography, we focus on path creation as the framework for understanding how, in a resort destination context, the shift from growth models to ones based on principles of sustainability are evolving. Path creation emphasizes the power of human agency by recognizing the influence of entrepreneurs in shaping their environments. In the case study of the mountain resort of Whistler, British Columbia, we focus on one key aspect of the discourse surrounding the transition in governance from growth towards sustainability – that of affordable housing. The data are drawn from key informant interviews, participant observation and community document sources. The findings demonstrate how, through 'mindful deviation' from a growth model approach, Whistler entrepreneurs were able to utilize the collective agency of the community, generated in support of a new governance model based on principles of sustainability, to address the pressing need for affordable employee housing. This resulted from the opportunity to host the 2010 Winter Olympic and Paralympic Games. Through the efforts of both individual and collective human agency Whistler entrepreneurs were able to persuade the local Olympic organizing committee to conform to the resort's sustainability mandate in the development of athletes' accommodation that would later serve as permanent resident-restricted housing. Overall, the study demonstrates the utility of employing a path creation lens as an analytical tool for understanding evolutionary change.

Introduction

In response to global forces, many nations have developed neoliberal modes of governance that embrace a 'growth first' ideology (Peck & Tickell, 2002). Concurrently, varying interpretations and applications of the concept of sustainability have become embedded in the political rhetoric of those seeking to achieve a more comprehensive and balanced set of environmental, social and economic priorities (McCool & Moisey, 2008; Westley et al., 2011). For many decision-makers, the concepts of growth and sustainability are viewed as antithetical (Peck & Tickell, 2002; Zovanyi, 2013). As Westley et al. (2011, p. 764) observe:

> the conceptual and institutional separation of social and ecological systems has contributed and continues to contribute to a misfit between ecosystem and governance systems. This separation is a strong contributor to the path dependence that makes it so hard to shift to sustainable trajectories.

In this paper, we employ an evolutionary economic geography (EEG) approach to identify factors influencing governance shifts in the mountain resort of Whistler, British Columbia, Canada from a growth-dependent model towards one grounded in principles of sustainability. The lens of path creation (Garud & Karnøe, 2001) is used as an analytical tool to help explain the emergence of this new governance approach. It highlights the roles of human agency and entrepreneurship as key factors in facilitating Whistler's 'mindful deviation' towards a sustainability-focused pathway. 'Mindful deviation' requires that entrepreneurs make a break from established institutional structures and practices by taking deliberate and conscious actions to reframe their thinking and approach along new pathways. Given the reputational capital that Whistler enjoys as an innovator in destination planning and management, this approach can serve as a bellwether for other destinations seeking to understand the critical elements underlying the adoption of new governance practices that embody sustainability principles.

To frame the study's focus, we first provide an overview of path creation and related EEG concepts followed by a summary of literature linking destination governance to issues of sustainability. We then present the empirical study of Whistler's governance journey along a new path towards sustainability. While the overriding theme of governance evolution in this case study emerges from more than two decades of multi-method field research in Whistler, the specific focus of this paper is on the role of human agency and entrepreneurship in effecting governance changes since around 2000. For this specific topic, we used a variety of approaches including analysis of official community documents and newspaper reports, key informant interviews and participant observation at community meetings. Based on findings emerging from our analysis, we subsequently describe the endogenous and exogenous factors that have resulted in a shift in resort governance away from a growth-oriented trajectory towards a more sustainability-focused path. We then provide a specific example of how this reorientation has manifested itself. The example illustrates how the influences of both individual and collective agency during the negotiation of an affordable housing legacy associated with preparations for the 2010 Winter Olympic Games (the Games) represent mindful deviation along Whistler's newly created path towards sustainability. We selected this case as an example of the complex and messy processes of resort governance because the issue of real estate development and the related concern about limited affordable housing supply were central to the debate concerning a transition from growth-oriented governance towards a more democratically engaged commitment to a sustainability path. In the subsequent discussion, we examine how the path creation constructs of mindful deviation and real-time influence were instrumental in shifting Whistler away from its growth-dependent path. We conclude by summarizing the key conceptual lessons derived from Whistler's experience and reflect on the resilience of Whistler's sustainability-focused governance path.

Destination governance and sustainability

In its broadest sense, the term 'governance' identifies 'who has power, who makes decisions, how other players make their voice heard and how account is rendered' (Institute on Governance, 2013, para.1). A wide spectrum of governance approaches can be identified in destinations worldwide (Laws, Richins, Agrusa, & Scott, 2011). Flagestad and Hope (2001) suggest a continuum of approaches ranging from community-focused to corporate-directed extremes. Beritelli, Bieger, and Laesser (2007) emphasize the importance of context and the stage of a destination's development. For instance, Murphy (2008) observes that the North American model of mountain resort development, that reflects frequent domination by corporate control, is distinct from those in Europe and Australia. Others suggest (Kemp, Parto, & Gibson, 2005; Painter, 2000) that since the late 1980s there has been a shift in many capitalist economies away from government as the key decision-maker towards a more neoliberal ideology that embraces wider stakeholder engagement resulting in a blurring of governance responsibilities between private and public institutions. Past research by Gill and Williams (2006) examining operating relationships between the mountain corporation and the resort community in Whistler, Canada, suggests that there are signs of convergence between the corporate and community models especially as companies invest more heavily in environmental and social responsibility practices. Dredge (2006a) indicates that such governance convergences make sense in tourist destinations comprised of complex multi-scalar systems of both public and private stakeholders. Interest in examining the functioning of these more complex destination governance models has increased substantially over the past decade, especially in Europe (Bodega, Cioccarelli, & Denicolai, 2004; Keller & Bieger, 2008; Svensson, Nordin, & Flagestad, 2005, 2006) and Australia (Dredge, 2006a, 2006b; Ruhanen, Scott, Ritchie, & Tkaczynski, 2010). As Svensson et al. (2006) observe, changes in governance strategies provide useful keys to understanding the dynamics and competitiveness of destinations. Reflecting the complexities of these emerging destination governance models, several studies have adopted network approaches for analyzing and understanding the preconditions for innovation in both structure and practice (Baggio, Scott, & Cooper, 2010; Beritelli et al., 2007; Erkus-Osturk & Eraydin, 2010; Graci, 2013; Guia, Prats, & Comas, 2006; Lazzeretti & Petrillo, 2006; Nordin & Svensson, 2005; Pforr, 2002). Recent work on the influence of entrepreneurs on destination governance suggests growing recognition of the importance of entrepreneurial reputation (Komppula, 2014; Strobl & Peters, 2013).

Hybrid combinations of corporate and community approaches to governance are increasingly linked to discourses on sustainable development through 'similar history and parentage' (Kemp et al., 2005, p. 13). However, both terms – 'governance' and 'sustainability' – whilst commonly used in governance discourse, are contested terms interpreted in multiple ways (Kemp et al., 2005; Ruhanen et al., 2010). Bramwell and Lane (2011) observe that the term governance has not been widely used in tourism contexts, although other related terms such as policy-making, planning and destination management fall within its realm. The term 'good governance' is increasingly used to imply approaches that embrace principles of sustainable practice such as: accountability; transparency; equitability and inclusiveness; responsiveness; effectiveness and efficiency; and openness and participation (Dorcey, 2004; Kemp et al., 2005; Stratford, Davidson, Griffith, Lockwood, & Curtis, 2007). As Bramwell and Lane (2011, p. 412) note in a special governance-themed issue of the *Journal of Sustainable Tourism* (2011, Vol. 19) '[t]ailored and effective governance is a key requirement for implementing sustainable tourism: it can enhance democratic processes, provide direction and offer the means to make practical progress' (Bramwell & Lane, 2011, p. 411). They also caution that governance guided by sustainability principles faces many obstacles due to the complexity of the tourism system, its related policy domains and the array of interests and priorities held by relevant actors. The papers assembled in that volume address such issues as theoretical frameworks; scalar aspects of governance; and, the ways in which sustainable tourism governance is evolving. Another recent special journal issue on destination governance in the journal Tourism Review (2010, Vol. 65), highlights the growing interest in how tourist destinations are organized, coordinated and governed through mechanisms of action and control. The articles in that publication focus on the reasons and conditions for implementing various styles of governance in planning and development processes (Pechlaner, Raich, & Beritelli, 2010).

In this paper, affordable housing development is used as an example of how social equity issues can be addressed within a sustainability governance context. Creating affordable employee housing is a necessary component to well-functioning communities but it is one of the more challenging 'wicked problems' that resort communities face. Externally driven real estate markets catering to high-paying amenity migrants (second home and permanent residents), typically drive tourism destination housing prices to levels not accessible to most resort employees (Marcelpoil & François, 2009; Moore, Williams, & Gill, 2006; Moss, 2006). While many resort destinations apply development charges to cover some of the costs of providing affordable employee housing, and some employers subsidize worker-housing costs, most resort areas still rely on surrounding 'down valley' communities to meet employee housing (Hartmann, 2006). Such realities do not enhance the social environment of the resort community, and in some cases lead to an erosion of service quality.

Evolutionary economic geography and path creation

The ideas of path dependency and the integral concept of 'lock-in' associated with the work of evolutionary economists such as David (1985) and Arthur (1989) have now diffused to other disciplines. At its core is the assumption that commitment to a path is determined by the cumulative results of small and impersonal historical events from which it is difficult to deviate. Path dependency 'is now widely understood as a plausible argument to describe inertia, stability and irreversibility in a broad range of contexts' (Meyer & Schubert, 2007, p. 23). While the notion of 'history matters' (David, 1994) underpins the concept of path dependency, geographers have added a spatial dimension defining the new disciplinary paradigm of EEG as 'the processes by which the economic landscape – the organization of economic production, distribution and consumption – is transformed over time' (Boschma & Martin, 2007, p. 539). They have primarily used this approach in understanding aspects of manufacturing and regional development especially with respect to notions of path dependence and lock-in. However, researchers have sought adaptations to what some consider narrow and restrictive assumptions of original path dependency theory (Martin, 2010). Notable amongst these alternatives is the concept of path creation (Garud & Karnøe, 2001).

Whereas path dependency approaches employ *post hoc* explanations to understand evolutionary change, path creation narratives focus on the real-time effects of human agency as manifested in the influence of entrepreneurs in shaping their environments. Two concepts, 'mindful deviation' and 'real-time influence', differentiate path creation from path dependency. Garud and Karnøe (2001, p. 2) formally define mindful deviation as: 'the ability to disembed from existing structures defining relevance and also the ability to mobilize a collective despite resistance and inertia that path creation efforts will likely encounter'. Related to the focus on human agency as opposed to historical incident as the determinant of path evolution, is the notion of 'real-time influence'. Given the complexity of the contexts in which human agency is situated, temporal agency is manifest in the ability of actors to utilize time as a resource in deciding when to act (Garud, Kumaraswamy, & Karnøe, 2010). Real-time influence means that there must be flexibility in the path so that actors can react to events that arise. Methodologically, as Garud et al. (2010, p. 770) point out, this means that when employing a path creation perspective it is necessary to 'place oneself at the time that events occurred even if one were looking at data gathered in the past'. They conceive of the path-creation perspective as one of 'being in the inside looking out' as opposed to the path-dependent approach of 'being outside looking in' and thus one best suited to a narrative approach.

The application of evolutionary economic approaches across varied disciplines has resulted in emerging complexity in the understanding of path-related processes. For example, while path dependency and path creation are understood by some to be alternate analytical perspectives for understanding evolutionary change, others have sought to integrate these two perspectives. Gáspár (2011, p. 94) considers this relationship with respect to futures studies and sees the interaction of path dependency and path creation as 'the bonds that tie the present to the past and to the future'. Schienstock (2007) in a study of techno-economic change suggests moving from path dependency to path creation as a method of better understanding recent institutional change. He argues that despite many nation-states retaining path dependent patterns of institutional continuity even under conditions of external shock to their political and economic environments, evidence from Finland, where a rapid economic transformation from a natural-resource-based to a more knowledge-based economy occurred during the 1990s, indicates that a path creation perspective with its greater emphasis on human agency is a more appropriate way to examine changing governance approaches. Stack and Gartland (2005) also support a path creation approach as a more appropriate lens through which to understand how entrepreneurs escape lock-in. Further evidence of the emerging understanding of the complexity of path-related development is the work of Strambach and Halkier (2013) who suggest the concept of 'path plasticity', whereby actors introduce innovations within a more flexible notion of path dependence that does not result in the creation of a new path but offers an alternate explanation of evolutionary change in some contexts. Meyer and Schubert (2007) in science, technology and innovation studies propose an integrated model of 'path constitution' that includes both path dependence and creation as components of a more elaborate understanding of path evolution.

Within tourism studies, the adoption of an EEG perspective is only emerging. Brouder and Erikkson (2013) used EEG theory to study the role of entrepreneurs' experience and location in influencing the spatial development of tourism firms. EEG perspectives have also been employed by Williams (2013) in an examination of mobilities and sustainability tourism and by Gill and Williams (2011) in a study of changing resort governance. Halkier and Therkelsen (2013) recently introduced in a tourism context the concept of 'path plasticity' to tourism studies as a more nuanced contribution to the understanding of path dependency in their study of coastal tourism in Denmark. In light of the emerging interest in such approaches, Ma and Hassink (2013, p. 89) suggest that the ongoing 'evolutionary turn' in economic geography 'could offer a powerful thrust to the theoretical discussion on tourism area evolution'. In their study of the Gold Coast, Australia, they argue that the related concepts of path dependence and coevolution offer new perspectives on Butler's tourism area life cycle model. The following case study of the forces influencing Whistler's shift from its long-standing growth-oriented governance approach to one based on principles of sustainability demonstrates how human agency and real-time exogenous and endogenous factors are integrally entwined in shaping new pathways.

Whistler's journey towards a sustainability-focused governance approach
Growth dependence
Whistler is an internationally renowned year-round mountain resort community located 120 kilometers north of Vancouver, British Columbia, Canada. It is considered to be

amongst the best mountain sports destinations in North America. Situated in the valley lands at the base of two converging mountains (Whistler and Blackcomb), the resort community has a resident population of around 10,000 citizens. It hosts about 2 million visitors annually, with visitation distributed almost equally between summer and winter seasons. It is the evolving nature of the destination's governance system that is the focus of this study.

Whistler was legally designated as a unique purpose-built resort community through an innovative Resort Municipality of Whistler (RMOW) Act enacted by the provincial government in 1975. This legislation gave distinctive financial and tax advantages to the new resort community in an effort to facilitate the creation of a comprehensive, integrated and innovative form of development. A local government (RMOW) was democratically elected and adhered to an official community plan (OCP) that articulated the objectives and policies guiding decisions on planning and land use management. Governance during the first two decades of the resort community's existence evolved from an initial growth machine regime, dominated by a group of elite decision-makers that included developers and municipal officials, to one of growth management facilitated by municipal government leaders who engaged local residents and other stakeholders in more consultative processes of decision-making (Gill, 2000). In 1989, under a new growth management strategy, a limit to resort growth of 52,500 bed units was established. The bed unit approach provided a readily understandable method for tracking the extent to which the growth of residential and commercial beds was approaching the resort's estimated overall water and sewage treatment capacity. As Gill (2007, p. 143) observed, over time bed units 'acquired value as both political currency in negotiating amenities for the community, and as symbolic currency representing environmental values and community control in the face of development pressures'.

Breaking the lock-in of growth dependence

Development commitments for build-out to the bed unit cap were reached around 2000. This precipitated the discourse within Whistler to shift from one focused on managed growth to one that diffused the long-established tight relationship between growth limits and environmental quality to a broader agenda (Gill, 2012). Politically, Whistler had a very stable local government that had held environmental issues as a high priority since the early 1990s. Indeed, both the municipal government and corporate businesses demonstrated considerable entrepreneurship in creating innovative environmental management strategies (Williams & Todd, 1997). Amongst these initiatives was the introduction in 1993 of a resort and community-monitoring program that formed the basis for public discussion on Whistler's progress on a range of economic, social and environmental issues at annual town hall meetings (Gill, 2000).

However, as housing prices soared during the 1990s and build-out to the 52,500 bed unit limit, accelerated residents became increasingly concerned about the availability of affordable housing for employees. Although developers were responsible for contributing to affordable housing costs as part of their development charges, rapid growth resulted in a severe shortage of affordable housing and for the first time this issue ranked as the most important quality of life issue for residents (Gill & Williams, 2008). Despite a history dating back to 1985 and the subsequent formation of a Whistler Housing Authority (WHA), dedicated to seeking and providing innovative ways of accommodating people working in Whistler, the resort municipality was well off its goal of having at least 75% of the community's permanent employees living within its boundaries (Dickinson, 2009). Without the infusion of financial resources captured from the development of new commercial and residential properties, where would the money for further affordable housing development come from? Further, given the long-assumed relationship between the established bed unit cap and environmental issues associated with water and sewer capacity, was it possible to build new employee housing units? It would seem that the RMOW was 'between a rock and a hard place'.

The solution to forging a new path arose unexpectedly in 2000 when the charismatic leader of The Natural Step (TNS) organization, Karl-Henrik Robèrt, visited the resort for a snowboarding holiday. TNS is an international non-profit research, education and advisory organization that uses a 'science-based' framework to help organizations and communities move towards sustainability (Robèrt, 2008). During his visit, Robèrt met with influential community leaders, who subsequently persuaded their organizations (including the RMOW and Whistler Blackcomb – the resort's mountain operator and largest employer) to sign up as 'early adopters' of TNS. This event and the impact that Robèrt had is well entrenched in the story of Whistler's journey towards a sustainability focused governance system. A quote on Whistler's website illustrates the impact Robèrt's perspectives had on the resort's ability to begin the discourse around sustainability:

> Life is about timing, and the timing was right! Whistler had always been proactive around the environment and other forward-looking issues, yet never defined its efforts in a formal definition of, or framework for, "sustainability". In fact, some local leaders were at that time seeking some way of communicating and engaging with the broader community about sustainability issues – and as luck would have it, they found their solution in Dr. Robèrt's presentations. (Whistler 2020, 2013, para.4)

Guided by TNS principles over a five-year period of significant stakeholder engagement, Whistler subsequently created its first comprehensive sustainability plan known as *Whistler 2020* (Whistler 2020, 2010). The first two years entailed an intense period of 'community conditioning' (Sailor, 2010) to establish a common understanding and appreciation of the meaning and language of sustainability. Stakeholder engagement remained high throughout the following three years of refining the *Whistler 2020* document that was adopted by council in 2005. Described as a shared vision, it became the highest level policy document for the resort community and was characterized as being 'long-term, comprehensive, community-developed, community-implemented and action-focused' (Whistler 2020, 2013, para.4).

To operationalize the vision, sixteen issue-specific task force groups comprised of a broad spectrum of community stakeholders were created. After filtering their proposed action plans using a matrix of sustainability criteria, recommendations for implementation were made to the RMOW and other agencies. The Whistler Centre for Sustainability was established at arm's length from the RMOW to facilitate stakeholder engagement in action-planning processes and to monitor community progress against prioritized sustainability goals. Execution of the proposed sustainability actions was the responsibility of 'Whistler 2020 partners' (a diverse group of organizations and businesses) and task force members. Comprised of about 160 individuals, this collective of stakeholders met annually to review progress on past recommended actions, evaluate current monitoring data, assess local and regional opportunities for action, and recommend future initiatives. A publically accessible interactive website provides transparency with respect to the overall process (www.whistler2020.com).

Negotiating affordable housing

In 2003, Vancouver and Whistler were named as hosts for the 2010 Olympic and Paralympic Winter Games. Whistler's recognition as a 'host mountain resort' (an Olympic first) and the appointment of two of Whistler's community leaders to the board of the Vancouver Olympic Committee (VANOC – the local host organizing committee) gave it significantly more formal status and power than it might otherwise have had to represent the community's interests. Whistler's engagement was motivated by potential opportunities to leverage Games legacies that would accelerate the attainment of some of the resort community's sustainability goals. Most importantly, its representatives convinced VANOC members to adopt guidelines, developed by Whistler, that clearly identified under what conditions Games initiatives would be encouraged in the resort, and how these initiatives would have to align with the destination's emerging sustainability priorities (Sheppard, Williams, & Gill, 2012). One of these priorities was to leverage a greater supply of affordable housing for Whistler's permanent employees.

By 2003, Whistler had already commenced the development of *Whistler2020*, and the RMOW decided to defer many decisions relating to the Games until the process was more evolved (Dickinson, 2009). Consequently, to ensure alignment with the sustainability strategy, decisions regarding housing the athletes were delayed until 2005 when *Whistler 2020* was adopted. Whistler's 'Resident Housing' task force was charged with addressing core issues surrounding the athletes' village development. In 2005, this 12-member task force consisted of an elected council member, an RMOW staff member, two WHA members, two WHA owners, a resident senior, a private developer, a realtor, a small business owner and a member of Whistler community services.

The original Olympic bid proposal envisioned locating the athletes' village in the Callahan Valley, 15 kilometers south of Whistler. This was in line with past Olympic Games practices of building such accommodation in secure, isolated sites for security reasons (Dickinson, 2009). However, to prevent unnecessary urban sprawl outside Whistler's boundaries the decision was made to establish the athletes' village on a reclaimed landfill site at the southern edge of the resort municipality (Dickinson, 2009). Post-Games, the development was to be primarily used for resident-restricted housing. To facilitate the creation of the proposed development, the RMOW negotiated three additional Olympic legacy agreements. These involved a boundary expansion, the transfer of 300 acres of provincial crown land to the municipality, and additional financial tools and resources. While acquiring additional provincial crown land provided the necessary physical site for the development, the creation of mechanisms to finance the project required an innovative management arrangement.

First, the RMOW decided to become the developer of the project and established the Whistler 2020 Development Corporation (WDC) to implement the development process, reduce the risk of financial losses, and ensure that innovative sustainability components were embedded in the village's design and development. With this management structure in place, the WDC garnered financing from several partners and subsequently built the $161 million, 350-unit Whistler athletes' village on time and on budget (Mason, 2009). In addition, it acquired favorable loan rates and made a decision to sell 10% of the village's housing units at full market price once the Games were over. Money from the sale of market-priced units was to ensure that the community would not be left with an unexpected financial burden caused by unforeseen costs. Further, Whistler in collaboration with 13 other newly designated resort communities in British Columbia lobbied the provincial government for additional ongoing financial mechanisms designed to address other resort community development challenges and opportunities. This resulted in Whistler receiving a greater portion of an already existing sales tax on hotel accommodation that generated around $6 million, one-third of which was earmarked for affordability enhancing initiatives, including housing.

Unlike the relatively short-lived athletes' villages constructed for many other Games, Whistler's village was designed to be a permanent resident neighborhood and a model for sustainable living. After the Games it was renamed Cheakamus Crossing and is now one of only 20 Canadian developments designated as a pilot project for Leadership in Energy & Environmental Design – Neighbourhood Development (LEED-ND) which sets the highest standards in green neighborhood design.

Discussion

The preceding case study described a useful context within which to discuss how mindful deviation and real-time influence – two key constructs of path creation – were instrumental in the creation of Whistler's new path towards sustainability. The success of the resort community in shifting the governance systems towards the sustainability model was largely shaped through mindful deviations from past approaches. This is illustrated in the example of the negotiations surrounding the development of the Olympic athletes' villages where through the human agency of individuals and organizations *Whistler 2020* principles were embedded into all of the resort's Olympic initiatives. The role of real-time influence is also demonstrated in the coincident timing of the Games with the emergence of Whistler's new governance path towards sustainability and the urgency of capitalizing on the Games while 'the getting was good'. The following discussion elaborates on these issues.

Entrepreneurship and mindful deviation

The role of entrepreneurs is often underestimated in models of destination competitiveness (Komppula, 2014). However, the power of human agency is critical to creating the momentum and know-how needed to shift governance paths (Beritelli, 2011a). As Stack and Gartland (2005, p. 421) observe, 'entrepreneurs often need to change the endogenized social practice, regulations or institutions away from an accepted, comfortable or optimized structure'. In Whistler's case, both external and internal entrepreneurs played influential roles in moving it along its customized sustainability journey.

A particularly important external influence was the internationally recognized social entrepreneur Karl-Henrik Robèrt, founder of TNS. His charisma and leadership qualities, complemented by the set of readily understandable TNS 'scientific principles' helped him communicate the legitimacy of the TNS approach for Whistler, as well as inspire local leaders to become 'early adopters' (Gill & Williams, 2008). To a large extent, his efforts in Whistler helped destabilize a growing stalemate amongst community stakeholders concerning how best to proceed beyond the established bed unit growth limits.

Notable among the 'early adopters' of the TNS and the subsequent development of *Whistler 2020* were an entrepreneurial group of political and administrative officers in the RMOW, Whistler Blackcomb administrators and several other small business operators. Their interpersonal relationships and stated commitment to TNS principles helped build the collective community consensus, confidence and momentum needed to proceed with *Whistler 2020*'s development and implementation. As Damaskie (2007, para. 5) observed:

> [f]or me, the beauty of *Whistler2020* and the high level of community involvement in our comprehensive sustainability plan is the shared values and language created through a very motivated, informed dialogue which creates an understanding of where we are now and where we want to be in the future.

Internally, two bureaucratically based entrepreneurs played particularly influential roles in not only paving the way for the development and implementation of *Whistler2020*, but also in establishing the formal and informal processes for garnering strategic sustainability focused legacies from the 2010 Olympic Games. These individuals were the RMOW's mayor (Ken Melamed) and chief administrative officer (Jim Godfrey). Like bureaucratic entrepreneurs in other municipal management positions (Teske & Schneider, 1994), they nurtured changes in Whistler's governance orientation through a combination of quiet but persuasive interpersonal skills, as well as creative community stakeholder engagement processes. Their leadership led to the creation and formal adoption of *Whistler 2020* as the resort community's comprehensive sustainability plan. Recognizing the immense opportunity the Olympics offered Whistler, Godfrey then left his RMOW position and assumed the role of executive director of Whistler's 2010 Games. This shift provided him with the level of entrepreneurial flexibility needed to guide the resort's engagement in the Games in ways that mindfully deviated from traditional Olympic short-term development goals, towards more Whistler-specific, sustainability-focused outcomes. In 2006, he delivered to Whistler's Council a strategic framework that clearly articulated a blueprint for gaining a wide range of benefits for the resort community that aligned with *Whistler2020* aspirations (RMOW, 2008). In a post-Games presentation, Mayor Melamed stated in reference to Jim Godfrey that, 'it goes without saying that there are few people who have the strategic ability to understand the way to get to success'. Among many other post-Games commentaries, one reporter stated: 'If there is one man responsible for the success of the 2010 Olympic Games in Whistler, it probably would be Jim Godfrey' (Smysnuik, 2010). In keeping with reported findings from Beritelli's (2011a, 2011b) case studies concerning cooperative behavior amongst tourism destination actors, Godfrey's ability to muster collective action that supported Whistler and VANOC goals lay not so much in his formal professional bonds, but more in informal linkages built around mutual trust and understanding fortified by effective and frequent communication with influential political and community stakeholders.

Collective human agency in the form of the WDC was central to extracting affordable housing benefits from the Games. Its governance was guided by *Whistler 2020* principles and priorities, and directed by a seasoned board of directors familiar with the processes needed to expediently develop master plans, create realistic business plans, review development proposals, award contracts and monitor construction progress. One of the most critical partnerships established was with the WHA. Because of its past community actions, respect and expertise, its leadership group had the community's 'social license to operate' required to lead discussions with Whistler stakeholders. Consequently, it was enlisted by the WDC to expedite community workshops designed to identify the nature and type of homes, and the support services needed in this planned neighborhood. These and other alliances created the web of support needed to bring the affordable housing initiative to fruition on time and on budget, as well as have it contribute in a meaningful way to Whistler's shift to a more sustainability focused governance path.

As Dickinson (2009, p. 14) observes:

> The ingenuity and creativity of WDC in meeting these diverse needs should not be understated; it has created a multipurpose neighborhood with housing that will welcome athletes during the Games and become a thriving, affordable community afterwards.

Real-time influence

Several real-time events provided 'forks in the road' that pushed Whistler off its growth-oriented governance path. Initially reaching its bed-unit cap in 2000 marked a crisis point with respect to lock-in to a model of continuing growth and development that had characterized Whistler's entire existence (Gill & Williams, 2011). Ultimately, the decision to challenge the growth path was a political one whereby the imperative for ever-increasing returns was weighed against the desires of the electorate for a more sustainability focused approach. To understand how the new pathway came about, the notion of 'real-time influence' is useful. As Garud and Karnøe (2001, p. 22) observe, [t]ime becomes a resource that offers entrepreneurs options to strike at the right time and place'. In particular, two real-time events played important roles. The first was an endogenous event – the escalating cost of housing during the 1990s and the concurrent lack of affordable housing in the resort. The other was exogenous – Whistler's designation as the Host Mountain Resort for the Games and the perceived challenges the Olympics would bring in the form of escalated house prices, and additional development within Whistler's boundaries.

Coinciding with the need for the RMOW to approve development beyond the long established 52,500-bed unit cap in order to address looming affordable housing needs, was the introduction of TNS. Its emergence provided an unanticipated platform for decoupling increased housing development concerns from environmental quality issues that the community believed to be escalating because of an unbridled pattern of growth in preceding years. TNS's focus on a broader sustainability agenda that addressed environmental as well as social concerns fitted very well with public sentiment for an alternative governance focus. By customizing this agenda to their situation, the community was able to find a politically astute solution that allowed them to expand the discourse beyond the limits to growth, as established in the bed-unit debate, to the broader mandate of sustainability. It allowed community leaders to embrace social concerns around affordable housing while at the same time not abandoning the long-held environmental interests of residents. This initiative represented a substantive 'mindful deviation' by them, and the introduction of TNS provided a real-time opportunity to make this shift.

The timing of the awarding of the Games was also significant with respect to real-time influence. It occurred in 2003 when the resort community was already embarked on the TNS pathway to developing its own vision and priorities. This coincidence of events determined Whistler's process of shaping the management of the Games development. The relationship between these two events reflects Garud and Karnøe's (2001) observations on 'real-time influence' that all actions have real-time consequences on the path in the making. Being able to respond to the real-time urgency of VANOC wanting Olympic athletes' housing in place well in advance of the Games, as well as accommodating the real-time pressure and influence of community stakeholders seeking sustainability 'wins' from the project, meant that the WDC had to strategically use the collective social capital of its staff and advisors to establish partnerships and alliances that would keep the project moving forward. In addition, the real-time urgency of the Games meant that if VANOC was to be persuaded to support Whistler's sustainability goals, decisions about how this was to occur would have to be made on a clearly articulated basis. The TNS and its successor *Whistler2020* provided the vision, values, priorities and directions needed to guide such decisions in a timely manner.

Conclusions

In this paper, we have sought to demonstrate that entrepreneurs and real-time influence — key components of a path-creation lens — have resulted in mindful deviation in the resort of Whistler from its previous growth-focused path towards one of sustainability. Although the findings of a single case study cannot be generalized, the results of our study offer support to the utility of a path-creation lens in understanding evolutionary change. As we have demonstrated, the power of human agency, both individually and collectively, was critical to the successful shifting of Whistler's development along a more sustainable pathway. The findings reinforce recent research in destination governance that highlights the importance of entrepreneurs in destination governance (Beritelli, 2011a; Komppula, 2014; Strobl & Peters, 2013).

The case study also highlights the importance not only of individual human agency but also collective action. As Williams, Gill, and Ponsford (2007) have previously observed, collective agency in the form of a 'social license to operate' is an essential component in the exercise of power. In Whistler, the collective power of a wide range of stakeholders in support of a new sustainability path was very evident in the decade leading up to the Games. However, in the post-Games era, subsequent effects of real-time influence resulted in many stakeholders contesting the priorities and related programs embedded in *Whistler2020*. A new council was elected in November 2011 that reflected the changing realities of Whistler's economy that, buffered for a few years by the effects of hosting the Olympics, felt the delayed impact of the economic recession. With a shift in political power that favored economic development over sustainability, many of the operational programming priorities supporting *Whistler2020* were compromised. The task forces were essentially abandoned and funding for community engagement on sustainability issues was substantially cut in favor of economic development priorities. In addition, the governance effects of broader Supreme Court of Canada rulings affirming aboriginal rights and title to traditional territories in British Columbia, as well as specific land-use agreements negotiated by First Nations within and adjacent to Whistler prior to the Games are emerging as factors potentially shaping the resort's governance trajectory. For instance, in their agreement with Whistler, First Nations exercised specific development rights on designated tracts of land within the community's boundaries. Not only did this development escalate Whistler's long-standing bed-unit growth cap but it also legally and symbolically affirmed First Nations' presence and potential areas of influence in the resort's governance. Most recently, this influence has extended to local First Nations taking legal actions to contest their perceived lack of opportunity to help shape Whistler's newly crafted Official Community Plan (Barrett, 2014). Only time will indicate how and to what extent this emerging relationship between First Nations and Whistler will shape the resort communities sustainability focused governance path.

Undoubtedly a major challenge to embedding a new long-term governance path towards sustainability is the often short-term nature of political decision-making. Consequently, the power of entrepreneurs to effect change may be fleeting and there may be a loss of institutional memory by community stakeholders and those in political office.

As Garud and Karnøe (2001, p. 20) assert: '[t]hose who attempt to create new paths have to realize that they are part of an emerging collective and that core ideas and objects will modify as they progress from hand to hand and mind to mind'. Those in Whistler who have sought to develop an innovative comprehensive sustainability governance model may be reassured by the fact that the model they developed was designed to be 'flexible and scalable' and *Whistler2020* remains as a high-level policy document even if its current implementation is limited. Further, the governance model developed has received much attention from other resorts worldwide. Garud and Karnoe's (2001) definition of the concept of mindful deviation acknowledges that path creation efforts will encounter resistance and inertia and they emphasize the need for entrepreneurs to be not only path creators but also path managers. As Meyer and Schubert (2007, p. 267) observe, 'path creation is not a solitary act but requires a long process of continual path creating and stabilizing events'. However, the resilience of the newly created pathway in Whistler is an issue for further study that can only be revealed over time. A retrospective path-dependency lens could reveal that the events during the past decade of Whistler's history did not constitute a fundamental break from the lock-in of growth dependency but could be interpreted perhaps as an example of path plasticity.

In conclusion, the study of Whistler's governance transformation strengthens the argument for adopting an EEG approach as a theoretical perspective in understanding change in resort destinations. While the evolution of tourism destinations has been a long-standing area of interest for tourism geographers, even predating Butler's (1980) seminal work on the resort cycle, EEG perspectives offer new opportunities for understanding the drivers of change over both *space and time*. Although the study presented here has employed case study research, EEG approaches encompass any type of research methodology that is grounded in evolutionary theorizing (Boschma & Frenken, 2007). This can be applied at various scales from the micro to the macro to consider such destination elements as the firm, sector or network, as well as regional development and policy. As such it offers opportunities to theoretically conceive of destination change from a more holistic perspective. In a resort destination context, recent studies on network analysis (e.g. Bodega et al., 2004; Lazzeretti & Petrillo, 2006), innovation (e.g. Guia et al., 2006), entrepreneurship (e.g. Komppula, 2014), policy (e.g. Dredge, 2006b) and governance (e.g. Bramwell & Lane, 2011; Gill & Williams, 2011; Svensson et al., 2006), although not necessarily couched in EEG concepts, could all be conceived of as being component parts of a broader theoretically linked domain. As an understanding of evolutionary economic processes evolves, so too does its theoretical development. In this study of Whistler, the lens of path creation was adopted. As such it represents a more recently developed construct in EEG that, with its associated notions of mindful deviation and real-time influence, applies new concepts to understanding how destinations evolve. The dynamic and evolving nature of the EEG approach offers exciting potential for tourism geographers to explore new, uncharted terrain.

Acknowledgements

The authors gratefully thank the many people in Whistler who have willingly shared their insights into the resort community's journey towards sustainability.

Funding

This work was supported by the Social Sciences and Humanities Research Council of Canada [grant number 410-2011-0752].

References

Arthur, W. B. (1989). Competing technologies, increasing returns, and 'lock-in' by historical events. *Economic Journal, 99*, 116–131.

Baggio, R., Scott, N., & Cooper, C. (2010). Improving tourism destination governance: A complexity science approach. *Tourism Review, 65*(4), 51–60.

Barrett, B. (2014, February16). First Nations OCP petition hearings wrap-up. *Pique Newsmagazine*. Retrieved May 31, 2014, from http://www.piquenewsmagazine.com/whistler/first-nations-ocp-petition-hearings-wrap-up/Content?oid=2545369

Beritelli, P. (2011a). Cooperation among prominent actors in a tourist destination. *Annals of Tourism Research, 38*(2), 607–629.

Beritelli, P. (2011b). *Tourist destination governance through local elites: Looking beyond the stakeholder level* (Cumulative post-doctoral thesis). Institute for Systematic Management and Public Governance, Centre for Tourism and Transport. St. Gallen, Switzerland.

Beritelli, P., Bieger, T., & Laesser, C. (2007). Destination governance: Using corporate governance theories as a foundation for effective destination management. *Journal of Travel Research, 20*, 1–12.

Bodega, D., Cioccarelli, G., & Denicolai, S. (2004). Evolution of relationship structures in mountain tourism. *Tourism Review, 59*(3), 13–19.

Boschma, R., & Frenken, K. (2007). Introduction: Applications of economic geography. In K. Frenken (Ed.), *Applied evolutionary economics and economic geography* (pp. 1–26). Cheltenham: Edward Elgar.

Boschma, R., & Martin, R. (2007). Editorial: Constructing an evolutionary economic geography. *Journal of Economic Geography, 7*, 537–548.

Bramwell, B., & Lane, B. (2011). Critical research on the governance of tourism and sustainability. *Journal of Sustainable Tourism, 19*(4–5), 411–421.

Brouder, P., & Eriksson, R. H. (2013). Staying power: What influences micro-firm survival in tourism? *Tourism Geographies, 15*(1), 125–144.

Butler, R. W. (1980). The concept of tourism area cycle of evolution: Implications for management of resources. *The Canadian Geographer, 24*(1), 5–12.

Damaskie, K. (2007, May 11). Whistler 2020. Smells like keen spirit. *Pique Newsmagazine*. Retrieved September 10, 2013, from http://www.piquenewsmagazine.com/whistler/whistler-2020/Content?oid=2156975

David, P. A. (1985). Clio and the economics of QWERTY: The necessity of history. *American Economic Review, 75*, 332–337.

David, P. A. (1994). Why are institutions the 'carriers of history'?: Path dependence and the evolution of conventions, organizations and institutions. *Structural Change and Economic Dynamics, 5*(2), 205–220.

Dickinson, C. (2009). *The Whistler Housing Authority story: A history of affordable housing in Whistler*. Whistler: Whistler Housing Authority.

Dorcey, A. H. J. (2004). Sustainability governance: Surfing the waves of transformation. In B. Mitchell (Ed.), *Resource and environmental management in Canada: Addressing conflict and uncertainty* (pp. 528–554). Don Mills, Toronto: Oxford University Press.

Dredge, D. (2006a). Networks, conflict and collaborative communities. *Journal of Sustainable Tourism, 14*(6), 562–581.

Dredge, D. (2006b). Policy networks and the local organization of tourism. *Tourism Management, 27*, 269–280.

Erkus-Osturk, H., & Eraydin, A. (2010). Environmental governance for sustainable tourism development: Collaborative networks and organisation building in the Antalya region. *Tourism Management, 31*(1), 113–124.

Flagestad, A., & Hope, C. (2001). Strategic success in winter sports destinations: A sustainable value creation perspective. *Tourism Management, 22*, 445–461.

Garud, R., & Karnøe, P (2001). Path creation as a process of mindful deviation. In R. Garud & P. Karnøe (Eds.), *Path dependence and creation* (pp. 1–41). Mahwah, NJ: Lawrence Erlbaum Associates.

Garud, R., Kumaraswamy, A., & Karnøe, P. (2010). Path dependence or path creation? *Journal of Management Studies, 47*(4), 760–774.

Gáspár, T. (2011). Path dependency and path creation in a strategic perspective. *Journal of Futures Studies, 15*(4), 93–108.

Gill, A. M. (2000). From growth machine to growth management: The dynamics of resort development in Whistler, British Columbia. *Environment and Planning A, 32*, 1083–1103.

Gill, A. M. (2007). The politics of bed units: The case of Whistler, British Columbia. In T. Coles & A. Church (Eds.), *Tourism, politics and place* (pp. 125–159). London: Routledge.

Gill, A. M. (2012). Shifting the discourse from growth to sustainability: New approaches in governance in resort destinations. In A. Kagermeier & J. Saarinen (Eds.), *Transforming and managing destinations: Tourism and leisure in a time of global change and risks* (pp. 345–352). Mannheim: MetaGIS-Fachbuch.

Gill, A. M., & Williams, P. W. (2006). Corporate responsibility and place: The case of Whistler, British Columbia. In T. Clark, A. M. Gill, & R. Hartmann (Eds.), *Mountain resort planning and development in an era of globalization* (pp. 26–40). Elmsford, NY: Cognizant Communication.

Gill, A. M., & Williams, P. W. (2008). From 'guiding fiction' to action: Applying 'The Natural Step' to sustainability planning in the resort of Whistler, British Columbia. In S. F. McCool & R. N. Moisey (Eds.), *Tourism, recreation and sustainability: Linking culture and environment* (2nd ed., pp. 121–130). Wallingford: CABI.

Gill, A. M., & Williams, P. W. (2011). Rethinking resort growth: Understanding evolving governance strategies in Whistler, British Columbia. *Journal of Sustainable Tourism, 19*(4–5), 629–648.

Graci, S. (2013). Collaboration and partnership development for sustainable tourism. *Tourism Geographies, 15*(1), 25–42.

Guia, J., Prats, L., & Comas, J. (2006). The destination as a local system of innovation: The role of relational networks. In L. Lazzeretti & C. Petrillo (Eds.), *Tourism local systems and networking* (pp. 57–66). Oxford: Elsevier.

Halkier, H., & Therkelsen, A. (2013). Exploring tourism destination path plasticity: The case of coastal tourism in North Jutland, Denmark. *Zeitschrift für Wirtschaftsgeographie, 57*(1–2), 39–51.

Hartmann, R. (2006). Downstream and down-valley: Essential components and directions of growth and change in the sprawling resort landscapes of the Rocky Mountain West. In T. Clark, A. M. Gill, & R. Hartmann (Eds.), *Mountain resort planning and development in an era of globalization* (pp. 278–293). Elmsford, NY: Cognizant Communication.

Institute on Governance. (2013). Defining governance. Retrieved September 20, 2013, from http://iog.ca/defining-goverance

Keller, P., & Bieger, T. (Eds.). (2008). *Real estate and destination development in tourism*. Berlin: Erich Schmidt Verlag.

Kemp, R., Parto, S., & Gibson, R. (2005). Governance for sustainable development: Moving from theory to practice. *International Journal of Sustainable Development, 8*(1/2), 12–30.

Komppula, R. (2014). The role of individual entrepreneurs in the development of competitiveness for a rural tourism destination – a case study. *Tourism Management, 40*, 361–371.

Laws, E., Richins, H., Agrusa, J., & Scott, N. (Eds.). (2011). *Tourism destination governance: Practice, theory and issues*. Wallingford: CABI.

Lazzeretti, L., & Petrillo, C. L. (Eds.). (2006). *Tourism local systems and networking*. Oxford: Elsevier.

Ma, M., & Hassink, R. (2013). An evolutionary perspective on tourism area development. *Annals of Tourism Research, 41*, 89–109.

Marcelpoil, E., & François, H. (2009). Real estate: A complex factor in the attractiveness of French mountain resorts. *Tourism Geographies, 11*(3), 334–349.

Martin, R. (2010). Roepke lecture in economic geography-rethinking regional path dependence: Beyond lock-in to evolution. *Economic Geography, 86*(1), 1–27.

Mason, G. (2009, July 10). In praise of village. *The Globe and Mail*. Retrieved March 24, 2012, from http://www.theglobeandmail.com/news/national/in-praise-of-village/article4278800/

McCool, S. F., & Moisey, R. N. (2008). Introduction: Pathways and pitfalls in the search for sustainable tourism. In S. F. McCool & R. N. Moisey (Eds.), *Tourism, recreation and sustainability: Linking culture and the environment* (2nd ed., pp. 1–16). Wallingford: CABI.

Meyer, U., & Schubert, C. (2007). Integrating path dependency and path creation in a general understanding of path constitution: The role of agency and institutions in the stabilisation of technical institutions. *Science, Technology and Innovation Studies, 3*, 23–44.

Moore, S., Williams, P.W., & Gill, A. (2006). Finding a pad in paradise: Amenity migration's effects on Whistler, British Columbia. In L.A.G. Moss (Eds.),*The amenity migrants: Seeking and sustaining mountains and their culture* (pp. 135–147). Wallingford, UK: CABI.

Moss, L. A. G. (Ed.). (2006). *The amenity migrants: Seeking and sustaining mountains and their cultures*. Wallingford: CABI.

Murphy, P. E. (2008). *The business of resort management*. Oxford: Elsevier.

Nordin, S., & Svensson, B. (2005). The significance of governance in innovative tourism destinations. In P. Keller & T. Bieger (Eds.), *Innovation in tourism: Creating customer value* (pp. 159–170). St Gallen: AIEST.

Painter, J. (2000). State and governance. In E. Sheppard & T. Barnes (Eds.), *A companion to economic geography* (pp. 359–376). Oxford: Blackwell.

Pechlaner, H., Raich, F., & Beritelli, P. (2010). Editorial: Destination governance. *Tourism Review, 65*(4), 3–3.

Peck, J., & Tickell, A. (2002). Neoliberalizing space. *Antipode, 34*(3), 380–404.

Pforr, C. (2002). The makers and the shakers of tourism policy in the Northern Territory of Australia: A policy network analysis of actors and their relational constellations. *Journal of Hospitality and Tourism Management, 9*(2), 134–151.

RMOW. (2008). *Delivering the dream: 2010 Winter games strategic framework summary*. Whistler: The Resort Municipality of Whistler. Retrieved August 20, 2013, from http://www.whistler.ca/2010-games/planning-for-success/delivering-dream

Robèrt, K.-H. (2008). *The Natural Step Story: Seeding a quiet revolution*. Gabriola: New Society Publishers.

Ruhanen, L., Scott, N., Ritchie, B., & Tkaczynski, A. (2010). Governance: A review and synthesis of literature. *Tourism Review, 65*(4), 4–16.

Sailor, L. (2010). *Conditioning community: Power and decision-making in transitioning an industry-based community* (PhD dissertation). Department of Recreation and Leisure Studies, University of Waterloo, Ontario.

Schienstock, G. (2007). From path dependence to path creation: Finland on its way to the knowledge-based economy. *Current Sociology, 55*(1), 92–109.

Sheppard, V., Williams, P. W., & Gill, A. M. (2012). Adaptability and resiliency in sustainability focused governance. In *AIEST Conference Proceedings, Khon Kaen, Thailand August 26–30, 2012*. St. Gallen: AIEST, University of St. Gallen.

Smysnuik, S. (2010, October 8). Jim Godfrey presented with Freedom of Municipality Award for applying The Natural Step Framework during the Olympics. *Pique Newsmagazine*. Retrieved September 11, 2013, from http://www.naturalstep.ca/jim-godfrey-presented-with-freedom-of-municipality-award-for-applying-the-natural-step-framework-during-vancouver-olympics

Stack M., & Gartland, M. P. (2005). The repeal of prohibition and the resurgence of national breweries: Productive efficiency or path creation. *Journal of Management History, 43*(3), 420–432.

Strambach, S. & Halkier, H. (2013). Editorial: Reconceptualizing change - path dependency, path plasticity and knowledge construction. *Zeitschrift für Wirtschaftsgeographie, 57*(1–2), 1–14.

Stratford, E., Davidson J., Griffith, R., Lockwood, M., & Curtis, A. (2007). *Sustainable development and good governance: The 'Big Ideas' on Australian NRM* (Report No. 3 of the project 'Pathways to good practice in regional NRM governance'). Hobart: University of Tasmania.

Strobl, A., & Peters, M. (2013). Entrepreneurial reputation in destination networks. *Annals of Tourism Research, 40*, 59–82.

Svensson, B., Nordin, S., & Flagestad, A. (2005). A governance perspective on destination development – exploring partnerships, clusters and innovation systems. *Tourism Review, 60*, 32–37.

Svensson, B., Nordin, S., & Flagestad, A. (2006). Destination governance and contemporary development models. In L. Lazzeretti & C. Petrillo (Eds.), *Tourism local systems and networking* (pp. 83–96). Oxford: Elsevier.

Teske, P., & Schneider, M. (1994). The bureaucratic entrepreneur: The case of city managers. *Public Administration Review, 54*(4), 331–340.

Westley, F., Olsson, P., Folke, C., Homer-Dixon, T., Vredenburg, H., Loorbach, D., ... van der Leeuw, S. (2011). Tipping toward sustainability: Emerging pathways of transformation. *Ambio, 40*, 762–780.

Whistler 2020. (2010). Whistler 2020: Moving toward a sustainable future. Retrieved July 29, 2010, from http://www.whistler2020.ca

Whistler 2020. (2013). Whistler's journey. Retrieved August 20, 2013, from http://www.whistler2020.ca/About/the_natural_step
Williams, A.M. (2013). Mobilities and sustainable tourism: Path creating or path dependent relationships? *Journal of Sustainable Tourism, 21*(4), 511–531.
Williams, P.W., & Todd, S. (1997). Towards an environmental management system for ski areas. *Mountain Research and Development, 17*(1), 75–90.
Williams, P. W., Gill, A. M., & Ponsford, I. (2007). Corporate social responsibility at tourism destinations: Towards a social license to operate. *Tourism Review International, 11*(2), 133–144.
Zovanyi, G. (2013). *The No-growth imperative: Creating sustainable communities under ecological limits to growth.* Abingdon: Routledge.

Collaboration and Partnership Development for Sustainable Tourism

SONYA GRACI

ABSTRACT *For many years, the need to improve sustainability in the tourism industry has been widely recognized. Many destinations have attempted to move toward sustainability, but unfortunately, have been hindered in their attempts by a lack of collaboration among stakeholders that is necessary to support their sustainability agendas. Collaboration, specifically through multi-stakeholder partnerships, has been seen as an effective way to support initiatives in tourism development. Through the lens of Gray's collaboration theory and Selin and Chavez's tourism partnership model, the success of collaboration and partnerships in tourism development on the island of Gili Trawangan, Indonesia, will be examined. Through a multi-method approach consisting of an environmental audit and semi-structured interviews, this paper explores the implementation of a multi-stakeholder partnership. The partnership that has been developed, called the Gili Ecotrust, provides an example of successful collaboration, leading to the implementation of innovative sustainability initiatives on the island.*

Introduction

The island of Gili Trawangan, Indonesia, is a destination that is primarily focused on dive tourism and is currently in the growth stage and rapidly moving toward the consolidation stage of its tourism lifecycle. For many years, Gili Trawangan was primarily underdeveloped; however in the span of the last decade, the selling of land to Westerners has resulted in rapid development. The island community, which is composed of mostly Westerners and local Indonesians, has become increasingly concerned with the state of the environment on the island. Gili Trawangan and its sister islands, Gili Meno and Gili Air, are located in an area with a great deal of marine diversity. The islands are currently located in the West Nusa Dua Marine Park, however this has been largely in name only and has not resulted in any involvement from the provincial government that has authority over the marine park. Despite its marine park status, there has been no implementation of initiatives by the marine park to protect the increasingly threatened marine diversity. Increasing traffic from boats, improper anchoring, rapid development on the island and overuse through fishing, diving and glass bottom boats has led to the fast decline of the marine environment. Tourism development has led to the degradation of the coral reefs, beach erosion and a large amount of rubbish littering the island. Illegal building on the beach and lack of planning has resulted in overcrowding and pressure on the existing infrastructure. In order to combat the effects of tourism development and maintain some ecological integrity on the island, a multi-stakeholder partnership was implemented in 2002. It is through this partnership that the island has attempted to move the sustainability agenda forward. This paper will focus on the progression of this partnership to illustrate how a successful collaboration can be established.

Literature Review

Tourism is often described as one of the world's largest industries on the basis of its contribution to global gross domestic product (GDP), the number of jobs it generates and the number of people it transports. Developing countries currently have only a minority share of the international tourism market (approximately 30%), with this number continuing to grow. International tourism arrivals in developing countries have grown by an average of 9.5% per year since 1990, compared with 4.6% worldwide (Tearfund 2002). In many Lesser Developed Countries (LDCs), tourism is significant to the economy and is generally growing (Tearfund 2002). The contribution that tourism makes to national economies is also far more pronounced in LDCs (United Nations World Tourism Organization [UNWTO] 2006). As many authors and government reports have outlined (World Travel and Tourism Council [WTTC] 1995, 1999; Weaver 2001; UNWTO 2005; Goeldner & Ritchie 2006) and recent events (hurricanes, tropical storms, 2004 Tsunami) have demonstrated, there is a need to move toward more sustainable forms of development to ensure long-term viability. Many small islands, particularly those with warm climates, depend heavily on sun, sea and sand as tourist attractions, and it is these resources that their industries have traditionally been based upon. Many of the problems that small islands face relate directly to their insular geography and fragile environmental characteristics (Kerr 2005; Scheyvens & Momsen 2008), and although they are benefiting from increased economic gain from tourism, they are also experiencing many negative environmental, economic and social consequences. Some of the issues and impacts affecting destinations include dependency of a host community's economy on tourism; competition; leakage; government debt to finance development; loss of habitat areas and resources due to development and pollution; decline in biodiversity of species and ecosystems; erosion; loss of natural and archeological heritage in the face of rapid expansion; sea, land, noise and air pollution; increased congestion and strains on infrastructure; encroachment of buildings, facilities and roads to the coastline, crowding and pressure on services; and displacement of the local population (Graci

& Dodds 2010). The characteristic complexities related to planning, development and management in island destinations give rise to resource management and governance issues, particularly relating to the potential success of sustainable development planning and strategies (Douglas 2006; Scheyvens & Russell 2012). It is important for small island states, dependent on tourism, to take control and manage their tourism industries. Far too many islands are facing detrimental effects from poor planning and governance. Many islands are facing beach erosion, water pollution, waste management issues, energy crises, coral reef destruction, acculturation and leakage (Graci & Dodds 2010). Strategies to influence tourism development can and have been implemented in some small islands with success. In order to overcome the challenges with managing island destinations in a sustainable manner, innovative initiatives can help to identify practical ways in which to move forward. Innovative initiatives can consist of varying forms, and in several destinations have enabled the progression of sustainability through the principles of long-term planning, collaboration, education, the conception of dialogue and creating a cohesive vision for the destination. To move toward sustainability, island destinations require the participation of the local people, the definition of long-term strategies, a carefully designed tourism plan, intensive capacity building and training of both national public officials and management in the destination and infrastructure support (Hashimoto 2002; Fennell 2003; UNWTO 2006; Graci & Dodds 2010).

Collaboration is considered to be essential in moving the tourism industry toward sustainability. Throughout the literature, cross-sector partnerships are recommended for their likelihood to result in sustainable development outcomes (Selin 1999; Bramwell & Alletorp 2001; Bramwell & Lane 2005). A central role for sustainable destination management involves bringing together different organizations in order to establish common goals and create a framework for joint action (Berresford 2004). The UNWTO revealed that public–private partnerships are the key principle for successful destination management (Foggin & Münster 2003). Participants that have traditionally acted in isolation from each other need to learn how to cooperate (Halme 2001). As no one organization does, or can deliver tourism development, a collaborative multi-stakeholder approach is necessary.

Collaboration through partnerships is described as a loosely coupled system of organizations and individuals that belong to various public and private sectors, who come together in order to reach certain goals, unattainable by the partners individually (Selin 1999; Fadeeva 2005). Collaboration is defined by Gray (1989: 5) as 'a process through which parties who see different aspects of a problem can constructively explore their differences and search for solutions that go beyond their own limited vision of what is possible.' Therefore, a collaborative alliance is an inter-organizational effort to address problems too intricate to be effectively resolved by independent action (Gray & Wood 1991). Collaboration is the evolving process of alliances working together in a problem domain (Gray 1989; Medeiros de Araujo & Bramwell 2002; Plummer *et al.* 2006; Jamal & Stronza 2009). The process has the potential to allow organizations to pool their knowledge, share expertise, capital and other resources (Plummer *et al.* 2006). The groups working together may therefore gain a competitive advantage. In addition, policies, implementation and enforcement of plans and regulations resulting from collaboration may be more accepted by individuals and organizations who were involved in creating them (Medeiros de Araujo & Bramwell 2002). It has also been argued that this practice of collaboration is part of a moral obligation to involve affected parties throughout any decision-making processes (Medeiros de Araujo & Bramwell 2002).

An inclusive collaborative approach has the ability to create social capital and thus contributes to the development of more sustainable forms of tourism (Kernel 2005). As indicated by Carbone (2005), a true partnership between the producer (the environment, the local culture and the people), the supplier (the tourism industry) and the consumer (the tourist) is critical for integrating community needs with the sustainable use of the environment while providing profits to the stakeholders involved. It is through partnerships that organizations, government and communities are able to collectively address concerns and determine mutually agreed upon objectives that will benefit all stakeholders involved, thus embarking on a more sustainable approach to tourism development. The purpose of a partnership is to eventually produce consensus and harmony that will lead to new opportunities and innovative solutions. Partnerships must include the views of all stakeholders within a destination and identify various roles and responsibilities for each stakeholder so that they can contribute to the overarching goal of moving the destination toward a more sustainable management of tourism. The key elements of a partnership are that all

- stakeholders are interdependent;
- solutions emerge by dealing constructively with difference;
- joint ownership of decisions is involved;
- stakeholders assume collective responsibility for the future direction of the domain; and
- partnerships remain a dynamic, emergent process (Gray 1989: 11 in Selin 1999: 262).

These key elements are the underlying principles for a multi-stakeholder partnership, which provides a cohesive environmental vision, enabling the tourism destination to focus resources, share information, increase environmental and social action in the destination, learn from the leaders and ultimately protect the resources that sustain the destination. Collaboration leads to the sharing and implementing of ideas as well as creative methods to deal with solutions.

Gray (1996: 61–65) outlined a three-phase framework for the collaboration process. The first phase, for problem setting, requires that multiple stakeholders agree on what the problem is, and that the problem is important enough to work with others to find a solution. In addition, this phase must ensure that all stakeholders are included to fully understand the process. If key stakeholders are excluded from this phase, Gray argues that this could cause technical or political problems during the implementation phase of collaboration (Gray 1989; Medeiros de Araujo & Bramwell 2002; Jamal & Stronza 2009). The second phase, of direction setting, focuses on establishing rules, groups and agreements between the stakeholders. In addition, phase two requires the exploration of options through discussing the interests and values of each group, then finally reaching an agreement to proceed with a particular course of action (Medeiros de Araujo & Bramwell 2002; Jamal & Stronza 2009). The last phase of collaboration sees the implementation of the chosen course of action, requiring support and structure, including monitoring for compliance (Medeiros de Araujo & Bramwell 2002; Jamal & Stronza 2009).

Although collaboration theory has many potential advantages, there are some important difficulties and obstacles involved. Collaboration requires frequent and regular meetings involving discussion and decision-making with various individuals or organizations (Medeiros de Araujo & Bramwell 2002). This type of demanding schedule can be problematic for many who wish to be involved. It is possible that financial and time constraints can be difficult to overcome, creating a barrier to participation in regular meetings (Medeiros de Araujo & Bramwell 2002). Therefore, certain groups may dislike or refuse to work together thereby hindering the collaboration process (Medeiros de Araujo & Bramwell 2002; Jamal & Stronza 2009).

The application of collaboration theory in tourism planning, management and development has become very prevalent over the past decade to help manage emerging environmental issues: climate change, biodiversity loss, resource depletion and impacts from globalization (Selin 1999; Plummer *et al.* 2006; Jamal & Stronza 2009). Since tourism is a complex industry that impacts several groups (Hardy & Beeton 2001; Medeiros de Araujo & Bramwell 2002; Jamal & Stronza 2009), this poses a challenge in terms of implementing collaboration (Medeiros de Araujo & Bramwell 2002). Specifically in tourism, each group will differ in terms of their interests at a local, regional or national scale as well as their influence over decision-making (Jamal & Stronza 2009).

Selin and Chavez (1995) developed a model of the evolution of tourism partnerships based on Gray's seminal work. They proposed that tourism partnerships progress through five stages: antecedents, problem setting, direction setting, structuring and outcomes (Selin & Chavez 1995; Plummer *et al.* 2006). Figure 1 outlines Selin and Chavez (1995) tourism partnership model.

Selin and Chavez's (1995) model begins with an antecedent that causes the partnership to be initiated. Crisis, such as serious marine biodiversity loss in a dive tourism destination, is frequently an antecedent that initiates tourism partnerships. In addition to a crisis, a broker or convener may initiate the process. From this environmental context, partnerships evolve through problem setting, direction setting and structuring, resulting in the outcomes of the partnership (Selin & Chavez 1995). Throughout this model, it is evident that a common vision among stakeholders is an important

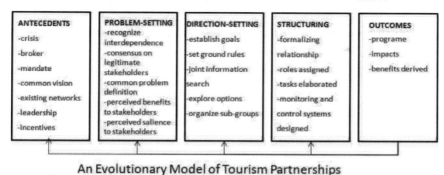

Figure 1. Tourism partnership model. *Source:* Selin and Chavez 1995: 848.

aspect of tourism partnership formation. Existing professional or social networks helps naturally develop relationships and expand their past or present work toward the goals of the partnership (Selin & Chavez 1995). A strong-willed, enthusiastic leader is often the catalyst for partnership development in tourism, as are incentives (including grants) and the vested interest of stakeholders (Selin & Chavez 1995). Areas that are likely to experience successful partnership development have a strong sense of community, which helps motivate participation in the partnership (Selin & Chavez 1995). Small islands are thought to be ideal settings for partnership collaboration as they commonly have a strong sense of community, along with existing networks.

Collaboration through partnership development involves initiating dialogue and creating relationships between stakeholders in order to tackle a common issue. Each stakeholder brings forth individual strengths such as knowledge, expertise and capital, and is more effective as part of a joint effort rather than an individual one. By working together, stakeholders can exchange information, learn from one another, develop innovative policies, adapt successfully to a changing environment and channel energy toward a collective good (Carr *et al.* 1998; Kernel 2005).

This paper utilizes Gray's (1989) collaboration theory and Selin and Chavez's (1995) model to examine collaboration in tourism development on the island of Gili Trawangan, Indonesia. On this island, they have utilized stakeholder engagement and planning to develop a multi-stakeholder partnership aimed at addressing sustainability, resulting in success with the implementation of several innovative initiatives.

Study Area

Gili Trawangan is a small island located among the Gili Islands, off the coast of Lombok in Indonesia, in a designated marine protected area, the West Nusa Dua

Figure 2. Map of Gili Trawangan, Indonesia. *Source:* Graci and Dodds 2010: 122.

Marine Park. Figure 2 identifies the location of Gili Trawangan in relation to other islands in Indonesia.

Gili Trawangan is approximately three by two kilometers in area, has low-lying topography with a small hill to the south, rising to 72 meters above sea level (Hampton 1998). Gili Trawangan is the most developed of all three Gili Islands (the other two islands being the newly developed Gili Air and the mostly undeveloped Gili Meno). Gili Trawangan has an approximate population of 474 families, composed of roughly 1,900 local people, along with numerous expatriates living on the island (Graci 2007). The majority of land use on the island is related to tourism, with the remainder being coconut plantation and small fields of agricultural crops and livestock. In recent years, however, the majority of undeveloped land is quickly being sold and developed, drastically increasing the amount of people who live and visit the island. Gili Trawangan is a sun, sand and sea destination, with tourism being the dominant economic activity on the island, as more than 80% of the families on Gili Trawangan are employed by tourism in some form (Graci 2007). The main tourism season is June–September with smaller peaks in December, January and February (Hampton 1998; Graci 2007). Gili Trawangan is not a very developed tourism destination in terms of mass tourism resorts, infrastructure or services. The main tourists on Gili Trawangan are backpackers and dive tourists, but as the island is rapidly developing and more accommodations are being built, this is changing. Previously there were only two high-end resorts and few mid-level accommodations on the island, but as of 2010, several new mid- and high-end small-scale accommodations were being built. Island transportation consists of non-motorized sources such as bicycles and cidomos (horse drawn carts), with mostly unsealed dirt roads and few paved roads. The island has limited fresh water shipped in barrels from the mainland on a daily basis. Only the high-end resorts, mid-level accommodations and restaurants use fresh water (Hampton 1998; Graci 2007). The island's energy source is based on a generator and there are many power outages throughout the course of a day. In the last few years, there has been an increase in the number of daily boats bringing tourists to the island, with direct transport from Bali. This has changed the nature of tourism on the island, as a more diverse clientele has begun to visit. Numerous accommodations have pools, there is horseback riding offered on the island and several high-end and culturally diverse dining establishments have opened catering to more of the mass tourist culture. These recent changes have resulted in the island beginning to move from the development stage to the consolidation stage of the tourism lifecycle.

Methodology

This paper is based upon fieldwork that was conducted in Gili Trawangan, Indonesia, over three visits in May–July 2005, October–November 2005 and December 2007. Research was also conducted in the summer of 2010 but focused on specific aspects of waste management and sea turtle conservation. A case study approach was undertaken for this study that consisted of an in-depth investigation of the issues surrounding tourism development and sustainability in Gili Trawangan. The case study approach presented the opportunity to apply a multi-method approach to a unique setting (Sommer & Sommer 1992). The first phase of this research consisted of undertaking an environmental impact assessment in 2005 to determine the environmental and social impacts occurring through tourism development on the island. In addition, 45 in-depth, semi-structured key informant interviews were conducted with a cross section of stakeholders including the local community, local government, western businesses, local businesses, employees and tourists. The interviews identified the barriers to implementing sustainable tourism initiatives on the island, the history of development and sought to investigate innovative ways to move the sustainability agenda forward. The environmental impact assessment and interviews formed the basis for a sustainable tourism strategy for the island. The strategy recommended the development of a multi-stakeholder partnership and subsequent actions that needed to be addressed. The sustainable tourism strategy was released in February 2006 and formed the basis for the actions that have been implemented on the island. In 2007, follow-up interviews were conducted with 20 of the original stakeholders interviewed in 2005 in addition to 20 interviews with stakeholders that were new to the island but showed an interest in the development of sustainability initiatives. These interviews sought to determine the cause for the slow progression of the implementation of the sustainable tourism strategy and to identify further strategies to ensure ease of implementation. New issues that have developed on the island were discussed. A snowball sampling method was used to recruit key informants for the interviews. This technique is used in social science research for developing a research sample where existing study subjects recruit future subjects from among their acquaintances. This research technique works well as a breadth of key stakeholders can be identified (Sommer & Sommer 1992). Through the various phases of research conducted on the island using multiple methods, a multi-stakeholder partnership was developed and sustainability initiatives were implemented.

Results

This study sought to determine the success of the multi-stakeholder partnership that was developed on Gili Trawangan to guide the implementation of sustainability initiatives. The stakeholders involved prior to and during the implementation of this partnership included representatives from the expatriate and local tourism businesses, local government, and community which includes expatriates living on the island as well as local Indonesians, tourists and employees.

An Evaluation of the Gili Trawangan Multi-Stakeholder Partnership

Challenges to Sustainable Tourism Development

Over the last number of years, Gili Trawangan has faced many challenges regarding sustainable development and maintaining the ecological integrity of the island. The main issues on the island have related to waste management, coral reef degradation, beach erosion, unplanned or unauthorized development, illegal fishing and tension between the westerners living on the island and the locals. It is also riddled with an unresponsive provincial government that does not provide any financial assistance to the island and a corrupt local government that is appointed through a feudal system of ownership versus a democratic election. Many of the locals on the island live in poverty.

In 2002, the Gili Ecotrust was organized by a number of the dive shops on the island. The purpose of the Ecotrust was to collect and manage a dive tax (initially at US$3 per diver and US$1 per snorkeler) which was used to pay local fisherman to stop detrimental fishing practices and to hire a patrol boat for the area. When the Ecotrust was first developed, despite the numerous ideas for how to increase sustainability in Gili Trawangan, and a common belief by a number of business owners that current practices were inadequate, there was a lack of momentum to move forward and implement initiatives. The lack of momentum was a result of the 'pass the buck' mentality, where everyone believed that they were too busy to contribute to the development and implementation of initiatives. Despite the concern that the environment on the island was degraded, several business owners did not want to take responsibility for implementation, especially when it involved time and money. It was evident that several of the business owners on the island had numerous complaints about the management of the environment, yet it was difficult to rally support in terms of volunteer time to manage the systems on the island. For example, only one business owner in conjunction with the local government managed the eco-tax funds to pay the fishermen, a practice that was not looked upon favorably as a sustainable solution by many of the business owners; however, no other solutions were put forth. The business owners felt that it was an ineffective method, as one patrol boat was unable to guard all areas around the island and this did not deter fisherman from the neighboring islands of Bali and Lombok. The payment did not encourage education on the reasons not to fish or skills training for the fisherman, rather just supported inaction.

Another challenge with the Ecotrust was that one person managed the funds and day-to-day workings of the Ecotrust, in addition to running their own successful dive business. It was not plausible for one person to voluntarily in his/her minimal spare time to manage the organization effectively. Despite the ideas and enthusiasm from other stakeholders on the island, no one was willing to take responsibility. This lack of responsibility was evident with the organization of a beach clean-up team that was funded by the Gili Ecotrust. The beach clean-up team was supported by all businesses participating in the Ecotrust; however, without any management, direction or motivation on how to proceed with the clean-up on a regular basis, it quickly ceased (Graci 2007).

Another challenge to sustainability on the island is due to corruption of the local government. On the local level, corruption occurred through the random pricing structure that government-appointed businesses charge in terms of waste collection. Expatriate businesses are charged an inflated rate over local businesses, despite the success or size of the business. These fees are based on personal relationships so that one expatriate business owner can pay up to triple the amount for the same services as another, who has a good relationship with the waste collection agency (Graci 2007). This has led to businesses on the island not wanting to participate in the waste management system. The disparity of policies on the island is dependent upon personal relationships, bribes and government corruption. This has led to the frustration of the stakeholders, particularly in terms of volunteering time and money to implement sustainable tourism initiatives. Many initiatives have been funded independently and several stakeholders felt powerless to oppose the current structure for fear of making their own lives difficult and negatively affecting their business. Physical attributes such as infrastructure, or lack thereof, are also an impediment. Gili Trawangan currently ships in barrels of fresh water on a daily basis to the island. Structures such as sewage treatment plants (sewage is currently either disposed of in homemade septic tanks, to the sea or open pits on the side of the road in the village) cannot be built, as salt water will degrade the infrastructure. In addition, technology continues to be a challenge. Even if initiatives such as solar power or a sewage treatment plant were installed, it would be difficult to fix or adjust technologies due to the remoteness of the island and lack of skill and cost. Space is also an issue on the island, as many businesses would like to install composters to dispose of their own organic waste, but do not have the space available (Graci 2007). Despite the fact that several of the tourists on Gili Trawangan supported a sustainability strategy and have no issue contributing to the eco-tax while diving or snorkeling, many tourists were not necessarily aware of the environmental issues, nor do they factor this into their motivations for visiting this destination. Tourists on Gili Trawangan are party tourists and divers. The majority of tourists are young (18–24 years old) backpackers and due to the inexpensive nature of their experience on this island, do not demand a higher quality of sustainability (Dodds *et al.* 2010). Therefore, the tourists will contribute their one-time fee of US$6 if they are diving or US$1 if they are snorkeling, but will not pay higher premiums for sustainability initiatives nor factor this into their decision when choosing an establishment to eat or stay. They are also satisfied with the status quo and despite attempts at banishing water bottles on the island, still consume water in bottles and contribute to the ever-growing waste problem on the island. This is due to the disconnection of the tourists with the rest of the island, as tourists on Gili Trawangan are not usually exposed to the village or are unaware of any of the issues. As with many paradise islands, tourists are only exposed to the beach, bars, restaurants and diving; however in the recent years, the loss of several of the beaches has led to massive overcrowding on the one beach that is left on the island. Tourists have commented that the island is becoming overcrowded and displeased with the state of the beach. They have also commented on the rubbish on the island, which many times is littered in public areas.

Overcoming Challenges: The Implementation of a Multi-Stakeholder Partnership

Despite the number of challenges that this island is facing, they have moved forward and have implemented a number of innovative initiatives driven by the implementation of a multi-stakeholder partnership.

The Antecedent Stage

In the island of Gili Trawangan, the antecedent to this partnership was the concern among the local community and businesses that the degradation of the environment would lead to the eventual demise of this tourism destination. Due to the crisis that arose because of coral bombing and other detrimental fishing practices, stakeholders joined together to formally manage the crisis. The Ecotrust formally began to monitor illegal fishing through providing financial incentives to fisherman to stop illegal fishing practices and hiring a patrol boat for the area.

Partnerships are also championed by a strong leader whose energy and vision mobilized others to participate (Selin & Chavez 1995). It was due to the vision of one dive shop owner that the Ecotrust was born and continued to gain momentum. As this dive shop owner had a good working relationship with the other stakeholders (such as the locals, other businesses and government), she took charge to manage the Ecotrust in the early years. She managed the collection of funds, holding of meetings, managing complaints and implementing the initiatives until 2007 when an environmental coordinator was hired.

In addition, as it is a very small island, there was a common vision among all stakeholders to protect the resources of the island, as it is their livelihood and home. Partnerships can also be encouraged by providing incentives to potential partners. In order to collaborate on protecting the marine environment, incentives were provided to the fisherman to stop illegal fishing and cease with harmful coral bombing practices as well as to the dive shop owners to participate in order to protect their business investment. As well, the existing networks of the island that result due to living in a small communal space with little development for many years encouraged collaboration.

The Problem-Setting Stage

In the problem-setting stage, consensus is reached on who has a legitimate stake in an issue. Stakeholders start to appreciate the interdependencies that exist among them and realize that problem resolution will require collective action. The participants begin to mutually acknowledge the issue that brings them together. The goal of this stage is to have stakeholders communicate about the issue and eventually act upon it. Having stakeholder involvement ensures that they will remain committed to the process of partnership development.

The problem-setting stage becomes an avenue for dialogue and collaboration among stakeholders, which in the case of Gili Trawangan included the local community, local businesses, expatriate businesses, employees, tourists and local government. Consultation was conducted with all stakeholders to identify the major issues on the island. Communicating about their concerns, stakeholders were able to brainstorm innovative methods to deal with the issues on the island. The consultation identified that waste management, coral reef degradation, beach erosion, health impacts through burning of waste and lack of local community involvement to participate in decisions regarding the island and the tourism industry were some major issues. Rapid and unsound developments such as building on the beach were also major areas of concern to the stakeholders. The consultation was used as the basis for a sustainability strategy that was developed for the island to prioritize initiatives and identify a form of collaboration to manage the implementation of the strategy.

The Direction-Setting Stage

In the direction-setting stage, collaboration evolves into a direction-setting stage where participants begin to identify a common purpose and shared interpretations of the future emerge as stakeholders identify commonly held beliefs and vision (Selin & Chavez 1995). This process is facilitated by the setting of goals and ground rules and by organizing subgroups to examine specific issues.

After the consultation occurred in the previous stage, a sustainability strategy was developed that focused on setting a mission statement to provide a clear direction toward achieving the common goal of sustainability. It incorporated best practices of sustainable tourism development worldwide and identified initiatives that can be implemented on the island.

The underlying principle of the sustainability strategy was to protect the environment by implementing a series of goals and objectives. It was also to ensure that there was dialogue and transparency occurring among the stakeholders to facilitate the buy-in and motivation to implement the initiatives. The need for a multi-stakeholder partnership to increase accountability and manage the implementation of projects was also recommended. The partnership was structured with the use of sub groups to explore options and gather support to accomplish the goals and objectives identified in the strategy.

The Structuring Stage

The purpose of the partnership, which has been incorporated into the structure of the Gili Ecotrust, was to be the avenue to initiate dialogue among all stakeholders and to create a plan for the island that everyone can adhere to. The formalization of the partnership mirrors phase four of Selin and Chavez's (1995) model which is the structuring phase. This phase formalizes the collaboration and its relationships, elaborates on the tasks necessary to achieve the goals and develops the systems for implementation. Stakeholders involved in the partnership were designated various roles and responsibilities for an environmental coordinator and the stakeholders involved in the sub-groups. Formalizing the partnership enables the stakeholders to focus resources, share information, increase environmental action and learn from the leaders. At this stage, it was identified that the role of the Gili Ecotrust was to

- make decisions and oversee the implementation of the sustainable tourism strategy;
- provide guidance and information to the community via community meetings and workshops;
- organize project teams to implement the sustainability initiatives;
- manage the eco-tax;
- provide accountability for finances and decisions made; and
- provide a mechanism for complaints on the management of the environment.

The formalized Ecotrust has been the avenue to ensure that the goals of the strategy are being achieved.

The Outcome Stage

At this stage, the programs that were developed by the collaboration are being implemented and the benefits derived from the collaboration. The Ecotrust, which is currently managed by an environmental coordinator, has succeeded in reaching this stage of the collaboration as it has implemented a number of initiatives garnering positive impacts on protecting the environment. It has also ensured collaboration through enabling stakeholders to voice their concerns while also becoming involved in major issues on the island. Monthly meetings with business owners, local governments and the community are held in order to work together to tackle the issues on the island.

The Gili Ecotrust now has the participation of numerous stakeholders on the island and has been responsible for working with the local community in order to monitor the surrounding area to ensure illegal fishing is not occurring. It is also working with the local school to educate children about waste disposal and how to protect the coral reefs, beginning dialogue on how to manage waste on the island, starting a waste separation program, organizing beach and coral clean-ups and ensuring that the horses that work the cidomo carts have constant access to freshwater and are treated humanely. Each dive shop has sponsored its own biorock in front of their properties. The biorocks provide low-level electrical current to a structure, which is placed under water and eventually grows into a coral reef balmy. This balmy attracts fish and leads to the regeneration of the coral reef. Plans for a waste management and green sea turtle conservation strategy were being explored in 2010. The environmental coordinator has now been hired full time and is currently learning the local language in order to negotiate contracts with waste management organizations and the government. Even if all the initiatives identified in the strategy are not implemented immediately, success is evident through the formation of a partnership that has brought together various stakeholders on the island to create dialogue and build relationships. This partnership will also lead to the sharing of information and best practices. By including locals in public consultation meetings, the local level of education is being raised and cultural exchange is occurring. This has, and will lead to new knowledge and overcoming challenges. Through the involvement of locals, empowerment has resulted. The partnership has led to increased accountability among the government, locals and westerners. This has also led to a cohesive environmental vision and language, where all who live on Gili Trawangan want to protect the resources that sustain the island and continue living in a clean environment.

Discussion

Despite efforts from a number of local businesses to further sustainability initiatives on the island of Gili Trawangan, challenges to sustainable tourism implementation still exist. The purpose of developing and implementing a collaborative partnership is to provide a holistic approach to sustainable tourism implementation that includes all stakeholders. This case study identifies that collaboration through multi-stakeholder partnerships can successfully lead to the implementation of programs and initiatives that can move a destination toward sustainability. In the beginning stages of collaboration, it is necessary to identify the challenges and work with all stakeholders to determine a collective vision. Increasing levels of local involvement and considering the views of all stakeholders are pertinent in achieving sustainable tourism measures, as they bring together a wider group of stakeholders with common interests (Farrell 1994; Middleton & Hawkins 1998; Tosun 2001; Puppim de Oliviera 2003). Further, residents are regarded as the rightful custodians of an area, and their needs should not be overridden by outside interests (Din 1993; Ruhanen 2008). Each stakeholder has a different view, and in order to achieve sustainable tourism, multiple stakeholders working together in collaboration to achieve goals, which benefit the greater good, is important. Collaboration and participation are needed in order to address the overall concept of the public good as well as environmental and social concerns in the context of development rather than solely market interests. It also must be mindful of the many other sectors – taxation, transportation, housing, social development, environmental conservation and protection and resource management. As these different industries all affect tourism, it cannot operate in isolation, and in order for successful island sustainable tourism to result, it must benefit more than just the business owners (Graci & Dodds 2010).

The case study of Gili Trawangan identifies that managing relationships with primary stakeholders can result in more than just continued participation. By developing long-term relationships with primary stakeholders, a set of value-creating exchanges happen that are relational rather than transactional since 'transactional interactions can be easily duplicated and thus offer little potential for competitive advantage' (Hillman & Keim 2001: 127). Collaboration and mutual trust leads to better cooperation and long-term viability, however this will only be successful if the process is open, consultative and aims to set objectives where each stakeholder will benefit. Effective stakeholder management will build trust and give stakeholders a sense of empowerment and ownership in the development process.

Once the problem is defined, it is necessary to establish goals as well as roles and responsibilities to achieve these goals. In Gili Trawangan, information was sought through consultation and conducting an environmental audit. This fed into a strategy that achieved buy-in from all stakeholders. The nature of the partnership was also one that fostered continuous dialogue and involvement as well as was financially stable through the collection of an eco-tax. The funds collected provided the ability to hire an environmental coordinator that was responsible for the day-to-day tasks related to the partnership. This also increased the level of success of the collaboration because this person acted as the link between all stakeholders. As it was the responsibility of the coordinator to ensure that tasks were completed and that communication did not break down, tasks were implemented to achieve the stated goals. In addition, monthly meetings and constant communication and consultation included all stakeholders in joint decision-making and ensured that the process was dynamic leading to its success. This case study has identified that momentum and good will are not enough, a collaborative effort toward sustainability is necessary for success.

It is recommended that this case study be taken as a good example of collaboration. Despite the number of challenges that this island has and currently is facing, due to collaboration, constant dialogue, a common vision and working together, challenges have and continue to be overcome. Selin and Chavez's (1995) tourism partnership model has identified the stages that a partnership can go through and this paper has used a case study to illustrate this. It is recommended that further tourism partnerships be analyzed to identify whether the challenges faced are similar and whether the partnership has followed the progressive stages as identified by Selin and Chavez (1995).

Conclusion

The multi-stakeholder partnership that developed as a result of collaboration in Gili Trawangan followed the five stages as identified by Selin and Chavez (1995) in their collaboration model. The island of Gili Trawangan went through the first phase when a crisis regarding illegal fishing and bombing developed and through leadership created the Gili Ecotrust to deal with these issues. This led to the problem-setting phase where a common vision and problem definition was identified, stakeholders consulted and collaboration began to occur. The third phase led to the goals being set, information sought out and options explored. Sub-groups to tackle certain initiatives were organized. The fourth phase consisted of formally structuring the partnership through hiring a full-time coordinator and assigning key roles and responsibilities to the stakeholders involved. The fifth stage led to the development of key outcomes such as the installation of a number of biorocks on the island, the beginning of a waste collection and management system, initiatives for turtle conservation and dialogue being created among stakeholders. Following Selin and Chavez's (1995) model which was built on the principles of Gray's collaboration theory, the multi-stakeholder partnership developed in Gili Trawangan can be considered successful and innovative in terms of sustainable tourism development.

References

Berresford, J. (2004) *Tourism in the Region*. Regional Review Hearing Report, pp. 1–11.
Bramwell, B. & Alletorp, L. (2001) Attitudes in the Danish tourism industry to the roles of business and government in sustainable tourism, *International Journal of Tourism Research*, 3, pp. 91–103.
Bramwell, B. & Lane, B. (2005) Sustainable tourism research and the importance of societal and social science trends, *Journal of Sustainable Tourism*, 13(1), pp. 1–3.
Carbone, M. (2005) Sustainable tourism in developing countries: Poverty alleviation, participatory planning and ethical issues, *The European Journal of Development Research*, 17(3), pp. 559–565.
Carr, D. S., Selin, S. W., & Schuett, M. A. (1998) Managing public forests: Understanding the role of collaborative planning, *Environmental Management*, 22(5), pp. 767–776.
Din, K. (1993) Dialogue with hosts: An educational strategy towards sustainable tourism, in: M. Hitchcock, V. King, & M. Parnwell (Eds) *Tourism in South-East Asia*, p. 32 (New York: Routledge).
Dodds, R., Graci, S., & Holmes, M. (2010) Does the tourist care? A comparison of visitors to Koh Phi Phi, Thailand and Gili Trawangan, Indonesia, *Journal of Sustainable Tourism*, 19(2), pp. 207–222.
Douglas, C. H. (2006) Small island states and territories: Sustainable development issues and strategies – Challenges for changing islands in a changing world, *Sustainable Development*, 14, pp. 75–80.
Fadeeva, Z. (2005) Translation of sustainability ideas in tourism networks: Some roles of cross-sectoral networks in change towards sustainable development, *Journal of Cleaner Production*, 13(2), pp. 175–189.
Farrell, B. (1994) Tourism as an element in sustainable development, in: V. Smith & W. Eadington (Eds) *Tourism Alternatives*, pp. 115–132 (Bognor Regis, UK: John Wiley).
Fennell, D. (2003) *Ecotourism, 2nd ed.* (London: Routledge).
Foggin, T. & Münster, D. O. (2003) Finding the middle ground between communities and tourism, *Africa Insight*, 33(1/2), pp. 18–22.
Goeldner, C. R. & Ritchie, J. R. (2006) *Tourism: Principles, Practices, Philosophies* (New Jersey: John Wiley).
Graci, S. (2007) Accommodating Green: Examining barriers to sustainable tourism development. Paper presented at the TTRA Canada conference, Montebello, Quebec.
Graci, S. & Dodds, R. (2010) *Sustainable Tourism in Island Destinations* (London: Earthscan).
Gray, B. (1989) *Collaborating* (San Francisco: Jossey-Bass).
Gray, B. (1996) Cross-sectoral partners: Collaborative alliances among business, government and communities, in: C. Huxham (Eds) *Creating Collaborative Advantage* (London: Sage).
Gray, B. & Wood, D. (1991) Collaborative alliances: Moving from practice to theory, *Journal of Applied Behavioral Science*, 27(1), pp. 3–22.
Halme, M. (2001) Learning for Sustainable Development in Tourism Networks, in: *Ninth International Conference on Sustainability at the Millennium: Globalization, Competitiveness and the Public Trust* (Bangkok: Greening of Industry Network).
Hampton, M. P. (1998) Backpacker tourism and economic development, *Annals of Tourism Research*, 25, pp. 639–660.
Hardy, A. & Beeton, R. (2001) Sustainable tourism or maintainable tourism: Managing resources for more than average outcomes, *Journal of Sustainable Tourism*, 9(3), pp. 168–192.
Hashimoto, A. (2002) Tourism and sociocultural development issues, in: R. Sharpley & D. J. Telfer (Eds) *Tourism and Development: Concepts and Issues*, pp. 202–230 (Clevedon: Channel View Publications).

Hillman, A. J. & Keim, G. D. (2001) Shareholder value, stakeholder management and social issues: What's the bottom line? *Strategic Management Journal*, 22, pp. 125–139.

Jamal, T. & Stronza, A. (2009) Collaboration theory and tourism practice in protected areas: Stakeholders, structuring and sustainability, *Journal of Sustainable Tourism*, 17(2), pp. 169–189.

Kernel, P. (2005) Creating and implementing a model for sustainable development in tourism enterprises, *Journal of Cleaner Production*, 13, pp. 151–164.

Kerr, S. A. (2005) What is small island sustainable development about? *Ocean & Coastal Management*, 48, pp. 503–524.

Medeiros de Araujo, L. & Bramwell, B. (2002) Partnership and regional tourism in Brazil, *Annals of Tourism Research*, 29(4), pp. 1138–1164.

Middleton, V. & Hawkins, R. (1998) *Sustainable Tourism: A Marketing Perspective* (Oxford: Butterworth-Heinemann).

Plummer, R., Telfer, D., & Hashimoto, A. (2006) The rise and fall of the Waterloo-Wellington Ale Trail: A study of collaboration within the tourism industry, *Current Issues in Tourism*, 9(3), pp. 191–205.

Puppim de Oliviera, J. A. (2003) Government responses to tourism development: Three Brazilian case studies, *Tourism Management*, 24(1), pp. 97–110.

Ruhanen, L. (2008) Stakeholder participation in tourism destination planning, *Tourism Recreation Research*, 34(3), pp. 283–294.

Scheyvens, R. & Momsen, J. H. (2008) Tourism and poverty reduction: Issues for small island states, *Tourism Geographies*, 10(1), pp. 22–41.

Scheyvens, R. & Russell, M. (2012) Tourism, land tenure and poverty alleviation in Fiji, *Tourism Geographies*, 14(1), pp. 1–25.

Selin, S. (1999) Developing a typology of sustainable tourism partnership, *Journal of Sustainable Tourism*, 7(3&4), pp. 260–273.

Selin, S. & Chavez, D. (1995) Developing a collaborative model for environmental planning and management, *Environmental Management*, 19(2), pp. 189–195.

Sommer, B. & Sommer, R. (1992) *A Practical Guide to Behavioural Research. Tools and Techniques* (New York: Oxford University Press).

Tearfund. (2002) *A Call to Responsible Global Tourism*, Report, UK. Available at http://www.tearfund.org (accessed 21 February 2010).

Tosun, C. (2001) Challenges of sustainable tourism development in the developing world: The case of Turkey, *Tourism Management*, 22, pp. 289–303.

Weaver, D. (2001) Mass tourism and alternative tourism in the Caribbean, in: D. Harrison (Eds) *Tourism and the Less Developed World: Issues and Case Studies*, pp. 161–174 (Wallingford, UK: CABI).

World Travel and Tourism Council (WTTC). (1995) *Agenda 21 for the Travel & Tourism Industry – Towards Environmentally Sustainable Development* (London: WTTC).

World Travel and Tourism Council (WTTC). (1999) *Travel & Tourism – Millennium Vision* (London: WTTC).

United Nations World Tourism Organization (UNWTO). (2005) *Definition of Sustainable Tourism*. Available at http://www.worldtourism.org (accessed 17 June 2007).

United Nations World Tourism Organization (UNWTO). (2006) *Tourism Barometer*. Available at http://www.world-tourism.org/facts/menu.html (accessed 15 February 2007).

Beyond the Beach: Balancing Environmental and Socio-cultural Sustainability in Boracay, the Philippines

LEI TIN JACKIE ONG, DONOVAN STOREY & JOHN MINNERY

ABSTRACT *Though considered the 'number one beach' of the Philippines, Boracay has been through periods where it has been considered as an example of environmentally and socially unsustainable development. In response there have been a number of programmes since the late 1990s aiming to improve Boracay's sustainability. In these, significant attention has been given to the aesthetic landscape of tourism's consumption, most especially 'the beach' and associated water quality. This paper further examines the dynamic growth of coastal tourism development and sustainability practices in Boracay, inclusive of broader socio-economic and cultural change and impact. The intent is to highlight those aspects of contemporary resort growth that need greater attention by policy makers and planners. While a number of interventions have led to improvement of the 'visual' environment, the concept of environmental sustainability needs to be expanded beyond visual cleanliness and more effort is still required on social and cultural sustainability.*

Introduction

Coastal tourism is one of the most popular and fastest-growing areas of global tourism (Orams 1999; Hall & Page 2006; Agarwal & Shaw 2007; Pforr & Dowling 2009) because 'coasts offer the best opportunities for leisure, physical activities and pleasure for all age and social groups' (Gormsen 1997: 39). To capitalize on domestic and international demand for coastal tourism, many developing countries have invested a great deal in promotional and hard infrastructure (R. A. Smith 1991; 1992; Wong 1998; Gössling 2004; Kay & Alder 2005: 39; Glavovic & Boonzaier 2007; León 2007; Murray 2007; Scheyvens & Momsen 2008). In Asia, coastal tourism has grown significantly in the past three decades and this trend is very likely to continue (Bui 2000; Wong 2003; Smith & Henderson 2008). However, despite the fact that coastal areas are popular places for recreation and tourism, the study of coastal tourism is 'limited as compared with other forms of tourism' (Agarwal & Shaw 2007: 1). Particularly notable is that most of the research which does exist is 'Western in orientation' (Smith & Henderson 2008: 271). The research reported here contributes to the small but growing literature on the impact of the rapid increase in coastal tourism in the southeast Asian context.

Coastal tourism is almost totally dependent on the attractiveness of the natural coastal environment to lure visitors. So coastal tourism poses particular sustainability demands, as it is more affected than other tourism locations by the impacts of environmental degradation (especially of water quality); congestion, in part due to the limited access points for coastal locations; problems of social integration, as migrants often are a major source of labour; and the fickleness of tourism, as tourists may eventually seek out 'another beach' (Gilbert, 1949; Franz 1985; R. A. Smith 1991; 1992; Wong 1993; 2003; Gómez & Rebollo 1995; Gormsen 1997; Murray 2007; Scheyvens & Momsen 2008). With the increase in demand for development, the pressures generated from human activities inevitably impact on coastal ecosystems. In recent years concerns have included the vulnerability of such environments to global climate change and sea-level rise (Beatley *et al.* 2002; Kay & Alder 2005; Harvey, 2006; Phillips & Jones 2006). Although many of the threats to the sustainability of coastal tourist locations can be managed, in many situations coastal tourism development has taken place rapidly and in an *ad hoc* manner, and often in the absence of long-term strategic planning (Smith 1997; Swarbrooke 1998; Kay & Alder 2005; Chua 2006).

Nevertheless, in part driven by the call for greater attention to sustainable development through national planning (Pigram 1990; Inskeep 1991; Lélé 1991; Swarbrooke 1998; Caffyn & Jobbins 2003; Brenner 2005; D'Hauteserre 2005; Bramwell & Lane 2010), growing concerns about the impacts of global climate change, and also through the efforts of international agencies such as the United Nations Environment Programme (UNEP) and the World Tourism Organisation (UNWTO), in recent years there has been much more concern given to the future sustainability of coastal tourism destinations (Ruhanen-Hunter 2006). A number of nations with coastal zones have now put integrated coastal management strategies into practice (UNEP and ICLEI 2003; Chua 2006). Nevertheless, there remain few rigorous studies addressing sustainable tourism at the implementation or operational level in developing country contexts, including Asia (Butler 1999; Bui 2000; Dodds 2007; Dodds & Butler 2009), especially beyond those understanding sustainability simply in terms of environmental conservation. This paper seeks to examine the value of an expanded concept of sustainability in understanding and responding to the dynamic growth of coastal tourism development in Boracay in the Philippines. It examines and evaluates sustainability policies and planning practices with the focus on both social and environmental aspects. The ultimate objective is to highlight how sustainability can and should be broadened away from concerns focused solely on the beach, to understand and respond more inclusively to equally pressing threats which lie 'beyond the beach'.

Boracay Island, the Philippines

Boracay is but one of 7,000-plus islands in the Philippines. It is a small tropical island of about 1,006 ha located in the Aklan province in the Western Visayas Region, 315 km south of Manila (DOT 2008a). Boracay is particularly small, being only 7 km in length and 1 km in width. The island is famous for its 'powdery' white beaches and attracted 634,363 tourists in 2008, generating 11.66 billion pesos (approximately $US250 million) for the Philippines' economy. Due to its popularity among tourists and its economic significance to the country, the Philippine government has declared the island as a national 'gem' and, as such, it is also designated as the country's 'number one beach' (DOT 2008a).

Tourism started to boom in Boracay only in the 1970s after its 'discovery' by foreign backpackers (V. L. Smith 1992; DOT 2008a). Prior to the 1970s, Boracay was a remote island with a small population of local Ati people located in several fishing villages (IFC 2005; DOT 2008a). Recent change, wrought by tourism and associated urbanization, has thus been both rapid and profound. The early impacts of coastal tourism development in Boracay are well documented by V. Smith (1990; 1992; 2001) and, to some extent, Trousdale (1999) and Carter (2004), who highlighted a number of negative environmental impacts and social dislocation, especially to the indigenous Ati people. Although the Philippines government recognized the consequences of unplanned development as early as the 1980s, and responded in the form of both the Helberg Plan in 1982 and the Boracay Development Master Plan (BDMP) in 1990, both plans are widely portrayed as largely failing to regulate the impacts of the tourism juggernaut (Trousdale 1999; IFC 2005; DENR 2008; DOT 2008a).

The 'wake-up' call to the Philippine government and tourism operators came in the form of the 1997 coliform outbreak, which was reported by the Department of Environment and Natural Resources (DENR) and later widely publicized in the national and international media. The incident and impact of the coliform crisis were reported by Trousdale (1999: 840–1):

> On June 30, 1997, the people of Boracay Island, Philippines were shaken by the news from the Department of Environment and Natural Resources that the crystal clear swimming waters off Boracay's internationally renowned Long Beach were contaminated with high levels of coliform blamed on inadequate sewage treatment. As a result, the dramatic 100% increase in tourist arrivals between 1995–96 was nearly matched by a dramatic 70% decline in the months that followed the announcement. The livelihoods of residents who had grown dependent on tourism suddenly became imperilled, billions of pesos in capital investments were threatened, and the image of Philippines' tourism suffered.

The coliform incident in 1997 not only stirred up concern among Boracay's stakeholders, it also generated world-wide interest among various international organisations, such as the Japan International Cooperation Agency (JICA), the Canadian Urban Institute (CUI) and the World Bank–International Financial Corporation (IFC), to conduct studies to help to improve the sustainability of the island. On the national and sub-national level, realizing the great potential of Boracay as a world-class coastal destination could be lost due to unregulated development, the Philippines government initiated programmes to rectify the problems.

Sustainability Initiatives and Implementation

Serious planning toward moving Boracay along a sustainable path dates back to initiatives of the Department of Tourism (DOT) as early as 1984 (Trousdale 1999; DOT 2008a). The DOT had recognized that appropriate planning was required to cater for the rising demand in visitorship to the island in the late 1980s so it formulated the Boracay Island Master Plan (BMDP) in 1990. However, this plan failed to be fully implemented due to the changes to the powers of the DOT resulting from nation-wide decentralization programmes initiated through the Local Government Code (LGC) in 1991. The responsibility for developing and managing Boracay Island was then transferred from the DOT to the Local Government Unit (LGU) (Trousdale 1999; DOT 2008a). However, the LGU was inadequately prepared to oversee the day-to-day administration of Boracay. As it lacked both human and financial resources, there was a notable failure in implementing the BMDP. Hence, in 2004 the national government appointed the Eminent Persons Group, led by the Tourism Secretary, to oversee the sustainable development of Boracay Island's tourism under Executive Order No. 377 (DOT 2008a). At the same time, the DOT was given the mandate to exercise administrative control over Boracay Island under Memorandum Order No. 214 in 2006 (Burgos 2008a; DOT, 2008a). This meant the power to manage the island shifted back from the local to the national level.

Since the DOT took back administrative control there have been a series of initiatives, including rejuvenation, greening and cleaning-up programmes. These initiatives and sustainability programmes include the following:

1. having a consultancy team appointed by the IFC (under the World Bank) to study the tourism potential of the island in 2005;
2. having a field survey and evaluation of the Environmental Infrastructure Project conducted by Normura Research Institute, Japan, a consultancy appointed by JICA in 2005;
3. creating the Boracay Solid Waste Management Master Plan through the Department of Boracay Solid Waste and Treatment in 2007;

4. providing 1.75 million pesos (approximately $US38,900) funding to the Rotary Club of Boracay for a one-year campaign against dengue fever. The project was launched after a rise in dengue cases in Aklan during the wet season in 2007;
5. providing 1.85 million pesos (approximately $US40,000) funding to the Boracay Chamber of Commerce and Industry (BCCI) for the solid waste management programme in 2007;
6. producing the Boracay Environmental Master Plan through DENR in 2008; and
7. producing the Comprehensive Land Use Plan (CLUP) by hosting workshops for stakeholders in 2008.

The sustainability programmes and projects implemented by the DOT have increasingly also been in partnership with a number of NGOs. This has included a greater focus on programmes incorporating education and information on sustainability for both visitors and employees. Programmes include the posting of notices to remind tourists to keep the environment clean or providing briefing sessions on marine life protection to scuba divers. Other programmes include training for employees focusing on the 3Rs (Recycling, Reuse, Reduce), energy-saving initiatives, and best water practices. To date, however, the focus on sustainability has been almost exclusively on the physical environment and, more specifically, the aesthetic quality of the beach. Much less effort and attention has been given to broader social and livelihood impacts of rapid growth, and the declining quality of services and infrastructure for a growing number of Filipino migrants who have come to Boracay to find jobs, social opportunity and to otherwise enjoy 'the good life'.

Research Approach and Focus

Boracay has often in the past been cited by scholars as a classic example of rapid coastal tourism development with undesirable outcomes (V. L. Smith 1990; 1992; 2001; Wong, 1998; Trousdale, 1999; Carter 2004). Although the Philippines government has made attempts to introduce policies and has initiated a series of clean-up programmes aiming to improve Boracay's environmental sustainability, the broader challenges and responses to sustainability on a rapidly developing and relatively isolated resort island have been examined less and so are not as well understood. This paper attempts to at least partially fill that gap.

The primary data for this research paper consisted of personal interviews using semi-structured questionnaires as well as site observations. Secondary data included official statistics and data from government agencies, a literature review of government policies and an archival review of news clippings and historical data on tourism development. The research thus used official data relating to environmental and social sustainability but expanded this to include government and non-government perceptions of the effectiveness of the various sustainability initiatives. It relied on official

Table 1. Key indicators for the research evaluation framework

Environmental and resource management	Socio-cultural well-being

• Building control
  – Set back from the beach
  – Environmentally sensitive design (e.g. Public green cover and architectural design)
• Nature conservation works
• Level of beach erosion
• Solid waste management
  – Waste disposal methods/waste collection programme/waste bins
• Waste water treatment management
• Water-saving practices
• Energy-saving practices
• Recycling practices
• Air pollution
• Water quality and pollution management
  – Coliforms and water pollution index
  – Sewage pollution
• Noise level
• Traffic congestion
	• Local ownership
	• Population distribution and density
	• Gap between the poor and wealthy
	• Local attitudes toward tourists
	• Local satisfaction with tourism
	• Women's status
	• Crime incidence
	• Cultural preservation and efforts in preservation of traditional values
	• Overall quality of life, such as:
	  – Housing
	  – Sanitation
	  – Potable water
	  – Energy supply
	  – Literacy rate
	  – Health services

data of environmental impacts rather than on collecting new data. The research analysis was structured around a series of widely accepted indicators of sustainability providing a framework to assess and measure programmes (UNEP & WTO 2005: 72). The key indicators used for the research are shown in Table 1.

The fieldwork, interviews and surveys were conducted from 4–22 January 2009. Of the 67 stakeholders interviewed, 44 were from the private sector (mostly private tourism operators), 11 from local NGOs, while 12 interviews were with officials from the public sector. The selection of stakeholders was based on a snowballing approach for both the government and non-governmental sectors and a sampling approach for the private sector. In this way, a wide range of opinions were canvassed and a full spectrum of stakeholders involved in understanding the drivers of change in Boracay, the key dimensions of sustainability and the nature and success of planning responses.

Environmental Sustainability Practices

The majority of businesses in Boracay showed strong awareness of the importance of having and enforcing environmental protection and resource management programmes in relation to tourism. Currently, awareness is also mediated by the presence of several international organizations working on ecosystem integrity, including CUI, IFC, JICA and Greenpeace. The particular presence of Greenpeace's programme to

Table 2. Survey findings on environmental and resource management

	Sector			
	Public ($n = 12$)	Private ($n = 44$)	NGOs ($n = 11$)	Overall ($n = 67$)
Survey questions: Our operation has successfully implemented:	Average mean score (1 = strongly disagree, 5 = strongly agree)			
A. Energy-saving methods	3.30	4.11	3.60	3.91
B. Water-saving methods	3.50	4.11	3.50	3.92
C. Waste water reduction and management	3.64	4.23	3.80	4.06
D. Reduction of water pollution	3.64	4.18	4.00	4.06
E. Prevention of beach erosion	4.00	3.77	4.00	3.85
F. Recycling practices	4.70	4.70	4.55	4.68
G. Reduction of rubbish on the beach	4.50	4.43	4.55	4.46
H. Tourism has significantly helped to improve environmental protection	4.64	4.59	4.45	4.58

Source: Fieldwork survey and interview in Boracay, Philippines, 4–22 January 2009.

promote the 'Save Boracay, Save Climate' campaign has created awareness of the dual challenges of environmental protection and climate change. In addition, civil society groups, such as the Boracay Foundation Incorporation (BFI) and the BCCI, have been active in spearheading a number of environmental programmes and workshops for business operators and community groups. The BFI is currently encouraging their members to practise conserving energy by turning electricity off when not in use; to walk in order to lessen pollution and congestion; and to not use plastic. Table 2 indicates that respondents felt that most businesses have implemented fairly broad strategies to lessen their environmental impact.

The strategies employed by government authorities in Boracay include a solid waste segregation programme, operating a centralized sewage treatment plant, and the drawing up of master plans for land use and environmental management. Almost all the stakeholders interviewed felt that Boracay has a range of environmental management programmes, and that these have generally been well implemented and that penalties are enforced.

Solid Waste Management and Rubbish Reduction

As a result of the IFC's Technical Assistance Project in 2005 and JICA's assistance from 1995, there has been more attention paid to solid waste management (SWM) on the island. Currently, SWM is implemented at the barangay (village or community) level, and each barangay has a Material Recovery Facilities (MRF) plant. Typical solid waste practices consist of 'collection; recovery of recyclables, composting of organic wastes and transfer of residuals to a holding area in Barangay Kabuilihan in Mainland Malay' (DOT 2008a: 60). The MRF plant segregates and processes about 100 m³ of waste each day generated from residential, government offices and commercial establishments (Municipality of Malay *et al.* 2008). Of the 100 m³ of waste generated, 37 percent are biodegradable, 39 percent recyclable and 24 percent are residuals.

The MRF plant project was spearheaded by the BCCI with the support from the local government in April 2008. The project has been successful across stakeholders and households and is becoming a successful model for other provinces in the Philippines. According to stakeholder interviews (Fieldwork survey and interview in Boracay, Philippines, 4–22 January 2009), SWM policy is strictly implemented in Boracay and there would be 'no collection of the garbage if the garbage is not properly segregated' between biodegradable and non-biodegradable waste. Indeed, a few well-established resorts even operate their own mini-MRF on site. Consequently, Boracay has become 'garbage-free' in the main tourist areas and beaches. The improvement in SWM is a far cry from the IFC's observation in 2005 that 'waste separation is not widely practiced and community-based solid waste management systems at the barangay level have not been initiated' (IFC 2005: 93).

Water and Energy

There were mixed responses regarding success of the implementation of water- and energy-saving methods (Table 2). Stakeholders indicated that Boracay still struggles with water and electricity shortages. Currently, water and electricity are imported from the Aklan mainland through underwater cables and a marine pipe. Business operators were more positive in their response than the public sector and NGOs regarding the success of the implementation of water-saving methods as there is a direct incentive for business operators because water saving has a great impact in their business operation cost. Thus, it is important to save water to trim costs. Measures adopted by business operators for water saving include using recycled water for watering plants and informing guests of how to save water by placing notices in the guest rooms.

Electricity outage is common in Boracay during the peak tourist season, and the majority of businesses have a generator on stand-by. Methods of conservation include having energy-saving bulbs, using 'key-tabs' and putting up notices in the guest rooms to remind guests to turn off electricity when leaving the rooms. A few of the more well-established hotels have installed solar panels.

Water Quality and Sewage Treatment

As a result of the coliform crisis in 1997, a centralized community water treatment plant was installed in Boracay to improve water quality (IFC 2005). Studies conducted by Takano (2006) and DENR in 2007 (Table 3) reveal that there has been

Table 3. Annual comparative average concentration of pH, total & faecal coliform in Boracay coastal water, 2005–7

Parameter	2005	2006	2007	DENR standard, Class SB
pH	8.2	8.1	8.08	6–8.5
Total coliform (MPN/100 ml)	114.0	632	59	1,000
Faecal coliform (MPN/ 100 ml)	50	80	31	200

Source: DENR (2008: 60).

an improvement in water quality (DENR 2008; DOT 2008a). The comparative study conducted by the DENR over a period of three years shows a decrease in the coliform levels and water pH. The water quality for the entire stretch of Boracay coastal waters reveals that physical and chemical characteristics and bacteriological analyses in terms of total and faecal coliform are within the acceptable levels (DENR 2008: 60; Takano 2006). The decrease in the coliform level is attributed to the increase in the number of sewerage system connections and the operation of the sewage treatment plant on the island. The majority of private sector businesses are now connected to the centralized waste water treatment plant operated by Boracay Water Supply System (BWSS).

Although progress has been made on water quality, poor drainage and the capacity of the sewerage systems are affected by the uncontrolled development and deforestation of the island (Lujan 2003; Burgos 2008b; DENR 2008; DOT 2008a: 61). Due to these reasons, the public sector and NGOs are less positive than the private sector about the management of waste water and water pollution issues (Table 2). In fact, a number of new and smaller businesses are known to be unconnected to the BWSS due to the limitations of the centralized treatment plant. Those establishments that are not connected 'either have their own septic tanks or are illegally discharging sewage into the storm drain or somewhere else' (DOT 2008a: 61).

The inefficiency in the water drainage system not only causes sewage outflow and water contamination but also contributes to mosquito breeding and water-borne infectious diseases. In fact, 'business owners especially the foreigners would use mineral water to brush their teeth or shower due to sense of unease in the water quality' (Takano 2006: 14). Moreover, water-borne infectious diseases were common prior to 2003 (Takano 2006: 14). Attempts have been made by the Boracay Rotary Club (an NGO) with the support of local government to fight dengue fever after an outbreak in 2007. Currently, the Department of BWSS is putting up a proposal to the national government to mitigate the drainage and sewage problems for Boracay but systems which have been established recently are already under threat of being overrun by development. Such problems are not only coastal. According to the DENR's recent inventory survey of the island (DENR 2008), which is also clearly evident to visitors, freshwater swamps, mangroves and woodland are 'highly threatened by development'

Figure 1. Beach erosion and adaptation. *Source*: Fieldwork survey and interview in Boracay, Philippines, 4–22 January 2009.

(DOT 2008a: 51). Much of the forested areas and wetlands have been cleared for building construction over recent decades, which has additionally severely impacted on wildlife (DENR 2008). Nevertheless, little action has been taken to address the issue except in the planting of more palm trees and gardening plants to green the environment.

Beach Erosion

Although a large majority of the stakeholders felt that there has been success in managing and preventing beach erosion, it remains a cause of concern on the island (see Figure 1). Beach erosion is very obvious along Bulabog Beach where the roots of coconut trees are highly exposed and even paved roads have been damaged. However, the majority of stakeholders suggested that beach erosion was not caused by the unregulated construction of seawalls and resort development literally on the beach, but by either 'natural' processes or even global warming. Most suggestions for addressing beach erosion were to build even more seawalls to protect what sand still exists. A number of business operators also 'dressed up' the roots of coconut trees in order to hold sand on beaches, protect the trees and also protect their properties from high tides.

The rapid rate of erosion has recently created enormous concern on Boracay. In 2009 the BCCI was asked by its members to act, and subsequently engaged an expert from the UNESCO National Committee on Marine Science to study the cause of erosion and the potential hazard that erosion would pose to the island and especially to tourism (Servando 2009). The study found that unchecked development and unregulated seawall construction were negatively impacting on natural tidal movements and sand deposits (Servando 2009).

Summary

Boracay continues to face a number of well-known threats to its environmental sustainability and meeting these challenges is critical to the future of its tourism industry. The recent verdict of the IFC team (2005: 83) was that 'the environmental situation in the island is extremely bad' and this view was shared by a number of stakeholders during field interviews. These stakeholders were clearly aware of the impact of development: they felt that there were 'a lot of bulldozers' and 'too much mushrooming' in the island and they would like 'less building construction' to be carried out (Fieldwork survey and interview in Boracay, Philippines, 4–22 January 2009). Even air pollution is becoming an issue with the increase in visitor arrivals and motor vehicle numbers. Approximately 65 percent of the stakeholders interviewed felt there had been an increase in traffic congestion on the island and 'it is one of the major issues in the island' (Fieldwork survey and interview in Boracay, Philippines, 4–22 January 2009). Air pollution and traffic congestion are worst along the Main Road of Boracay during the peak hours (both the morning and evening times). This is due to the narrow road width and the traffic system which operates on the 'One-Entry/Exit Policy' that allows tourists to arrive and leave the island only from the main Cagban Jetty Port through the Main Road (DOT 2008a).

The Human Dimensions of Sustainability: A Tale Less Told

The environmental threats to Boracay's tourism success and very sustainability are considerable and pose planning challenges which have been more evident in recent years. The threat to 'the beach', as the aesthetic signifier of sustainability, is clearly paramount. Nevertheless, much less has been written on the human factors of sustainable development, especially as they relate to rapid socio-cultural change and uneven economic opportunity. The remainder of this article aims to identify and evaluate these pressures, and argues that they constitute as great a threat to the island's sustainability as the more readily identifiable pressures on the environment. In so doing, the authors aim to progress a broader agenda of understanding the sustainability of small island tourism development.

With the dramatic influx of tourists to Boracay, socio-cultural change and transformation has been inevitable. In the interviews, the majority of stakeholders identified the positive socio-cultural changes from the impact of tourism development (Table 4). However, those in the private sector tended to be more positive, while community leaders and NGOs were much more critical of tourism's impacts on the socio-cultural well-being of the community. In particular, the large influx of foreign workers and immigrants competing for jobs and infrastructure facilities and services has become a source of tension. Some stakeholders also indicated their concerns about the rise in prostitution (see also Zabal 2009).

Migration and Social Change

According to official statistics, Boracay's population will grow from 16,530 persons in 2007 to 26,123 persons in 2017, an increase of 58 percent (DENR 2008;

Table 4. Survey findings on socio-cultural well-being

	Sector			
	Public (n = 12)	Private (n = 44)	NGOs (n = 11)	Overall (n = 67)
Survey questions:	Average mean score			
Tourism in this area increases:	(1 = strongly disagree, 5 = strongly agree)			
A. Number of people living in poverty	2.45	2.93	2.82	2.83
B. Gap between the poor and the wealthy	3.09	3.23	3.09	3.18
C. Women's status	3.73	3.66	3.55	3.65
D. Education opportunity	3.91	3.70	3.91	3.77
E. Awareness of local cultural tradition and values	3.36	3.61	3.00	3.48
F. Local arts and craft production	3.91	4.02	3.30	3.89
G. Historical and cultural conservation	3.55	3.48	3.50	3.49
H. Crime incidence	2.36	2.48	2.80	2.51
I. Congestion (in terms of traffic)	4.00	3.40	4.10	3.61
J. Negative impacts on local cultural values and traditions	3.09	3.02	3.27	3.08
K. Effort in preservation of traditional festivals, social values and cultural diversity	3.91	4.00	4.09	4.00
L. Overall quality of life	4.09	3.80	4.00	3.88
M. Tourism should be developed further in this area	4.09	3.89	3.73	3.89

Source: Fieldwork survey and interview in Boracay, Philippines, 4–22 January 2009.

DOT 2008a). The high population growth is caused by natural growth and tourism development, typically the latter, which has accelerated urbanization and economic activity and attracted large numbers of people from other parts of the Philippines to seek jobs in the island (DOT 2008a). Although official statistics state that migrants constitute about 24 percent of the total population of Boracay (DOT 2008a), a more commonly held position is that migrant workers make up as much as 40 percent of the island's population (IFC 2005: 21). The majority of 'new' migrants are Muslims from Mindanao in the southern Philippines, which has experienced a protracted civil and military conflict. Migrant workers typically operate outriggers, work as vendors (mostly in the informal sector) and act as construction workers. Despite their critical role in the island's economy, migrants are often referred to as the 'number one' social problem by community leaders (Fieldwork survey and interview in Boracay, Philippines, 4–22 January 2009). There has even been a petition to the LGU to identify the real size of the migrant population working and living on Boracay, as well as calls for limits to be placed on future migration.

Competition for employment remains the greatest single source of tension. In recent years employment has become highly competitive and many migrants come to Boracay with experience in tourism-related businesses. Migration has also accelerated population growth, with family members joining initial migrants over time, thus accelerating the pressures on basic services, such as water, housing, health, education and other social services. Land use has also come under considerable pressure in any areas left outside of tourist-related activities. Indeed, land for housing and settlement is the current source of much conflict both within 'domestic' populations and between locals, investors and tourists, who find themselves increasingly in competition for the limited land resources of the island (DOT 2008a: 90). In interviews, long-term residents tended to be less tactful; migrants were blamed for deteriorating environmental conditions as they 'lack sanitary awareness'; 'they don't pay tax'; 'they earn money and leave' and so on. Several respondents suggested 'outsiders' should be allowed to operate a business on the island only if they paid a hefty deposit (Fieldwork survey and interview in Boracay, Philippines, 4–22 January 2009).

Approximately 70 percent of the stakeholders in the survey felt that tourism has helped to improve women's status in Boracay. Those in private business and in the public sector were more positive about women's status than the NGO sector. They claimed that tourism has provided more job opportunities for women and thus they are more independent economically. Moreover, they felt that there were equal opportunities for women in society as 'there are many women in the island holding managerial posts in the private sector and civil society organizations. Those who were more negative about women's status felt that there is 'an increase in the number of woman-related illnesses' and the 'rise in prostitution' (Fieldwork survey and interview in Boracay, Philippines, 4–22 January 2009) on the island despite a ban on prostitution in 2003 (Aguirre 2003; Zabal 2009). Again though, prostitution was blamed on migrants bringing in the 'sex trade' to take advantage of tourism. In addition, it was claimed that many women are still subjected to 'family violence' at home (Fieldwork survey and interview in Boracay, Philippines, 4–22 January 2009).

There is a clear perception of increasing levels of crime and of an increased presence of police and coast guards. Respondents felt that most crime in Boracay involved youth, either as victims of the sex trade or human trafficking or as perpetrators of petty theft, often as part of organized crime networks. In recent years this has led to the Boracay Social Welfare Department (BSWD), together with police and business operators, working with EPCAT (End Child Prostitution Pornography and Trafficking). Night curfews are in place for children for many beach areas at night. Moreover, recent public campaigns have targeted prevention of child-sex tourism. NGOs, such as the Kiwanis Club of Boracay, have additionally been involved in running arts courses for the island's growing number of street children.

Although crime rates are, in practice, comparatively low in Boracay, declining perceptions of safety are reported. Many interviewees felt 'less safe now as compared to the past' (Fieldwork survey and interview in Boracay, Philippines, 4–22 January 2009). One interviewee noted that 'there were fewer people in the past and everyone knew everyone, but with more people now we have to be careful at night as we don't know a lot of the new people' (Fieldwork survey and interview in Boracay, Philippines, 4–22 January 2009). The change in the social fabric from a simple island lifestyle around a small community to a commercialized tourist destination has resulted in a more heterogeneous population and a greater level of unfamiliarity and, hence, reduced perceptions of safety.

Inequality amid Plenty

Increasing social tension between 'local' and 'migrant' populations undoubtedly reflects the growing inequality evident on the island. While Boracay's reputation for wealth and beauty has attracted many, the benefits of tourism have been unevenly felt. While the majority of respondents felt that livelihood opportunities remain, poverty had resulted from problems of unaffordability; 'although there are jobs available for the poor and uneducated ones, the prices of commodities have gone up' (Fieldwork survey and interview in Boracay, Philippines, 4–22 January 2009). Thus, in real terms, poverty is becoming more widespread. This has led to an increase in practices of begging, though respondents claimed that 'the beggars are from other islands' (Fieldwork survey and interview in Boracay, Philippines, 4–22 January 2009).

More critical were the views of Boracaynons who argued that increasingly those who were benefiting from the tourism pie were the 'resort owners' and 'investors from outside' who are 'not Boracay originals' (Fieldwork survey and interview in Boracay, Philippines, 4–22 January 2009). In particular, Boracay's growth was seen as disadvantaging and further marginalizing native Ati people. As one NGO commented 'the natives are not benefitting as they are mainly employed as beach cleaners and have no land title'. Those concerned about quality of life in Boracay argued that life 'is not about quantity but about values' (Fieldwork survey and interview in Boracay, Philippines, 4–22 January 2009). They felt that there was 'too much entertainment around the islands' and 'while the rest of the Boracaynons are improving their life, the small handful of minority group – the native people – their life is still living in poor conditions' (Fieldwork survey and interview in Boracay, Philippines, 4–22 January 2009).

Land prices in Boracay have sky-rocketed in recent decades. From about $US1 per m^2 in 1978 (V. L. Smith 1992), land values escalated to about $US1,100 per m^2 in 2009 (Boracay Business Centre 2009). Moreover, the average rate of increase for the three barangays in Boracay between 1995 and 2005 was 333 percent for coastal areas and 600 per cent for housing districts (Takano 2006: 15). This rapid increase in land prices is driven by a shortage of land and the development of higher density development. Housing prices have risen in concert – beyond the scope of many locals' and migrant workers' financial capacities. While sanitation and water provision have improved in recent years, the great majority of households are not connected to these systems due to the cost of supply and use.

With the increase in demand for prime land for tourism-related development, land shortages and constraints for further development imply that the problem of affordable housing will be exacerbated in future. Currently 53 percent of households in Boracay do not have ownership of the lots they occupy and the majority of them are living in temporary housing units (DOT 2008a). In response, local authorities have proposed a plan to resettle the population to the mainland in the CLUP (DOT 2008b). This plan, if materialized, will have great socio-economic and cultural impact on the local Boracaynians, particularly the Ati minority.

Dislocation and Relocation: Ati and Tourism

Stakeholders in the interviews tended to associate Boracay's traditional culture and its conservation with the Ati-Atihan Festival that takes placed in January each year and the 'Pina' textile production from the Aklan Province or other provinces in the Philippines. Stakeholders who provided positive responses about the awareness of cultural traditions and values cited the 'Ati minority' and 'the celebration of the Ati-Atihan' (Fieldwork survey and interview in Boracay, Philippines, 4–22 January 2009). Those who felt negative about the awareness of cultural tradition and values felt that Boracay has 'no tradition and culture' as 'the island was very remote thirty years ago' and thus 'culture never stays in Boracay' (Fieldwork survey and interview in Boracay, Philippines, 4–22 January 2009). In addition, these stakeholders claimed that the island has been branded as a 'liberated culture' as 'everything on the island is about business' and the wide range of arts and craft products in Boracay 'are not outputs from local Boracaynons but elsewhere from Philippines or from Indonesia' (Fieldwork survey and interview in Boracay, Philippines, 4–22 January 2009).

Although the cultural image of Boracay appears to be 'weak' (DOT 2008a: 11), a high percentage of the stakeholders (approximately 83%, see also Table 4) felt that tourism has helped to preserve traditional festivals, social values and cultural diversity. Still, it is arguable whether indigenous populations have benefited from commercialization and, indeed, the commodification of their culture. The problem was expressed eloquently in one interview:

> In the past, the Atis depended on food from nature, the root, the plants and vegetables. But now with tourism development, nature is taken by tourism. Forest is taken for development or protected. Ati can no longer fish at Bulabag at certain times of year. There were times, we had to beg milk to save the babies. There is also fear of danger of eviction to other islands. They (the government) have given designated land here but only words that the land would be given. No black and white given yet. However, promise still remains a promise... They now have water and electricity but still use the well water for doing washing as

water and electricity are expensive for them. Some even have television. The real problem to the native is the land.

Conclusions

To date there has been an *ad hoc* approach to sustainably managing coastal tourism development in Boracay, primarily orientated to maintaining the aesthetic appeal of the beach and coastal area. Increasing evidence is to be found of the incidence and impacts of traffic congestion, air pollution, water pollution, beach erosion and deforestation. While programmes relating to 'cleaning' the environment are widely implemented and seen as largely successful, concepts of sustainability will clearly need to be expanded beyond that of visual cleanliness.

This research has shown that greater attention also needs to be given to the impacts of coastal tourism on social and cultural sustainability. The experience of Boracay provides lessons that are applicable to other tourism-dependent communities. Many concerns were identified through the current research. Of particular note is the growing tension between the economic development which tourism drives and the livelihoods of local residents. In the case of Boracay the problems are compounded by the presence of the original island inhabitants. In-migration of people attracted by the opportunities offered by tourism can create tensions between the new arrivals and local inhabitants, as well as increased demands on physical and social infrastructure. There is also a 'dark side' to the opportunities offered through increased tourism, which can include prostitution, exploitation of children and women and increased crime.

In Boracay there have been a number of initiatives taken that attempt to address these social and cultural problems but with very variable degrees of success. The responses from people interviewed for the research seem to indicate that there are both structural and specific problems to be addressed. The structural problems include the rapid rise in land, housing and other costs concomitant with increased population and economic activities competing for access to a limited supply of land. These are problems faced in any rapidly growing urban area, but they are exacerbated in coastal tourism areas through the concentration of human activity on 'the beach' as well as the socio-cultural differences between tourists, migrants and the permanent population. On the other hand, tourism seems to have mainly a positive impact on the status of women in areas like Boracay. The more specific issues flow from the loss of a sense of community with increased population and the retention of more than a superficial form of cultural practice.

The shift in management power of the island from the local to the national level demonstrates that in order to manage tourism development more sustainably and effectively, 'intervention and regulation by the state' is essential (Bramwell & Lane, 2010: 3) as the state has the human capacity, financial resources and power which the local authority might be lacking. In addition, the sustainability of coastal tourism development depends on partnership, co-operation and co-ordination among the various key stakeholders in monitoring the outcome of tourism operations and practices (Trousdale 1999; McAlpine & Birnie 2005; Beritelli *et al.* 2007). The partnerships among the state and the key stakeholders at different levels of tourism development are crucial as sustainable tourism has been viewed increasingly as needing an 'adaptive management' tool to 'enhance its resilience to disturbance rather than to achieve stability' (Farrell & Twining-Ward 2005 in Lu & Nepal 2009: 13). Thus, besides implementing environmental regulations or sustainability policies, government should consider working more closely with a broad range of stakeholders. In many instances, NGOs play an important role in advancing the implementation of sustainability programmes and creating awareness and educating the public and policy makers (Strange & Baley 2008: 119).

There is a high level of commitment from NGOs together with some of the established hotel operators for the implementation of sustainability programmes set out by the government or by NGOs. The majority of the business stakeholders in Boracay are well aware of the concept of sustainable tourism development in relation to small island environments and are making efforts to operationalize sustainable tourism practices. They do, however, place greater emphasis on environmental sustainability rather than social or cultural sustainability. In addition, there is a lack of effort by smaller firms which have limited financial resources, and some of the bigger resorts which have links with the government, in addressing both facets of sustainability. Thus, more incentives and knowledge assistance will need to be provided for the smaller firms by the tourism-related organizations or authorities as these firms have strong direct linkages with the local economy and livelihoods (Bui 2000).

'Achieving sustainability takes time' (Alampay 2005: 20) and tourism policy makers need to recognize there is no short-cut approach to the sustainability of Boracay's tourism by adopting *ad hoc* 'problem-avoiding' approaches (Smith & Eadington 1992; Gunn 1994; Murphy 1994 in Bui 2000: 242). It requires commitment and participation from all levels of stakeholders, and the community (Butler 1999), to achieve an 'absolute sustainability' (Gössling *et al.* 2009: 6). This also ultimately requires moving the sustainability of Boracay's tourism 'beyond the beach'.

References

Agarwal, S. & Shaw, G. (2007) Managing coastal tourism resorts: A global perspective, in: S. Agarwal & G. Shaw (Eds) *Managing Coastal Tourism Resorts: A Global Perspective*, pp. 1–18 (Clevedon and Buffalo: Channel View Publications).
Aguirre, J. A. (2003) Sex trade ban working in reverse for Boracay, *The Daily Tribune*, 1 December 2003. Available at http://trafficking.org.ph/v5/index.php?option=com_content&task=view&id=509&Itemid=56 (accessed 30 September 2008).
Alampay, R. B. A. (2005) The challenge of sustainable tourism development in the Philippines, in: R. B. A. Alampay (Ed.) *Sustainable Tourism: Challenges for the Philippines*, pp. 1–22 (Makati

City: Philippine APEC Study Center Network and the Phillippine Institute for Development Studies).
Beatley, T., Brower, D. J. & Schwab, A. (2002) *An Introduction to Coastal Zone Management* (Washington, D.C.: Island Press).
Beritelli, P., Bieger, T. & Laesser, C. (2007) Destination governance: Using corporate governance theories as a foundation for effective destination management, *Journal of Travel Research*, 46(1), pp. 96–107.
Boracay Business Centre (2009) *Boracay Business Centre: Boracay Island Real Estate*. Available at http://www.boracayinfo.com/ (accessed 31 March 2009).
Bramwell, B. & Lane, B. (2010) Sustainable tourism and the evolving roles of government planning, *Journal of Sustainable Tourism*, 18(1), pp. 1–5.
Brenner, L. (2005) State-planned tourism destinations: The case of Huatulco, Mexico, *Tourism Geographies*, 7(2), pp. 138–164.
Bui, T. T. (2000) Tourism dynamics and sustainable tourism development – Principles and implications in Southeast Asia, Doctoral dissertation, Nanyang Technological University, Singapore.
Burgos N. P. (2008a) Gov't appoints new Boracay czar, *The News Today Online*, 13 February. Available at http://www.thenewstoday.info/2008/02/13/govt.appoints.new.boracay.czar.html (assessed 31 August 2008).
Burgos, N. P. (2008b) Flooding threatens to sink tourism in Boracay, Inquirer.net, 7 January. Available at http://services.inquirer.net/print/print.php?article_id=20080107-110795 (accessed 31 March 2008).
Butler (1999) Sustainable tourism: A state-of-the-art review, *Tourism Geographies*, 1(1), pp. 7–25.
Caffyn, A. & Jobbins, G. (2003) Governance capacity and stakeholder interactions in the development and management of coastal tourism: Examples from Morocco and Tunisia, *Journal of Sustainable Tourism*, 11(2/3), pp. 224–245.
Carter, R. W. (2004) Implications of sporadic tourism growth: Extrapolation from the case of Borocay Island, The Philippines, *Asia Pacific Journal of Tourism Research*, 9(4), pp. 382–404.
Chua, T. (2006) *The Dynamics of Integrated Coastal Management: Practical Applications in the Sustainable Coastal Development in East-Asia* (Quezon City: Partnerships in Environmental Management for the Seas of East Asia (PEMSEA)).
DENR (2008) *Borocay Environmental Master Plan (BEMP)* (Boracay, Philippines: Department of Environment and Natural Resources).
D'Hauteserre, A. (2005) Tourism, development and sustainability in Monaco: Comparing discourses and practices, *Tourism Geographies*, 7(3), pp. 290–312.
Dodds, R. (2007) Sustainable tourism and policy implementation: Lessons from the case of Calviá, Spain, *Current Issues in Tourism*, 10(4), pp. 296–322.
Dodds, R. & Butler, R. W. (2009) Inaction more than action: Barriers to the implementation of sustainable tourism policies, in: S. Gössling; M. C. Hall & D. B. E. Weaver (Eds) *Sustainable Tourism Futures: Perspectives on Systems, Restructuring and Innovations*, pp. 43–57 (New York: Routledge).
DOT (2008a) *Boracay Island Comprehensive Land Use Planning (CLUP): Volume I* (Boracay, Philippines: Department of Tourism).
DOT (2008b) *Boracay Island Comprehensive Land Use Planning (CLUP): Volume II* (Boracay, Philippines: Department of Tourism).
Farrell, B. & Twining-Ward, L. (2005) Seven steps towards sustainability: Tourism in the context of new knowledge, *Journal of Sustainable Tourism*, 13(2), pp. 109–122.
Franz, J. C. (1985) Pattaya-Penang-Bali: Asia's leading beach resorts (Part-two), *Tourism Recreation Research*, 10(1), pp. 25–30.
Gilbert, E. W. (1949) The growth of Brighton, *The Geographical Journal*, 114(1), pp. 30–52.
Glavovic, B. C. & Boonzaier S. (2007) Confronting coastal poverty: building sustainable coastal livelihoods in South Africa, *Ocean & Coastal Management*, 50(1–2), pp. 1–23.

Gómez, M. J. M. & Rebollo, F. V. (1995) Coastal areas: Process, typologies and prospects, in: A. Montanri & A. M. Williams (Eds) *European Tourism: Regions, Spaces and Restructuring*, pp. 111–126 (Chichester: John Wiley & Son).

Gormsen, E. (1997) The impact of tourism on coastal areas, *GeoJournal*, 42(1), pp. 39–54.

Gössling, S. E. (2004) *Tourism and Development in Tropical Islands* (Cheltenham: Edward Elgar).

Gössling, S., Hall, C. & Weaver, D. (2009) Sustainable tourism future, in: S. Gössling, M. C. Hall & D. B. E. Weaver (Eds) *Sustainable Tourism Futures: Perspectives on Systems, Restructuring and Innovations*, pp. 1–15 (New York: Routledge).

Gunn, C. A. (1994) *Tourism Planning: Basic Concepts, Cases*, 3rd ed. (Washington, D.C.: Taylor & Francis).

Hall, C. M. & Page, S. J. (2006) *The Geography of Tourism and Recreation: Environment, Place, and Space* (New York: Routledge).

Harvey, N. (2006) *Global Change and Integrated Coastal Management: The Asia–Pacific Region* (Dordrecht, The Netherlands: Springer-Verlag).

IFC (2005) *Assessment/Identification of Private Investment Opportunities in the Island of Boracay/Philippines* (Philippines: International Financial Corporation).

Inskeep, E. (1991) *Tourism Planning: An Integrated and Sustainable Development Approach* (New York: Van Nostrand Reinhold).

Kay, R. & Alder, J. (2005) *Coastal Planning and Management* (London: Taylor & Francis).

Lélé, S. M. (1991) Sustainable development: A critical review, *World Development*, 19(6), pp. 607–621.

León, Y. M. (2007) The impact of tourism on rural livelihoods in the Dominican Republic's coastal areas, *Journal of Development Studies*, 43(2), pp. 340–359.

Lu, J. & Nepal, S. K. (2009 Sustainable tourism research: an analysis of papers published in the *Journal of Sustainable Tourism*, *Journal of Sustainable Tourism*, 17(1), pp. 5–16.

Lujan, N. (2003) *Boracay's road to ruin*, Philippine Centre for Investigative Journalism, 20–21 January. Available at http://www.pcij.org/stories/print/boracay.html (accessed 1 July 2008).

McAlpine, P. & Birnine, A. (2005) Is there a correct way of establishing sustainability indicators? The case of sustainability indicator development on the island of Guernsey, *Local Environment*, 10(3), pp. 243–257.

Municipality of Malay, National Solid Waste Management Commission and JICA (2008) *Master Plan on Solid Waste Management for Boracay Island and Malay, 2007* (Philippines: Nippon Koei Corporation).

Murphy, P. E. (1994) Tourism and sustainable development, in: W. Theobald (Ed.) *Global Tourism: The Next Decade*, pp. 274–290 (Oxford: Butterworth-Heinemann Ltd).

Murray, G. (2007) Constructing paradise: the impacts of big tourism in the Mexican coastal zone, *Coastal Management*, 35(2), pp. 339–355.

Orams, M. (1999) *Marine Tourism: Development, Impacts and Management* (New York: Routledge).

Pforr, C. & Dowling, R. (2009) Coastal tourism development: Planning and managing growth, in: R. Dowling & C. PFORR (Eds) *Coastal Tourism Development*, pp. 3–13 (New York: Cognizant Communication Corporation).

Phillips, M. R. & Jones, A. L. (2006) Erosion and tourism infrastructure in the coastal zone: Problems, consequences and management, *Tourism Management*, 27(3), pp. 517–524.

Pigram, J. J. (1990) Sustainable tourism – policy considerations, *Journal of Tourism Studies*, 1(2), pp. 2–9.

Ruhanen-Hunter, L. M. (2006) Sustainable tourism planning: An analysis of Queensland local tourism destinations, Doctoral dissertation, University of Queensland, Australia.

Scheyvens, R. & Momsen, J. H. (2008) Tourism and poverty reduction: issues for small island states, *Tourism Geographies*, 10(1), pp. 22–41.

Servando, K. (2009) Boracay threatened by erosions, *Newsbreak Online*, 19 March 2009. Available at http://www.newsbreak.ph/2009/03/18/boracay-threatened-by-erosions/ (accessed 12 June 2009).

Smith, R. A. (1991) Beach resorts: A model of development evolution, *Landscape and Urban Planning*, 21(3), pp. 189–210.

Smith, R. A. (1992) Conflicting trends of beach resort development: a Malaysian case, *Coastal Management*, 20, pp. 167–187.

Smith, R. A. (1997) The environment and its role in sustainable tourism – lessons from Pattaya and Pahang, in: *1st International Conference on Sustainable Tourism Development*, May 22–23, Hue City, Vietnam, pp. 37–43 (Singapore: Nanyang Technological University).

Smith, R. A. & Henderson, J. C. (2008) Integrated beach resorts, informal tourism commerce and the 2004 tsunami: Laguna Phuket in Thailand, *International Journal of Tourism Research*, 10(3), pp. 271–282.

Smith, V. L. (1990) Geographical implications of 'Drifter' tourism Boracay, Philippines, *Tourism Recreation Research*, 15(1), pp. 34–42.

Smith, V. L. (1992) Boracay, Phillippines: a case study in 'Alternative' tourism, in: V. L. Smith & W. R. Eadington (Eds) *Tourism Alternatives: Potentials and Problems in the Development of Tourism*, pp. 135–157 (Philadelphia: University of Pennsylvania Press).

Smith, V. L. (2001) Power and ethnicity in 'Paradise' Boracay, Phillippines, in: V. L. Smith & M. Brent (Eds) *Hosts and Guests Revisited: Tourism Issues of the 21st Century*, pp. 141–152 (USA: Cognizant Communication Corporation).

Smith, V. L. & Eadington, W. R. (1992) *Tourism Alternatives: Potentials and Problems in the Development of Tourism* (Philadelphia: University of Pennsylvania Press).

Strange, T. & Bayley, A. (2008) *Sustainable Development: Linking Economy, Society, Environment* (Paris: OECD).

Swarbrooke, J. (1998) *Sustainable Tourism Management* (UK: CABI Publishing).

Takano, M. (2006) *Boracay Environmental Infrastructure Project*. Available at http://www.jica.go.jp/english/operations/evaluation/oda_loan/post/2006/pdf/project16_full.pdf (accessed 20 April 2008).

Trousdale, W. J. (1999) Governance in context: Boracay Island, Philippines, *Annals of Tourism Research*, 26(4), pp. 840–867.

UNEP & ICLEI (2003) *Tourism and Local Agenda 21: The Role of Local Authorities in Sustainable Tourism* (Paris: UNEP).

UNEP & WTO (2005) *Making Tourism More Sustainable: A Guide for Policy Makers* (Paris: United Nations Environment Programme; Madrid: World Tourism Organisation).

Wong, P. P. (1993) Island tourism development in Peninsular Malaysia: environmental perspective, in: P. P. Wong (Ed.) *Tourism vs. Environment: the Case for Coastal Areas*, pp. 83–98 (Dordrecht: Kluwer Academic).

Wong, P. P. (1998) Coastal tourism development in Southeast Asia: relevance and lessons for coastal zone management, *Ocean & Coastal Management*, 38, pp. 89–109.

Wong, P. P. (2003) Tourism development in Asia: patterns, issues, and prospects, in: L. S. Chia (Ed.) *Southeast Asia Transformed: A Geography of Change*, pp. 409–442 (Singapore: Institute of Southeast Asian Studies).

Zabal, B. R. B. (2009) Sex workers also coming in droves to Boracay, *Manila Bulletin*, 15 March. Available at http://www.mb.com.ph/node/199042 (assessed 5 May 2009).

Community sustainability and resilience: similarities, differences and indicators

Alan A. Lew, Pin T. Ng, Chin-cheng (Nickel) Ni and Tsung-chiung (Emily) Wu

ABSTRACT
Sustainability has been a core conceptual framework for community development since the approach was popularized in 1987, although in its essence it reflects a long history of environmental conservation reactions to industrialization. Resilience, as a framework for understanding and approaching community development, emerged more gradually out of ecological studies in the 1980s, but has only recently, since the mid-2000s, emerged as a focus of public interest as a way of responding and adapting to the planet's growing anthropogenic changes. For many, sustainability and resilience are slightly nuanced perspectives on the same phenomenon. For others, however, there are distinct differences between them, with sustainability's conservation goals being in opposition to the adaptation goals of resilience. Two major reasons for these confusions are (1) both concepts are defined and used in many different ways to achieve a variety of political goals that may not reflect their core definitions, and (2) both concepts share similar goals and some common approaches, such as a focus on climate change and seeking a balance between humans and nature. Returning to the core definitions of conservation and adaptation helps to clarify their similarities and differences, as well as to articulate indicators for understanding how each applies to community tourism development. Indicators from research in rural Taiwan tourism communities were therefore based on responses to the questions: What does the community want to conserve and how do they want to do it (sustainability)? What do they want to change and how do they want to do it (resilience)? Preliminary results suggest that the new ideal community is the one that is both sustainable and resilient.

摘要
可持续性概念自从1987年流行以来一直是社区发展的核心概念框架，尽管它实质上反映了长期以来环境保护对工业化的回应。然而，恢复力作为一个理解和研究社区发展的研究框架，在八十年代逐渐从生态研究中脱胎而出，但是直到最近，也就是2000年代中期（2005年左右），开始作为一种响应与适应这个地球日益加剧的人类活动变化的方法，而成为公众利益的焦点。对很多人来说，可持续性和恢复力只是对同一现象有细微差别的研究视角；但是，对另一些人来说，它们之间又存在明显的不同，可持续性的目标是保护，而恢复力的目标是适应。这些混淆之所以存在的两个主要原因是：(1) 这两个概念都以很多不同的方式界定与使用，以达到形式各样的政治目标，但是这些政治目标可能并未反映它们的核心定义；(2) 这两个概念有共同的类似目标和一些共同的研究方法，比如关注气候变化和寻求人与自然的平衡。回归这两个概念保护与适应的核心内涵有助于理解它们的相似与差异之处，同时也有助于阐明它们各自适用于社区旅游发展的指标。台湾乡村旅游社区发展的指标是基于对以下问题的回应：社区想保护什么?可持续性?和社区想改变什么?恢复力?。初步的结果表明，新的理想社区是那种既可持续又具恢复力的社区。

Introduction

Sustainable development has been a popular conceptual framework since the World Commission on Environment and Development (WCED) issued its report, *Our Common Future*, to the United Nations in 1987 (Brundtland, 1987; Hardy, Beeton, & Pearson, 2002). Also known as the *Brundtland Report*, its goal was to define a global agenda to address the deterioration of natural and social environments that has been accelerating since the industrial revolution (Butler, 1998; Hall, Gossling, & Scott, 2015; Hall & Lew, 2009). Although never mentioned in the 1987 report, tourism interests were quick to adopt the idea of sustainable tourism as the application of sustainable development to tourism activities (Hall & Lew, 1998).

Sustainable development, or sustainability, continues to maintain a dominant role as the preferred development paradigm for most policy and program actions taken by governments, communities, and businesses today (Anderies, Folke, Walker, & Ostrom, 2013). This has come, at least in part, from the idealistic nature of the goals for sustainability in creating a better world than what we have now. However, with the growing threats of anthropogenic changes (Steffen, Crutzen, & McNeill, 2007; Walker & Salt, 2006; Zalasiewicz, Williams, Steffen, & Crutzen, 2010), especially those that are weather and climate related, there are some doubts that sustainability alone is an effective response (Allison et al., 2009; Fiksel, 2006; Leichenko, O'Brien, & Solecki, 2010). No matter how sustainable an individual person, community, or a single country is, global greenhouse gases continue to increase at an unabated rate, the world's flora and fauna biodiversity continues to decrease, and human population growth and migration will be a continuing challenge for decades to come, accompanied by income and social inequities (Davidson, 2010; World Economic Forum, 2015). Despite achieving the greatest advances in technology and science that humankind has known, global governance under the sustainability paradigm does not appear to be capable of fully addressing these issues, which are only likely to intensify with major climate shifts and increasing globalization on the horizon.

With these concerns in mind, interest in social and community resilience as an alternative development model has grown rapidly since the mid-2000s. In general, resilience thinking emphasizes adaptation to change instead of sustainability's emphasis of conservation and mitigation. The relationship between sustainability and resilience approaches, however, has been a confusing one that has not been made clearer with the recent proliferation of papers on resilience topics (Meetow & Newell, 2015). This research commentary presents a framework for clarifying the similarities and differences between sustainability and resilience by focusing on their core differences of conservation and adaptation. Based on these definitions, indicators of each at the community development scale are presented, derived from research into tourism-oriented communities in rural Taiwan.

The framework builds on the notion that sustainability and resilience are distinct conceptual paradigms (Anderies et al., 2013; Jeuch & Michelson, 2011; McLellan, Zhang, Farzaneh, Utama, & Ishihara, 2012; Prasad et al., 2009; Tobin, 1999). Derissen, Quaas, and Baumgärtner (2011) define this difference as one where sustainability mitigates change by maintaining resources above normative safe levels, whereas a resilience approach adapts to change by building capacities to return to a desired state following a disruption. Even within resilience theory, we hold that evolutionary resilience (the idea that change is a constant and stability is an illusion) provides the most compelling ontological model of the role of change in community and global contexts (Davoudi, 2012; Simmie & Martin, 2010). Evidence from the literature, however, indicates that many researchers do not agree that sustainability and resilience are two different perspectives. Instead, it is common to hold that resilience and sustainability are essentially the same (Adger, 2003; Edwards, 2009; Farrell & Twining-Ward, 2005), or that resilience is a key indicator of sustainability (Magis, 2013; Schianetz & Kavanagh, 2008; Walker & Salt, 2006), or that sustainability is the broad social goal and resilience is how it can be implemented (Anderies et al., 2013; Fiksel, 2006).

Confusing sustainability and resilience

The confusion between sustainability and resilience has two basic sources. The first is the weak, and sometimes even sloppy, conceptualizations and definitions that researchers often use for the two terms. Sustainability is sometimes used in only the narrowest dictionary definition of the word 'sustain,' meaning to maintain a status quo and to not disappear (Sayer & Campbell, 2004, pp. 38–40). This definition tends to be more common among popular business interests (not scholars) who seek to maintain a healthy economy, and for whom the environmental origins of sustainable development are secondary, at best (Carroll, 2011; Wilson, 2012).

At the opposite extreme is the tendency to define sustainability as including every possible 'good' condition available to human societies and their preferred natural environments. This definition emerges from the *Brundtland Report*'s widely quoted definition of sustainable development as development that ensures the well-being of people both today and in future generations (Brundtland 1987: Chapter 2, Section 1). Well-being is a very broad concept and one person's well-being can be very different from another's. The approach is more common among environmental, social, and political interest groups, and may include reducing carbon use, conserving cultural heritage, ensuring gender equity, creating livable wage jobs, ensuring an open government, safeguarding religious freedom, supporting performing arts, alleviating poverty, and much more. Such an all-encompassing approach to sustainability is similar to the comprehensive urban planning model, which became popular in the early 1900s with Daniel Burnham's plan for Chicago (Smith, 2006). That approach, however, has been criticized by planners for being based on the unrealistic assumptions of synoptic (all seeing) and perfect knowledge, resulting in flawed and unrealizable policies and plans (Friedmann, 1971).

Proponents of resilience sometimes define sustainability within the framework of resilience. Redman (2014), for example, equates sustainability with adaptation and the qualities of incremental change, responding to shock and maintaining previous order. Resilience, on the other hand, is equated to transformation and the qualities of major change, anticipatory pre-action, and creating a new and open-ended order. These definitions are more closely aligned with resilience responses to slow-change variables and fast-change variables, and reflects a common approach of making slow change synonymous with sustainability (Walker, Carpenter, Rockstrom, Crépin, & Peterson, 2012).

Similar sustainability definitional issues arise in tourism studies. For example, an all-encompassing approach to sustainable tourism is the Global Sustainable Tourism Council's criteria for sustainable tourism destination development (GSTC, 2013). This is typical of many UN documents that need to address the special interests of the widest possible global constituencies, and in the process can become too general for practical implementation. While this approach to sustainability might be good comprehensive planning and might even result in good community development, it goes beyond the original environmentalist values of sustainable development that were at the core of *Our Common Future* in 1987.

The primary goal of *Our Common Future* was to reinforce a clear environmental ethic and a strong conservation approach that was meant to both protect existing resources, as well restore selected past resources and ecological systems. This is sometimes referred to as environmental sustainability. What made this commission different from past conservation movements was the recognition that protecting the environment could not be successful without a strong human development component. The commission, therefore, sought to integrate the goals of development activists (mostly from the global south) with those of environmental activists (mostly from the global north).

By deconstructing the origins of sustainable development, we suggest that the concept is best defined in terms of its core goals of protecting and maintaining natural and cultural resources for the future and mitigating undesirable change. This is a much more narrow definition of sustainable development than the comprehensive planning approach, but it is widely recognized through sustainability efforts to reduce the consumption of carbon and other natural resources, increase biodiversity, protect tangible heritage artifacts, and revitalize intangible cultural traditions. A good example of sustainable tourism that is defined in terms that are more true to the original core definition of sustainable development is the European Commission's (2013) *European Tourism Indicators System for Sustainable Destination Management*.

Sustainability that adheres to *Our Common Future*'s definition of conservation values is less confusing than vague dictionary definitions and idealistic all-encompassing definitions. Both of these latter definitions frequently include elements of resilience thinking and, therefore, lead to blurred understandings of both sustainability and resilience.

Resilience has its conceptual origins in physics, ecology, and disaster management (Davidson, 2010). It is about adaptation, including building human resource capacities to change in efficient ways, creating learning institutions that can address changing circumstances while maintaining core values, understanding feedback loops in dynamic social and environmental systems, and generally encouraging flexibility, creativity, and innovation in the culture of a community. Like sustainability, understandings of resilience can

Table 1. Similarities between sustainability and resilience.

Assumptions	Harmony between human society and the natural environment is possible
Research focus	Social and ecological systems; climate change impacts; globalization; community development
Methods	Climate change policies and actions, especially governance; education and learning as implementation tools
Goals	System survivability, security and well-being (social and biodiversity); sense of place and belonging (heritage)

Source: Authors

sometimes be confused by the use of simplified dictionary definitions of resilience. And as with sustainability, this is most often found among business interests, although 'business resilience' is a distinct subfield of resilience research that has its own evolving conceptual basis (Goble, Fields, & Cocchiara, 2002). Social ecologists, on the other hand, approach resilience from a dynamic adaptive systems perspective, applying quantitative models that attempt to mimic real-world feedback loops to monitor change in key system variables (Anderies et al., 2013; Fiksel, 2006; Jeuch & Michelson, 2011; Schianetz & Kavanaugh, 2008; Strickland-Munro, Allison, & Moore, 2010). While dynamic and adaptive system models offer considerable understanding of the complexity of the modern world, they are difficult to translate into practical and accessible policies and actions for local stakeholders.

In addition to definitional issues, the second reason for the confusion between sustainability and resilience among researchers is that the two approaches share some important assumptions, methods, and goals (Table 1). Possibly, the most important of these are (1) the goal of system survivability, which is inherent in most systems, and (2) the assumption that there exists a state of harmony between how human societies function within the larger context of our natural world. For both sustainability and resilience, these two assertions give rise to research questions about how to best ensure the survival of the system and how to best achieve its state of harmony. In addition, they both tend to focus their research on the topics of natural ecosystems, the development of human communities, and climate change. These common goals and research topics make it seem like sustainability and resilience are the same thing. However, the way they frame, study and resolve their research questions are very different from one another.

Table 2. Differences between sustainability and resilience.

	Sustainability	Resilience
Assumptions	Stability and balance are the norm (or are at least possible)	Nonlinear and unpredictable change and chaos are the norm
Goals	Normative Ideals (culture, environment and economic conservation; intergenerational equity; fairness)	Strategic, dynamic and self-organizing systems; learning institutions and innovative cultures
Research focus	Environmental and social impacts of economic development and growth; over use of resources; carbon footprints	Natural and human disaster management; climate change impacts; social capital and networks
Methods	'Wise Use' resource management; mitigation or preservation against change; recycling and 'Greening'; education for behavior change	Reducing vulnerability and increasing physical and social capacity for change (flexibility, redundancy); system feedback and performance; education for innovation
Criticism	Poorly defined and highly politicized	Does not address the causes of social and environmental change

Source: Authors

Using the definitions outlined above for sustainability and resilience helps to articulate the many deeply fundamental differences between the two paradigms (Table 2). The most significant difference is in their basic ontological assumptions about the nature of the world: whether it is normal to be in a state of stability and balance, or in a state of change and even chaos. To be sustainable requires that some sense of stability is possible, and that it is important to understand and manage impacts that disturb that stability. However, human experience seems to be telling us that we live in a chaotic world that requires an understanding of how our environments and societies operate as complex adaptive systems (Calgaro, Lloyd, & Dominey-Howes, 2014; Farrell & Twining-Ward, 2005; Schianetz & Kavanagh, 2008). Evolutionary resilience, in particular, suggests that all systems are in a constant state of adaptation within an ever-flowing field of change (Davoudi, 2012; Simmie & Martin, 2010). These different assumptions lead to different research goals, different ways of defining research problems, and different sets of solutions to contemporary challenges.

Conflicts may even arise between sustainability and resilience approaches in terms of how a cultural or natural resources should be managed. Politically, sustainability initiatives have become highly polarizing, due largely to their normative idealism. This has limited some of their potential impacts, and its supporters have tended to be associated with liberal political orientations. Due to its still relatively new status, resilience has experienced less of this, with proponents often claiming it is non-normative (Anderies et al., 2013). However, it has also been increasingly criticized as supporting a conservative neoliberal agenda that, by focusing on adaptation, avoids the root causes of environmental and social changes and may give license to development and resource exploitation (Evans & Reid, 2015; MacKinnon & Derickson, 2012).

Sustainability and resilience indicators

While they share some common views, sustainability and resilience, as defined in this review, mostly offer distinct perspectives on the contemporary challenges of human society. From a policy perspective, neither of these are inherently better than the other – they just offer communities different choices. Thus, faced with the modern challenges of climate change and natural disasters, economic and cultural globalization, and numerous other predictable and unpredictable drives of change, communities need to continually ask themselves two questions:

(1) *What do we want to protect and conserve, and to keep from changing?* (sustainability)
(2) *What do we want to adapt and* change *into something new, and maybe better?* (resilience)

Based on the goals of a community, sustainability may be a preferred approach for some resources and challenges, while resilience may be preferred for others. Determining the answers is not easy, as they reflect the values of a community and may be highly contested among community interests. Changes in these values are often reflected in political outcomes, and sustainability and resilience approaches are the basis of many political debates, although the terms are seldom used directly in this way.

The conceptual framework outlined here has been used to evaluate the relationship between sustainability and resilience in an ongoing research project assessing the

Table 3. Sample tourism indicators of community sustainability and resilience.

Category	Sustainability Indicators	Resilience Indicators
Local government budgeting	Conserving community resources - *Effective environmental conservation, protection* and *restoration* - *Programs for conserving* and *teaching cultural traditions*	Building community capacity for change - *Level of infrastructure construction for education/interpretation* and *resource access* - *Programs for innovative tourism developments* and *marketing*
Environmental knowledge	Maintaining traditional resource uses - *Level of locals' traditional environmental knowledge* - *Level of traditional practices* and *uses of resources by locals*	Creating new environmental knowledge - *Participation of locals* and *tourists in environmental education programs* - *Innovative uses of traditional knowledge by locals*
Community well-being	Preserving cultural traditions - *Strength of traditional livelihoods, especially natural resource based*	Improving living conditions and employment - *Rate of unemployment* and *youth outmigration* - *Rate of employment in tourism*
Social support systems	Providing social welfare and equity - *Support for elderly* and *underprivileged populations*	Supporting social collaboration - *Rates of participation in religious* and *other local organizations*

Source: Authors

development of rural tourism communities in Taiwan. Field work was conducted in eight communities across four geographic contexts: coastal wetlands, high mountains, agricultural lands, and island. In qualitative interviews with community leaders, we used the two questions posted above to define indicators of sustainability and resilience (Table 3).

Interviews with community leaders were structured through four categories that respondents would be familiar with and which are often associated with sustainability and resilience. For each of these four categories, we unpack the interviews to identify indicators that reflect sustainability (conservation, restoration, and change avoidance) and resilience (adaptation and innovation). In the category of environmental knowledge, for example, a high rate of participation in environmental education programs was considered an indicator of resilience because it increased the potential of community members to utilize local resources in times of unexpected need. On the other hand, a high level of traditional resource use was considered sustainability because it conserved a traditional cultural system. (While traditional resource uses could also contribute to resilience in some cases, they could just as easily engender path-dependent barriers to innovation.)

These categories and indicators appear to be effective for understanding sustainability and resilience in tourism communities in Taiwan. Modifications might be needed for other contexts. Some preliminary results from the Taiwan research are available online at Collaborative for Sustainable Tourism and Resilient Communities (2015).

In general, the better a community is able to conserve (or sometimes recover) that which they cherish, the more successful they are at sustainability. Similarly, the better a community is able to adapt and change in areas that they want to see development, the better they are at resilience. On the other hand, the inability to protect a community's resources against change, or being forced by external forces to change something in directions deemed undesirable by a community, reflects disempowered states of sustainability and of resilience, respectively.

Due to the fundamental role of these two concepts in contemporary community development, a new goal should be to create sustainable and resilient communities — communities that demonstrate strength and vision in both sustainability and resilience (Tobin,

1999). Our preliminary findings in Taiwan indicate that rural tourism communities that have strength in both sustainability and resilience may be more dynamic and forward looking than those that mostly emphasize sustainability or resilience (CSTRC, 2015). Further, in some instances, successful sustainability initiatives might even hinder resilience, because such communities have fewer incentives to adopt resilience policies. Sustainability and resilience independently are insufficient in today's world. However, to create resilient and sustainable communities first requires a clear understanding of what sustainability is and what resilience is, upon which more effective planning and development models can then be built. All systems have some degree of sustainability and some degree of resilience. The issue is how to best manage and strengthen these to create dynamic and successful communities.

Acknowledgements

Thanks to Joseph Cheer (Monash University) for comments on an early draft of this paper. A very early draft of this paper by the same authors was published as 'Similarities and Differences between Community Resilience and Sustainability' in the Tourism Place blog at http://www.tgjournal.com/tourism-place-blog/similarities-and-differences-between-community-resilience-and-sustainability on 27 October 2015.

Disclosure statement

No potential conflict of interest was reported by the authors.

ORCID

Alan A. Lew http://orcid.org/0000-0001-8177-5972
Pin T. Ng http://orcid.org/0000-0002-5018-9513
Chin-cheng (Nickel) Ni http://orcid.org/0000-0002-7178-8558
Tsung-chiung (Emily) Wu http://orcid.org/0000-0003-0057-1199

References

Adger, W. N. (2003). Building resilience to promote sustainability. *IHDP Update*, *2*, 1−3.

Allison, I., Bindoff, N., Bindschadler, R., Cox, P., de Noblet-Ducoudre, N., England, M., … Weaver, A. (2009). *The Copenhagen diagnosis: Updating the world on the latest climate science*. Sydney: The University of New South Wales, Climate Change Research Centre.

Anderies, J. M., Folke C., Walker B., & Ostrom E. (2013). Aligning key concepts for global change policy: Robustness, resilience, and sustainability. *Ecology and Society*, *18*: 8. doi:10.5751/ES-05178-180208

Brundtland, G. H. (1987). *Report of the world commission on environment and development: Our common future*. New York, NY: United Nations. Retrieved from http://www.un-documents.net/our-common-future.pdf

Butler, R. (1998). Sustainable tourism − looking backward in order to progress? In C. M. Hall & A. A. Lew (Eds.), *Sustainable tourism: A geographical perspective* (pp. 25−34). London: Addison Wesley Longman.

Calgaro, E., Lloyd, K., & Dominey-Howes, D. (2014). From vulnerability to transformation: A framework for assessing the vulnerability and resilience of tourism destinations. *Journal of Sustainable Tourism*, *22*, 341−360.

Carroll, A. (2011). *8 Steps to a sustainable business*. Bank of Ireland, All About Business. Retrieved from http://www.allaboutbusiness.ie/hub/article/8_steps_to_a_sustainable_business

Collaborative for Sustainable Tourism and Resilient Communities. (2015). *Sustainability and resilience to disturbance and change in rural Taiwan communities*. Retrieved from http://www.tourismcommunities.com/taiwan-project.html.

Davidson, D. J. (2010). The applicability of the concept of resilience to social systems: Some sources of optimism and nagging doubts. *Society and Natural Resources*, *23*, 1135−1149.

Davoudi, S. (2012). Resilience: A bridging concept of a dead end? *Planning Theory and Practice*, *13*, 299−333. doi:10.1080/14649357.2012.677124

Derissen, S., Quaas, M. F., & Baumgärtner, S. (2011). The relationship between resilience and sustainability of ecological-economic systems. *Ecological Economics*, *70*, 1121−1128.

Edwards, C. (2009). *Resilient nation*. London: Demos.

European Commission. (2013). *European Tourism Indicators System for sustainable destination management*. Retrieved from http://ec.europa.eu/enterprise/sectors/tourism/sustainable-tourism/indicators/index_en.htm

Evans, B., & Reid, J. (2015). Exhausted by resilience: Response to the commentaries. *Resilience*, *3*, 154−159.

Farrell, B. H., & Twining-Ward, L. (2005). Seven steps towards sustainability: Tourism in the context of new knowledge. *Journal of Sustainable Tourism*, *31*, 109−122.

Fiksel, J. (2006). Sustainability and resilience: Toward a systems approach. *Sustainability: Science Practice and Policy*, *2*, 14−21.

Friedman, J. (1971). The future of comprehensive urban planning: A critique. *Public Administration Review*, *31*, 315−326.

Global Sustainable Tourism Council. (2013). *Global sustainable tourism council criteria*. Retrieved from https://www.gstcouncil.org/en/gstc-criteria/sustainable-tourism-gstc-criteria.html.

Goble, G., Fields, H., & Cocchiara, R. (2002). *Resilience infrastructure: Improving your business resilience*. Somers, NY: IBM. Retrieved from https://www.ibm.com/smarterplanet/global/files/us__en_us__security_resiliency__buw03008usen.pdf

Hall, C. M., Gossling, S., & Scott, D. (2015). The evolution of sustainable development and sustainable tourism. In C. M. Hall, S. Gossling & D. Scott (Eds.), *The Routledge handbook of tourism and sustainability* (pp. 15−31). Oxford: Routledge.

Hall, C. M., & Lew, A. A., eds. (1998). *Sustainable tourism: A geographical perspective*. London: Addison Wesley Longman.

Hall, C. M., & Lew, A. A. (2009). *Understanding and managing tourism impacts: An integrated approach*. Oxford: Routledge.

Hardy, A., Beeton, S., & Pearson, L. (2002). Sustainable tourism: An overview of the concept and its position in relation to conceptualizations of tourism. *Journal of Sustainable Tourism, 10*, 475–496.

Jeuch, C., & Michelson, E. S. (2011). Rethinking the future of sustainability: From silos to systemic resilience. *Development, 54*, 199–201.

Leichenko, R. M., O'Brien, K. L., & Solecki, W. D. (2010). Climate change and the global financial crisis: A case of double exposure. *Annals of the Association of American Geographers, 100*, 963–972.

MacKinnon, D., & Derickson, K. D. (2012). From resilience to resourcefulness: A critique of resilience policy and activism. *Progress in Human Geography, 37*, 253–270.

Magis, K. (2013). Community resilience: An indicator of social sustainability. *Society & Natural Resources: An International Journal, 23*, 401–416.

McLellan, B., Zhang, Q., Farzaneh, H., Utama, N. A., & Ishihara, K. N. (2012). Resilience, sustainability and risk management: A focus on energy. *Challenges, 3*, 153–182.

Meetow, S., & Newell, J. P. (2015). Resilience and complexity: A bibliometric review and prospects for industrial ecology. *Journal of Industrial Ecology, 19*, 236–251.

Prasad, N., Ranghieri, F, Shah, F., Trohanis, Z., Kessler, E., & Sinha, R. (2009). *Climate resilient cities: A primer on reducing vulnerabilities to disasters.* Washington, DC: The World Bank. Retrieved from http://bit.ly/1643fsf (library subscription service).

Redman, C. L. (2014). Should sustainability and resilience be combined or remain distinct pursuits. *Ecology and Society, 19*, 37.

Sayer, J., & Campbell, B. M. (2004). *The science of sustainable development: Local livelihoods and the global environment.* Cambridge: Cambridge University Press.

Schianetz, K., & Kavanagh, L. (2008). Sustainability indicators for tourism destinations: A complex adaptive systems approach using systemic indicator systems. *Journal of Sustainable Tourism, 16*, 601–628.

Simmie, J., & Martin, R. (2010). The economic resilience of regions: toward an evolutionary approach. *Cambridge Journal of Regions, Economy and Society, 3*, 27–43.

Smith, C. (2006). *The plan of Chicago: Daniel Burnham and the remaking of the American City.* Chicago, IL: University of Chicago Press.

Steffen, W., Crutzen, P. J., & McNeill, J. R. (2007). The Anthropocene: Are humans now overwhelming the great forces of nature? *Ambio, 36*, 614–621.

Strickland-Munro, J. K., Allison, H. E., & Moore, S. A. (2010). Using resilience concepts to investigate the impacts of protected area tourism on communities. *Annals of Tourism Research, 31*, 499–519.

Tobin, G. A. (1999). Sustainability and community resilience: The holy grail of hazards planning? *Environmental Hazards, 1*, 13–25.

Walker, B. H., Carpenter, S. R., Rockstrom, J., Crépin, A. -S., & Peterson, G. D. (2012). Drivers, "slow" variables, "fast" variables, shocks, and resilience. *Ecology and Society, 17*: 30.

Walker, B. H., & Salt, D. (2006). *Resilience thinking: Sustaining ecosystems and people in a changing world.* Washington, DC: Island Press.

Wilson, F. (2012). How to be in business forever: A lesson in sustainability. *ACV blog.* Retrieved from http://avc.com/2012/10/how-to-be-in-business-forever-a-lesson-in-sustainability/

World Economic Forum. (2015). *Global Risk 2015*, 10th ed. Geneva: World Economic Forum. Retrieved from http://reports.weforum.org/global-risks-2015/

Zalasiewicz, J., Williams, M., Steffen, W., & Crutzen, P. (2010). The new world of the Anthropocene. *Environmental Science and Technology, 44*, 2228–2231.

Evolutionary economic geography: reflections from a sustainable tourism perspective

Patrick Brouder

ABSTRACT

Evolutionary economic geography (EEG) is receiving increasing attention from tourism geographers with over 30 publications explicitly incorporating EEG into tourism between 2011 and 2016. Many of these contributions are conceptual, which is not surprising given the novelty of EEG within economic geography, in general, and tourism, in particular. However, a sizeable number of these are built on detailed case studies, using EEG as an analytical lens rather than as a conceptual point of departure. Thus, many tourism researchers have found that EEG has great potential for understanding change in tourism destinations. In this *Research Frontiers* paper I critically reflect on this early research of EEG in tourism geographies from a sustainable development perspective. In the cases presented, EEG offers a fresh understanding of two related challenges in each of two separate aspects of sustainable tourism development. First, pro-growth governance models can be disrupted by engaged local stakeholders in order to make tangible sustainability gains but these gains remain precarious over time as pro-growth governance models prove tenacious in the very long-term. Second, regional institutional legacies hamper new path emergence in two ways – through institutional inertia which keeps the region's focus on past success in other sectors and through the (possibly competing) institutional imperatives of the dominant and emerging tourism sub-sectors or sub-regions. These challenges are illustrated through two complementary Canadian cases drawn from the extant literature – the mass tourism destination of Niagara and the resort community of Whistler. I highlight how a sustainable tourism perspective can also help to critique EEG theory and empirics in line with other recent political economy critiques in economic geography. I conclude that sustainable tourism, at its best, is an established reflexive lens which will help to develop, validate, and challenge aspects of EEG theory within tourism studies, in particular, and economic geography, in general.

摘要

演化经济地理学逐渐引起旅游地理学者的关注，在2011–2016期间有30多篇文章明确地把演化经济地理学融合进旅游研究中。这些文章多是概念性的文章，这一点也不意外，这是因为演化经济地理学即使在经济地理学中也是一个比较新的研究领域， 更不要说在旅游研究中了。但是，这些文章中有相当一部分是建立在详细的案例研究基础上，把演化经济地理学作为分析工具，而不是研究的概念起点。因此，很多旅游研究人员发现，演化经济地理学对于理解旅游目的地的变化有很大潜力。在本研究前沿文章中，我从可持续发展的视角批判性地反思了演化经济地理学在旅游地理学方面的早期研究。在本部分的案例研究中，演化经济地理学对于理解可持续发展中两个相关的挑战提供了新鲜的理解:第一，当地旅游发展的利益相关者为了获取可见的持续性收益，造成前增长管制模型会受到当地地方利益相关者的干扰。虽然该模型从长期来看是强韧的，但是可持续性收益随着时间发展表现出不确定性。第二，区域制度以两种方式阻碍新路径的出现，一是制度惯性，使该区域聚焦于其它部门过去的成功经验;二是主导性旅游分部门或亚区域与新出现旅游分部门或亚区域的 (可能是竞争性的) 制度性强制力。这些挑战通过取自现有文献的两个互补性的加拿大案例 (尼亚加拉大众旅游目的地和惠斯勒度假胜地社区) 进行了说明。我强调可持续旅游视角如何有助于评论经济地理学中与其它晚近政治经济学有关的演化经济地理学理论与实证结果。我发现，可持续旅游充其量可以作为一个明确的、反思性的透镜，助于发展、验证与挑战经济地理学特别是旅游研究中演化经济地理学理论。

Introduction

In the introduction to a recent special issue of *Tourism Geographies* (Volume 16, Issue 4), the editors wrote that 'the incorporation of EEG to better understand how tourism evolves through time and influences regional development offers a promising avenue of research and theory building in the economic geography of tourism' (Ioannides, Halkier, & Lew, 2014, p. 536). EEG (evolutionary economic geography) emerged as a new sub-field of economic geography within the last decade (Boschma & Frenken, 2006; Boschma & Martin, 2010) and its immediate impact has raised the question of whether this constitutes an 'evolutionary revolution' (Coe, 2011) with evolutionary thought proving useful in many economic studies.

In the years since Coe asked this question EEG has grown further, quickly finding its way onto the pages of *Tourism Geographies* (Brouder, 2014a, b; Brouder & Eriksson, 2013a; Chen & Bao, 2014; Gill & Williams, 2014; Ma & Hassink, 2014; Niewiadomski, 2014; Sanz-Ibáñez & Anton Clavé, 2014) as well as other leading tourism journals (Anton Clavé & Wilson, 2017; Brouder & Eriksson, 2013b; Brouder & Fullerton, 2015; García-Cabrera & Durán-Herrera, 2014; Gill & Williams, 2011; Ma & Hassink, 2013; Sanz-Ibáñez & Anton Clavé, 2014; Williams, 2013). One edited volume has emerged on *Tourism Destination Evolution* (Brouder, Anton Clavé, Gill, & Ioannides, 2017) and several authors have published on EEG and tourism in non-tourism journals (Brouder & Ioannides, 2014; Halkier & Therkelsen, 2013; Larsson & Lindström, 2014; Randelli, Romei, & Tortora, 2014). Thus, EEG is helping to bridge the gap between economic geography and tourism theory (Ioannides & Brouder, 2017; Ioannides, 2006) and this has the potential to be a two-way bridge.

Sustainable tourism is 'knowledge and research on sustainable development in the context of tourism' (Butler, 1999, p. 8) and has been criticised for being too simplistic and inflexible (Hunter, 1997) and for sustaining capitalism (Fletcher, 2011) while others defend its close affinity with political economy due to the collective action required to make any form of sustainable governance work (Bramwell, 2011). While acknowledging the critiques and the dilution of the term, I sympathise with Bramwell's approach and see sustainable tourism as an interesting nexus of political economy and economic geography in a tourism context.

The development of tourism partnerships, for example, is an interesting empirical arena for linking political economy (sustainable tourism) and economic geography (EEG) in order to investigate whether (unsustainable) path dependence can be challenged through new (sustainable) path creation (cf. Bramwell & Cox, 2009). If tourism is to be sustainable, it is important to study how that is achieved. For example, Mellon and Bramwell found that sustainable tourism does not develop in isolation but rather 'sustainable tourism-related policies co-evolved with, and through, policies for community well-being, actor participation, and sustainable development' (Mellon & Bramwell, 2016, p. 15). Thus, one may ask whether EEG research to date has taken the notions of community, participation, and sustainability seriously enough. While the majority of EEG studies have focused on regional economies or high-growth sectors (Coe, 2011), as EEG develops there is more interest in localised (e.g. destination) studies which necessarily bring questions of resident communities to the fore.

In this paper, I critically reflect on the early studies of EEG in tourism geographies from a sustainable development perspective. Specifically, I examine the theory and empirics of EEG and tourism in the two distinct extant cases of Whistler and Niagara in Canada (Gill & Williams, 2011, 2014; Brouder & Fullerton, 2015, 2017). I ask what the key findings from these studies of EEG and tourism tell us about sustainable development in tourism and by linking these to sustainable tourism development I take EEG theory to a place where it rarely has been but where there is ample space for it to go (Essletzbichler, 2009), that is, its place in understanding economic evolution in a normative (progressive) sense (Essletzbichler, 2012).

Literature review

A perennial question in regional development studies is: why do some regions prosper while others struggle over time? Reframing that question in a destination evolution context: why do 'some destinations appear better at adapting to changing circumstances'?, as Halkier and James (2017) ask, finding their answer in resilience theory. Notions of resilience have received significant interest with both EEG (Boschma, 2015) and tourism (Lew, 2014) scholars identifying the need to understand the role of regional shocks as well as slow changes affecting a region's ability to prosper over time. This regional resilience approach is perhaps best conceptualised by Pike, Dawley, and Tomaney (2010) who focus on adaptation and adaptability, i.e. the tension between a region's ability to make focused, rapid change and its ability to diversify and nourish more long-term possibilities. In this way, resilience closely matches sustainable tourism as each is criticised for 'sustaining capitalism' and being too simplistic/conservative (MacKinnon & Derickson, 2013) while still looking to the future.

From the political economy perspective, both sustainable tourism and resilience are potentially innovative approaches to research which empower communities (Bramwell & Lane, 2012). One significant innovation is Lew's (2014) model of scale, change, and resilience in tourism, which captures much of the dynamic facing tourism entrepreneurs (both slow changes and sudden shocks) and links individuals (entrepreneurs) to a higher scale (community) while also answering the call to be bottom-up (MacKinnon & Derickson, 2013). However, resilience may be found wanting through its downplaying of government and sociocultural factors (Hassink, 2010) – particularly important aspects of sustainable tourism.

Within EEG, many studies focus on struggling regions 'locked-in' to formerly prosperous paths which are now seen as problematic for long-term regional development. Tourism scholars have drawn parallels between this picture and the post-zenith phase of uncertainty found in Butler's Tourist Area Cycle of Evolution (Brouder & Eriksson, 2013b; Butler, 1980; Ma & Hassink, 2013). It is also worth noting that Butler's seminal paper was inherently concerned with the sustainability of destinations as he stated 'a change of attitude is required on the part of those who are responsible for planning, developing, and managing tourist areas… They could then be more carefully protected and preserved' (Butler, 1980, p. 11). Thus, there is a normative focus in tourism evolution from its earliest academic models that is not usually as prominent in EEG studies which tend towards a narrower (firm) focus although whether such a narrow approach is best for EEG remains contested (Essletzbichler, 2009; MacKinnon, Cumbers, Pike, Birch, & McMaster, 2009; MacKinnon & Derickson, 2013).

Although questions persist around what exactly is being 'sustained' in sustainable tourism (Saarinen, 2006), the goal of sustainability has brought a rich conceptual palette to tourism studies – including complexity theory with a focus on Complex Adaptive Systems (Farrell & Twining-Ward, 2004; Meekes, Parra, & de Roo, 2017). Complexity theory is also one of the three theoretical antecedents to EEG (along with path dependence and generalised Darwinism) (Boschma & Martin, 2010). While little has been written in EEG on how to properly couple the human and natural systems (e.g. Patchell & Hayter, 2013), the question of limits to growth in sustainable tourism has primacy (Saarinen, 2013) and what is prioritised (community, environment, economy) is, at least in part, a normative decision.

The complexity of tourism development is also reflected at the policy level and in discourse. Saarinen (2004) discussed the competing discourses existing around tourism development noting that there is often a dominant discourse and that there may be several (possibly competing) discourses present. Brouder (2014b) implicitly supports this argument by putting it in a path development (EEG) context with tourism occurring in regions where it is not necessarily the dominant sector and where the tourism sector may be made up of multiple (possibly competing) paths. If we accept that varying discourses and/or paths exist and that they may even be in competition with each other, we may be inclined to ask: how does sustainable tourism emerge in a given destination and can it impact local development?

Hall (2011) highlights the paradox of sustainable tourism as a highly diffused concept among academics and practitioners but one which has not stemmed the growing environmental impact of tourism development. For example, sustainable tourism planning often leads to improved indicators and management plans but runs the risk of paying little more than lip-service to real change. Hall (2011) asks why this fails to impact the dominant policy paradigm, noting the lack of any significant evidence that entrenched policy paradigms can be unsettled. This resonates with sustainable tourism practitioners who all too often find their innovative endeavours stifled by an unreceptive institutional environment (Carson & Carson, 2017; Ruhanen, 2013). Thus, there are two 'evolutionary challenges' to sustainable tourism – the dominant growth paradigm which permeates much tourism development discourse and the related dominance of one (or few) institutional assemblage(s) supporting this growth. It is the unquestioned centralisation of tourism development *tout court* which creates an abundance of space for the former and which eliminates a diversity of challenges to the latter.

Sustainability praxis

I now present two illustrations of tourism destinations in Canada drawn from the extant literature on EEG and tourism – the Resort Municipality of Whistler near Vancouver, British Columbia and the Niagara Region near Toronto, Ontario. Each of these destinations faces challenges to sustainable development and tourism is a major economic sector in each. Their stories offer further insights and new challenges to the application of EEG in tourism.

Whistler's 'Mindful Deviation' facilitating sustainable tourism development?

Whistler is a resort community 120 km north of Vancouver. It is primarily a winter sport resort but is increasingly diversifying into the other seasons. It has a population of 11,000 and receives over two million visitors annually (Gill & Williams, 2011). The evolution of Whistler as a tourism destination has been a long-term focus of research for Gill (2000), whose early research examined the transition of Whistler's development approach from one characteristic of a 'growth machine' to one of 'growth management.' This early evolutionary research demonstrated the growing importance of social and environmental concerns in the discourses around economic development. A much more inclusive, participatory governance model of sustainability was in place in the years leading up to the 2010 Vancouver Winter Olympics – Whistler's role as a host mountain facilitated much support and funding for the new approach to flourish (Gill & Williams, 2011). Gill and Williams (2014) described this new path creation as 'mindful deviation' where entrepreneurs and policy-makers were able to co-opt the community in order to move away from an unsustainable growth trajectory and realise some key sustainability goals for Whistler (e.g. affordable community housing). However, the 'protective space' afforded by the Olympics has fallen away in the years since and Whistler's sustainability agenda has been supplanted by a resurgent growth agenda in response to a post-Olympic hangover (Gill & Williams, 2017). The future of Whistler as a sustainable destination is again uncertain but the recent purchase of the resort infrastructure by Vail Resorts (who include the environment and community as key stakeholders alongside guests, employees and shareholders) (Vail Resorts, 2016) is an interesting new development.

The case of Whistler demonstrates that evolutionary change towards sustainable development can be successful over time but that any success remains tentative as political change can alter the institutional imperative and lead the destination down a new, and potentially less sustainable, path. The combination of the end of fixed-term institutional support (from the Olympics) and external global pressures (from real estate markets) combined to undermine sustainable development goals, at least in the medium-term. Whether institutional support for long-term sustainable development has been supplanted or merely suppressed is a central research question and here empirical work in tourism can contribute to EEG theory by better conceptualising the suppressed voices in a plethora of regional development cases.

Niagara's 'Institutional Inertia' inhibiting sustainable tourism development?

Niagara is an amalgamated region of 12 municipalities 100 km south of Toronto. It is primarily a summer mass tourism destination but is also diversifying its seasonal offerings. The Niagara region has a population of c.430,000 and receives c.14 million visitors annually. Tourism is arguably the most resilient sector of the economy as agriculture and manufacturing have contracted in recent decades (Brouder & Fullerton, 2015). However, despite significant innovative small-scale tourism growth across the region, two institutional barriers persist. In theory, as economies evolve 'old institutions are challenged and individuals with particular skill sets become marginalised' (Brouder & Ioannides 2014, p. 422) but how this plays out in reality is highly contested with intra- and inter-sectoral inhibitors present and the interplay between inhibitors and innovators defines institutional evolution.

The first barrier in Niagara relates to the path dependent 'institutional inertia' which is a legacy of Niagara's industrial glory days – when high wages and full employment were the norm for most communities (Brouder & Fullerton, 2017). Thus, the collective institutional memory persists and policy-makers are reluctant to embrace the relatively low-paying, precarious employment opportunities typical of most mass tourism in the region. The second barrier has to do with the internal 'institutional imperatives' of the tourism sector in the region – with the mass tourism destination of Niagara Falls focused on continuing capital investment so that the central stakeholders there have a revenue-capturing focus which serves to hinder many tourists from spreading out across the region (Brouder & Fullerton, 2017). Meanwhile, as small-scale tourism continues to grow across the wine region and rural communities away from Niagara Falls, these communities are beginning to form 'institutional imperatives' of their own – with localised destination management organisations finding their voice in regional planning. The question remains as to whether this voice is promoting a more sustainable new path for the regional tourism economy by being closer to local communities.

The case of Niagara shows that evolutionary theory when applied in even a relatively small geographical region cannot escape normative questions of what sustainable development really means. It is imperative to ask going forward whose development agenda counts in terms of regional institutional support for different types of tourism development and how do regions evolve over the long-term as co-evolving local tourism paths compete. Here tourism can contribute to EEG theory by nuancing the debates around related diversification since the developments across the Niagara region, while related, are each linked to different institutional environments, thus questioning the nature of co-evolution in this case as the co-evolving institutions are very different depending on the particular type of tourism.

Discussion and conclusion

In comparing the illustrations of Whistler and Niagara, two related challenges in each of two separate aspects of sustainable tourism are apparent. First, pro-growth governance models can be disrupted by engaged local stakeholders in order to make tangible sustainability gains but these gains remain precarious over time (as evidenced by Whistler's recent recidivism) as pro-growth governance models prove tenacious in the very long term (cf. Hall, 2011). Second, regional institutional legacies (Carson & Carson, 2017) hamper new path emergence in two ways – through institutional inertia which keeps the region's focus on past success in other sectors and through the (possibly competing) institutional imperatives of the dominant and emerging tourism sub-sectors or sub-regions (cf. Brouder & Fullerton, 2017).

Future research on EEG and sustainable tourism should focus on three key areas. First, how might pro-growth governance models be supplanted in the long-term? This requires not just a medium-term change in direction but an actual evolution towards a new way, which Hall (2011) sees little evidence for as yet although physical and social proximity to the community may ultimately yield a more sustainable sectoral evolution (cf. Mellon & Bramwell, 2016). Second, how will EEG broaden to incorporate normative goals (e.g. environmental and social goals), reflecting advancements in political economy and resilience (cf. Essletzbichler, 2009; Lew, 2014; Pike et al., 2010)? Third, how can EEG theory be used to 're-frame' sustainable tourism research, as Saarinen (2013) calls for? For instance, if we can use the concept of 'sustainability' to decentralise the tourism growth-first imperative (Saarinen, 2013), then we can also push the research frontiers of EEG and tourism by using the concept of sustainable development as a critical lens on EEG in tourism studies, and vice versa.

It is known that bottom-up change is occurring but the processes which facilitate or suppress such changes, as well as the related institutional environment (Carson & Carson, 2017; Ruhanen, 2013) are not very well understood and these processes offer rich empirical ground. Tourism geographers can create a two-way bridge with EEG scholars by highlighting some marginalised voices and by nuancing the understanding of co-evolution. Ultimately, sustainable tourism demands a rethinking of EEG studies in tourism which broadens the scope of institutional actors involved and reorients research towards grassroots stakeholders who are closer to their communities and should have a better vision of what their own sustainable future should be (MacKinnon & Derickson, 2013) including tourism's place in it.

Disclosure statement

No potential conflict of interest was reported by the author.

References

Anton Clavé, S., & Wilson, J. (2017). The evolution of coastal tourism destinations: A path plasticity perspective on tourism urbanisation. *Journal of Sustainable Tourism*, *25*(1), 96–112.

Boschma, R. (2015). Towards an evolutionary perspective on regional resilience. *Regional Studies*, *49*(5), 733–751.

Boschma, R., & Frenken, K. (2006). Why is economic geography not an evolutionary science? Towards an evolutionary economic geography. *Journal of Economic Geography, 6*, 273–302.

Boschma, R., & Martin, R. (Eds.). (2010). *The handbook of evolutionary economic geography*. Cheltenham: Edward Elgar Publishing.

Bramwell, B. (2011). Governance, the state and sustainable tourism: A political economy approach. *Journal of Sustainable Tourism, 19*(4–5), 459–477.

Bramwell, B., & Cox, V. (2009). Stage and path dependence approaches to the evolution of a national park tourism partnership. *Journal of Sustainable Tourism, 17*(2), 191–206.

Bramwell, B., & Lane, B. (2012). Towards innovation in sustainable tourism research? *Journal of Sustainable Tourism, 20*(1), 1–7.

Brouder, P. (2014a). Evolutionary economic geography: A new path for tourism studies? *Tourism Geographies, 16*(1), 2–7.

Brouder, P. (2014b). Evolutionary economic geography and tourism studies: Extant studies and future research directions. *Tourism Geographies, 16*(4), 540–545.

Brouder, P., Anton Clavé, S., Gill, A., & Ioannides, D. (Eds.). (2017). *Tourism Destination Evolution*. London: Routledge.

Brouder, P., & Eriksson, R. H. (2013a). Staying power: What influences micro-firm survival in tourism? *Tourism Geographies, 15*(1), 124–143.

Brouder, P., & Eriksson, R. H. (2013b). Tourism evolution: On the synergies of tourism studies and evolutionary economic geography. *Annals of Tourism Research, 43*, 370–389.

Brouder, P., & Fullerton, C. (2015). Exploring heterogeneous tourism development paths: Cascade effect or co-evolution in Niagara? *Scandinavian Journal of Hospitality and Tourism, 15*(1–2), 152–166.

Brouder, P., & Fullerton, C. (2017). Co-evolution and sustainable tourism development: From old institutional inertia to new institutional imperatives in Niagara. In P. Brouder, S. Anton Clavé, A. Gill, & D. Ioannides (Eds.), *Tourism destination evolution* (pp. 149–164). London: Routledge.

Brouder, P., & Ioannides, D. (2014). Urban tourism and evolutionary economic geography: Complexity and co-evolution in contested spaces. *Urban Forum, 25*(4), 419–430.

Butler, R. W. (1980). The concept of a tourist area life cycle of evolution: Implications for management of resources. *The Canadian Geographer, 24*(1), 5–12.

Butler, R. W. (1999). Sustainable tourism: A state–of–the–art review. *Tourism Geographies, 1*(1), 7–25.

Carson, D. A., & Carson, D. B. (2017). Path dependence in remote area tourism development: Why institutional legacies matter. In P. Brouder, S. Anton Clavé, A. Gill, & D. Ioannides (Eds.), *Tourism destination evolution* (pp. 103–122). London: Routledge.

Chen, G., & Bao, J. (2014). Path dependence in the evolution of resort governance models in China. *Tourism Geographies, 16*(5), 812–825.

Coe, N. M. (2011). Geographies of production I: An evolutionary revolution? *Progress in Human Geography, 35*(1), 81–91.

Essletzbichler, J. (2009). Evolutionary economic geography, institutions, and political economy. *Economic Geography, 85*(2), 159–165.

Essletzbichler, J. (2012). Generalized Darwinism, group selection and evolutionary economic geography. *Zeitschrift für Wirtschaftsgeographie, 56*(3), 129–146.

Farrell, B. H., & Twining-Ward, L. (2004). Reconceptualizing tourism. *Annals of Tourism Research*, 31(2), 274–95.

Fletcher, R. (2011). Sustaining tourism, sustaining capitalism? The tourism industry's role in global capitalist expansion. *Tourism Geographies, 13*(3), 443–461.

García-Cabrera, A. M., & Durán-Herrera, J. J. (2014). Does the tourism industry co-evolve? *Annals of Tourism Research, 47*, 81–83.

Gill, A. M. (2000). From growth machine to growth management: The dynamics of resort development in Whistler, British Columbia. *Environment and Planning A, 32*, 1083–1103.

Gill, A. M., & Williams, P. W. (2017). Contested pathways towards tourism destination sustainability in Whistler, British Columbia: An evolutionary governance model. In P. Brouder, S. Anton Clavé, A. Gill, and D. Ioannides (Eds.), *Tourism destination evolution* (pp. 43–64). London: Routledge.

Gill, A. M., & Williams, P. W. (2011). Rethinking resort growth: Understanding evolving governance strategies in Whistler, British Columbia. *Journal of Sustainable Tourism, 19*(4–5), 629–648.

Gill, A. M., & Williams, P. W. (2014). Mindful deviation in creating a governance path towards sustainability in resort destinations. *Tourism Geographies, 16*(4), 546–562.

Halkier, H., & James, L. (2017). Destination dynamics, path dependency, and resilience: Regaining momentum in Danish coastal tourism destinations? In P. Brouder, S. Anton Clavé, A. Gill, & D. Ioannides (Eds.), *Tourism destination evolution* (pp. 19–42). London: Routledge.

Halkier, H., & Therkelsen, A. (2013). Exploring tourism destination path plasticity: The case of coastal tourism in North Jutland, Denmark. *Zeitschrift für Wirtschaftsgeographie, 57*(1–2), 39–51.

Hall, C. M. (2011). Policy learning and policy failure in sustainable tourism governance: From first- and second-order to third-order change? *Journal of Sustainable Tourism 19*(4–5), 649–671.

Hassink, R. (2010). Regional resilience: A promising concept to explain differences in regional economic adaptability? *Cambridge Journal of Regions, Economy and Society, 3*(1), 45–58.

Hunter, C. (1997). Sustainable tourism as an adaptive paradigm. *Annals of tourism research, 24*(4), 850–867.

Ioannides, D. (2006). The economic geography of the tourist industry: Ten years of progress in research and an agenda for the future. *Tourism Geographies, 8*(1), 76–86.

Ioannides, D., & Brouder, P. (2017). Tourism and economic geography redux: EEG's role in scholarship bridge construction. In P. Brouder, S. Anton Clavé, A. Gill, & D. Ioannides (Eds.), *Tourism destination evolution* (pp. 183–193). London: Routledge.

Ioannides, D., Halkier, H., & Lew, A. A. (2014). Evolutionary economic geography and the economies of tourism destinations. *Tourism Geographies, 16*(4), 535–539.

Larsson, A., & Lindström, K. (2014). Bridging the knowledge-gap between the old and the new: Regional marine experience production in Orust, Västra Götaland, Sweden. *European Planning Studies, 22*(8), 1551–1568.

Lew, A. A. (2014). Scale, change and resilience in community tourism planning. *Tourism Geographies, 16*(1), 14–22.

Ma, M., & Hassink, R. (2013). An evolutionary perspective on tourism area development. *Annals of Tourism Research, 41*, 89–109.

Ma, M., & Hassink, R. (2014). Path dependence and tourism area development: The case of Guilin, China. *Tourism Geographies, 16*(4), 580–597.

MacKinnon, D., Cumbers, A., Pike, A., Birch, K., & McMaster, R. (2009). Evolution in economic geography: Institutions, political economy, and adaptation. *Economic Geography, 85*(2), 129–150.

MacKinnon, D., & Derickson, K. D. (2013). From resilience to resourcefulness: A critique of resilience policy and activism. *Progress in Human Geography, 37*(2), 253–270.

Meekes, J., Parra, C., & de Roo, G. (2017). Regional Development and leisure in Fryslân: A complex adaptive systems perspective through evolutionary economic geography. In P. Brouder, S. Anton Clavé, A. Gill, & D. Ioannides (Eds.), T*ourism destination evolution* (pp. 165–182). London: Routledge.

Mellon, V., & Bramwell, B. (2016). Protected area policies and sustainable tourism: Influences, relationships and co-evolution. *Journal of Sustainable Tourism, 24*(10), 1369–1386.

Niewiadomski, P. (2014). Towards an economic-geographical approach to the globalisation of the hotel industry. *Tourism Geographies, 16*(1), 48–67.

Patchell, J., & Hayter, R. (2013). Environmental and evolutionary economic geography: Time for EEG2?. *Geografiska Annaler: Series B, Human Geography, 95*(2), 111–130.

Pike, A., Dawley, S., & Tomaney, J. (2010). Resilience, adaptation, and adaptability. *Cambridge Journal of Regions, Economy, and Society, 3*(1), 59–70.

Randelli, F., Romei, P., & Tortora, M. (2014). An evolutionary approach to the study of rural tourism. *Land Use Policy, 38*, 276–281.

Ruhanen, L. (2013). Local government: Facilitator or inhibitor of sustainable tourism development? *Journal of Sustainable Tourism, 21*(1), 80–98.

Saarinen, J. (2004). Destinations in change: The transformation process of tourist destinations. *Tourist Studies, 4*(2), 161–179.

Saarinen, J. (2006). Traditions of sustainability in tourism research. *Annals of Tourism Research, 33*(4), 1121–1140.

Saarinen, J. (2013). Critical sustainability: Setting the limits to growth and responsibility in tourism. *Sustainability, 6*(1), 1–17.

Sanz Ibáñez, C., & Anton Clavé, S. (2014). The evolution of destinations: Towards an evolutionary and relational economic geography approach. *Tourism Geographies, 16*(4), 563–579.

Vail Resorts. (2016). *Vail Resorts Management Company 'what we believe'*. Retrieved October 31, 2016, from http://www.vailresorts.com/Corp/info/what-we-believe.aspx

Williams, A. M. (2013). Mobilities and sustainable tourism: Path-creating or path-dependent relationships? *Journal of Sustainable Tourism, 21*(4), 511–531.

Index

Note: **Bold** page numbers refer to tables and *italic* page numbers refer to figures.

Aboriginal tourism 58
accessible tourism 51–2
accountability 83–4, 197, 198, 204–5, 209
affordable housing 218, 220–1
Airey, D. 193
all-inclusive tourism 46–7
Alonso, A. F. 193, 210
Alpine Convention 33
alternative tourism 16–17, 21, 53
Andriotis, K. 152
animal rights 100, 103, 106
Apollo tour operator: activities 93; buffering/decoupling 102, 106; coercive isomorphism 100; in complex institutional environments 104–5; critical case approach 92; CSR and sustainability 93–4; data collection and analysis 92; ECPAT Code 94–5; by Fotios Costoulas 93; institutional pressures 101, 105; mimetic isomorphism 99–100; negotiating and influencing CSR and sustainability 102–3; normative isomorphism 100–1; organizational learning 103–4; social components of **94**; SOS Children's Villages 95; Statement of Commitment on Human Rights 96–7; strategic positioning 101; Suppliers' Code of Conduct 96; Travelife sustainability system 95–6; turnover 93
Arthur, W. B. 218
Ashley, C. 69, 70, 77
Ateljevic, I. 193
athletes' village 222–3
Ati-Atihan 264
Atkinson, R. 196
Ayikoru, M. 193

Bakker, M. 47
Barrado, C. 136
Basic Orientations for the Sustainability of European Tourism 133
Baumgärtner, S. 272
beach erosion 259, *259*

Beaumont, N. 198
Becker, C. 35
Bell, S. 135
Beritelli, P. 194, 196, 216, 224
Berno, T. 119
Biddulph, Robin 6
Bieger, T. 216
Blackstock, K. 135
Blancas, F. J. 141
Bofill, J. 136
Bonaire's tourism policy 122
Boracay Foundation Incorporation (BFI) 256
Boracay Island, Philippines: air pollution and traffic congestion 260; beach erosion 259, *259*; Boracay Foundation Incorporation 256; Boracay Island Master Plan 253; Boracay Water Supply System 258; coliform outbreak 252–3; cultural image 264–5; data collection 254–5; Department of Tourism 253–4; dislocation and relocation 264–5; electricity outage 257; environmental and resource management 255–6, **256**; indicators for research 255, **255**; inequality 263–4; initiatives 265–6; isolated resort island 254; land and housing prices 263–4; Material Recovery Facilities plant 256–7; migration 260–2; rubbish reduction 256–7; sewage treatment 258–9; social change 262–3; socio-cultural well-being 260, **261**, 265; solid waste management 256–7; sustainability initiatives and implementation 253–4; tourism product 252; unplanned development 252; water quality 257–8, **258**; water-saving method 257
Bossel, H. 137
bottom-up approach 141, 193, 283, 286
bottom-up globalization 124
Brain, R. 195
Bramwell, B. 14, 15, 20, 193, 195, 210, 217, 282
Britton, S. 68
Brohman, J. 68
Brouder, P. 8, 219, 283

Brundtland Commission Report of 1987 13, 30, 31, 271, 272
de Bruyn, C. 193, 210
buffering 98–9, 102
Bulger, S. M. 154
Bulkeley, H. 196
Burns, P. 81–3
business resilience 274
Butler, G. 57
Butler, R. W. 6, 133, 143, 219, 227

capacity of tourism 2
Cape Town Declaration 53
Carbone, M. 120, 124, 235
carrying capacity 6, 19–20
Carter, R. W. 252
Castellani, V. 141
Cater, E. 35, 36, 42
Chavez, D. 236, 244, 247
Cheakamus Crossing 223
Chin-cheng Ni 8
Choi, C. 195
Choi 137
Chok, S. 80–1
Christie, I. T. 68
Churchill, G. A. 152, 160
coastal tourism 7–8, 250–2, 265–6;
  see also Boracay Island, Philippines
Coccossis, H. 14
The Code in Sweden 94–5
Coe, N. M. 281
coercive isomorphism 98, 100
cognitive/mimetic isomorphism 98–100
coliform outbreak 252–3
collaboration theory 7, 234–7, 243–7;
  see also tourism partnership model
Collaborative for Sustainable Tourism and Resilient Communities 276
Commission of the European Communities 37
Communal Areas Management Programme for Indigenous Resources (CAMPFIRE) 184
community-based tourism 53
Community Environment Fund 184
community sustainability and resilience: business resilience 274; challenges 275; comprehensive urban planning model 272–3; Daniel Burnham's plan for Chicago 272; definition 272–4; differences **274,** 275; *European Tourism Indicators System for Sustainable Destination Management* 273; evolutionary resilience 275; Global Sustainable Tourism Council's criteria 273; *Our Common Future* 273; rural tourism in Taiwan 276–7; similarities 274, **274**; tourism indicators 275–7, **276**; well-being 272–3
Companies Act 2013 83
Complex Adaptive Systems 283

complexity theory 283
conformity 34, 98, 99
Connell, J. 115
corporate social responsibility (CSR) 6–7, 56; Burns' model 78–9; business 77; capacity 79; Development First planning 78–9, **79** (*see also* Development First framework); emerging economies 77; ethical principles 83; growth of 76; motivating factors 77; pro-poor tourism (PPT) 79–80; reporting and accreditation initiatives 77–8, 83–4; Tourism First approach 78, 79, **79**
Craik, I. 18
Craik, J. 18
Cyprus Sustainable Tourism Initiative (CSTI) 203
Cyprus Tourism Organisation (CTO): accountability 204–5; data analysis 202–3; data collection 201–2, **202**; effectiveness 206–7; key tourism indicators by region 201, **201**; map of Cyprus 199, *199*; network governance 201; power and involvement 207–9; regional tourism boards 200; stakeholder identification 203; Strategic Plan 200; structure 206–7; sustainability approach 200; sustainable tourism awareness 203–4; tourism development policies 200–1; tourism product of Cyprus 199–200; transparency 204–5

Daniel Burnham's plan for Chicago 272
Dann, G. 124
David, P. A. 218
Dawley, S. 282
decentralisation of authority 193
decoupling/buffering 98–9, 102
Delmas, M. A. 98, 101
Delphi technique: advantage 186–7; analysis 172–3; application of 186; Chi-square analysis 172; criteria 170; Delphi process 168–9; indicators of sustainable tourism 136, 137; marine ecotourism 169; objectives 167; participants 170–2, **171**; RAND Corporation 168; survey materials 169–70; Sustainable Nature-based Tourism Assessment Toolkit (SUNTAT) 172
'democratization of tourism' 124
Department of Tourism (DOT) 253–4
Deptford 57, 61
Derissen, S. 272
destination governance 216–18, 220;
  see also Whistler entrepreneurs
DeVellis, R. F. 152
Development First framework: assessment 83; characteristics 81; community development projects **82,** 82–3; development thinking 79; ideas 78–9, 82; Third Way 78; *vs.* Tourism First approach **79**

Dickinson, C. 225
dive tourism 232; *see also* Gili Ecotrust
Dodge, M. 55
Dome Hotel 59, 61
Dredge, D. 198, 209, 210, 217
Dubai Report 96–7, 101
Dullstroom 57

Earth Summit 1992 30
Echtner, C. M. 166, 185
eco-tax 242, 245, 247
ecotourism 17, 22, 119
Ecotrust *see* Gili Ecotrust
ECPAT Sweden 94–5
effective tourism 193, 197–8, *199,* 204–9
Elkington, J. 166
embeddedness 34
enclave tourism 46–7
English Tourism Council 133
entrepreneurship 47, 105, 206, 210, 216, 223–5
Erikkson, R. H. 219
European Community Models of Sustainable Tourism project 133
European Tourism Indicators System (ETIS) for Sustainable Management at Destination Level 142, 273
European Union's Fifth Environmental Action Programme 32
evolutionary economic geography (EEG) 7, 8, 216, 218–19, 227; complexity theory 283; discourses and/or paths 283; dominant policy 283–4; in journals 281; Niagara Region near Toronto 285; political economy 282–3; pro-growth governance models 285–6; regional economies 282; resilience theory 282; Resort Municipality of Whistler 284; tourism partnerships 282
evolutionary resilience 272, 275
exclusive enclaves 49

Fair Trade in Tourism (FTT) 54
Fair Travel 102
Farmaki, Anna 7
Favela 55
Felipe, J. C. 136
Felipe, J. J. 136
Ferreira, S. 183, 184
Filho, W. L. 119
Flagestad, A. 216
formalization 34, 244
French Institute for the Environment 133
Friends of the Earth 41

Gartland, M. P. 219, 223
Garud, R. 218, 225, 227
Gáspár, T. 219
Gerdrup, Anna Cederberg 55

Getz, D. 20
Ghosh, R. N. 119, 121
Gibbs, D. 41
Gibson, R. B. 197
Gili Ecotrust: antecedent stage 243; corruption of local government 241–2; direction-setting stage 244; eco-tax 247; green sea turtle conservation 245; illegal fishing 243; lack of responsibility 241; multi-stakeholder partnership 239–40, 242–6; outcome stage 245–6; primary stakeholders, relationship with 246; problem-setting stage 243–4; purpose of 240–1; role of 244–5; Selin and Chavez's model 244–5, 247–8; stakeholders consultation 243–4; structuring stage 244–5; study area 237–9, *238*; sustainability strategy 244; waste management 245–6
Gili Meno and Gili Air 232
Gili Trawangan, Indonesia 232, 237–9, *238*
Gill, A. M. 7, 210, 217, 219, 220, 226, 284
global governance 271
Global Sustainable Tourism Council (GSTC) criteria 273
global tourism 2, 67, 68, 75, 142, 250
Godfrey, Jim 224
Goodall, B. 35, 36, 42
Good Hotel in Amsterdam and London 58
Goodwin, H. 68, 80
Gothenburg 55, 56
Graci, Sonya 7
Gray, B. 234–6
Great Limpopo TFCA: Community Environment Fund 184; 'essential' factors 184, 185; Gonarezhou portion 183–4; interstitial areas 181, *182*; joint-ventures 181, 183; Makuleke people 181, 183; tourism partnerships 183
'green' consumer movement 40–1
green economy 70–1
greenhouse gases 271
green tourism 16–17
Group for Development and Environment 36, 42
Gunn, C. 20

Halkier, H. 219, 282
Hall, C. M. 196, 198, 209, 283, 286
Ha Long Bay, Vietnam 47
Hampton, M. 47
Hanekom, Derek 57
Harcourt, W. 82
Harrison, D. 117, 118, 121
Hassink, R. 219
Haysom, G. 69, 77
Higgins-Desbiolles, F. 57, 80
Holcomb, J. L. 78
Hope, C. 216

Host Mountain Resort for the Games 219, 225; *see also* Whistler entrepreneurs
Hotelplan 34–5
Housner, L. D. 154
Huberman, M. 202
Hunter, C. J. 132

inclusive business 6, 47, 48, 69–71, 75
inclusive development 5, 48, 49, 56
inclusive growth approach 47
inclusive tourism 6; *vs.* accessible tourism 51–2; all-inclusive tourism 46–7; changing the tourism map 55–6; *vs.* community-based tourism 53; concept 46–8; constraints 59–60; decision-making 56–7; definition 48–9; elements of 49–50, *50*; enclave tourism 46–7; ethical production and consumption 48; exclusive enclaves 49; inclusive business 47; inclusive development 48; inclusivity 89; local people as producers 54; mutual understanding and respect 57–8; non-mainstream consumers 54–5; overlapping concepts 50–1, **51**; *vs.* peace through tourism 52–3; power relations 58–9; *vs.* pro-poor tourism 52; *vs.* responsible tourism 53; self-representation 58; social benefits of 57–8; *vs.* social tourism 52; strategic priorities 91; types of 89; *see also* Apollo tour operator
indicators of sustainable tourism: challenges 143; characteristics 134, 142; complex indicators 136–7, **137**; criteria and conditions **134**, 134–5; definition 134; English Tourism Council 133; French Institute for the Environment 133; global and holistic sustainability 141–4; index of sustainability 136–7, 142–3; set of indicators 135–6, 142–3; simple indicators 135–7; transition to sustainability 132–3; types of 135; use of indicators 137, **138–40**, 141–3
Inskeep, E. 20
institutional inertia 285, 286
institutional theory: coercive isomorphism 98, 100; cognitive/mimetic isomorphism 98–100; decoupling 98–9, 102; institutional pressures 98, **99,** 101; normative isomorphism 98, 100–1; pursuit of legitimacy 98; use of 97
International Centre for Responsible Tourism 53
international tourism 68
International Tourism Receipts (ITR) 112
International Union of Official Travel Organizations 149
International Year of Sustainable Tourism for Development 4

Jamal, T. B. 166, 185
James, D. 134
James, L. 282
Jayawardena, C. 195

Jenkins, C. L. 121
Jeyacheya, J. 47
Johns, N. 197

de Kadt, E. 36, 41
Kalisch, A. 77
Karnøe, P. 218, 225, 227
Kavanagh, L. 134
Kemp, R. 197
Kenis, P. 196, 211
Ketola, T. 77
Kiss, A. 185
Kitchen on the Run project 58
Kitchin, R. 55
Ko, T. G. 133
Kreutzwiser, R. 20
Kuoni Group CSR strategy 93–4

labour rights 96–7, 102, 106, 120, 121
Laesser, C. 216
Land and Agrarian Reform Program 183–4
Lane, B. 193, 217
Lawson, V. 48
Lazarsfeld, P. 152
Leadership in Energy & Environmental Design-Neighbourhood Development (LEED-ND) 223
Lei Tin Ong 8
Lesser Developed Countries (LDCs): collaboration process 234–5; Gray's collaboration theory 235–6; inclusive collaborative approach 235; innovative initiatives 234; insular geography and fragile environmental characteristics 233; multi-stakeholder partnership 235–6 (*see also* Gili Ecotrust); resource management and governance 234; Selin and Chavez's tourism partnership model 236–7, *237*
Lew, A. A. 8, 282
Lewis, J. M. 196
Lew's model 282
life cycle model (Butler) 219
Likert, R. 169
Liu, Z. 166
Liu, Z.-H. 121
Local Government Code (LGC) 253
Locke, R. M. 77
Lockington, D. 134
Long, P. H. 47
Lynch, P. 197

Macbeth, J. 80, 81
McCool, S. F. 135, 141
McElroy, J. L. 141
Magdas Hotel in Vienna 58
Ma, M. 219
Manning, T. 136
Maori people 58
marine ecotourism 169

marine park 232–3
Marques, J. C. 49
Marsh, J. 20
Marzo-Navarro, Mercedes 7
mass market 22, 53, 60, 91
mass tourism 17, 21–2, 78, 90
Material Recovery Facilities (MRF) plant 256–7
Matthews, A. 58
Mayer, A. L. 136
Meadows, D. H. 19
Mellon, V. 282
Messerli, H. R. 47
Meyer, D. 80
Meyer, U. 219, 227
Miles, B. 202
Millennium Development Goals (MDGs): contemporary tourism scholarship 69; corporate supply chains 69; Global South 67; global tourism 68; goals and targets 66–7; green economy 70–1; inclusive business 69–70; linkage development 70; poverty reduction 66–8; pro-poor tourism (PPT) 67–8; tourism capacity and willingness 68; tourism-led development 68
Miller, G. 137, 143, 169
Milne, S. 122, 193
mindful deviation 216, 218, 223–5, 284
Minnery, John 8
MNCs 90, 101, 103–5
Momsen, J. H. 7, 80
Montanari, Armando 6
Moore, S. A. 141
Morrison, A. 197, 198
Morse, S. 135
Mowforth, M. 60, 80
multinational tourism corporations 75–6
multi-stakeholder partnership 235–6, 239–40, 242–6
Munt, I. 60, 80
Murphy, P. E. 216

National Trust 41
nature-based tourism 166; *see also* trans-frontier conservation areas (TFCAs)
The Natural Step (TNS) organization 221, 223–6
neocolonialism 112
neoliberalism 59–60, 80, 215
Neto, F. 119, 166
network governance 196
New York Dialogue 69–70
Noel Josephides of Sunvil Holidays 39
normative isomorphism 98, 100–1

objectification 58
Ochheuteal Beach in Cambodia 49
Okumus, F. 78
Oliver, C. 98, 101
Oppermann, M. 112

organizational learning 103–4
orphanage tourism 58
Our Common Future 273
outbound tour operators 89, 90; *see also* Apollo tour operator

Pappalepore, I. 57
partnerships 7, 32, 34, 59, 66, 67, 233–48, 254, 266, 282
Parto, S. 197
path constitution 219
path creation concept: mindful deviation 216, 218, 223–5; *vs.* path dependency 218–19; real-time influence 218, 225–6
path dependency theory 218–19
path plasticity 219
Patterson, D. J. 195
Payne, R. 20
peace through tourism 52–3
Pearce, P. L. 56
Pedraja-Iglesias, Marta 7
Peters, B. 198
Pierre, J. 198
Pigram, J. J. 37
Pike, A. 282
Pingeot, L. 56
Pin Ng 8
Plog, S. C. 23
Polley, A. 141
Ponsford, I. 226
Potter, R. 121, 122
poverty alleviation: agriculture–tourism linkages 70; contemporary tourism scholarship 69; corporate supply chains 69; green economy 70–1; inclusive business 69–70; linkage development 70; pro-poor tourism 67–8; retained tourism revenue 70; tourism value chains 70
poverty reduction: Bonaire's tourism policy 122; governments of SIDS 121; initiatives and subsidies 124; local participation and agency 124–5; metropolitan ties 122–3; neoliberal agendas 121–2; private sector tourism operators 123; tourism planning 124–5; 'Travelers' Philanthropy' approach 123
Prat, A. G. 17
Preferred Code 114
Preston-Whyte, R. A. 186
Priestley, G. K. 18
Private-Community Partnerships in Uganda 59
pro-growth governance models 285–6
pro-poor tourism (PPT): aim of 67–8; benefits 114–15; concept 113, 125; corporate social responsibility 79–80; definition 113; *vs.* inclusive tourism 52; PPT Partnership 113–14; strategies of 114
Provan, K. G. 196, 211

public-private partnerships (PPPs) network 193, 197–8
Pulido, J. I. 141

Quaas, M. F. 272

real-time influence 218, 225–6
Redman, C. L. 273
regional tourism governance: accountability and effectiveness of 204–5, 209, 210; challenge 210; changing nature of 195–7; decentralisation of authority 193, 209; delegation of authority 193; effectiveness 197–8, *199*; good governance, principles for 197; network theory 195–6, 209; power and involvement 207–10; public-private partnerships (PPPs) 197–8; regional characteristics 210; stakeholders 203, 209–10; sustainability 194–5; variables 197; *see also* Cyprus Tourism Organisation (CTO)
regional tourism organisations (RTOs) 192, 202–9
regulation theory: 'green' consumer movement 40–1; intra-generational equity 41; local control 38; political practices 40; production and consumption 40; small firms and local areas 38–9; social norms and cultural values 41; tour companies role and practice 39; value of 42
resilience theory 272, 282; *see also* community sustainability and resilience
Resort Municipality of Whistler (RMOW) Act 220, 284
responsible tourism 53
Rio Earth Summit in 1992 165
Ritchie, B. 197
Ritchie, J. R. B. 80
Robèrt, Karl-Henrik 221, 223
Robinson, J. 166
Rogerson, C. M. 6, 57, 75
Ruhanen, L. 197, 198
rural tourism 7; content and construct validity 155–6; data collection 152–4; development 150, 159, 160; economic sustainability 150, 156, **156,** *157*; El Palmar 154, *154*; environmental sustainability 151, **158,** 158–60, **159,** *159*; indicators 151–2, **153,** 160–1; requisites 151; research limitations 161; resident opinions 160; sampling 152; sociocultural sustainability 150–1, **157,** 157–8, *158,* 160; stakeholder groups 159–60; sustainability descriptives 155, **155**; in Taiwan **276,** 276–7; Tierra de Palmares 160; tourism product 159; variables 160

Saarinen, J. 6, 7, 75, 149, 211, 283, 286
Sala, S. 141

Sánchez, M. 141
Scandinavia 92
Scheyvens, R. 2, 5–7, 68, 80, 195
Schianetz, K. 134
Schienstock, G. 219
Schilcher, D. 80
Schubert, C. 219, 227
Scott, N. 197
Seely, R. L. 169
Seiver, B. 58
self-regulation 6; Alpine Convention 33; alternative 37; challenges 36–7; codes of behaviour 35; community level 34; cost-effective 34–5; definition 31; effectiveness 35–6; external costs and benefits 36; gaps 42; Hotelplan 34–5; limitations 37, 41–2; marketing advantages 35–6; neoliberal beliefs 32; partnerships 32; provincial-level 33–4; resource use 36; state regulation 32–3; Strategic Concept for Weisensee 34; Tyrolean Environmental Seal of Quality 33–4; voluntary codes 35; *see also* regulation theory
Selin, S. 236, 244, 247
Sharpley, R. 75, 79, 81, 160
Sharma, A. 68
Shaw, G. 31
Shyst Resande 100
Siddique, M. 121
Sinclair, T. 68
Sirakaya, E. 137
small island developing states (SIDS): challenge control elites 120–1; control over tourism 118; economic vulnerabilities 117–18, 125; ecotourism 119; environmental vulnerabilities 118–19, 125; external shocks 117; foreign exchange 116; as holiday destination 116; Maldives 120; material poverty 119; metropolitan ties 122–3; natural resource 118; neocolonialism 112; poverty of opportunity 119 (*see also* poverty reduction); primary production 117–18; social impacts of tourists 120; social sustainability 119–21; tourism and 111–12; tourism market 115–16; tourism revenues 116; well-being meetings of 115
Smeets, E. 134
Smith, A. 57
Smith, V. 252
social tourism 52
Sofield, T. 67
Solidarity Tourism Company 59
solid waste management (SWM) 256–7
SOS Children's Villages 95
Spenceley, A. 7, 80, 181, 185
Stack, M. 219, 223
staged inclusivity 102
Statement of Commitment on Human Rights 96–7
Stewart, Gordon 'Butch' 123

Storey, Donovan 8
Strambach, S. 219
Strategic Concept for Weisensee 34
Suppliers' Code of Conduct 96, 100
Sureda, B. 136
sustainability 31–2, 42
Sustainable Development Goals (SDGs) of 2030 Agenda for Sustainable Development: capacity of tourism 2; challenges 3; core 74–5; Global South 3; goals **3**, 3–4; International Year of Sustainable Tourism for Development 4; sustainable solutions 5; tourism geographers 5; World Bank Group 4
Sustainable Nature-based Tourism Assessment Toolkit (SUNTAT) 167, 172
sustainable performance index (SPI) 141
sustainable tourism 1–2, 6; action strategy 24, **25**; alternative/green tourism 16–17, 21; appropriate tourist 17; Brundtland Commission 13–14; carrying capacity 19–20; control of development and operation 21; definition of 13–15, **14**, 23; economic geography 281–5; environmental concern 18; future 24; good, common and best practices 41–2; ideological and philosophical concept 15–16; interpretation, ways of 14–15; marketability 17, 24; mass/conventional tourism 17, 21–2; mass market 22; measurement of sustainability 20–1, 24; performance 42; quality and attractiveness 22–3; resource and environmental management 12; tourist sites 18–19
Svensson, B. 217
Swarbrooke, J. 167
SwedWatch 100, 102

Takano, M. 257
Telfer, D. J. 70, 75, 79, 81
Therkelsen, A. 219
'Third Way' 78
Third World countries 113
Thomas, R. N. 122
Tierra de Palmares 154, 160
Tikitut initiative 56
Timothy, D. 56
Tkaczynski, A. 197
Toffel, W. M. 98, 101
Tomaney, J. 282
Torres-Delgado, A. 7, 149, 211
Torres, R. 80
Tourism First approach 78, 79, **79,** 83
Tourism Geographies 281; carrying capacity 6; coastal tourism 7–8; collaboration and partnership 7; corporate social responsibility 6–7; evolutionary economic geography analysis 7, 8; governance 7; inclusive tourism 6, 7; regulation theory 6; rural tourism 7; tourism and poverty reduction 7; Virtual Special Issue 2, 6
tourism partnership model 236–7, *237,* 244–5, 247–8
Tourist Area Cycle of Evolution 283
Touristik Union International of Germany 39
Tour Operator Initiative 101
tour operators: inclusiveness *89,* 89–91; institutional theory 97–9, **99**; large tour operators 90–1; mass tourism 91; sector 90–1; sustainability practices 91–2; travel market 89; *see also* Apollo tour operator
Towards Shared Responsibility 32
trans-frontier conservation areas (TFCAs) 7–8; characteristics 167; consultation 167–8 (*see also* Delphi technique); co-operative wildlife management 167; economic factors 173, 175, **176–7**; environmental factors 177, **178–9**, 179; essential and incompatible factors 173, **173**, 186; fragmentation 166–7; Great Limpopo TFCA 181–5; policy and planning factors 173, **174–5**; research 167–8; social factors 179, **180–1**, 181; tourism 167
transparency 134, 198, 204–5, 209, 221, 244
'Travelers' Philanthropy' approach 123
Travelife sustainability system 93, 95–6, 101
Tren Ecuador 54, 60
Tribe, J. 193
Trousdale, W. J. 252
Tsung-chiung Wu 8
Twining-Ward, L. 143
Tyrolean Environmental Seal of Quality 33–4

United Nations Development Programme (UNDP) 78
United Nations Environment Programme (UNEP) 150, 251
United Nations Millennium Development Goals (UN MDGs) 2; *see also* Millennium Development Goals (MDGs)
United Nation World Tourism Organization (UNWTO) 4, 5, 66
Upchurch, R. S. 78
Uprising Resort 55, 61
Utting, P. 49

Vancouver Olympic Committee (VANOC) 222
Vaughan, R. D. 152
Vinzón, Lucia 7
Virtual Special Issue (VSI) 2
voluntourism 58
von Hayek, E. A. 32
Von Malmborg, F. 209

Wall, G. 13, 16, 70
Warren, C. 80, 81

Watson, H. K. 186
Weaver's argument for Sustainable Mass Tourism 78
well-being 272
Westley, F. 215
West Nusa Dua Marine Park 232, 237–8
Weterings, R. 134
Wheeller, B. 15, 20, 31, 132
Whistler 2020 221
Whistler entrepreneurs: affordable housing 220–1; athletes' village 222–3; bed unit approach 220, 225; Cheakamus Crossing 223; community stakeholders 221; destination planning and management 216; evolutionary economic geography 216, 218–19, 227, 284; Games initiatives 222; growth dependence 219–20; mindful deviation 216, 218, 223–5, 284; The Natural Step 221, 223–6; official community plan 220; path creation 218–19, 226, 227; Resort Municipality of Whistler Act 220; *Whistler 2020* 221, 223–4, 226; Whistler 2020 Development Corporation 222
Whistler Housing Authority (WHA) 220
White, V. 134
Wilkinson, P. F. 115
Wilkinson, R. 198
Williams, A. M. 6, 31, 219
Williams, P. W. 7, 210, 217, 219, 226, 284
2010 Winter Olympic Games 216, 222, 284
World Bank Group 4
World Commission on Environment and Development (WCED) 271
World Congress against Commercial Sexual Exploitation of Children 94
World Conservation Union 166
World Parks Congress 166
Wu, M. Y. 56

Zahra, A. L. 198
Zapata, M. J. 198
Zhao, W. 80